D1568928

The Battle for Western Europe, Fall 1944

TWENTIETH-CENTURY BATTLES
Edited by Spencer C. Tucker

The Battle of An Loc
James H. Willbanks

The Battle of Heligoland Bight
Eric W. Osborne

The Battle of Leyte Gulf: The Last Fleet Action
H. P. Willmott

*The Battle of the Otranto Straits: Controlling the
Gateway to the Adriatic in World War I*
Paul G. Halpern

Battle of Surigao Strait
Anthony P. Tully

The Brusilov Offensive
Timothy C. Dowling

D-Day in the Pacific: The Battle of Saipan
Harold J. Goldberg

The Dieppe Raid: The Story of the Disastrous 1942 Expedition
Robin Neillands

Midway Inquest: Why the Japanese Lost the Battle of Midway
Dallas Woodbury Isom

Operation Albion: The German Conquest of the Baltic Islands
Michael B. Barrett

The Second Battle of the Marne
Michael S. Neiberg

The Battle for
Western Europe
Fall 1944

An Operational Assessment

John A. Adams

Indiana University Press

BLOOMINGTON & INDIANAPOLIS

This book is a publication of

Indiana University Press
601 North Morton Street
Bloomington, IN 47404-3797 USA

www.iupress.indiana.edu

Telephone orders 800-842-6796
Fax orders 812-855-7931
Orders by e-mail iuporder@indiana.edu

♾ The paper used in this publication meets the minimum requirements
of the American National Standard for Information Sciences—Permanence
of Paper for Printed Library Materials, ANSI Z39.48-1992.

Manufactured in the United States of America

Library of Congress Cataloging-in-Publication Data

Adams, John A., [date]
  The battle for Western Europe, Fall 1944 : an operational assessment / John A.
Adams.
       p. cm. — (Twentieth-century battles)
  Includes bibliographical references and index.
  ISBN 978-0-253-35435-8 (cloth : alk. paper) 1. World War, 1939–1945—Campaigns—
Western Front. I. Title.
  D756.A19 2010
  940.54'21—dc22

                                                                    2009035159

1 2 3 4 5 15 14 13 12 11 10

A proud son of Little Rock, Arkansas, Charles B. MacDonald graduated from Presbyterian College during the first part of World War II. Commissioned through ROTC, he scarcely had time to put away his diploma before becoming a twenty-one-year-old captain and replacement rifle company commander in the famous 23rd Infantry, 2nd Division. He joined his new unit in September 1944 in the southern tip of the Huertgen Forest near the Monshau Corridor just as the bloody battles for that ill-starred piece of ground began. Captain MacDonald fought through the fall's Huertgen fights and the winter's Battle of the Bulge, earning the Silver Star, the Bronze Star, and finally the Purple Heart for wounds received 17 January 1945. After convalescing, he returned to his regiment and fought in the final battles in Europe.

Right after the war, he wrote what is still widely read as a classic description of infantry combat, *Company Commander*. In 1948 Charles joined the project within the U.S. Army Center of Military History charged with writing the official history of the war. MacDonald authored three of the widely acclaimed "Green Books," including *The Siegfried Line Campaign*, which covers many of the events covered by this book. During the writing of those volumes, he personally inspected the original of every official document that was used to compile an accurate and complete record of events. MacDonald stayed with the project, rising to become the Center's deputy director, until 1979, when he retired. In addition, he wrote several non-official volumes, including *The Mighty Endeavor*, his recounting of the campaign for Western Europe from D-Day to VE Day. A consummate raconteur, a meticulous historian, and an objective recorder of the facts, he melded the skills of a historian with the experiences of a frontline veteran and produced much of value for generations that follow. Most historians consider him the most knowledgeable student of the fall 1944 campaign.

In recognition of the sacrifices Charles and his compatriots made in the fall of 1944 and of the quality of the record he assembled for those of us who wish to learn from their heroic efforts, this work is dedicated to the memory of

Charles B. MacDonald

1922–1990

Historian and Captain of Infantry

Contents

Maps

Preface

Look at some old news footage taken in France during late August 1944. Under brilliant sunshine, columns of speeding Sherman tanks race ahead, looking to catch fleeing Germans. Overhead, P-47 fighters swoop by, machine-gunning anything ahead of the armor that looks even suspicious. Certainly, the horrid Nazi monster must be on its last legs.

View news film clips taken four months later. Snarling Panther tanks emerge from the cold, dense morning mist, spitting fire at retreating Americans looking to simply get out of the way of the hulking, advancing monsters.

What happened?

Conventional wisdom holds that the Allies, due to some supply problems, poor theater strategy, and inter-Allied squabbling, lost their opportunity to finish the Nazis in the early fall of 1944. Maybe the Allies could have marched all the way to Berlin.

Readers more familiar with the details of that period recall debate among the Allied generals about a "narrow thrust" versus a "broad advance" toward Germany. The narrow thrust advocated by the British field marshals would have concentrated the limited supply of Allied strength into a single "full-blooded" thrust north of the Ardennes and into the heart of Germany. Some American generals proposed giving the rampaging U.S. Third Army more supply and letting its commander perform a similar feat through Lorraine and into the Saar.

Instead, Eisenhower, and more properly his Allied SHAEF staff, promulgated what has been dubbed a "broad front strategy." That strategy dictated that the Allies complete a continuous front from the North Sea to the Swiss border. Detractors claimed this meant little more than "everyone attack all the time." Rather than run out of steam, this faulted strategy dissipated the limited head of Allied steam and prevented the Allied engine from further eastward movement in the fall of 1944.

In the pages that follow, SHAEF planning machinery and existing constraints will be more closely examined. What develops is a far more intricate plan formulated by Eisenhower and his staff than is commonly recognized. Describing its important working parts, it will be called the "two phase, two thrust" theater strategy.

First, what was the overall objective, the grand strategic objective, that the theater strategy was supposed to achieve? Eisenhower and Marshall agreed emphatically: destruction of the German armed forces, the Wehrmacht, in the field. Most Allied generals repeated this goal. The British field marshals did, too, but in practice they wandered away from this objective in favor of seizing geography (Berlin) and war-making potential (the Ruhr) deep within Germany.

As will be demonstrated below, Eisenhower did not advocate a simple "everyone charge" approach. He and his staff created an offensive with a strong primary thrust and a smaller secondary one—standard practice among those planning an offensive. But this basic notion was encased in a two-phased pair of operations. First the Wehrmacht would be forced into decisive battle west of the Rhine and destroyed, while the logisticians created a solid base of supply. In a second phase, the Rhine would be crossed and final dismemberment of the Nazi monster completed.

Was this a war-winning theater strategy? *Or did Eisenhower's two principal army group commanders, Field Marshal Montgomery and General Bradley, botch this plan in its execution?* This will be examined closely. Were several subsidiary opportunities also missed?

A long time ago along some sun-baked, long-forgotten dirt road, a dust-covered, sweat-streaked, cursing quartermaster must have mouthed, "tactics is the art of what is logistically possible." As is often the case, logistics dominated events in Western Europe during the fall of 1944. Chapter 2 is devoted to deriving the elements of the iron logistical calculus that governed decision making. (Those readers who can't stand numbers can skim over this chapter without losing the thrust of the argument.) Throughout the remainder of the story, logistics will constantly interrupt with its overpowering base tones.

Many good people provided comment on and support for this work. I wish to especially thank the hard-working archivists at the U.S. Army Military History Institute at the Army War College in Carlisle Barracks, Pennsylvania, the Marshall Library at Virginia Military Institute, and the

Eisenhower Library in Abilene, Kansas. Especially I thank David J. Haight at the Eisenhower Library for his patient and thoughtful guidance into the extensive holdings at that facility.

I also wish to thank Professors Malcolm Muir and Spencer Tucker for their friendship and encouragement. Finally, kudos to Indian River County, Fla. Library for maintaining a handsome collection of World War II literature.

In a work this size, several errors inevitably will creep in. I retain sole responsibility for their presence.

John Adams
Vero Beach, Florida

Abbreviations and Acronyms

AD	Armored Division
ADSEC	Advance Section, forwardmost COMZ section.
AEF	World War I American Expeditionary Force
AFHQ	Allied Force Headquarters
CCA	Combat Command A (B,R), regimental-sized combat groups found in American and French armored divisions
CCS	Combined Chiefs of Staff, American and British Chiefs meeting together.
C&GS	Command & General Staff School (Ft. Leavenworth)
COMZ	Communications Zone; logistical organization behind Army Group rear Boundary
Cobra	Code name for American breakout attack from Normandy
Comet	British operation to gain the Rhine that preceded Market Garden
COSSAC	Chief of Staff to Supreme Allied commander
D+21	21 days after D-Day
Division Slice	Division plus supporting and logistical troops. A division averages 15,000 troops. A division slice can total 45,000 troops
Dragoon	Invasion of Southern France, September 1944. Earlier called ANVIL
DUKW	Amphibious 2½-ton truck useful in unloading ships out of port and crossing rivers
ETO	European Theater of Operations
FFI	French Forces of the Interior; the Marquis underground
G-1	Personnel staff section, division HQ or higher
G-2	Intelligence staff section
G-3	Operations staff section

G-4	Logistics (supply) staff section
Goodwood	Attempted British breakout attack that preceded Cobra
ID	Infantry Division
JCS	Joint Chiefs of Staff, U.S. chiefs
Market Garden	Montgomery's airborne assault (market) and ground attack (garden) to seize a bridgehead across the Rhine at Arnhem
MLR	Main line of resistance primary defensive positions, usually dug in. Outposts are out front.
MTO	Mediterranean Theater of Operations
NATOUSA	North African Theater of Operations, U.S. Army. Supplied Dragoon until 15 September.
OB West	Oberbefehlshaber West; highest German HQ in the West (Rundstedt's HQ)
Overlord	Code word for Normandy invasion plans and follow-up
RAF	Royal Air Force
RCT	Regimental Combat Team; infantry regiment reinforced usually by an artillery battalion plus engineer, tank, and antitank companies
SHAEF	Supreme Headquarters, Allied Expeditionary Force (Eisenhower's HQ)
SOP	Standard Operating Procedure
TACHQ	Headquarters operate in up to three locations simultaneously; Rear (administrative), Main, and TAC (tactical—a small forward HQ with the commander and a small staff). Montgomery liked to operate from TACHQ. Eisenhower and Bradley did so less frequently.
TOT	Time on Target artillery barrage, timed so all shells hit simultaneously
PzD	Panzer Division
PGD	Panzer Grenadier Division
Queen	Major First/Ninth Army offensive, November 1944
Red Ball	Express truck route to move supplies to First & Third Armies
ULTRA	Secret intelligence garnered from reading German radio codes
VGD	Volks Grenadier Division. Smaller, less well armed infantry division
Wehrmacht	German Armed Forces
Zone of Interior	Term for the continental United States

The Battle for Western Europe, Fall 1944

1

Culmination

I have used one principle in these operations . . . and this is to fill the "unforgiving minute with sixty seconds of distance run." That is the whole art of war, and when you get to be a general remember it. . . . I have never given a damn what the enemy was going to do or where he was. What I have known is what I intended to do and then have done it. By acting in this manner I have always gotten to the place he expected me to come about three days before he got there.

George Patton, letter to his son, 21 Aug. 1944

On 6 June 1944, forever "D-Day," five Allied divisions stormed the Normandy beaches. Seven weeks of frustrating fighting in the Bocage, the hedgerow country, followed. Territorial gains were smaller than planned, and casualties were staggering. The opposing armies deadlocked.

To break the impasse, U.S. First Army brilliantly executed a penetration attack—Cobra—on 25 July. (See map 1.1.) Omar Bradley, the First Army commander, envisioned a major air strike to create a hole in a narrow section of the front and then positioned concentrated American ground power, echeloned in depth, to rip that hole open. On the day before the attack, Dwight Eisenhower, supreme allied commander—"Ike"—cabled Bradley: "My high hopes and best wishes ride with you on your attack today . . . [conditions thus] allowing you to pursue every advantage with an ardor verging on recklessness and with all of your troops."[1] Subsequently he signaled, "We will crush him [the enemy]."[2]

Bradley entrusted Major General "Lightning Joe" Collins and his VII Corps with executing the breakout. VII Corps, brought to the size of a mini-army with three infantry and two armored divisions, made the main effort. After an incredible air bombardment that included most of Eighth Air Force's heavy bombers, American infantry moved forward. Bombing

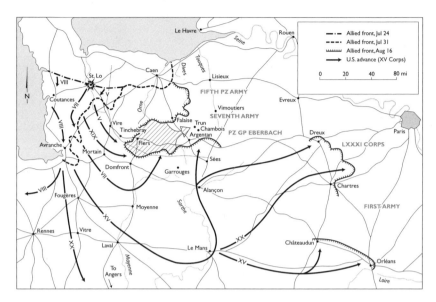

Map 1.1. Normandy Breakout

and shelling had disintegrated Panzer Lehr. In some sectors Americans advanced against little opposition except wreckage and bomb craters. In others Germans shuffled into the breach put up fierce resistance. Initial infantry advances were slow as GIs picked their way between broken limbs, deafened and dumbfounded German survivors, and bomb craters. Would this be another of a string of failed attempts to break free of seemingly unmovable German defenses that had hemmed in the Allies for the last seven weeks?

Constant Allied grinding had worn the Germans down. Earlier attacks (such as Goodwood) ordered by British General Bernard Montgomery, overall land commander, and executed by Lieutenant General Miles Dempsey's British Second Army, while unsuccessful at creating a breakout, had pulled most German armored reserves over to the British sector.

German defenses before VII Corps lacked depth. Although a clear breakout had not occurred by early morning of the second day, Collins smelled German defenses melting. Without hesitation, he gambled and committed his exploitation force, 2nd Armored Division (2AD) and 1st Infantry Division (1ID) specially motorized for this role, to push through. The initial Cobra plan envisioned a penetration of German lines, then a left hook to cut off Germans opposing the rest of First Army. The exploitation force was to consolidate on a line between Coutances and Caumont, well inside of Normandy.[3] This would have created a sack less than 25 kilometers deep and brought American spearheads to rest pointed at the west coast of Normandy 20 kilometers north of Granville.

By the 27th a clear penetration was developing. Bradley, who had not scripted what was to happen after the first three days, made the decision to commit several corps into the exploitation. Neither Bradley nor anyone else envisioned what actually happened next. Tankers found daylight. Racing southward, they took first Coutances, then Granville, then Avranches. American armor started barely 30 kilometers from the American D-Day beaches. On the 28th, Bradley ordered Collins to open up full-scale exploitation. To support the Americans, Montgomery ordered British Second Army to execute Operation Bluecoat, a shift of resources from its left flank to its right, and to begin attacking at Caumont, near the inter-army group boundary on 30 July. The Allied ground force commander was doing his job. However, the official American historian complained, "If the original intention was to hold German forces in place . . . , Blue Coat came too late."[4] The American attack had begun on the 25th. After 1,200 bombers pounded frontline German defenders, British 11th Armored Division moved out smartly. Exploiting a gap in German lines they uncovered, British tankers moved onto high ground east of Vire.

By the 31st, VII Corps armor crossed the Normandy-Brittany border—a 120-kilometer advance in six days. And little but open road and a few German stragglers lay ahead of the American tanks (map 1.1.) From that point on, the Americans ad-libbed based on the opportunities that lay before them.

The first of August brought about preplanned changes in the Allied command structure that reflected the increased size of their forces that had landed on the continent. Dwight David Eisenhower remained the Allied supreme commander; British Air Marshal Arthur Tedder was his deputy. At the next level British Admiral Bertram Ramsay commanded all naval forces and British Air Marshall Andrew Cunningham commanded the tactical air forces. After 1 September, General Eisenhower would also act as overall ground commander. Before that date British General Bernard L. Montgomery remained temporarily in overall command of all Allied ground forces for the month of August. As his commander, General Dwight Eisenhower—supreme commander—said, "one battle, one commander." In addition, Montgomery retained his "permanent" command of 21st Army Group, which included British Second Army (Lieutenant General [LTG] Miles Dempsey) and Canadian First Army (LTG Henry D. G. Crerar). LTG Omar N. Bradley moved up the newly created 12th Army Group, which contained his old command, U.S. First Army (now under LTG Courtney Hodges), and newly formed Third U.S. Army (LTG George S. Patton).

Again, as part of the plan, the rampaging spearheads came under Patton. Actually he had been "observing," kibitzing and urging Collins on, for several days. From the beginning, planners and generals alike knew that port capacity to supply the invaders would be at a premium. During June, GIs struggled to wrest the port of Cherbourg from the tenacious Germans. When they finally captured their objective, the Americans took control of one of the most thoroughly wrecked harbors in military history. Most supplies would continue to land over the beach. This was something no logistician thought was possible. While they might cope for a little while longer in summer weather, real ports would be needed by fall.

During World War I, the doughboys and most of their supplies debarked from their trans-Atlantic crossing onto the deep water quays of Brest. Those facilities lay at the tip of Brittany, 300 kilometers west of Avranches. But Berlin was 1,200 kilometers to the east! Which way should 12th Army Group go? Patton knew, but even he was hesitant to say, since the slapping incident in Sicily that had almost sent him home in disgrace.

During the first week of August, Patton's lead divisions ran amuck, but in the wrong direction. Overlord planning designated the 14,000-ton capacity of the large ports in west Brittany as Third Army's objective. Sixth Armored wound up on the outskirts of Brest. Fourth Armored pulled up in front of the Bretagne port of Lorient.

Nearly every senior Allied commander itched to go east—toward the heart of Germany. Patton was one of the most vocal. But he was allowed to turn only one of his four corps toward the center of Nazi power.

In June, Montgomery's planners had studied Allied objectives beyond Brittany. By the 2nd of August, Eisenhower urged Montgomery to begin exploiting east. As Ike cabled the American chief of staff, General George C. Marshall, who was back in Washington, "I would consider it unnecessary to detach any large forces for the Conquest of Brittany, and would devote the great bulk of the forces to the task of completing the destruction of the bulk of the German Army" to the east.[5] On the 3rd, Eisenhower traveled to the continent to confer with Bradley and Montgomery. On 4 August, Montgomery ordered a major departure from Overlord. His stated intent was to force the Germans back against the Seine, trap them there as Allied airpower had dropped all the bridges, and destroy them. U.S. First Army was to turn east as well as Patton's three corps that had been moving south. Twenty-First Army Group was to attack southward into the developing sack no later than 8 August.

Developments in Normandy were also being monitored closely in Germany. On 2 August, Hitler ordered a full panzer army to attack westward near the little town of Mortain toward Avranches. His goal was to cut off Patton's Third Army and seal off the Allied breakout.

INTERLUDE

While Eisenhower had to deal with the fear of stalemate in Normandy during July and the planning to break out, the British decided to again raise objections to the planned invasion of southern France (Dragoon). Montgomery had originally objected to a landing in southern France in February.[6] That operation was also motivated by the overarching battle of the ports. Supreme Headquarters, Allied Expeditionary Force (SHAEF) planners and Eisenhower wanted the huge capacity of the port of Marseilles on the south end of their projected line to complement the port of Antwerp on the north. Forces for this operation were to be taken from the Italian campaign, effectively stalling its advance just north of Rome, which was captured on, of all days, the 5th of June.

Any detached strategist would immediately concur with taking resources away from a subsidiary theater to focus on the decisive one. But the British had a political agenda in the eastern Mediterranean not shared by the Americans. They wanted to regain their prewar sphere of interest in that part of the world.

Much of this inter-Allied fight was carried out among the Combined Chiefs. When Marshall, in support of Eisenhower, proved immovable, Churchill attempted to get around him by haranguing Eisenhower, who, conveniently, was in London.

On the 4th, Eisenhower learned Churchill had appealed to President Roosevelt about Dragoon, code name for the invasion of southern France. All of this forced Eisenhower to cable Marshall on the 5th of August:

> I learn that the Prime Minister has sent a message to the President relating to Dragoon. I will not repeat nor under any conditions agree at this moment to a cancellation of Dragoon.[7]

On the 7th, Churchill met with Eisenhower at his forward headquarters, Shell burst, in an apple orchard in western France. For six hours, while Patton's breakout was unfolding and the Falaise Gap was forming, the prime minister pleaded, cajoled, and threatened Ike while trying to convince him to support canceling the invasion of southern France and accepting reinforcements via Brest instead. During Ike's 9 August meeting at 10 Downing Street, Churchill again picked up his cudgel and beat the SHAEF commander further about the issue. Finally the invasion itself went off with few casualties on the 15th. The Marseilles docks, the real prize, were captured intact. Soon supplies and vehicles were swinging onto them from shipside. Until the end of the war, Marseilles would rival Antwerp in the tonnage landed.

While carefully and tactfully guiding his subordinates in the middle of a decisive battle, Ike has to deal with prime ministerial interference in a separate but critical part of his campaign. Imagine what one of Ike's days must have been like!

Hitler attempted to isolate the American breakout with an armored counterattack at Mortain. Its objective was to slice through to the coast at the juncture of Normandy and Brittany. If it had been successful, Third Army would have been cut off and the Allied breakout contained.

American forces, especially the 30th Infantry Division (30ID), frustrated Hitler's ill-conceived effort to cut off Third Army. A subaltern could see that German strength was far insufficient to achieve this objective. Many Allied generals rated the Mortain counterattack as one of Hitler's greatest blunders of the Western campaign. By forcing this attack, Hitler had placed most of his armor in the wrong end of a sack developing between the American and British army groups. A great opportunity, a "once in a century" opportunity in Bradley's words, developed.

By 7 August the Americans had stopped the German attack at Mortain. Hitler demanded that the effort be redoubled no earlier than the 11th. Meanwhile Bradley's armies were marauding to the south and east. By the 11th a sack was forming. Its open end was Falaise, at the opposite end and 60 kilometers away from Mortain. Virtually the entire German Seventh Army as well as Panzer Group West was in the bag. If the Allies could seal it shut, Army Group G would be finished.

On the evening of 6–7th Eisenhower penned into a memorandum about Dragoon:

> The attack by the Canadian Army this morning south from Caen met the stiffest kind of resistance and has not made much progress. It therefore appears to me that the American right wing on this front should swing in closer in an effort to destroy the enemy by attacking him in the rear. On a

visit to Bradley today I found that he had already acted on this idea and had secured Montgomery's agreement to a sharp change in direction toward the Northeast instead of continuing directly toward the East, as envisaged in M517 [Montgomery's most recent field order of 6 August, which directed a wider swing to the east to Paris and the Seine by Third Army].[8]

Despite what he said to Eisenhower, Bradley hesitated. On the 9th, Patton wrote, "If I were on my own, I would take bigger chances than I am now permitted to take. Three times I have suggested risks and been turned down and each time the risk is warranted."[9] Patton kept working on permutations that maximized the amount of combat power he could send east. Unknown to each other, both Patton and Montgomery favored a wide encirclement of retreating German forces by sending American forces westward down the Seine to the English Channel.

On the 11th Monty was assaying how best to close what had become known as the Falaise pocket. Initially Argentan appeared the best point for the northern pincer, Canadian First Army, to meet the southern one, Third Army, which had XV Corps in the lead. Eighty kilometers separated the two Allied forces.

Canadian II Corps was commanded by the highly regarded Lieutenant General G. G. Simonds. According to M517, Canadian First Army was to take Falaise. However Simonds's exploiting divisions, 4th Canadian Armored and Polish 2nd Armored, were new to combat and making mistakes expected of green units. Canadian II Corps had been bogged down for three days by skillful German resistance.

XV Corps, a component of Third Army, reached Argentan just before midnight. Now the gap was less than 40 kilometers. XV Corps commander, Major General Wade Haislip, signaled he had no orders to go beyond that city. However, he was prepared to advance northward until XV Corps linked with the Canadians. Doubting 21st Army Group's ability to reach Argentan, Patton called his boss Bradley, who had just been elevated to Commander 12th Army Group (First and Third American Armies). Patton requested permission to advance beyond the army group boundary. Stating he would rather have "a solid shoulder at Argentan than the possibility of a broken neck at Falaise,"[10] Bradley halted the American thrust.

If Bradley had given Patton permission to close the gap, history would have recorded it as a bold decision consistent with his *Commander's Intent* (close the gap). Bradley might have communicated more forcefully with his commander, Montgomery, who was temporarily overall ground commander as well as Commander 21st Army Group (British Second and Canadian

First Armies), but he didn't. Certainly this was not Bradley's most sterling hour. This will not be the last time a subordinate of one army displays less than sparkling communication skills with his commander in another color of uniform. A renowned American military historian, Carlo D'Este, is even more severe: "The crucial decisions were solely Bradley's. He created the Falaise Gap and ultimately he failed to close it."[11] Bradley apparently was afraid of the combat power that German units caught in the Falaise pocket still had. Major Alexander C. Stiller, an aide to Patton, records a meeting between Patton and Bradley about the time forward elements of Third Army reached the Seine. Bradley related to Patton that German forces still trapped were more than Third Army could contain at that juncture and advised him to keep open an escape route for them.[12]

However, it was up to Montgomery, as overall commander, to solve the problem. He had two choices: order Bradley forward or reinforce the Canadian effort. For two days he attended to neither. He hesitated. Martin Blumenson, in his book *The Battle of the Generals*, recounts the events that prevented a complete seal of the Falaise pocket. While most Wehrmacht equipment was destroyed or abandoned, two-thirds of the troops in the trap, 100,000+ of the 175,000, escaped.[13] Those uncaptured Germans would reappear to frustrate the Allies throughout the fall of 1944.

Patton wanted to take another shot at bagging and destroying the Germans fleeing Normandy. He wanted to create a second, wider, envelopment by turning his army seaward upon reaching the Seine. But his superiors had other priorities. The army group commanders, Montgomery and Bradley, had their vision on objectives farther to the east—Paris, the Meuse, and the German border. Ragtag troops in *feldgrau*,* crossing the Seine on rafts, did not seem to be a military impediment—so the army group commanders thought. Unless those stragglers found the time to re-equip and reorganize.

Failure to close the jaws at Falaise is identified as a major Allied failing. Hitler's "greatest blunder" wasn't fully capitalized on. Depending on the historian, error is charged to Bradley or Montgomery. Either way, this less-than-complete victory set the stage for the fall battles to come.

As early as 7 August, the time of the Mortain counterattack, Ike was looking at his options beyond the Seine. He communicated to Marshall that he wanted "to destroy as much of the enemy's Seventh Army this side of the Seine" and then "to cross the Seine before the enemy has time to hold it in strength, destroy his forces between the Seine and the Somme

---

*The color of German uniforms.

and secure the Seine ports."[14] Ike was looking ahead, looking deep. This is an essential skill for both chess masters and generals. Ike concentrated on two vital issues: the need for additional logistical (port) capacity and the destruction of his enemy in the field. This is a far better basis from which to derive a strategy than any set of geographic reference points or phase lines drawn before D-Day.

As late as 17 August, SHAEF continued to plan for a pause, which was to last thirty days, at the Seine.[15] Ike's first decision was to cancel this halt. On 19 August he decided to cross the Seine. Only a dunderhead would have slavishly adhered to the planned pause. When he is running, chase a broken enemy as far as you can.

However, as soon as Ike made that decision he knew the logistical machine would begin to run down. Ever since they had begun dealing with the problem of sustaining the invasion force, planners liked to quip, "the number of divisions required to capture the ports required to sustain the divisions exceeds the number of divisions the ports can supply." As overall ground commander, Montgomery understood this limitation better than most. Tonnage would be consumed more rapidly than it could be brought forward. At some point, even a small increase in enemy resistance would cause the Allies to halt. This was just as important a fact as the Germans running to get out of France.

Culmination "is the point in time and location where attacker's combat power no longer exceeds that of the defender. Here the attacker greatly risks counterattack and defeat and continues the attack only at great peril." "The art of the defense is to draw the attacker to his culmination, then strike when he has exhausted his resources and is ill-disposed to defend success-fully."[16] Attack is an exhausting endeavor. Grunts carrying a lot of equipment have to run, stumble, and crawl through mud while the bad guys shoot at them. Occasionally they have to shoot back. Only by luck does an attack go according to plan. With all the hot metal flying around, sticking one's head up is not the best idea. Attackers slogging across unfamiliar ground get disoriented. People get hurt. Others stop to help their buddies. Some get lost in all the noise and confusion. By the time the attacking unit gets to its objective, its combat power is likely to have been reduced. It is moving toward culmination.

As armies advance, it is almost axiomatic that their combat power begins to dissipate. Units begin to unravel as they maneuver forward. Casualties are only one grisly toll. Communications become severed, artillery falls behind, people get confused and lost. And the logistician almost always falls behind.

Be they carried in carts, wagons, or trucks, the supplies inevitably cannot move as rapidly as spearheads.

German commanders understood the process well. Often they would withhold their counterattack until their enemy reached culmination. Then the Germans would strike when their enemy was least able to resist. Ask virtually any veteran Allied tactical commander from World War II, and he will tell you that German counterattacks at that point were almost automatic. As much as they would deny it, senior commanders knew that Ike's decision to keep going also meant that the forces of culmination would accelerate their ever-tightening grip on the advancing Allied armies. Ike said:

> We have advanced so rapidly that further movement in large parts of the front *even against very weak opposition* is almost impossible. . . . The closer we get to the Siegfried line the more we will be stretched administratively and a period of relative inaction will be forced upon us. The potential danger is that while we are temporarily stalled, the enemy will be able to pick up bits and pieces of forces everywhere and reorganize them swiftly for defending the Siegfried line or the Rhine. It is obvious from an overall viewpoint we must now as never before *keep the enemy stretched everywhere.* [emphasis added][17]

Rapid advance and lagging logistics rapidly interacted to bring Allied spearheads to culmination. Yes, the Germans were disorganized and running. However, if Allied tanks had no gas, they had no ability to chase them. Vehicles break down under hard use. Mechanized units were melting away as tank after truck broke down at the side of the road. Artillery and engineers lagged behind faster-moving maneuver units. Fragmented forward infantry and tank units, without support and with no ammunition resupply, could get caught and chewed up by German defenders who had honed this skill for years on the eastern front. Despite reduced German ability to resist, the Allied attack machine was approaching culmination by late August. Forward tactical commanders railed at the logistical constraint and screamed to be given more. Eisenhower had to deal with the reality that until the supply trucks caught up, there just wasn't enough to go around.

Ike's communication showed a much better grip of the situation than his army group and army commanders. In mid-August reporters asked him, "how many weeks until the end of the war?" While the Allies were winning the Battle of France, that did not mean they had won the war. Eisenhower knew the Nazi monster may have been knocked down hard, but it was far from finished. Ike understood that he had neither sufficient troops nor sufficient logistical support to do everything.[18] After Cobra set the conditions for breakout, yelling "Charge!" had netted the Allies northern France and the Low Countries. Now, a more coherent plan had to be formulated. Ike stated that there was no point in closing on the Rhine until he had the combat power to do something about it.[19]

Eisenhower was very aware that Germany was regenerating its forces and that a large central reserve was being reconstituted.[20] He also knew a logistic pause inevitably would give the Germans additional time to buttress their defenses. Ike envisioned building a secure logistical base anchored on the high-capacity port of Antwerp, which was close to the German border. While the logistical strength for a deep thrust into Germany was developed, he wanted to pull German forces into decisive battles west of the Rhine, where their lines of communications would be more vulnerable.

Montgomery's and Eisenhower's strategic assessments could not have been more disparate.

Dragoon, the invasion of southern France, came ashore on 15 August. Resistance was light for the most part. Many of the static defense troops were Poles dragooned into the Wehrmacht, with little stomach for a fight. Spearheaded by U.S. 3rd Infantry Division, Allied troops raced north parallel to the Rhone River and caught many retreating Germans in a defile near Montélimar on the 28th. Artillery and air strikes churned the retreating forces into a bloody mob running away from mounds of flaming carnage. While many Germans escaped, 57,000 entered POW cages. Forces under Lieutenant General Jacob Devers's 6th Army Group linked up with elements of Third Army on 12 September. The Allied line now stretched from the North Sea to the Italian border. However, like its sister army groups, 6th Army Group had outdistanced its supply lines. Even though Marseilles was operating and French rails paralleling the Rhone were in decent shape, there wasn't enough transportation to bring supplies forward.

On 19 August, Eisenhower told his two army group commanders, Montgomery and Bradley, he intended to take personal command of the ground war as soon as SHAEF Forward HQ could be established on the continent. Monty deeply resented losing overall command of the ground war, especially to Eisenhower, whom he regarded as his military inferior. On this score, he was supported by General Alan Brooke. Chief of the Imperial Staff, Brooke was Monty's mentor, confidant, and superior within the British Army. These feelings may account for a great deal of Monty's adamancy in what was not a clear-cut decision. Montgomery would continue an unabashed campaign of his own to again become the overall ground commander by kicking Ike upstairs, where Monty thought he could do some good. Monty's efforts did more to split the alliance asunder than any other post-D-Day event.

Geographical objectives continued to fall with breathtaking speed. The Free French and the Americans entered Paris, 140 kilometers east of Falaise, on the 25th. Patton's spearheads crossed the Meuse, 260 kilometers east of Paris, on the 30th.

Initial kudos for rapid exploitation rightly were given to Patton and his Third Army. Toward the end of August, 21st Army Group's advance began to accelerate. In late August, Lieutenant General Brian Horrocks's 30 Corps, part of British Second Army, raced across northern France with 12 Corps in van. Dempsey's third formation, 8 Corps, was grounded back on the Seine so that its transport could be used for resupply.

Eisenhower recognized he had to stop some of his spearheads in order to provide fuel to keep the others moving. On 30 August, General Bull, Eisenhower's assistant operations officer, met with Generals Bradley and Patton in Chartres. He unequivocally laid down the gasoline law. Most of the fuel would be diverted to Montgomery's 21st Army Group. That which 12th Army Group did get would be supplied to First Army. Third Army was shut off. Patton fumed and railed. However, as Martin Blumeson states, "even in the darkest hours, Patton realized there was no conspiracy against him. There was insufficient transport to move the large stocks back in Normandy up to the front line troops pawing for the chance to continue their exploitation."[21]

MONS—OPERATIONAL MANEUVER OF AN ARMY

ULTRA, the Allied code-breaking operation that read ciphered German radio communications, identified a large gaggle of Germans retreating up the highway to Brussels that runs through Tournai. Elements of two panzer and as many as ten infantry divisions might be trapped.[22] Ike wanted to mount an airborne drop at Tournai to bag them. Tournai lay in Montgomery's sector. Bradley had little faith in either airborne forces or Montgomery. Understanding that the Germans had little chance of forming a coherent line west of the Meuse River, he was determined to capture what remained of Fifth Panzer and Seventh Armies.[23] Like Eisenhower and Marshall, Bradley strongly advocated concentration on the destruction of German armed forces in the field. The three corps of U.S. First Army, advancing northeast on parallel routes, had outdistanced retreating Germans. This is the dream of any pursuing army. Without consulting higher headquarters, Bradley turned First Army's pursuit from the northeast to the north—and

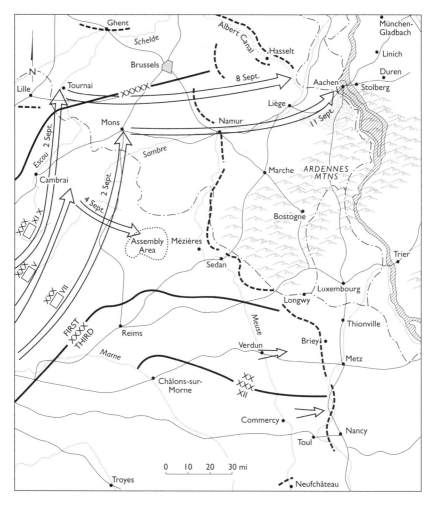

Map 1.2. First Army Pursuit to Mons

onto ground intended for 12th Army Group.[24] (Please see map 1.2.) If ULTRA was right, the flags of two panzer and ten infantry divisions might be caught up in a trap set by rapidly maneuvering U.S. First Army to cut the Lille-Brussels highway along its length. Destroying the remnants of two armies was consistent with Eisenhower's often stated intent.

Bradley focused on the enemy instead of the terrain. That is the mark of a good general. He directed XIX Corps of Hodges's First Army to interrupt its planned eastward pursuit and wheel left to cut the retreating Germans off. They were to turn north and capture Tournai. With little advance notice,

XIX Corps, commanded by Major General Charles Corlett, would have to turn 90 degrees and race 150 kilometers in forty-eight hours.

Warning orders for round-the-clock operations went out. Three divisions cranked up. Tankers, already bleary-eyed and hunched over with fatigue from the seemingly nonstop drive across France, knew more was in store before sleep could be had. The adrenaline high had long since faded into weariness. But Jerry was still running, so Americans kept pursuing. Trucks were stripped from corps artillery and anti-aircraft units. Elements of both 79th and 30th IDs were motorized so they could follow in the wake of 2nd Armored "Hell on Wheels."

2nd Armored's commander, General Edward Brooks, turned to his chief of staff and asked, "where the Hell is Ghent?" It was off the maps issued to the division.[25] At 0600 Hell on Wheels struck out toward Tournai in six parallel columns with two combat commands abreast.* Division Reserve, built around armored infantry, trailed closely behind. Some columns ran out of gas and lagged behind until resupplied. Belgians along the routes went crazy. One American had his nose split open by a beer bottle hurled up by a well-wisher.

But all was not cognac and roses. North of Hayrincourt, a number of Germans in a beet field decided to resist. Someone thought tanks could overrun the fields. Tankers could lean out their hatches and grenade foxholes as they went by. After the loss of several tank commanders, however, it was clear this wasn't such a good idea. Artillery was called in. Seven hundred rounds of airburst artillery dug out the dug-in defenders. Now the tankers had more prisoners than they could handle. Many dead were left among the beets.

At one point General Brooks, waiting by the roadside for one of his columns, was instead passed by a German one. The general got off a single round from the .50 caliber machine gun mounted on his armored car before it jammed. Colonel Hinds, commander of the armored infantry, had been conferring with Brooks. He expended a box of .50 caliber. He reached for another but found the box contained a brush and some shoe polish instead.

The senior officers radioed CCA (Combat Command A), warning them of the approaching target. Shermans blocked the Germans front and rear. Several half-tracks, which had maneuvered cross-country to get into position, slammed into the middle of the stalled German column. When

---

*Two combat commands and division reserve were in the 1944 "heavy" division structure, which applied to 2nd and 3rd Armored Divisions only.

it was over 2nd Armored counted 123 destroyed German vehicles and 300 *feldgrau*-clad bodies lying on the ground.[26]

Hell on Wheels reached their objectives with two hours to spare. Blocking positions were set up from Mons to Tournai. Resistance along the route of advance had been intermittent but sharp at times.

Initially, the prisoner haul was small. XIX Corps had arrived ahead of the bulk of the retreating Germans! As other American units forced them up the road, thousands would enter First Army POW cages. Soldiers from twenty German divisions were taken prisoner. Fast-moving armor had eliminated the need for a planned airdrop.

Lacking gasoline, 2nd Armored would remain around Tournai for three days. Finally some B-24s flew in gas. 79ID received initial priority so it could move south to reinforce Third Army. Finally XIX Corps, led by 113 Cavalry Group, moved out toward the Meuse.

XIX Corps was the left-most unit in First Army. Both V Corps and VII Corps conducted similar 90-degree right wheel maneuvers. V Corps ran out of gas before VII Corps did, thereby opening Collins's left flank. More importantly the turn would leave his right, facing toward Germany, completely open.

Lightning Joe called his boss and asked, "but who will fill the gap that will develop between my right and the Third Army?" Hodges's reply: "Joe, that's your problem."[27] Collins solved it by using a cavalry group ("mechanized" armored cars and light tanks) to guard his extended flank. It worked; VII Corps, its three divisions concentrated and oriented on the battle, raced ahead.

Cavalry watched the ever-widening opening on the right flank. The Germans had too many problems of their own to attempt to exploit a temporary advantage. The Americans maintained the initiative and exploited it to lethal advantage. Defend your weakness by getting the enemy to worry about his.

General Straube, commander of German LXXIV Corps, had neither instructions nor orders from above. He lashed two other formations, LVIII Panzer and II SS Corps, into a provisional army. Aware the American units in the area threatened to encircle his force, Straube decided to head toward Germany. The canals and marshy ground near Mons looked like a good route. Someone advised that a 25-kilometer gap in American dispositions existed around Mons and that the road through the town was the fastest way to the West Wall.[28]

Collins's lead division, 3rd Armored, took Mons. The town was eerily quiet. No Germans and few townspeople were in sight.[29] Large columns approached the town in administrative formation. German vehicles began driving up a straight stretch of highway leading into town. In the dark a German half-track all but crashed into a Sherman, and 75mm shells blew it apart. Third Armored tankers began dismantling the rest of the column with hot steel. Daybreak revealed a conglomeration of wrecks 2 kilometers long. Confused soldiers from both sides continued to blunder into one another. The forward echelon of 3rd Armored HQ, normally not in the line of direct fire, received a Distinguished Unit Citation for its role in shooting up German columns. In another instance of confusion an American MP calmly waved a Panther tank into an American motor park, where it promptly surrendered.[30]

Many Germans lost their will to fight and meekly entered captivity. Others fought like caged animals. In the confusion the headquarters of both LVIII Panzer and II SS Corps escaped. In places Americans had to use bulldozers to clear paths through the wreckage. But equipment operators had to be careful lest they hit hungry civilians who were already cutting steaks from the numerous dead horses still harnessed to what they had been pulling.

During the fighting around Mons, Collins became concerned that the way to the West Wall to the east might become blocked. He instructed his heavily reinforced 4th Cavalry Group, which had been guarding his flank, to seize bridges across the Meuse and to maintain contact with Third Army. By thinking ahead, Lightning Joe began to prepare for the next fight while his division commanders finished the current one. By the 4th, the situation had stabilized enough for Collins to dispatch the 3rd Armored toward Namur. One bridge was captured, and engineers emplaced another. First Infantry Division remained behind and continued to pick up prisoners.

Over twenty-five thousand Germans were taken prisoner.[31] This was roughly equal to the size of Students' First Parachute Army that would bring British Second Army's pursuit to a halt. In Bradley's opinion, German losses at Mons opened First Army's path to Aachen.[32] The Germans retreating from France who should have delayed First Army while the West Wall was manned were now in Hodges's POW cages.

This comparison underscores the frustration every Allied commander felt. Twenty-five thousand troops rushing pell-mell toward home are nothing more than a large juicy target. The same group placed in defensive formations by cohesive leadership can bar an army's advance. If only the Wehrmacht could be kept off balance while the Allies pushed all the way to Berlin.

Bradley's ad hoc maneuver also generated a protest about the zone incursion from Montgomery. Mons is about 50 kilometers northwest of Paris, and the fight there coincided with British Guards entering the Belgian capital. Those who criticized Bradley at Falaise said he should have ignored the army group boundary that separated the Americans and the ground needed to close the gap. This time he did. Initially 12th Army Group signaled that its subordinate units were too far along to recall. Then a much more binding restraint than an army group boundary took hold. The Americans ran out of gas.

The fighting around Mons fell within Ike's strategy—destroy German combat power west of the Rhine. Bradley's tactical good sense and swift execution by Corlett and Collins caged 25 percent of what slipped through at Falaise.

Mons also demonstrated how headstrong Bradley could be. The opportunity to "beat" both the British and the airborne spurred him on. He did overstep the boundary—with good results this time. That may have encouraged him to turn a blind eye to some orders in September—with far different results.

THE IMPENDING HALT

No wonder "victory disease" had become epidemic. Even the normally unflappable George Marshall issued a message on redeploying European Theater of Operations (ETO) army units to the Pacific, identifying the most likely date of German capitulation between 1 September and 1 November.[33] The stock market dropped in anticipation of lower profits—postwar. The war in Europe was just about over, wasn't it?

Then the gas ran out.

An under-channel pipeline brought fuel to a terminal in Bayeux. Insufficient transportation existed to move it to the spearheads. Patton's tanks ran dry on 28 August. For five days his columns were almost completely immobilized. Hodges met a similar fate on 2 September. While Montgomery was not completely stopped, he had resources to advance with only a single corps. Frustrated commanders from one end of the Allied line to the other clamored for supplies that the transportation system was incapable of delivering. Given the rapid advance of the prior three weeks, a five-day hiatus seemed to some a war-lengthening pause of the first magnitude.

Patton took the situation personally. Many authors write as if the shortage were a surprise and a mean trick conjured up by either sinister senior

American senior commanders, Monty, or gold-bricking supply "garitroopers." Some authors state that the gas halt was the cause for the entire stall in the fall. One of Patton's biographers wrote, "Five fateful days! It is possible that they added hundreds of days to the war in Europe!"[34]

However, those closest to data describing the supply situation knew this pause would come even before the first soldier dragged himself onto a Normandy beach. Before the invasion armada departed, logisticians, calculating mileages, fuel consumption rates, and the availability of trucks, knew there wouldn't be enough transportation to keep the spearheads moving. On 20 August, Eisenhower told reporters that supply lines were badly strained and that further advances would be almost impossible.[35] The date is important. Ike was ahead of his subordinates. While they imbibed the heady wine of pursuit, the supreme commander had a prescient view of what was to come.

Ike didn't have to be clairvoyant. All he had to do was to read the projections of his logisticians. Since the beginning of the pursuit, deliveries to the forward armies had not kept up with consumption.[36] Armies drew down the few days of reserve supplies they kept on hand to alarming levels. On 2 August, one day after the breakout began, SHAEF's chief of logistical plans noted that the supply shortage would soon reach major proportions.[37] By 11 August the planners concluded that no more than four divisions could be supported beyond the Seine. The initial Overlord plan built in a one-month pause on that river. A lot of numbers had been crunched to reach this conclusion.

Throwing away the plan that called for a pause at the Seine, the supreme commander said, keep on trucking. That was 19 August. Allied planners and senior commanders knew they advanced on borrowed time. During the run across France, supply shortfalls cumulated. For ten days logistical support spiraled downward. Finally the system broke down altogether.

In late August, an Allied opportunity existed because the Germans couldn't move units into holes fast enough. But an offsetting constraint existed. A German general remarked that "blitzkrieg is paradise for the tactician but hell for the quartermaster."[38] The Allies couldn't move supplies fast enough to capitalize on the opportunity. One condition was just as real as the other. No senior Allied commander should have been surprised. All through August, the logistics planners predicted the stoppage. Study after study was produced detailing the problems for anyone willing to listen.

An Allied logistical pause at the end of August was as unalterable a fact as the smoking German equipment back at Falaise. The logisticians knew they didn't have enough motor transport to sustain the pursuit. Operations officers had to take this fact, just like the weather forecast, and plan to adapt to it. If there was a forecast pause, create a plan that restarts the offensive in the most opportune manner.

The real surprise is that senior commanders did not do a better job of planning a restart of the offensive after the well-advertised logistics-induced halt finally occurred. Just maybe the pause would be too short to allow the Germans to recover. That wasn't the prudent planning assumption.

Any pause would allow the Germans time to scamper into the West Wall if not some river line farther west. During the last ten days of August, operational staffs at army group and above should have been working on forward plans predicated on logistical reality. There is scant evidence they did much else but listen to the euphoria that swept from less-informed quarters. Theater planners screamed the inescapable facts. Ike knew logistics would tether his armies west of the Rhine. Not downshifting to a gear that concentrated more combat power in fewer spearheads is the real reason for the first frustrations the Allies suffered as they restarted their advance in early September.

With data proving that a pause was inevitable, there is little excuse for army group staffs not to have put cohesive campaign plans together during the period between 20 August and 7 September. This was before frontline armies and corps became irretrievably committed in fights that would not achieve the theater plan. Most of the seeds that yielded bitter fruit for the Allies in late 1944 were planted in this time frame. Unmistakable signs of logistical strain had shown up in mid-August. On 19 August, U.S. First Army requested 62,000 tons be moved over a ten-day period to forward supply points near La Loupe, France. The logistical organization, the Communications Zone Advanced Base Section, replied it could transport only 26,000 tons for First Army in that period.[39] In order to make up the difference, First Army engineers dumped pontoons from their bridge trucks and employed them, along with dump trucks and most of the motor transport stripped from field army heavy artillery, to move the crates. Still First Army supply units ran out of many line items. What would happen if they advanced into Germany in September?

Logistical concerns would color, if not dominate, all Allied military decisions in the fall of 1944. But a five-day pause did not decide the campaign. Had the gasoline drought not existed, Patton probably would have leapt the Moselle, and Hodges might have opened a breach in the Siegfried Line. While tactically important, the logistically imposed pause dictated an early stop to the pursuit. Nevertheless, German defensive efforts would have forced a halt some dozens of kilometers farther east. British Second Army would cite increasing German resistance north of Brussels as limiting its advance. On 17 September, the opening day of Market Garden, a sharp counterattack around Lunéville would check Patton's advance. Even without a halt, unsupported spearheads would have run into resistance that could not have been overcome without concentration and a major fight.

Ike had experienced a similar supply problem before. In November 1942, he had dashed into Tunisia before his logistical base could sustain the thrust. His forces sat on their heels, out of supply, while the enemy maneuvered away from his attempt to crush them.[40] One might have expected Ike to have vividly recalled this lesson during August 1944.

Original Overlord planning envisioned a two-pronged attack toward the German border. Monty's group would advance across the north German plain past the Ruhr. Back in May when this outline was assembled, Eisenhower reasoned that the German Army could not afford to lose this industrial region and would give battle in order to defend it. He intended to destroy what remained of the Wehrmacht west of the Rhine as close to the German border as possible. If the combat units were destroyed, occupation of the industrial areas, Berlin, or any other geography would be of passing importance. Any "National Redoubt" in the southern mountains or any other bastion would be useless if there were no troops to mount an organized defense.

During the North African campaign of 1942 Montgomery had felt that Eisenhower's broad front in Tunisia dangerously overexposed American forces.[41] Apparently he was determined not to have the American amateur repeat his error.

Toward the end of August, even Ike showed some sign of the "victory disease." It shows up in the first line of FWD13765, which is the primary directive for September operations: "1. Enemy resistance on the entire front shows signs of collapse." It goes on to list enemy strength north of the Ardennes as two weak Panzer and nine infantry divisions "unlikely to offer any appreciable resistance if given no respite." Two panzer grenadier and four infantry divisions were listed south of the Ardennes, plus about 3.5 divisions in southern France. The document also warns of additional reinforcements from within Germany but doubts they will arrive in time.

But the disease never swept Eisenhower away. The parade into Paris would not continue on to Berlin unopposed. Some authors claim De Guingand, Monty's chief of staff, agreed with Eisenhower's position.[42]

2

Logistics

When action is proceeding as rapidly as it did across France during the hectic days of late August and early September every commander from division upward becomes obsessed with the idea that with only a few more tons of supply he could rush right on and win the war.

Dwight Eisenhower

The rest of our story is dominated by logistics—supply, transportation, and maintenance. Logistics define what is militarily possible. Tanks without gas cannot execute sweeping advances no matter how boldly the movement is drawn on the map. Artillery without ammunition generates no combat power. Even grunts need to eat. It has been said that "amateurs talks tactics, professionals talk logistics." "Eisenhower allocated supplies, and that was his real power."[1]

LOGISTICS DESCRIBED

Admiral King is said to have remarked, "I don't know what this 'logistics' that Marshall keeps talking about is, but I want to get some of it." In order to understand the implications of three logistical considerations—transportation, ammunition, and port capacity—that heavily influenced the fall campaign, one needs to know a little about the arithmetic of logistics. As always, the devil is in the details. And logistics is an enormous, maddening mass of them.

Logistics is "the science of planning and carrying out the movement and maintenance of forces."[2] "Logistics" is not some homogeneous bologna that can be sliced to order. To understand it a little better, logistics can be broken into four categories:

supply
maintenance
transportation
medical

During World War II, supply was broken down into five categories:*

Class I   rations
Class II   organizational equipment
Class III   fuel and lubricants (petrol, oil, and lubricants—POL)
Class IV   non-organizational equipment and construction materials
Class V   ammunition

Soldiers have a decided tendency to supplement their rations by scrounging. Small parties can live off the land for short periods. However, much of continental Europe was hungry in 1944. Soldiers gave away more than they took. Theater policy was not to acquire food on the continent unless a clear surplus existed in a locality. The American Army would need 3.5 billion lbs. of food by spring. Three hundred and forty liberty ships would be required to move it.

Class II and IV are frequently listed together. Replacement weapons and vehicles are examples of Class II supply. Construction materials—bridging, lumber, gravel, barbed wire—often make up a large portion of Class IV tonnage moved. However, additional tenting, flamethrowers, and cookstoves were also be listed under Class IV in the 1940s.

Construction consumed an enormous amount of tonnage. Seventy-three thousand five hundred tons of bridging were needed. Eighty million board feet of lumber would be consumed.[3] Reconstruction of the all-critical railroads required 47,000 tons of material.[4] Don't want to repair the railroads? You don't have the trucks to move what will be left at the depots.

Class III is principally gasoline. During World War II little gas was delivered below divisional level by bulk fuel tankers. Most was "decanted" into the familiar 5-gallon "jerry can." It was a laborious process. A lot of gasoline entered the continent via a pipeline laid across the channel and terminating in Bayeux. However, technical problems delayed operation until late August. "Pluto" (pipe laid under the ocean) pipelines began to operate just about the time of the gas drought.

---

*Five classes existed in World War II. Five additions exist in contemporary usage: VI—personal demand items (liquor, cigarettes, etc.), VII—major end items (tanks, bulldozers), VIII—medical, IX—repair parts, and X—non military.

First and Third Armies each burned about 400,000 gallons a day in their run across France. When set up, the Red Ball itself consumed 300,000 gallons a day.[5] Fuel comprised about 25 percent of the tonnage landed in France.[6] Petroleum tonnage is often excluded from port discharge totals because it is handled in segregated pumping facilities.

The greatest percentage of ammunition tonnage goes to the artillery. In operations around Aachen, First Army fired 300,000 rounds of 105mm ammo. Each weighed about 60 pounds crated. That equals about two shiploads just for the 105s. And First Army's fire plan during this period was constrained by shortage of available rounds. In a single month 6 million rounds of artillery and 2 million mortar rounds had been fired.

Tank ammunition in armored units takes considerable weight. However, tanks fire a lot less than howitzers. Tank ammunition was seldom a problem in this campaign. In infantry units, mortars are the big users. Rifle ammunition is a tiny sliver of tonnage.

Artillery ammunition is manufactured in lots. Slight variations exist between lots. Because these variations are just large enough to influence accuracy, cannoneers want all their ammunition for a given fire mission from the same lot. Frequently, lots became badly mixed in shipment. Attempts were made to re-sort it. But the system broke down. Unsorted ammunition was shipped. This added to problems of the artillery. Unsorted ammo resulted in less accurate shoots, an issue that is especially critical when firing close to friendly infantry.

Three elements are required for proper maintenance. First there must be organizations with properly trained mechanics and tools. That the U.S. Army had. Second is a good supply of parts. In the field maintainers make a lot of adjustments and switch out a lot of broken parts. Third is time to work on the equipment. Since the beginning of the Cobra breakout, that too was in short supply.

Replacement parts are, by far, the most complex element of Class II/IV supply. Think of the "exploded" diagram of an engine on the wall of an auto parts store. An enormous number of line items existed. No one had ever heard of a computer. All the records had to be kept by hand. Shops and supplies moved from place to place constantly. Keeping track of it all was next to impossible. A ton of repair parts is almost a meaningless notion. Piles of tires, transmissions, and engine blocks are of no use to a mechanic who needs to replace a punctured carburetor float.

During September, First Army received less than 10 percent of the ordnance repair parts requested. Often the required parts were missing, while much unwanted material was shipped instead. Out of frustration, First Army once sent an entire trainload of unwanted supplies back to ComZ (the Communications Zone: the rear area administered by the Services of Supply). They just moved the engine from the front of the train to the back. Third Army did the same with a train load of blacksmith's anvils. By October, there were no tires or tank tracks in Advance Section depots despite months of priority orders from the field armies.[7]

Mechanized armies have more maintainers than fighters. Much World War II mechanical paraphernalia needed a great deal of tinkering. Equipment operators/drivers were young. Nobody "owned" equipment, especially items that left units for repair. Much of it was abused, or at least ridden hard. Even combat damage added a little to the mountains of equipment broken from abusive overuse.

In addition to user maintenance, World War II maintenance was divided into direct support and general support. Broken equipment was evacuated from end users to direct support maintenance shops and then returned to users when fixed. This was a little like a good repair shop in town where you take your car or truck when it stops running altogether. General support units took heavily damaged or junked equipment and rebuilt it. Rebuilt equipment was placed back in supply channels for reissue. Divisional maintenance elements were designed to provide only 60 percent of the direct support load generated by daily operation and only 30 percent of the load generated by combat. That didn't include heavier repairs performed only at the general support level. To handle the heavier repairs and the workload overload, field armies have additional maintenance units in their rear echelon.

However, divisional maintenance units could not keep up with the rate of advance. Cumbersome non-divisional maintenance units and their heavy crates of spare parts had been left far behind during the rapid advance. Given the transportation drought, few means were available to move them forward. In fast-moving combat situations, maintenance is often deferred. Since Normandy, much equipment had been used hard. By early September, much Allied equipment was in ragged shape. There had been little time to pull maintenance. In September, the theater G4 estimated that 100,000 tons of replacement equipment was needed to re-equip the existing force and create a small reserve.[8] This was on top of daily consumption of rations, fuel, ammo, and so on, and independent of the transportation required to build up new units.

As their tanks break down, armored units slowly dissolve. One could recognize the route of advance of a tank unit in poor maintenance condition by the trail of broken-down vehicles alongside the road at seemingly regular intervals. For example 3rd Armored Division reported in early September that it had only 70 of 232 authorized medium tanks operational. The remainder were either deadlined for maintenance or missing altogether.[9] This diminution in strength parallels the problems wrought by the destruction of German equipment, which is more referenced by most authors. Missed maintenance can drop combat power as readily as missing gas or ammunition. Artillery units can't respond to fire missions if all their ammunition trucks are deadlined or their radios are busted.

Airplanes also wore out quickly. Contemporary jet engines operate thousands of hours before needing overhaul. In 1944 many piston aircraft engines were junked after a couple hundred hours in the air. By early August 1944 IX Tactical Air Command (TAC) was forced to stand down two of its six fighter groups each day for maintenance.[10]

Cold, wet weather brought with it trench foot and a plethora of additional maladies. Frontline infantry were most exposed to the elements. Sickness seriously reduced already anemic foxhole strength. Leaders paid close attention to the health of their men. The medical system was extremely important, and American medical support especially was outstanding. Operation of this critical system was not a limiting factor during the fall, so it will not be examined further.

"Personnel" is normally not considered "logistics." However, personnel replacement became very important in the fall campaign. The British Isles were out of men of prime military age. British commanders knew that 21st Army Group would see no more UK divisions and precious few replacements. Wreck a division in combat, and it was finished. There wasn't the manpower to reconstitute it. Before campaign's end, British 51st Division would be disbanded to supply replacements.

Similarly, the American Army ran short of riflemen. Planners hadn't recognized that most casualties would concentrate in one occupation specialty. During the fall rifle companies went short. Administrative units were combed for bodies. Usually, an outfit's "eight balls" (misfits) were offered up. Jailed American soldiers were offered pardons if they volunteered as infantry. More than a few eyebrows were raised when Ike offered rifleman status to "colored" service troops. Some black sergeants removed their stripes for the honor of carrying a rifle as private soldiers in service to their country.

One of the great organizational mistakes of the American Army of World War II was to assume replacement people were as interchangeable as replacement parts. Humans react to the people around them. The dynamics of small groups frequently dictates human behavior. "Buddies are forever." That can be doubly true in a combat unit. Most men don't fight for lofty ideals. They fight to protect their buddies. They fight so they don't disgrace themselves in front of their peers. In his famous study *Men under Fire* S. L. A. Marshall, official historian for the European Theater of Operations (ETO), stated: "The majority are unwilling to take extra-ordinary risks and do not aspire to a hero's role, but they are equally unwilling that they should be considered the least worthy among those present. . . . Social pressure, more than military training, is the base of battle discipline, and when that social pressure is lifted, battle discipline disintegrates."[11] Marshall noted that individuals cut off from their own small unit were not of much use. A lone retreating straggler stopped and placed in a battle position soon finds a way to slip away. Grab several from the same unit and put them into position, and they will again conduct themselves like soldiers.[12] Both the Germans and the British understood the phenomenon well. Many of their units recruited in a specific local area. New recruits trained together in a depot unit before shipping off to a frontline unit. In the British Army these units were often referred to as county regiments. As one Tommy put it, "The guys around me knew my father. I couldn't have them telling him I ran off or was a coward."

General Depuy, a battalion commander in World War II who rose to four-star rank and command of the Training and Doctrine Command, described the individual replacement problem. "These poor devils were sent us through the replacement system and often went into combat without even a chance to meet, much less know, the men with whom they fought. Many died never knowing what it was about."[13] During the fall campaign American frontline infantry units received a steady stream of replacements. A number died before knowing the names of their squad mates. Recovered wounded were often reassigned without regard to their former outfits. Some went AWOL to get back to their old buddies. Better attention to this problem would have raised the combat power of Eisenhower's armies.

But the British/German system had problems of its own. No one could predict which units would suffer casualties and need mass replacements Some replacement depots would be in surplus while other units were desperate for warm bodies. In late summer when British 21st Army Group was short 35,000 infantrymen, 52,000 were held in depots and training units in the UK.[14] Familiarity between assigners and those being assigned allowed many in depots of units not needing replacements to avoid being trans-shipped to those that did.

The eminent historian Forrest Pogue wrote the official history of the Allied Supreme Command in Europe. After studying the enormous logistical problems of late summer, he remarked:

> In hardly any respect were the allies prepared to take advantage of the great opportunity offered them to destroy the German forces before winter. The buildup of men and certain critical supplies in the United Kingdom, the arrival of divisions in France, the requisition and transport of civil affairs supplies, the organization for military government, the rebuilding of rail lines, the laying of pipelines, virtually the whole intricate military machine was geared to a slower rate of advance than that required in late August. Unfortunately the period of the great opportunity lasted only a few weeks and there was not sufficient time to make the necessary re-adjustments in the logistical machinery which would insure speedy victory.[15]

Pogue's observation contains a tone of surprise. But SHAEF planners were acutely aware of three major logistical shortfalls prior to the first paratrooper landing in Normandy. They knew because of those planning estimates.

Beyond establishment of the lodgment area, the Overlord plan seemed little more than a series of dates and phase lines. Many writers have commented on the ordinariness of Overlord projected phase lines; as if someone should have pulled a more creative guess from his head. They were not selected whimsically. Planners assumed that the Germans would vigorously defend each major river line. Montgomery himself drew the D+90 line along the Seine.[16]

Assumptions were made about when the Allies would reach a line and how many divisions would arrive. From this rough outline, planners calculated the number of gallons of gas required to move the divisions that far, the number of trucks needed to move the gas, the number of maintenance companies required to fix the trucks, and so on. Unlike a business plan presented to investors, a business operating plan contains no grand description of strategy. Rather it is page after page of numbers that tell each of the operating departments what is required of them in terms of output and when it is due. Like an operating plan in business, Overlord planners had to assemble the pieces in the right combinations and quantities to create the tools strategists and tacticians would require to do a job about the size that those phase lines assumed.

As an example of planning calculations, let's look at the requirement for rear area engineer general service regiments (GSR). One Engineer GSR can construct 12 miles of pioneer road a day or maintain 170 miles. Calculations based on estimated road usage indicated that 5 GSR, reinforced by two dump truck companies, would be required in the first six weeks of Overlord.[17]

Port capacity was the overarching logistical constraint. It dictated theater strategy. As one harried Overlord planner wrote: "The general principle is that the number of divisions required in order to capture the number of ports required to maintain those divisions is always greater than the number of divisions those ports can maintain."[18] Instead of heading toward Berlin, the plan directed the first offensive to go in the opposite direction, to capture the Brittany ports. Even with those docks in Allied hands, projections indicated that the Overlord plan would suffer from insufficient port capacity by D+120, or early October.

The second major constraint was the shortage of cargo trucks. Early in 1944, planners recognized there would not be enough trucks to support a major Allied advance beyond the Seine. The Allies didn't run out of gas in late August. They ran out of trucks to move it. Transportation shortfalls caused Ike to curtail the theater's secondary attack by Patton in September. A shortage of trucks predicted in May made the September halt inevitable.[19]

No one expected the campaign to unfold smoothly. War seldom does. But no one could have predicted the length of the Normandy stalemate or the rapidity of the breakout. What was predictable was that the advance would be anything but uniform, and that in itself should have generated a requirement for flexibility in the rate of development of the logistical base. What does a planner need to add flexibility to the logistics plan? More trucks. But allowances for this effect were not included computations of the need for transportation. Port capacity and transportation limitations interrelated and complicated each other.

A second great pause sets in during October and continues for the better part of a month. Its root grew from the third constraint. This time it was a shortage of artillery ammunition. Large-scale American combat operations became almost impossible for lack of fire support. Again, planners knew before the first attack transport left for the invasion beaches that there wasn't enough ammunition in theater to meet army and army group expenditure projections. And there wasn't enough production capacity back in the States to make up the shortfall. Parsimonious War Department planners vastly underestimated the need. Insufficient production was scheduled. Poor logistical management in the ETO reinforced the planners' beliefs. This would take time to correct. The artillery ammunition shortage was an American problem. British gunners had decent stocks throughout the war. Both Allies had insufficient truck fleets.

PROBLEMS WITH THE SERVICES OF SUPPLY

During World War II, the American Army was divided into three components: Air Forces, Ground Forces, and Services of Supply. Most organizations located behind the rear boundary of the numbered armies were Services of Supply units. In an active theater, the area that stretched behind the numbered armies was known as the communications zone (COMZ). This zone was, in turn, broken down into a series of base sections and an advance section that controlled operations immediately behind the field armies.

Lieutenant General J. C. H. Lee of the Army Service Forces commanded the Services of Supply in Europe. In addition, he was deputy commander for American forces in theater, second in rank only to Eisenhower. Lee had blanket procurement and contracting authority. He had been selected by General Brehon Somervell, the hard-working, if very bureaucratic and empire-building, head of Services of Supply, and by General Marshall. He was one of their most controversial choices. "He [Lee] was not normally concerned with the details of logistic administration . . . and had a reputation for attaching more importance to the outward appearance than the substance of things."[20] "The essential traits of those [logisticians] who succeed are great initiative, a 'can do' and a willingness to improvise, traits J.C.H. Lee lacked in abundance."[21]

Lee was a Regular Army engineer. A 1909 West Point graduate, he had also attended Command and General Staff School. During World War I, he served as chief of staff of 89th Division. In 1940, Brigadier General Lee commanded the San Francisco Port of Embarkation. A year later he commanded 2nd Infantry Division.

Controlling both the flow of supplies and paperwork, Lee held tremendous administrative power. He wielded it as skillfully as any senior level bureaucrat. A martinet, he ruled his domain with a heavy hand. A sycophant, he was not above presenting turkeys to senior field commanders just before they came in to complain about inadequate support and less than Herculean efforts by COMZ to put right a myriad of problems. Often his pettiness got under Ike's skin. For example, he caught Lee disapproving decorations approved by army group commanders. Ike wrote Lee forbidding him from doing it again.

Eisenhower did not trust either Lee or his organization.[22] As early as 1943 he described Lee to Somervell in less than glowing terms.[23] But, to accommodate Somervell's position that the logistics officer should be the number-two man in a theater, Ike had elevated Lee to deputy theater commander. Marshall had elevated Lee to three-star rank despite Ike's objection.

Lee lived high. His accommodations were always commodious and his table overflowing. He traveled on his own private train. Many found him remote, standoffish, and overly concerned with ceremonial deference to his rank. A subordinate's loyalty counted for more than his ability. The official historian euphemistically wrote, "Lee assigned some officers to positions of authority and responsibility whose qualifications were at time obscure."[24] Through them Lee maintained an iron grip, jealously defending his prerogatives over what he considered Services of Supply matters. Both hard working and very religious, Lee did put in long hours running his empire.

The official history euphemizes, "relations between the Communications Zone and the field commands were never completely cordial." There was a "general lack of confidence in the Communications Zone which was widely prevalent in the field commands."[25] Field commanders held a universally low opinion of Lee and his entourage. Patton remarked, "Lee is a glib liar."[26] Referring to the fall's supply problems, Patton wrote in his diary, "[H]e has failed in his supply setup. I cannot understand why Eisenhower does not get rid of him."[27] Many derisively dubbed J. C. H. Lee "Jesus Christ Himself." One joke making the rounds criticized God for beginning to think and act as if he were Lee.

Combat officers thought COMZ lacked the discipline for and commitment to getting the job done. At the height of the truck shortage at the end of August, Lee diverted precious transportation to move his bloated headquarters to Paris. Eight thousand officers and 21,000 men moved into the capital.[28] COMZ took over 167 hotels and its subordinate Seine Base Command another 129. By comparison, SHAEF and its organizations occupied only 25.[29] Ike was outraged at the amount of drinking and night clubbing American COMZ officers indulged in.

An official study of the history of logistics made an unfavorable comparison of Lee's operation: "[T]he Logistic structure was probably inferior to that devised during World War I."[30] Deficiencies in organization of port clearance, the depot structure, and inventory control were cited. The study also noted that the rapid exploitation across France seriously impacted the timelines logistic planners worked on. However, this disruption was nothing compared to what their German counterparts had to deal with. And they regenerated an army from the flotsam fleeing the disaster in France.

One logistician stood out from Lee's mediocrity. Major General Edward Plank, the Advance Section commander, did the best with what he received from the rest of COMZ. The supply system was designed to dump tonnage in the Advance Section, where trucks from the numbered armies picked it up. "The field commanders in the 12th Army Group were unanimous in expressing confidence in the ADSEC Commander, General Plank."[31] Plank instilled an urgency within his command to meet the needs of combat units, which was much appreciated.

The southern line of communications up from Marseilles was not under Lee's control until late in the fall. Instead it operated under the Mediterranean Theater of Operations, initially within the preview of General Devers. "Dissatisfaction with the service elements never reached such proportions on the southern line of communications."[32]

Knowing Lee's foibles and his ability to manipulate the system for his own benefit, "Beetle" Smith urged Ike to get rid of him as well as most of the base section commanders. After the war Smith stated: "Lee was a stuffed shirt. He didn't know much about supply organization."[33] Ike was to regret not taking the advice of his chief of staff.

Major General Everett Hughes had served under Ike since back in North Africa. In Europe, he served as a second set of eyes and ears for Eisenhower.[34] He was one of the biggest proponents of replacing Lee. During the Normandy campaign, an attempt was made to reorganize Services of Supply in ETO. Little came of it except some shuffling of the organization chart. Hughes railed that Ike wouldn't "make orders that stick."[35] Apparently Ike did not want to cross swords with Somervell. Eisenhower, ever the pragmatist, or politician if you wish, did not want to make enemies in high places on which he was dependent for support.

By the fall of 1944, Marshall recognized something was amiss with ETO's logistic leadership. He dispatched a respected leader, Lieutenant General Ben Lear, to ETO to replace Lee as deputy commander for American forces in the theater. Lear's third star predated Pearl Harbor, which made him senior to every American lieutenant general in ETO. When Lear arrived, Smith took him under his wing. Overwhelmed by the politics and suffering from a prostate problem, Lear declined to get sucked into the infighting between Lee and Eisenhower/Smith (Smith blamed Lee for the manpower shortage).[36] Ben Lear wound up as deputy theater commander for manpower.

Marshall did eventually catch on. The chief of staff thought the world of the chief of service forces, but after the war, General Marshall remarked, "Somerville did great things around the world. The only thing he failed to do was when I sent him to Europe to handle Lee. He didn't quite do it. Lee had been his room mate at college."[37]

Conversations about logistics revolve around tonnages. But there is an additional dimension to the problem. A logistician not only needs the materials and the brute force to move them, he needs the information to control the process. What good are supplies if the logistician can't locate them and identify who needs them? Information systems were not invented in the computer age. Before electronic boxes, information was controlled by legions of clerks wielding mimeographed forms, stubby pencils, and rubber stamps. The sheer volume of paper that had to be processed was overwhelming. For example, Bradley's 12th Army Group headquarters received 1,100 bags of mail a day.[38] But the information system lost track of incoming supplies from the get-go. It is sometimes said the American Army creates an "iron mountain" of supplies and then fights a war from it. Only nobody knew what was in the mountain.

Services of Supply never created a decent record-keeping system in the European Theater. The official history cites instances where supply officers simply ordered more from Stateside rather than try to search among the many depots and warehouses for material that was known to be on hand—somewhere. Material that is unidentified and unsorted is unusable. The transportation used to pile it up had been wasted. Services of Supply had two years' experience, from Guadalcanal to Italy, of difficulty in keeping records straight. ASF staff officers found "communications Zone's staff work had been below standard . . . it had failed to pay sufficient attention to the details of logistical management . . . had let things drift. . . . [I]t was constantly rushing to put out fires which it should have had the foresight to prevent," and it had an "ineffectual stock control system, inadequate signal communications and poor documentation."[39] If the "Organizers of Victory" prepared their combat troops for war, they did not do the same for their service support troops.

Patton summed up what many field commanders felt: "I stated they (COMZ) were too inflexible in their methods. If fighting troops had been equally inflexible, the war would have already been lost."[40] Nobody likes filling out forms in triplicate. The reason for the paperwork and procedure was to provide information, especially in the days before computers. To simultaneously have records in shambles and to have the end user complain about inflexibility is the worst of all worlds. It is the inability to control after inflicting all the pain of a control process.

REQUIRED TONNAGES

Supply consumption rates in the tables below were computed from U.S. Army experience in western Europe during World War II. The mix and rate of supply consumption varied with the type of combat. During the pursuit across France, a lot of gas but little ammunition was burned up. As armies engaged in heavy combat along the West Wall, mountains of shells passed through guns, and fuel consumption fell off.

Both the theater G4 (logistics officer) and 12th Army Group's G4 preferred to use 650 tons per division slice* per day delivered at the field army.[41] During a buildup stage a division slice would climb to 900 tons a day.[42] The extra tonnage allowed the reserve necessary to begin a major offensive. On top of this, 9th Air Force consumed 4,000 tons a day on the continent. In a pinch Bradley estimated he needed something on the order of 9,000 tons a day to keep his stocks even. That works out to 500 tons per division.

Additional tonnage would be consumed in the rear area bringing that tonnage to the front. Note that attacking units consume about twice as much tonnage as pursuing units. In other words, the ammo weighs a lot more than the gas. Just as the Allied armies reached the end of their logistical tether, they entered heavy combat along the West Wall and the Moselle. Just as the delivery system broke down, required tonnage doubled. To imply that the Allies almost made it without a pause along the German frontier is inaccurate.

British tonnage estimates were similar. Their planning assumptions were 520 tons at the army railhead plus 180 tons consumed along the lines of communication.[43] In early September, Monty's 21st Army Group cut down imports from 16,000 tons/day to 7,000 tons in order to free up trucks from port clearance operations.[44] A quick calculation of 520 tons times the

---

*A division slice includes all the non-divisional units associated with a combat division. For example, a typical division was supported, on average, by three non-divisional artillery battalions, two engineer battalions, two quartermaster and ordnance maintenance battalions, and a couple of hospitals, not to mention all the truck companies needed to keep supplies moving forward.

Table 2.1. Armored Division Supply

	Attack	Pursuit	Defense	Reserve
		Tons per day		
Class				
I	40	42	41	41
II & IV	137	46	40	44
III	103	174	56	44
V	375	66	400	0
	655	328	535	129

fourteen divisions in his army group indicates this was a pinch but would provide resupply consistent with sustained combat operations.

Pre-D-Day planners estimated ports allocated to the Americans and in Allied hands would have a port discharge capacity of 46,000 tons/day by D+90 (i.e., 4 September). American forces would need 40,000 tons of capacity, including construction and so on. At first glance this seems more than the immediate need. Much of the difference is accounted for by the tremendous need for material to repair damaged facilities and construct new ones, such as airfields, to support the Allies' forward advance.

But actual discharge capacity fell behind almost from the get-go. Planners estimated 25,000 tons/day capacity would be needed by the end of June. The actual rate was 19,000 tons/day. Add British and American requirements and one can easily see the pinch. Remember that equipment of new units coming ashore also had to be included. The 25,000-ton rate would not be reached until 21 July—almost a month behind schedule.

Mountains of supplies littered dumps in Normandy and England or remained unloaded in the fleet of cargo ships awaiting berths. With the exception of artillery ammunition, the problem wasn't material per se. It was putting the needed material up with the frontline troops hundreds of miles inland. Tonnage allocations—that is, tonnage movement allocations—determined who could mount an attack and who would sit on his heels. Supply priority is a principal tool with which to weight a main effort. Bradley was very much in the logistics loop. When Normandy Base Section was established on July 14, Bradley was to have final authority in all logistical matters except for priorities concerning the Air Force.[45]

At the beginning of the pursuit, deliveries to forward armies kept pace. First Army received, on average, 6,144 tons a day. Third Army, which moved out ahead, received 13,250 tons a day. Half of it was in gasoline. The

Table 2.2. Infantry Division Supply

	Tons per day		
	Attack of fortified Psn	Attack of hastily organized Psn	Pursuit
Class			
I	51	48	50
II & IV	55	55	41
III	44	75	136
V	430	386	69
	580	564	296

Source: FM101-10-1 Staff Officers' Field Manual Organizational, Technical, and Logistical Data, July 1971, Appendix B cites FM 101-10, Aug. 1949, from which this data was taken. Data reflects World War II in Europe experience.

transportation system could not maintain this pace as the armies moved eastward. From the beginning of the pursuit, shortage in lift appeared. Stocks at forward points began to decline as consumption outstripped arriving shipments.[46] SHAEF logisticians felt it would be infeasible to maintain anything but the smallest American force beyond the Seine.[47] Between 25 August and 12 September the Allied armies had advanced from the D+90 to the planned D+350 phase line. Nowhere was the transport available to cover such a huge variation in the ton miles that had to be moved. By the time the field armies reached the Seine, they had largely used up their operational reserves.[48]

During the pursuit, COMZ gasoline stocks were never exhausted. During the first half of August stored gasoline in Normandy increased from 25.8 million gallons to 27 million gallons.[49] That represented a 11.5-day supply at the rate 12th Army Group was burning it during the pursuit. Again, the shortage was not supply but transportation to move it forward.

On the 20th of August Third Army reserve stocks were down to one day's consumption of rations and gas and insufficient ammunition to resupply forward units with the amount consumed in two days of heavy fighting.[50] Despite the numbers, and the rate at which they were deteriorating, Patton continued to press his spearheads forward.

By the end of August First Army needed 5,500 tons/day. It received 2,225 tons per day on COMZ transportation. Another 800 tons moved by First Army trucks diverted from other duties that weren't supposed to be performing line-of-communications hauling.[51] The combined figure is half of receipts in mid-August when First Army was at the Falaise pocket.

Third Army had an even more voracious appetite. Patton's G4 wanted 6,000 tons for daily consumption. In addition, he identified a requirement to ship 12,500 tons of Class II and IV equipment (principally weapons) to replace that which had been lost or worn. To prepare for upcoming combat, Third Army wanted to build up a 15,000-ton ammunition reserve.[52]

Obviously, these tonnages were out of the question. On 30 August Bradley and his G4, Major General Raymond C. Moses, met with the theater G4, Brigadier General James Stratton. General Lee and his organization were taking a lot of heat for their inability to supply the forward armies. Twelfth Army Group estimated that it needed 20,000 tons a day to cover its armies, overhead, and necessary re-equipping. However, no one expected anything like this number to materialize.

Stratton estimated that by 2 or 3 September, COMZ could deliver 11,400 tons a day to the area of Chartres, 40 miles short of Paris and the Seine. Six thousand tons a day would come by truck, 5,400 tons by rail. After subtracting the needs along the line of communications, civil affairs, and the air force, 12th Army Group would receive 7,000 tons a day.[53] Even that was about 60 percent of what its forward divisions needed.

General Moses doubted COMZ could deliver anything of the sort. He had become very angry with repeated COMZ shortfalls and blamed most of the supply screwups on that organization. He was right. Stratton had promised more than COMZ could deliver. Because of poor record keeping, actual records are confusing and contradictory. First Army complained that COMZ fell short 1,900 tons a day during early September.[54] Third Army received an average of 2,620 tons, 40 percent of what Patton's divisions needed.[55]

During the week of 10–16 September, First Army receipts averaged 5,700 tons per day; Third Army, 3,700 tons. COMZ did not achieve its promised levels until mid-September. By that time, Bradley had decided to split supply tonnage evenly between First and Third Armies. The worst of the supply famine had passed. However, Army minimum daily resupply rates were nowhere near to being achieved. First Army set its minimum at 6,202 tons a day, Third Army at 6,665.[56]

Monty's 21st Army Group was suffering shortages as well. But they were nowhere near as severe as Bradley's problems. Moving parallel to the coast, 21st Army Group remained much closer to its depots and supporting entry ports. This reduced the tonnage expended moving tonnage forward. Still Monty was 250 kilometers from his nearest operating ports and 500 kilometers from his principal depot complex at Bayeux. To compound matters, 1,400 British three-ton trucks were deadlined because the manufacturer had supplied bad pistons. No replacement parts were available.

Twenty-First Army Group was at least 25 percent smaller than 12th Army Group. Monty's logistical tail was shorter. His forces were closer to the coast, and home base was just across the Channel. Despite these differences, Monty estimated he needed 12,000 tons a day, more than 12th Army Group was asking for.[57] For a short period he felt he could cut down to 7,000 tons. But "[a]s soon as I have Pas de Calais working, I would then require about 2500 additional 3 ton lorries plus an assured airlift averaging a minimum 1,000 tons a day to enable me to get to the Ruhr and finally Berlin."[58]

Compare Monty's calculations with those of Bradley's G4. The Englishman was by no means parsimonious. In chapter 4, we shall see the reason. Monty was calculating what he needed to support his alternative strategy, not what he needed for the tasks immediately before his army group.

TRANSPORTATION

At the beginning of September, the Allies did not lack for supplies. The beaches were piled high, and the ports were clogged. Normandy Base Section depots bulged with crates of every description. The problem was the lack of transportation to get what was needed to the armies approaching the German frontier. Over 90 percent of the tonnage that had been offloaded lay near the beaches.[59] There was a massive sorting problem. Truck companies were needed for "port clearance," that is, moving crates from the wharves and into supply dumps where they could be sorted and categorized. Remember, no one at the time had ever heard of a computer.

Before D-Day, planners had identified a shortage of truck transport.[60] U.S. Transportation Corps estimated that 240 truck companies would be needed in Europe. SHAEF planners came up with an estimate of only 100. The compromise was 160. But the mix of heavy line haulers was below Transportation Corps estimates. Seventy of the companies were to have heavy semitrailers. A requisition for them was placed in December 1943. Production snarl-ups prevented producing most of these tractor trailers by the end of May 1944. Instead of 10-ton semitrailers, most substitutions were "deuce and a halves" with some short-bed 6-ton tractor-trailers initially earmarked for the Ledo road thrown in.[61]

Blitzkrieg is characterized by sudden movements of large, supply-hungry mechanized forces. If the attacker achieves his desire in combat—sudden, deep advance—he undoubtedly has just increased the distance back to the railhead. Tanks can roll much faster than engineers can rehabilitate wrecked railroads. Whatever your logistician computed to support the force in a steady state, add for the need to move a lot of tonnage to forces that have become suddenly distant from the railhead. Additional trucks are required to pick up the load. What happens if the port is in the "wrong" place or the rails haven't been sufficiently repaired to take traffic? Trucks have to fill in this gap as well. Planners had not allowed for these contingencies.

The compromise on the number of truck companies had enormous strategic impact but went little noticed by senior commanders. The logistics staffs were well aware of the problem and had repeatedly flagged it. By D+41 only thirty truck companies were planned to be in the lodgment area to meet a daily movement requirement of 23,700 tons a day. General Moses, destined to be 21st Army Group's G4 but assigned to Monty's HQ for Overlord, expressed serious misgivings about the planned size of the truck fleet planned for D+41.[62] Logisticians warned that the armies would run out of supply at the D+90 phase line (about the Seine). Suddenly, the cargo truck became the most important weapon in Western Europe.

Shortfalls in many other supporting units, especially ordnance maintenance companies and heavy truck maintenance companies, were also projected.[63] That meant the existing truck companies would be wasting assets. The mechanics were not likely to keep up with an ever-lengthening deadline of broken vehicles.

Overlord logistical plans assumed the combat armies would be on the Seine in early September. Instead they were along the West Wall. Rail transportation should have done the heavy lifting. However, the rails in northwestern France had been thoroughly torn up. In order to protect and isolate the invasion area, Air Force bombers had conducted what now appeared to be an overly successful "Transportation Plan" designed to rip up Seine bridges and French railroad capacity.

To solve the transportation shortfall, why not rely on aircraft? As Eisenhower observed, the answer is "octane." An aircraft cannot move enough fuel tonnage to sustain itself at the far end of its journey. It is a relationship similar to calculations in the era before mechanization. A horse cannot pull a large enough wagon to carry its own fodder for an extended trip, say across a desert.

The tonnage that could be delivered by the entire Allied air transport fleet averaged about 650 tons a day. It could bring in 1,000 tons a day with a maximum effort.[64] That's enough to support one to two divisions. Air transport can move critical supplies quickly, but it cannot sustain an army. Desert Storm proved this was as true in 1991 as it was in 1944.

In 1944, the real tonnage mover was the railroad. Trains provided the heavy line haul. In the 1940s, a single track in the United States line could move ten 400-ton-capacity trains a day. A double track line allows for far more efficient operation. It can move 12,000 tons a day on thirty trains.[65] The Allies intended to rely on the excellent French railways for long distance hauling.[66] Overlord planners estimated each numbered army needed its own double track line. Trains were to move high tonnage items, such as artillery ammunition, bridging, and rations, to dumps directly behind each army. Army trucks would have to move supplies only from the railhead to tactical units. Planners assumed this would be no more than a 150-mile haul.

In Overlord, the high-tonnage transportation system was an oceangoing ship arriving at a deep-water port and transferring cargo onto a railroad, with operating railheads in close proximity to each numbered field army. Since the Civil War, armies have understood the need to destroy (or repair) the rails. Ask any Georgian about "Sherman bow ties" (rails stripped from roadbeds, heated, and then wrapped around trees). Logisticians pleaded with the air strategists not to bomb the French rail system any more than was absolutely necessary. What the Air Force didn't destroy, the Germans were likely to rip up as they retreated.

Standard 2½-ton trucks were frequently overloaded. Many carried over 4 tons a trip. Including the impact of larger semitrailers, the average truck involved in Red Ball averaged 5.9 tons.[67] The average train carried 1,000 tons.[68] A single train moved as much as four truck companies. One daily train delivered about as much as all the airlift available in ETO. Use of a single two-track line replaces eighty to one hundred truck companies!

In the attack on the railways, the primary objective was destruction of locomotives and associated repair facilities.[69] In Region Nord of France 1,500 of 2,000 assigned locomotives had been immobilized from either air attack, lack of maintenance, or lack of coal. Rundstedt's rail chief estimated that one hundred daily trains were required to sustain the Wehrmacht in France. By D-Day, average daily train movements had fallen to thirty-two. Eighteen of twenty-four Seine bridges between Paris and the sea had been dropped. Another three had been so weakened they were closed to traffic. Destroyed marshaling yards around the French capital were a real problem. Supplies were offloaded onto trucks, motored through the city, and reloaded onto undamaged lines going east and north. Paris itself required 1,500 tons a day to provide relief for the civilian population. Not until mid-September had reconstruction advanced to the point that trains could be routed through Paris.

Given the well-known trucking shortage, rehabilitation of the French railways took on added importance. General service engineers were switched from road maintenance to railroad rehabilitation, which was given highest priority.[70] Of course this would degrade the engineering effort to support the Red Ball trucking operation. So much for the planning calculation for GSR referred to earlier. Only two of the five engineer regiments assigned to this duty had any specialized training on railroad construction.[71] The biggest problem were bridges that had been destroyed along the right of way. By D+90, the rail system was not expected to go beyond Rennes.[72] Planners estimated 47,500 tons of construction material would be needed to push one double-tracked trunk line just that far. That tonnage requirement was on top off what the army groups were not getting but were screaming for.

Commanders from numbered army up understood the impact of a functioning rail line. Patton's disdain for things logistic was known by many. Seventh Army proposed to share the rail line between Toul and Nancy. Patton declared there would be no discussion of the subject. Rail capacity was absolutely essential to Third Army, and the line was being used to maximum capacity.[73] The status of even one trunk line became a subject of communication at the highest level. In his 24 August letter to Marshall, Ike cited the imminent opening of a double track line to Chartres. "This will ease our situation immeasurably."[74]

POL pipelines known as Pluto were planned to move a lot of Class III tonnage. But the Allies had little experience in the operation of flexible pipelines. Ten 3-inch lines were laid from the Isle of Wright to the Continent. Each line had throughput of 300 tons of gasoline a day. On the continent, three 6-inch lines (two truck gas, one aviation gas) were laid going forward. They had a combined practical capacity of 1,515 tons/day.[75] But pipelines are a little like railroads. They move tonnage efficiently but only over lines that have been pre-installed. Seven thousand engineers, including many former oil workers, labored to extend the system. The major limitation was the lack of trucks to deliver pipe.[76] Specialized parts were airlifted in from the United States.

Logisticians did make an attempt to adjust to the impending tonnage shortfall induced by the pursuit across France. Transportation officers established the "Red Ball Express" on 23 August. Two one-way routes were laid out from Saint-Lô to southwest of Paris. Only Red Ball vehicles were allowed on them. By this time, COMZ had 198 truck companies under its technical direction.[77] However, only 84 were under its direct control and hence available for line haul service. Initially, 67 truck companies were employed. Over half of the units had 2½-ton vehicles. Most companies contained 48 trucks.

Almost 500 tons were delivered the first day. The objective was to move 100,000 tons to the forward armies by 1 September. Rail could move only 25,000, tons so trucks had to move the remaining 75,000. Composite truck companies had been formed by withdrawing men and equipment from other organizations. Antiaircraft, artillery, and specialized engineers units were heavily drafted. So were the trucks of three American infantry divisions that were immobilized near the coast. Four days later 132 companies with 5,958 trucks were involved in the operation. On its best day 13,576 tons were moved. Red Ball fell just short of target.[78]

The Red Ball run was a 700-mile round trip. Most of the distance was covered at 20 mph. A round trip, including loading and unloading, took five days. With 6,000 trucks in operation, about 1,200 truckloads reached forward dumps daily. They averaged about 7,000 tons a day. That equated to less than one operational double-track rail line.

To control line haul trucking, a motor transport brigade was formed. By 31 August it controlled one hundred companies and had capability of moving 10,000 tons 100 miles/day. In November, large semitrailers began to enter the theater. Eighteen hundred trailers and 690 tractors entered France via the quays at Marseilles. Fourteen semitrailer companies became the principal gasoline haulers. Five had skid-mounted 750-gallon tanks, and nine had 2,000-gallon tank trailers.[79] By the end of 1944, 104 of 198 truck companies were still equipped with 2½-tonners.[80] The British added to their motor transport by shipping trucks not previously earmarked to leave the United Kingdom. Seventeen additional British truck companies arrived by early October.[81]

Widespread use of trucks instead of rails added greatly to the consumption of supply to move supply. Before Red Ball, the American Army consumed 800,000 gallons per day. Red Ball itself consumed 300,000/day.[82]

American logistics doctrine required the rearward echelon to deliver to the more forward one. For example COMZ trucks deliver to armies; army trucks deliver to divisions. Because of the tonnage starvation, armies sent their transport back toward the beaches looking for supplies. This also caused dislocation. Stripping army transportation would slow the advance of combat support units needed for heavy fighting in September.

First Army supplemented its forty-three quartermaster truck companies with an additional ten to twenty provisional companies.[83] Troops derisively dubbed provisional units "truck destroyer" companies. As with most levies,

commanders filled them with their least desirable soldiers. Without sufficient trained drivers, vehicles took a beating. Mechanics couldn't keep up
with the additional workload. By the end of September 1,500 trucks were
deadlined, awaiting someone to repair them.[84]

Some trucks committed to Red Ball were taken from port clearance,
thereby guaranteeing future snarl-ups on the docks. Backed-up, uncleared
ports meant incoming ships had to wait at anchor. The War Department
complained that these idle bottoms disrupted shipping schedules all over
the globe and therefore reduced sailing dates required to match projected
discharge levels. This backup meant there was no way to meet emerging
priorities—such as ammunition.

This was not the first time the Allies had run out of trucks. A large truck
shortage had also surfaced in North Africa.[85] As alluded to in chapter 1, Ike
had a similar experience in advancing beyond his supply transportation
capacity early 1943. The lesson wasn't learned.

Red Ball operated for only a short period. Rail reconstruction finally
solved the problem. By 18 September, through rails reached Liege.[86] By early
September gasoline pipelines reached 280 kilometers southwest of Paris.[87]
These remedies were too late to lay in tonnage for either Market Garden or
First Army's attack through the Aachen Gap.

Red Ball would not be the last time forward movement relied on trucks.
In the late winter of 1945, trucks delivered the bulk of tonnage to support
the exploitation into Germany. The "X, Y, and Z" routes benefited from the
Red Ball experience and greater availability of tractor-trailers for line haul.

Tracks north and east of Paris suffered little from either bombing or
fighting. Initial rail service to the combat armies began from Paris. In a
reversal of normal practice, supplies made the first leg from base section
dumps to the Paris marshaling yards by truck and then were placed on
the train. During October 798 freights arrived to Paris, and 999 departed
toward the front.[88] By 15 December 50,000 tons a day reached the city of
light. Twelve thousand tons a day came up from Marseilles by late October.

Trucks are mundane. But the shortage, predicted months before D-Day,
was the proximate cause for the end of the pursuit. If the production people could have traded a couple hundred bombers for the eighty missing
truck companies, they might have shortened the war. A few hundred fewer
heavy bombers would not have made an impact on the war's outcome. Ford
shouldn't have been making B-24s at Willow Run. Instead, tractor-trailers
should have been coming off the line.

THE WAR FOR PORTS

Planning for the cross-Channel attack had always revolved about port capacity.[89] In 1944, conventional wisdom held that invading armies must capture major ports or fail. Limited discharge capacity of the ports in northern France was a major headache. A large group of ports would need to be captured and placed into operation.

In 1944, a rule of thumb was a discharge rate for general cargo of 500 tons per day per ship. A typical ship might carry 5,000 tons. Both of these amounts are small by contemporary containerized rates, but these were the days of cargo slings and hooks. If each division required 500 tons of dry cargo a day, each fully worked berth could support one. Minimum air force requirements would require eight more. Cherbourg couldn't begin to fill the need.

As Overlord planners continued their calculations, they concluded there simply was not enough discharge capacity available. Engineers came up with a solution. They would build artificial ports at the invasion beaches. Code named Mulberry, floating caissons and piers would be towed across the Channel and installed. Ships could discharge directly onto them. Including Mulberry, total discharge capacity was just enough to support the planned buildup.[90]

Engineers did not think the Mulberry facilities would survive strong gales that came down the English Channel. The prefabricated ports were seen as a stopgap until sufficient port capacity was captured and rehabilitated. Until the July breakout, the biggest logistical concern was that port capture and therefore development was far behind plan.[91] Lack of progress toward the Breton and Seine ports was very worrisome. Fortunately over-the-beach daily throughput and the survivability of Mulberry far exceeded expectations.

During World War I, much of the AEF entered France by stepping onto the quays of the deep-water port at Brest. That port loomed large on the planners' ledger. It was the primary magnet pulling the Allied armies into Brittany. Deep-water ports were required to accept oceangoing ships sailing directly from the United States. Antwerp at the opposite end of the English Channel and Marseilles in the south of France offered the best alternatives. Even with the addition of Brest, projections indicated insufficient discharge capacity. To meet the need, a large artificial harbor was planned for Quiberon Bay on the south coast of Brittany.[92]

Cranes, warehouses, and rail facilities were required for port clearance. Logisticians anticipated that these facilities would be severely damaged. Extensive study had been conducted about the potential nature of damage and the resources required to repair it. Extensive bombing of the ports of Baltimore, Portland, Mobile, and Savannah was assumed. Engineers went about identifying what would be needed to reconstruct them. A list of equipment and materials was made. From this data, army engineers designed port reconstruction units and pre-stocked required material in England.[93] Extensive drawings were made of selected French ports, especially Brest.

Any general involved in D-Day planning was very aware of the port situation. As commander of the invading army group, Monty was keenly aware of the problem.

Distance between port and the front line obviously impacts the transportation problem. Cherbourg was the first port to be rehabilitated under the plan. It was a primary objective of the Normandy campaign. By the time Patton ran out of gas in late August, Cherbourg was the only major operating port in Allied hands. It would remain an important installation until VE Day. Cherbourg was supposed to discharge 20,000 tons a day. By the end of August only 12,900 tons a day were being offloaded. German demolitions proved more extensive than the engineers had anticipated. Only five of planned twenty-eight Liberty berths were free of debris and available.

The plan called for 14,000 tons a day to be coming off the docks of the Brittany ports. Now that the Brittany ports had been scratched off the rehabilitation list, logicians needed an early opening of Le Havre and Antwerp.[94] All senior commanders understood the need for these facilities.

The armies couldn't be moved closer to the existing ports. Therefore, ports closer to the armies had to be seized. Position is also critical. At best, a truck at 20 mph (33 kph) can perform only one 200-mile (333-kilometer) round trip a day. As a practical matter, including stops, fueling loading, and so on, trucks averaged only 400 kilometers a day. Therefore a port 200 kilometers closer to the front needs one truck less in the "pipeline" for each truck load delivered. Given the shortage of locomotives and rolling stock, a similar benefit is gained in rail operation. Again the critical importance of Antwerp is underlined. Omaha Beach to Aachen, scene of heavy fall fighting, is 570 kilometers. Antwerp to Aachen is 130 kilometers.

The initial Overlord requirement had been for 38,500 tons a day.[95] Without the beaches or Antwerp, planners feared capacity would be less than 20,000 tons a day. Without Brest, Le Havre, or Antwerp, 12th Army Group's

Table 2.3. Actual Discharge Rates of Ports Supporting U.S. Forces
(Short Tons per Day)

	Aug	Sept	Oct	Nov	Dec
Omaha Beach	12,603	8,800	4,634	485	
Utah Beach	6,791	5,425	2,628	466	
Cherbourg	9,634	11,360	13,209	15,655	9,036
minor Norman ports	4,529	3,617	2,125	1,760	1,834
minor Breton ports	342	2,717	2,808	2,315	987
Le Havre			2,230	5,371	5,999
Rouen			972	4,609	4,785
Antwerp				212	15,448
Northwest Europe	33,898	33,919	28,336	30,871	38,089
South of France	6,305	11,807	18,964	19,784	18,121
	40,202	43,727	47,300	50,656	56,210

Source: Derived from Ruppenthal, Logistical Support of the Armies, vol. 2, p. 124.
Note: Tonnages allocated to American forces only. Note the impact of both Antwerp and the
South of France, principally Marseilles.

port need was reaching crisis proportions. Emergency preparations to beach LSTs on the Calais coast were made.[96]

These were projections on which decisions were based. While they were correct in some details and not in others, reality proved to be as dreary as the planners' overall picture. As the official history states: "The logistic support of U.S. forces reached its lowest ebb in the month of October. At no other time during the eleven months of continental operations did the supply situation appear so unfavorable in all of its aspects. This can be attributed in large measure to the unsatisfactory port situation."[97]

When Ike elected to jump the Seine, planners estimated they would have to put 100,000 tons of supplies in depots of the Chartres-Dreux-Zloupe triangle by 1 September. Planners had projected 20 percent would come in by rail. With no operating railroads, trucks had to hump the load.

The field armies continued to feel the pinch. During the period 5–15 September First Army had received only 3,300 tons a day. Third Army received even less, 2,500 tons a day. Both armies were engaged in heavy combat. Neither was receiving even 500 tons per division per day. First Army was down to five days of ammunition.

Discharge rates across the invasion beaches continued to surprise planners. Virtually no one thought such tonnages could be achieved or sustained into September. However, the fall brought Channel storms that sharply reduced and then finally eliminated over-the-beach operations. In the Overlord plans, Brest and the other Brittany ports were supposed to take up the slack. However, Brest is 200 kilometers farther away from the West Wall than are the Normandy beaches. The spectacular race across France invalidated plans for Brittany port development.

Le Havre is third to Marseilles and Cherbourg among French ports. Situated at the mouth of the Seine, the port boasted fourteen basins and 13 kilometers of quays. It was the only English Channel facility, aside from Cherbourg, that could directly offload oceangoing Liberty ships. Rouen, the port capital of Normandy, lies 125 kilometers up the Seine from Le Havre. As long as the Germans held Le Havre, Rouen's outlet to the sea was blocked. Capable of taking a Liberty ship that had already discharged part of its cargo, this modest port had significant value.

During the fall, Cherbourg handled more cargo than anyone thought it could. Despite that good performance and the Seine ports' coming on line, total daily tonnage coming in to support the American armed forces dropped. Daily tonnage delivered in October was one-sixth less than August and September. The numbers of both squadrons and divisions on the continent were supposed to increase. Winter was coming on. Paris had to be supported. No wonder logisticians screamed to open Antwerp. Not until that port cranked up in December was the squeeze eased.

Table 2.3 also underscores the need for the invasion for southern France. In midsummer no one could predict with any certainty when Antwerp might fall or the state of demolition it might be found in. Brest was so thoroughly destroyed that no serious rehabilitation was attempted during the war. What if early fall storms smashed operations on the invasion beaches? Without either of these ports or Marseilles, the Allied buildup would have faltered. The entire front risked indefinite stalemate, which would have been disastrous for both the British and the Americans.

While northwest European tonnage dropped September to October, southern France (principally Marseilles) more than made up the difference. However, little of this came to the aid of Bradley's army group. Supplies coming up from the Cote d'Azur belonged to the Mediterranean Theater of Operations (MTO). The artificial barrier between MTO and ETO was difficult to pierce. This ridiculous bureaucracy-induced restriction added to the less than sterling record of American logistical management. In

November Patton began receiving 1,000 tons a day. Given the tonnages in table 2.3, this is not an impressive amount.

Supplies began landing on the quays of Marseilles in late September. But the truck shortage bit again. So few were available for port clearance that the Americans pressed local horse-drawn wagons into service.[98] As more equipment and capacity came on line, the logistics picture finally began to improve. By 1 November 1,100 trucks were available for port clearance.

On the other hand, the situation for Bradley's 12th Army Group was far worse than planned. During July, discharges averaged 20–25,000 tons a day against a requirement of 30,000.[99] Neither Brest nor the planned artificial port at Quiberon ever came on line. The invasion beaches received far more cargo than anyone had anticipated. But coming bad weather would inevitably close them down. Planners estimated they would shut down completely by September's end, so Le Havre and Rouen were welcome additions. Repairing damage in Le Havre from German demolition and British bombardment took a month. Civilians required relief supplies that hadn't been anticipated; Paris sucked in 2,400 tons a day. Bradley's spearheads were farther east than anticipated, and more importantly, they were much farther from railheads.

Bradley needed the additional divisions scheduled to arrive from the States. He planned to bring six newly arriving divisions up to the front in mid-October. Without additional deep-water quays, he would have trouble landing supplies for his existing divisions, let alone capacity for debarking new ones. The theater G4, Brigadier General James Stratton, projected that deliveries would not meet even minimum maintenance requirements until the end of October. He estimated the Americans would need a minimum of 22,000 tons a day to supply 12th Army Group and Ninth Air Force and establish minimum reserves.[100] That did not include capacity to replace badly worn equipment or land winter clothing. Neither did it allow for large Class IV requirements such as the 8,000 tons of bridging Montgomery assembled for Market Garden. It didn't cover the enormous tonnages required to restore port and railroads, which was the only way to ultimately solve the transportation problems.

Hitler understood the port problem. He counted on it. The fuehrer knew Antwerp was the key. In order to keep that Belgian port closed, Hitler ordered the use of his vengeance weapons, especially the V1. In response, an ad hoc air defense organization, Antwerp X, was formed to defend against the theater cruise missile (i.e., "buzz bomb") threat. Two American and a British anti-aircraft brigade set up gun lines to bring the noisy machines down. Of 4,883 buzz bombs launched against Antwerp in 154 days, 2,759 definitely headed toward the port area. Only 211 got through.[101]

AMMUNITION

The official history of logistical operations in Western Europe states, "In the eleven months no supply problem plagued U.S. forces more persistently or constricted their operations more seriously than the shortage of field artillery ammunition."[102] The primary problem was insufficient production. The root of that problem is a lesson on how bad data can screw up a war.

Because divisions in North Africa had been inactive in the spring of 1943, excessive stocks of artillery ammunition had built up. In response to criticism from a congressional committee about wasteful spending on munitions, the War Department cut back ammunition production. No one stopped to analyze the needs of units engaged in intensive combat against prepared positions. Usage based on division days in theater did not distinguish between inactive periods and time engaged in intensive combat. Revised War Department planning estimates were simply set too low.

Patton's estimates highlight the difference between the two measures. He felt he needed 60 rounds per day of 105mm and 40 per day of 155mm on a routine basis. During heavy combat, Patton knew he needed 350–400 rounds a day per howitzer.[103] The authorized expenditures for the European command were 40/day for the 105mm and 25 for 155mm howitzers.[104] During World War II British commanders planned on 150 rounds per tube during a major offensive. Contemporary American artillery allocation rates for direct support artillery is 140 rounds per day.[105]

Fighting in Italy quickly revealed the error. Computations derived from actual combat usage rates caused Overlord planners to double their estimates for artillery ammunition.[106] That happened in March 1944. But the War Department had a hard time believing ETO estimates of the amount of ammunition needed.[107] The bureaucratic response was that the theater's requisitions exceeded approved War Department expenditure levels. Senior officers were very concerned about cost. They thought theater planners were promulgating incredible projections. However, ETO wasn't the only group looking for more tonnage.

Planners within the theater didn't even agree among themselves. The closer one got to tactical organizations, the greater the estimate of ammunition requirements. By mid-May 1944 it was clear that armies and army group planners wanted more ammunition than the theater would have on hand, especially mortar and 105mm.[108] It turned out that theater planners and planners at lower echelons were working from quite different data bases and were using different units of measure. One level denominated requirements in "units of fire" while another calculated in terms of "days of supply." Calculations lacked credibility, which reinforced decision makers' reliance on rules of thumb. Given the downward bias of true requirements as one rose through the organization, one would have expected final allocations to be too low.

Prior to the first soldiers landing in Normandy, SHAEF ordnance officers understood there would be an ammunition shortage. So did any army or army group commander who was paying attention.

Neither computers nor real-time communications links existed. When planning calculations are challenged, a lot of "selling" must be done to convince decision makers to change their minds. Difficult and slow communication compounds the difficulty of this task. With numbers in doubt and communication difficult, the War Department continued to resist ETO's upward revision of estimated ammunition per day of combat. But even without their agreeing on the total need, it became clear to the War Department that production would be insufficient to meet demand.[109] In mid-April, the War Department indicated that artillery ammunition would be in worldwide shortage. Each theater would be put on allocation.

Belated orders for more ammunition were placed with industry. It was impossible to increase production in time to meet the projected needs. Propellant powder was particularly in short supply. Had AA ammunition manufacture been more severely cut back in 1943 when the Axis air threat had shriveled, more capacity would have been available to alleviate the field artillery ammo shortage. By the spring of 1944 construction of additional plants was given highest priority, but results would take time.

Ammunition shortages plagued initial operations in the Normandy lodgment area. As early as 15 June, First Army restricted the use of artillery ammunition. However, this was due more to offloading and distribution problems. Initially, expenditures had been below estimates. But hedgerow fighting tended to increase the depth and width of artillery barrages. Stocks on the continent declined rapidly. Shortages reached the critical level in July.[110] First Army chief of staff, General William G. Kean, expressed doubt that results justified the heavy firing. Corps and division commanders objected strenuously, stating that high-volume artillery fire saved lives and created higher rates of advance.[111] By the time of the breakout, it was very clear that ammunition was being consumed far more quickly than it was being landed. Reserves in the dumps of numbered armies were far below recommended levels. For example, First Army stocks were reduced from 157,000 tons to 12,000 tons by the end of August.[112] The fuel shortage also masked the full nature of the problem.

Despite heavy expenditures in Normandy, War Department functionaries continued to "edit" ETO requests "to prevent accumulation of excess in the ETO."[113] Washington-based officials pointed out that actual expenditures were falling below already approved consumption rates. They seemed oblivious to the counter-argument that shortage-induced rationing had restricted firing to a level well below what was desired. The War Department also suspected a good deal of ETO's ammunition problems resulted from the inability to offload ships already in the theater. During the first week in October, only one ammunition ship was unloaded. Thirty-five awaited space along the wharves.[114] Ammunition shortage was so bad that trucks loaded at shipside were dispatched directly to the front. Stocks in the UK became so badly depleted that training was curtailed and some units were sent to the continent without a basic load of ammunition.

The snarl-up in Lee's paperwork contributed to the problem. Again, the existence of one problem and bad data masked a more serious problem. Washington didn't believe Lee and his people.

Neither did the irascible 12th Army Group G4, General Moses. Lee's people had been fudging their 105mm availability by counting stocks out somewhere in the channel on ships they couldn't reach. Rather than argue, General Moses requisitioned 25,000 rounds in early October. Not a single shell came forward from COMZ.[115]

No one knew the right numbers, but everyone in ETO recognized there was a severe problem. In a cable to General Somervell, dated 8 August 1944, Eisenhower pleaded for more 81mm mortar and 155mm howitzer ammunition.[116] For the theater commander to recite ammunition expenditure rates to the head of army supply underscores the urgency of the problem. By that date, the issue at Falaise had yet to be decided. The dash to the Seine and the German border lay in the future. Ike was pleading that 390,000 rounds of the July allotment be released in the United States for shipment. In the supreme commander's words, "I consider it imperative that tactical commanders' requirements for the next 30 days be met in full." Many in channel communications and analyses preceded Eisenhower's personal intervention.

Exploitation warfare of the last two weeks in August required little artillery ammunition expenditure. For the month of August, First Army expended 100 tons per division slice per day, about one third of what active combat required.[117] These lighter expenditures tended to mask ammunition requirements during heavy combat in the fall.

Despite Lee's citation of the ammunition shortage, the War Department remained adamant.[118] ETO had squadrons of transport ships waiting to unload on the continent. War Department officials thought backlogged cargoes, not the amount of ammunition manufactured, were the real culprit. Based on the August numbers, the European Theater was to reduce the idle ship backlog by 75. Instead, by 31 October, the backlog had risen to 183 ships, not counting an additional 60 at dockside.[119] Ports were backed up so badly that 15 partially laden ships were sent back to America.[120] It is easy to understand why the logisticians—and Eisenhower—so urgently wanted Antwerp's voluminous docks.

The shipping and ammunition problems became so severe that Ike dispatched three major generals (Clay, Bull, and Lord) to Washington to plead SHAEF's case. The War Department said they could have all the ships they could handle, but they couldn't handle what was already in theater.[121] Demurred shipping, including that in the Pacific, was so severe that the Joint Chiefs brought the issue up with the president.

By late summer, everyone was looking for data to justify positions. But no reliable figures were to be had. As a result, gun crews didn't have the shells to respond to the infantry's request for support. The War Department cleaned out all available 8-inch and 240mm ammunition available in the Zone of Interior and shipped it to the ETO on two fast freighters.

Despite the ammunition shortage, ETO proceeded to shoot itself in the foot. The theater ordnance officer, apparently infected with the "victory disease," predicted a "surprise for the people back home." Major General Henry Sayler stated that ETO would soon stop ordering ammunition. Given current shortages, field commanders went ballistic. Brigadier General John Hinds, 12th Army Group artillery officer, demanded that COMZ then remove current artillery ammunition rationing. That is exactly what 12th Army Group did. Army group stocks were released to the field armies for the period 2–11 September for consumption far in excess of what COMZ delivered. The Army Group G4, General Moses, took care that the chief of staff and Bradley understood the risks entailed. This was a decision of enormous impact. The logisticians were betting a major and irreplaceable chip. If the tacticians played it wisely, it could buy their way through the West Wall. We shall see in chapter 5 that Bradley and Hodges did not play their hand well and squandered this bet. They were not ready to execute what made sense to the officers doling out dwindling ammunition stocks: concentrate, go for broke, and bash through the wall early.

In early September, ammunition consumption sky rocketed. Third Army gunners along the Moselle near Nancy and Metz were especially active. By mid-September, it was clear the bet had not been won. On 16 September, 12th Army Group estimated that artillery ammunition would run out by 10 October.[122] Further, the War Department had not released sufficient stocks to replenish the emptying ammo dumps.

During October ETO submitted its request for November loadings. It pleaded they not be "edited" or compared with prior usage, as assaulting the West Wall would be artillery intensive.[123] Instead, November's requests for ammunition were reduced:

Type	% Reduction
81mm mortar	74%
105mm howitzer	49%
155 howitzer	44%
155 gun	64%

Decreasing the time required to ship ammunition from port to artillery piece was another way of easing the shortage. During the fall the journey took forty-six days: twenty-three days awaiting discharge, fifteen days unloading, and eight days coming forward. The trip from the United States took an additional fifty days.[124] It took a two-star inspector from the States, Major General Leroy Lutes, to identify the problem. Reduced delivery time would not be felt until after the Battle of the Bulge. Part of the reason why planners in the United States were slow to recognize the ammunition problem was their lack of faith in ETO logisticians. Given the inability to shorten demurrages and discharge time despite the ETO-forecasted shortage, one can understand why those Stateside planners felt this way.

MOVING THE AIR FORCE

Fighter bombers in 1944 had a combat radius of only a few hundred miles with a useful load. Allied spearheads racing across France were outdistancing the umbrella afforded by tactical air. If the ground armies had reached the Rhine in early September as Patton and the other army commanders strained to do, they would have done it with very limited air cover. Accounts of the fall's fighting include a surprising number of air raids on forward positions by the Luftwaffe.

Capture of partially demolished German airfields near and just east of Paris provided great potential for moving Ninth Air Force closer to its targets. But in the crunch of tonnage trying to move forward, IX Engineer Command had great difficulty getting materials delivered that were required to renovate the damaged bases.[125] For a period, interruption of general-purpose bomb delivery limited tactical operations. Air forces require huge tonnages of ordnance, fuel, support equipment, and airfield-building materials. Four thousand tons a day was a small price to pay for tactical air superiority.

During August and September IX Engineer Command, which supported all of Ninth Air Force, constructed sixty airfields. Most fighter groups moved three times, and one moved five times.[126]

Bradley approved increased priority for matting, bombs, and aviation gasoline to keep Ninth Air Force running. Movement of IX Bomber Command into the airfields around Paris had not been planned. As rail service to Paris improved, B-25s and -26s moved into the area.

CAMPAIGN PLANNING AND LOGISTICAL CONSTRAINTS

A myth about American logistical prowess has developed. The record demonstrates that American logistical management was far from perfect. If Army Service Forces were as competent as their tactical counterparts in 12th Army Group, perhaps the supply constraints would not have been as binding. Certainly the ammunition-induced October pause would not have been so severe.

The near-miracle German combat power regeneration has already been alluded to. Despite strategic bombing, air interdiction at all levels, and shortages of key materials, the Germans got the job done. Their adaptation was a marvel in responsive control.

On the other hand, Allied generals were far less successful in adapting to the realities of their logistical environment. As a group, Allied operational commanders seemed to view logistical constraints as aberrations that somebody else was supposed to fix. Montgomery demonstrated insensitivity to the war for the ports when, as Overlord ground commander, he was acutely aware of its importance. American generals gave insufficient thought to the tradeoffs between today's artillery preparation and the future requirements of the campaign plan of even a few weeks hence. No one wanted to acknowledge that transportation limitations had to be systematically addressed rather than wished away.

As the story unfolds in subsequent chapters, inability to properly calculate logistical arithmetic and plan battles accordingly is a major failure and a principal source for much of the Allied frustration in the fall of 1944.

3

SHAEF's Plan

You will enter the continent of Europe and, in conjunction with other nations, undertake operations aimed at the heart
of Germany and the destruction of her armed forces.

Combined Chiefs of Staff Instructions to Eisenhower, Supreme Commander

Even before D-Day, the SHAEF plan envisioned a main effort north of
the Ruhr and a secondary effort to the south aimed at the Saar.[1] (Map 3.1
displays the Allied position as of 10 September and shows key geographical
points.) The initial strategy for advance beyond the Rhine was codified in a
SHAEF G3 planning document dated 3 May 1944, entitled "Post Neptune
Courses of Action After Capture of the Lodgement Area,"[2] attributed to a
group of three British staff officers headed by Brigadier Kenneth McLean.
McLean had been a member of Morgan's planning staff from the beginning
of invasion planning. In this document, four options for eastward advance
were outlined. The two potential objectives were the war industries in the
Ruhr Valley or Berlin. Ike rejected Berlin as the primary objective.[3] Instead
he focused on the Ruhr. An official British history uses this nomenclature:
primary thrust north of the Ardennes and a "secondary thrust through the
Saar."[4] But Ike's primary target was not the productive capacity. As we shall
see, Ike had the German Army itself squarely in his sights.

Sixth Army Group, advancing up the Rhone valley from landings in
the south of France, would come even with Third Army's attack toward the
Saar and protect that army's flank. As a result, a continuous front would be
established from the North Sea to the Swiss border. While this attack plan
had a primary and a secondary effort, it became tagged the "broad front."

After reviewing the weakened state of German resistance in some detail,
a SHAEF G3 planning study at the beginning of September recommended

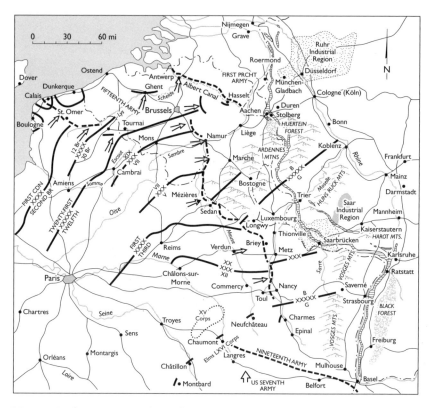

Map 3.1. Situation 10 September and Key Geography

that Bradley be given the option of moving one of the corps of first Army south of the Ardennes to reinforce Patton's drive on the secondary axis toward the Saar. The staff estimated this could be done without removing the priority of logistical support in the north. Clearly SHAEF staff remained committed to the two-pronged strategy. So did Eisenhower.

Montgomery recognized that limited ability to deliver supply tonnage to frontline units would hobble further Allied advance. In order to advance further, the Allies must carefully pick only the most important advance and push all support to that one effort. Monty demanded that the Allies concentrate most of their divisions (about forty) into a single "full-blooded" concentrated thrust into the heart of Nazi Germany. This concentrated mass would cross the Rhine on a narrow front, move north of the Ruhr on the north German plain, and head straight toward Berlin. A grouping of forty divisions "need fear nothing," including German counter-efforts. At least three field armies, Canadian First, British Second, and a reinforced American First, would be formed into a single army group for the thrust. Of course such an endeavor would need a single commander to guide it on its way.

Debate between these two alternatives generated an enormous amount of heat that almost led to Ike confronting his superiors with the choice of "Monty or me." A great deal of ink has been spilt over the years reporting, analyzing, and arguing the merits and intra-Allied politics of this difference of opinion.

Field Marshal Montgomery was a brilliant practitioner of what military men refer to as the *operational level* of war. *Tactics* are what leaders execute when in contact with the enemy. In World War II, operations at corps level and below were tactical. Most decisions at army level were tactical. Decisions made by the Combined Chiefs, like the instructions to Eisenhower "to enter western France and proceed to the heart of Germany" are *strategic*. To achieve strategic goals, armies can't just fight anywhere they, by happenstance, collide with the enemy. Since the time of Napoleon, more than one battlefield victory has been required to win a war. A single victory no longer creates enough damage to force our opponent to submit to our strategic will. A campaign plan, usually created at the theater (SHAEF) or army group *operational level*, must precipitate a series of battles at the proper time and place to force the enemy to acquiesce, and thereby we achieve our *strategic* goals. The operational level creates campaigns designed to bring about battles under conditions favorable to us that are fought by tacticians. The series of *tactical* victories, in the combination laid out in the *operational level plan*, achieve the objectives designated by the *strategy*.

Above all, Montgomery understood the need for concentration at the decisive point to win a battle required by the campaign plan and the mechanics of massing both forces and logistics to achieve that concentration. His masterful execution of the battle of El Alamein in North Africa is exemplary. Americans sometimes forget that Montgomery was the overall ground commander at D-Day and the subsequent Normandy campaign. The landings themselves were another masterpiece at assembling a complex organization to accomplish a difficult military feat. Reading how Montgomery describes the intricacies of the amphibious landing organization underscores his expertise. Eisenhower's chief of staff, the gruff General Bedell "Beetle" Smith, stated, "I am no Montgomery lover but I give him his full due and believe that for certain types of operations [such as the Normandy invasion] he is without equal."[5] The principles of concentration and objective are honored by virtually every practitioner of military science. As will be developed in subsequent chapters, the lack of concentration in

American campaign plans at the operational level became a source of great frustration. Montgomery's overall criticism of the American approach to war had some foundation in fact.

As insufferable as the feisty British general was, he truly admired the breadth of Eisenhower as a man and leader of a national coalition. Noted Eisenhower biographer and World War II historian Carlo D'Este observed, "Whatever their later quarrels, Montgomery's admiration for Eisenhower was unequivocal."[6] However, D'Este also observed, "Montgomery never considered Eisenhower anything other than an amateur soldier who lacked vital command experience he himself had attained. Ability was the foundation upon which Monty judged others. . . . Eisenhower had not met his rigid standard."[7] In other words, Montgomery judged Eisenhower as not skilled at the operational level.

Not all of Monty's detractors were American. Feuds that reached all the way back to North Africa pitted several RAF officers, including Tedder and Coningham, against Montgomery, whom they considered overbearing and insufficiently appreciative of the role of air support in his successes.[8] During July, when Allied ground forces under Montgomery's command seemed to have stalemated against German defenses, Tedder pressed Ike to relieve the British general. While as frustrated as his deputy supreme commander, Ike never seriously entertained the option, which would have jeopardized the combined command structure.

While he could be insufferable, Monty had a way of inspiring the common soldier, American and British alike. The *London Daily Telegraph* described Chester Wilmot's *The Struggle for Europe* as "A classic of contemporary history." Wilmot states, "There was a marked element of professional vanity in Montgomery's make up. He was frequently dogmatic" and his "appearance of conceit was emphasized by his disregard for social graces."[9] But he received fierce loyalty from his subordinates and rank-and-file British "Tommies."

Sometimes Montgomery is criticized for being less able to improvise and conduct a war of movement. However, the rapid advance of his 21st Army Group through France and the Low Countries once breakout occurred must dampen some of those comments. Once they got going, British, Canadian, and Polish forces moved out smartly.

Montgomery was attuned to the logistical requirements to support large operations. He paid careful attention to the buildup of supplies before a major endeavor. As overall ground commander of the Normandy invasion, he was very aware of the "port dilemma." Until Antwerp or a similar-sized deep-water port close to the German border was placed in Allied operation, the Allies simply couldn't support all the divisions they had at their disposal with the fuel and ammunition needed for heavy mobile combat. Citing the limitations that would hamstring the Allies as they moved beyond the Seine, Montgomery recognized that Allied ability to transport supplies sufficient to sustain even his forty-division force wasn't really there. Logisticians thought they might support twelve divisions beyond the Rhine, a force about the size of Dempsey's Second Army. Therefore, Montgomery insisted that all other ground forces drawing succor from the ports along the Channel coast and Brittany needed to cease movement and conserve their ammunition. A truncated Third Army (Patton) would stand in place. The forces coming up from the landings in the south of France would tag up as they came even with the Third. Virtually all supplies and air power would support the main effort, Montgomery's forty-division push.

Montgomery declared that his approach to warfare was completely different from Eisenhower's:

> My military doctrine was based on unbalancing the enemy while keeping well balanced myself. I planned always to make the enemy commit his reserves on a wide front in order to plug holes in his defenses; having forced him to do this, I then committed my own reserves on a narrow front in a hard blow. I always sought to create fresh reserves quickly. I gained the impression that the senior officers at Supreme Headquarters did not understand the doctrine of "balance" in the conduct of operations. Eisenhower's creed appeared to me to be that there must be aggressive action on the part of everyone all the time. Everyone must attack all the time.[10]

While recounting the heated debate over the "full-blooded thrust" versus "broad front" argument, Montgomery made some disparaging remarks about Eisenhower's military expertise. "His ignorance as to how to run a war is absolute and complete."[11]

Virtually everyone acknowledges Ike's skill at holding together Allied organizations that might otherwise devolve into mush and in interfacing with senior civilian leaders. Napoleon once remarked, "Let all of my enemies be allies."

Britain's chief of the Imperial Staff, Field Marshal Brooke, viewed Ike as a "staff officer with little knowledge of the realities of the Battlefield . . . obsessed with the logistical problems . . . a believer in the classic Civil War doctrine of frontal assault, of 'Everybody attacks all the time.'"[12] Given the close communication between the two field marshals, this assessment was a shared belief. Brooke confided in Montgomery, "You have always told me, and I have agreed with you, that Ike was no commander, that he had no strategic vision, was incapable of making a plan or of running operations when started."[13] Brooke was the one man Monty truly feared. On the subject of Ike, the two field marshals were in complete agreement. Nigel Hamilton, Montgomery's principal biographer, states that "Brooke and Monty lost confidence in Eisenhower as a field general," when they felt Ike in early July grossly misinterpreted Montgomery's operational plan to pull the Germans onto 21st Army Group so that Bradley could break out "from the back of the scrum."[14] Brooke remarked of Montgomery, "He is probably the finest tactical general since Wellington, but on some of his strategy and especially on his relations with the Americans, he is almost a disaster."[15]

E. K. G. Sixsmith, deputy director of staff studies at the British War Office during World War II, suggests that some of the venom be drained from Brooke's comments. "It can hardly be doubted that Brooke underestimated Eisenhower."[16] Sixsmith points out that Brooke was bitterly disappointed that he was not appointed supreme commander, a role Churchill had promised him earlier in the war when the British were the undisputed senior partner. Second, "Brooke and Marshall were men of a very different stamp and rarely saw eye to eye."[17] The differences between the two army chiefs devolved to their prodigy.

GENERAL EISENHOWER'S PHILOSOPHY OF WAR

Virtually every critic agrees that Eisenhower had a winning way with people. He was a keen observer of humans and had the knack of threading his way through interpersonal minefields without setting them off. Stephen Ambrose was fond of saying that "Eisenhower would stay up all night winding up jack-in-the-boxes and carefully placing them around the conference room. Then next day he would feign sincere surprise as they went off according to his plan." Eisenhower is the acknowledged master at getting a lot of powerful, disparate, and highly opinionated people to move along in the same general direction. One thing a man tasked with such a difficult task cannot do is take a lot of time explaining in public how his ideas shaped the course of that direction.

British General Sir Charles Guthrie, commander of NATO's Northern Army Group in 1993, stated that "Eisenhower was probably the 20th Century's greatest master of coalition warfare."[18] Ike's ability to corral the disparate personalities and national agendas and head them in the same general direction was an enormous skill valued by all. The final volume in the official army history observed: "Eisenhower's ability to manage his sometimes quarrelsome subordinates, as well as to fend off their political chiefs and preserve the alliance, may have been the most accurate measure of his success in the art of generalship."[19] But what did he know about tactics and strategy? Militarily, did Ike know what he was doing?

Eisenhower did not see combat during World War I. The noted Australian historian Chester Wilmot selected slightly more neutral terms than Brooke and Montgomery. But he was no fan of Ike.

> Eisenhower was conscious of his lack of experience in the tactical handling of armies and this gave him a sense of professional inferiority in dealing with men like Montgomery and Patton who had been through the mill of command at every level. Because he had no philosophy of battle which he himself had tested in action, Eisenhower was reluctant to impose his own ideas, unless the decision was one which he, as Supreme Commander, had to make. As a general rule, he tended to seek the opinions of all concerned and work out the best compromise . . . he had a remarkable capacity for distilling the counsel of many minds into a single solution.[20]

Eisenhower ran the only tank training school in the States during 1917–18. During the interwar period, he participated in the development of American armor. Both Patton and Ike commanded tank battalions at Ft. Meade. Despite their very different personalities, the two tank officers became fast friends.[21] In 1920 both published their views on armored warfare; Eisenhower in the *Infantry Journal*, Patton for the *Cavalry Journal*. Both agreed that tanks used en masse could break through or envelop enemy positions, penetrate into the enemy's rear, and spread confusion and havoc. Both got in trouble with their respective service chiefs.

Fox Conner, Pershing's operations officer in World War I, was widely regarded as the real brains of the AEF. As members of Pershing's First Army staff during World War I, Conner and Marshall spent many hours discussing tactics and strategy. Marshall did not have a lot of exposure to the writing of Clausewitz. Conner and Marshall spoke in terms of Grant and his Wilderness Campaign that relentlessly ground Lee's army down, regardless of distractions. Recall that Clausewitz set out to codify Napoleon's approach to and philosophy of war. It was the emperor himself who stated that battles are fought not to capture territory but to destroy enemy armies.

After the war, Conner took a liking to the young Eisenhower and asked that he be assigned to him. Pershing intervened, and Ike was detailed as Conner's executive officer in the 20th Brigade in the Panama Canal Zone. The older man ensured that Ike read deeply into military literature. He tutored Ike on the decisions of many great commanders. Under Conner's mentoring, Ike worked through Clausewitz three times. In 1964, after an outstanding military career and two terms as president, Ike told his biographer, "Fox Conner was the ablest man I ever knew."[22] Ike described his three years in Panama as "sort of a graduate school in military science." In retirement, Ike volunteered that *On War*, Clausewitz's masterpiece, was by far the most important military book he ever read.[23]

At the level of campaign planning, Clausewitz admonished the general to carefully study all aspects of his opponent. Identify the one (or sometimes the few) "hub(s) of enemy strength," foci Clausewitz labeled "center(s) of gravity," from which the enemy's power emanated. Then the general must create a plan that focuses *all* available combat power to destroy that center of gravity. Destroy it, and enemy ability to resist falls apart. Concentrate less than all strength on destroying the center of gravity and the enemy is likely to deploy all his strength against yours—and win. All secondary uses of power, all side issues and campaigns, must be ruthlessly chopped away to concentrate enough strength to destroy the enemy's most essential source of strength. Easy to say; extraordinarily tough to do. The more complex the Allied side is at the national political level, the greater the centripetal forces pulling at the strategist's attempt to concentrate on the critical enemy center of gravity.

What was *the* center of gravity of Nazi Germany? The airmen had a straightforward answer: Germany's ability to build the machines of war. Destroy those factories by strategic bombardment and the German Army will fall apart without need of a titanic land struggle. Many army generals had a similar selection. While their campaign plan was completely different, they identified the strategic objective, *the center of gravity*, as capturing the twin geographical sites of German economic power—the Ruhr and the Saar.

A traditional objective has been the enemy's capital. Destroy it—and its central government—and the opposing state (not the people or their culture) is destroyed. In advocating a forty-division mass driving straight to Berlin, Field Marshal Montgomery was placing himself in this time-honored camp.

General George Marshall, the American chief of staff and principal architect of the strategy to achieve the goals President Roosevelt had so clearly laid out, would have none of the above argument. In a dictatorial state as tightly controlled as the one created by the monster Hitler, only the destruction of the German armed forces would bring down the hated Nazi state. Churchill, fearing the bloodletting of a direct confrontation with the Wehrmacht, wanted a strategy of slicing down the Nazi state through a series

of peripheral cuts—at Europe's "soft underbelly," in the eastern Mediterranean (where Britain had imperial interests not shared by the United States)
and in Scandinavia. Marshall would have none of this either, except when
force-fed by his commander in chief, as in North Africa. General Marshall
wrote out one of the most succinct statements of a strategy: "You will enter
the continent of Europe (via Northwestern France??), and in conjunction
with other nations, undertake operations aimed at the heart of Germany and
the destruction of her armed forces." In the field, Eisenhower was his own
man. Marshall went to great lengths not to interfere. Back in February 1943,
when the campaign in Tunisia was raging, Marshall wrote Eisenhower not
to worry about reporting back to Marshall but to concentrate on the battle
in front of him. Marshall wrote, "it did our business to support you and not
to harass you."[24]

Clausewitz said concentrate all available military power on what he
defined as the enemy's center of gravity—the one essential element of power
around which holds everything together. While that element is not necessarily the enemy's army in the field, the World War II version against Germany
came down to that. While Marshall was far less familiar with Clausewitz,
he admired Grant's ability to focus exclusively on the Army of Northern
Virginia as the Confederacy's linchpin of Confederate power. Despite many
distractions across an entire continent, Grant focused his campaign on Lee's
army and simply would not let up. On this concept of destroying the enemy's
army instead of taking geography or sites of economic value, Eisenhower
and Marshall agreed. When Eisenhower completed a solution, the highest
praise Conner conferred was "You handled that just the way Marshall would
have done."

During the years Ike headed the War Plans Division prior to coming
to Europe, Marshall and Ike spent a lot of time working closely together.
Eisenhower and Marshall were in complete agreement about how to end
World War II in Europe. "Both believed that defeating the enemy in the
shortest possible time was essential; and both believed the United States
should bring all of its resources to bear" on defeating the German army in
western Europe.[25] Directly attack the center of Nazi power, its field army,
and destroy it as fast as possible. Democracies have a tendency to tire of
extended military stalemate. Destroy the enemy before the people tire of
the conflict.

Most major authors have not commented on the strong Clauswitzian
vein in Eisenhower's military thinking. At the national strategic level, Clausewitz wrote of the "holy trinity"—the People, the Army, the Commander.

Especially in a democracy, the people must be behind the army and its commander in chief (president), or a war cannot be prosecuted very long. Marshall and Eisenhower worried that the indirect attacks on Europe's periphery so favored by the British might so extend the war that cracks would appear in the holy trinity. Most observers recognized that Ike understood better than any other Allied officer in Europe in 1944 the value of maintaining solidarity with the citizens back home and the need for bringing the war to the quickest, least costly conclusion. But this might be filed under "political general skills" ceded by his British critics.

The mechanics of large-unit operations are taught at the Command and General Staff College. Because of Eisenhower's early outspokenness about the value of tanks, the chief of infantry blocked Eisenhower from attending this key school. Conner wangled Ike's assignment as a recruiter in Denver and told Ike to take it without question. Recruiters came under the control of the adjutant general, not their service chiefs. From this posting, the adjutant general assigned Ike to Command and General Staff School, thereby endrunning the chief of infantry's efforts to squelch the upstart tanker.

Ike entered the school with Patton's Leavenworth notes under his arm. During the year, Ike and Gee Gerow, future V Corps commander, set up a CP upstairs in Ike's quarters. Eisenhower graduated at the top of his 275-member class in 1926. Ike was to say later that "I know of no single year in my whole service that I go back to in my memories more than my student year at Leavenworth."[26]

Neither schoolhouse nor maneuver ground is a substitute for direct combat experience. However, Eisenhower clearly was literate in the operational art and theater strategy. While he may not have had Montgomery's direct combat experience, neither did Monty have Ike's years of experience as a theater commander. Since the beginning of American involvement in November 1942, Ike had been a senior commander.

A text on the principles of war written by the head of the Army War College during the 1920s stated, "I wish to stress the point, that warfare means fighting and that war was never won by maneuvering."[27] William Naylor, an influential senior Leavenworth instructor, maintained "that the correct application of firepower and the frontal infantry assault could breach any defense."[28] Most American officers believed that mass armies had become too unwieldy to maneuver on the battlefield. "Frontal assault was the only recourse."[29]

"Eisenhower did not believe in the doctrine taught at C&GS."[30] His pattern of thinking remained that of a tank officer. Use armor's inherent mobility to envelop your enemy and drive deep into his rear. Instead, official doctrine stated that "the primary mission of the tank is to facilitate the uninterrupted advance of the rifleman in the attack."[31]

A less-cited conclusion of the May 1944 SHAEF G3 planning papers is the deduction that "[t]here will be no great disparity in land forces for a considerable period," maybe eight months. The analysis concluded that, because of Allied logistical constraints, both sides might have on the order of thirty-five divisions in the main battle area. "We must avoid a line of advance which leads us to a head on collision with the main GERMAN forces without the opportunity for maneuver." Advancing on only single axis to the north was rejected, as "[i]t leads only to a head on collision of the opposing forces on a narrow front, with no opportunity to maneuver."[32] At the decisive point of attack, the attacker must have at least three times the combat power of the defender in order to prevail. If there is parity up and down the line, this can be obtained locally only if the attacker can concentrate swiftly before the defender can counter-maneuver. This is what the SHAEF planners were flagging. The worse course of action is a generalized frontal attack, which results in a series of one-to-one attacks that are far more likely to fail than to succeed. As a tanker, Eisenhower understood the need for rapid maneuver and the need for a main effort on which to concentrate attacking force. The unfortunate labeling of subsequent SHAEF strategy as "broad front" connotes a series of one-to-one attacks. Eisenhower understood the difference and focused on maneuver. The planners also stated the Allies should advance on more than one axis of advance "to keep the Germans guessing as to the direction of our main thrust, cause them to extend their forces, and lay the German forces open to 'defeat in detail' [a term used to denote breaking the enemy into smaller subunits and then picking them off one by one]."[33]

The Louisiana maneuvers of 1941 was the first large exercise to shake down Marshall's newly constructed army. Second Army, eight divisions strong, attacked the Third Army. It was the largest force-on-force maneuver in U.S. Army history. Eisenhower served as chief of staff to Third Army commander Lieutenant General Walter Krueger. Together, the two of them cooked up Third Army's plans. There is some argument whether Kruger or Eisenhower outlined the big picture. Everyone agrees Eisenhower handled the myriad details required to execute it. In the first problem, Third Army defended while Second Army attempted to outflank with Patton's 2nd Armored Division (2AD). Eisenhower had very definite concept of defense. Using air scouts, Third Army identified 2AD's thrust before it made contact.

Ike shuffled forces to block and completely shut down the "enemy" attack. In other words, maneuver even in the defense. Patton attempted to bull ahead and soon got himself into a lot of tactical trouble. In the second problem, Third Army, with Patton now on their side, executed a much wider maneuver as its attack on Second Army. It succeeded in getting completely behind the defenders and was crushing them when umpires called a halt. In both cases Kruger and Eisenhower used maneuver to gain decisive results.

Marshall and Lieutenant General Lesley McNair, commander of the Army Ground Forces, thought little of the maneuver performance of most senior American field commanders. Marshall noted Ike as one of the few standouts among a group of dismal performers during the Louisiana maneuvers.[34] By no means do war games compare with the battle experience of Montgomery or Brooke. But Eisenhower's record demonstrates he understood and could handle the mechanics of large-unit operations. He was tactically literate.

Ike received some public notoriety when Drew Person reported that Eisenhower "conceived and directed the strategy that routed Second Army."[35] His operations used trucks to shuttle troops across broad distances, which retained flexibility. Orders he drafted were clear, were straightforward, and produced good results with minimum risk.[36] This was about as good a reference on large-unit operations as any American officer could receive in 1941.

Omar Bradley, Ike's senior American subordinate, stated, "Eisenhower showed himself to be a superb tactician with a sensitive and intimate feel of the Front." Bradley recalled that Ike's tactical direction was often confided in private conversations with his army group commanders and that he had a good feel for the front.[37] However, in his later 1982 biography, Bradley implied that Eisenhower's tactical understanding didn't match his own.[38]

Patton felt Ike did not provide his commanders with sufficient guidance in "grand tactics" a term that loosely coincides with the operational level of war.[39] This is a weakness that the record bears out. Many military analysts embrace "mission" orders, where the superior tells his subordinate what to do but not how to do it. However, if the superior provides insufficient guidance, and especially does not provide enough supervision in execution, he risks his plan devolving into uncoordinated jabs by subordinates that do not have sufficient impact by themselves to unhinge the enemy.

Combat is a very physical endeavor. However, strategy is an intellectual pursuit. The best battalion commander, the man that can connect with his troops and lead them into the assault, is not necessarily going to excel at weighing the tradeoffs every strategist must make. Ike didn't have "muddy boots" in his kit. But he spent years working both at national strategy and at handling the enormous pressure of a wartime theater commander, experience Montgomery didn't have.

Is this Clausewitzian connection the artifact of an overzealous author? After the 2 September 1944 meeting at Chartres with Eisenhower, Bradley, and Hodges, Patton wrote in his dairy; "Ike was very pontifical and quoted Clausewitz to us, who have commanded larger forces than C ever heard of."[40]

Destruction of the German armed forces: one can't get more Clausewitzian than that. Marshall had a kindred spirit in his protégée, General Eisenhower. From the beginning, Eisenhower developed his campaign plans in a manner to bring the German Army into decisive combat *on terms most advantageous to the Allies.* One needs to look deep into the record to find the consistent theme. But it's there. Eisenhower's direct communications to his superiors and subordinates are full of examples. Start with Ike's communications with Marshall during the opening campaigns in France.

CABLE S 56677 EISENHOWER TO MARSHALL
AUGUST 2, 1944—TOP SECRET

"From the beginning, Montgomery, Bradley and I have agreed that we should attempt to maneuver and attack so as to pin down and destroy substantial portions of the enemy in our immediate front so as to have a later freedom of action. The alternative would be merely a pushing back with the consequent necessity for slowly battling our way toward necessary geographical objectives."

". . . [We will] devote the great bulk of the forces to the task of completing the destruction of the German Army, at least that portion west of the Orne [River]."

". . . The next step would be aggressive action toward the north east to destroy the bulk of German mobile forces, all generally located along our present front and stretching up to include Pas de Calais."[41]

CABLE FWD 12674 EISENHOWER TO MARSHALL
AUGUST 7, 1944—TOP SECRET EYES ONLY

"We have three objectives as follows:

  a. To secure Brittany ports quickly . . .

b. To destroy as much of the enemy's Seventh Army as possible this side of the Seine.

c. To cross the Seine before the enemy has time to hold it in strength, destroy his forces between the Seine and Somme and secure the Seine ports.

Plans are being made for a strong airborne force . . . to facilitate the advance and assist in the destruction of the enemy."[42]

CABLE S 57189 EISENHOWER TO MARSHALL
AUGUST 9, 1944—TOP SECRET EYES ONLY

"Under my urgent directions all possible strength in France is being turned to the destruction of the forces now facing us. I am not, repeat, not willing to detach from the main army at this juncture additional forces merely in order to save a week or so in the time of capturing the Brest peninsula ports."[43]

TO GEORGE CATLETT MARSHALL
AUGUST 11, 1944—SECRET

"Dear General:
My entire pre-occupation these days is to secure the destruction of a substantial portion of the enemy forces facing us."[44]
The primary objective of destroying German forces is repeated in virtually every order issuing new plans that Ike sent out during this campaign.
Note two subcurrents that run under this theme of destroying enemy forces. Eisenhower recognized that the closer a battle is to where supplies are being landed on the continent, the easier it is for the Allies to support the endeavor logistically. He repeatedly emphasized destroying the Germans on the near side of the next river. This point becomes crucial in the orders for the beginning of September. Second, Eisenhower, an old armor enthusiast, underscores the benefit of seeking an open flank and fighting a mobile war where Allied materiel superiority can kill lots of Germans with the least cost in Allied blood. It was what Ike did in the Louisiana maneuvers.
The focus on destroying German forces as far west as possible is reflected in SHAEF planning documents written even before D-Day. "We must do our utmost to prevent a German withdrawal 'according to plan.'"[45] That is, chasing Germans back to Germany does not accomplish the Allied objective. German forces must be destroyed in the west so they can't resist again.

"The attack aimed at the Ruhr is likely to give us every chance of bringing to battle and destroying the main German forces."[46]

As frequently happens, logistics dominated Allied operational planning in Western Europe throughout 1944. D-Day planning was dominated by the need to secure enough port capacity to sustain the number of troops the Allies wanted to bring ashore. The references in the Eisenhower-to-Marshall cables above about Brittany ports are to the overriding concern among senior commanders about port capacity. Many of the minor channel ports catered to small coastal vessels carrying cargo across the channel. The miles of Antwerp's deep-water quays had always figured large in D-Day planning estimates. *No one understood this better than the highly competent overall commander of D-Day landing forces—Montgomery.* Deep-water quay capacity was also the reason Eisenhower became willing to risk blows with Prime Minister Churchill to retain the landings on southern France to secure the high-capacity deep-water port of Marseilles.

Eisenhower constantly juggled the need to provide additional logistical capability to unleash more combat power to smash Wehrmacht combat formations. Ike was not a logistics expert. Like many officers he avoided entanglement in the intricacies of the quartermaster, ordnance man, and transportation manager. But he understood the broad implications of supply tonnages, distances, and port capacity.

The closer to Allied ports German forces could be forced into decisive combat, the easier became the Allied logistical problem. From the beginning of the campaigns for Western Europe, this became important in Eisenhower's thinking. The last thing Ike wanted to do was to keep "pushing back" intact German forces onto their Fatherland, regardless of the speed of advance throughout the pursuit across France and the Low Countries.

In *Crusade in Europe* Eisenhower stated:

> This purpose of destroying enemy forces was always our guiding principle; geographical points were considered only in relation to their importance to the enemy in the conduct of his operations or as centers of supply and communications in proceeding to the destruction of enemy armies and air forces. . . . If we could overwhelmingly defeat the enemy *west* of the river [Rhine] it was certain that the means available to him for later defense would be meager indeed.[47]

Ike even reiterated the destruction of the German Army as his prime objective in a letter home to his wife.[48]

This is not to say that Montgomery, or any other senior commander, did not concentrate on the destruction of enemy forces. His 21st Army Group

Order M518 concentrated on maneuvers to finish what remained of the German army between the Seine and the Loire and said, "This will suit us very well." The intent of M519 on the 20th: "We will now complete the destruction" of German forces caught in the Falaise Gap. In early September Monty sent Ike a separate cable restating his intention to destroy enemy forces.[49]

While Ike did have a good education in strategy and the operational art, two years as supreme commander in the Mediterranean had made him a shrewd pragmatist.[50] Mistakes in Tunisia and at Salerno and Anzio had taught their expensive lessons. Joseph P. Hobbs points out that Eisenhower sought to retain as much flexibility as possible.[51] He accomplished this by laying out broad outlines and leaving his subordinates to work matters out in detail. These are "mission"-type orders favored in American (and German) doctrine. Tell a subordinate what to do and let him determine how to do it. Communications between Eisenhower and his subordinate commanders underscore the point.

In North Africa and Italy, Ike saw what masters at defensive warfare and delay the German soldier and the German leadership were. Wehrmacht training and doctrine had devised many ingenious way to stop an opposing force in its tracks. Eisenhower had learned not to give them the opportunity. Allied airpower and mechanization gave his forces tremendous advantages—but only if they didn't become bogged down, as in Italy, when German defenders could easily stop up a few routes of advance. A mobility differential would be useful only *if* the Allies retained freedom of action.

To summarize Eisenhower's approach to war:

- The objective is not geographical; it is the German Army.
- Engage the Wehrmacht west of the Rhine as close to Allied logistical bases as possible.
- Destroy it in a war of maneuver,
- Retain the advantage of Allied mobility by retaining the ability to shift the point of main effort.
- Do not allow the Germans to counter-concentrate against a single Allied axis of advance.
- Maintain logistical balance.
- Retain options as long as possible.

As his theater orders continued to repeat, movement against the Ruhr—and the Saar—was to force the Wehrmacht into decisive battle *as far west* as possible. The farther west the decisive battles, the closer they would be to the overstretched Allied logistical system and the larger grouping of Allied divisions and firepower that could be employed to crush the Nazis.

Somehow Montgomery lost this crucial point. Assuming his grouping of forty divisions marching toward Berlin was logistically feasible, capture of that city did not assure the destruction of the Third Reich. Moscow's fall to Napoleon did not bring down the hated czar. German planners had already planned a "southern redoubt" in the mountains of Bavaria. As Napoleon said, the object is to destroy armies, not to capture geography. Ike *never* took his eye off this ball. Monty's gaze was less focused.

A critical task Ike ably completed was keeping in harness a number of very independent-minded "horses" of the Allied stable. Eisenhower worked tirelessly to motivate his team and to keep them engaged within the general scheme of the Allied plan. Ike's running up and down his line of commanders, like a coach in a football game, was more an encouragement to each to put forth his best than a statement of Ike's strategic concept.[52]

HOW SHAEF PLANS WERE FORMULATED

First of all one must realize that SHAEF plans were a team effort. The military prowess of a group of American and British officers is reflected in the final product. The "two phase, two thrust" strategy is more properly labeled a SHAEF plan than an Eisenhower plan. Montgomery tended to hatch his own strategies virtually alone at a small TAC HQ. Only a small group of his liaison officers, typically captains or majors, were present. On the other hand, one of Ike's great qualities was his ability to pull the best out of a group of people.

Let's review some of Ike's key team members.

Ike relied heavily on his chief of staff, Lieutenant (later full) General Walter Bedell "Beetle" Smith. In fact many American officers felt that Beetle was more in control of operations than Ike. However, that was never true. Ike had a way of exerting more control than a casual observer was likely to pick up. Eisenhower was very plugged in to everything that was going on. "Behind the disarming smile was a calculating shrewdness." "Beneath his image as proselytizer of Allied unity existed a vast amount of indirect, carefully concealed exercise of authority. Eisenhower always sought to operate through others with his part known only to a few."[53] His nonconfrontational style led many to underrate Ike's knowledge of affairs. To protect his own interpersonal capital, Eisenhower used Smith as his "son-of-a-bitch." Beetle relished the role. He was an indispensable instrument of control whom Ike wielded with great skill.

Beetle had seen quite a bit of soldiering prior to serving on higher staffs. He joined the Indiana National Guard in 1911 and rose to first sergeant in two years. Commissioned through ROTC before shipping to France during World War I, Smith fought in the Battle of the Marne and was badly wounded. After the war he gained a Regular Army commission and stayed with the colors. In the thirties, he served on faculty of the Infantry School, where Marshall recognized Beetle's ability. A hard-driving martinet with an enormous capacity for organizing staff work, Beetle prided himself on being a "square-wheeled son-of-a bitch." Ike depended more on Beetle's military judgment than anyone else's, with the possible exception of Bradley. Beetle was the one man Marshall thought of denying Ike. The chief of staff found his services in Washington that valuable.

Smith was strong on the principle of unity of command. At times he felt Ike didn't have the moral courage to stand up to Montgomery.[54] By 1944, Smith had grown weary of Eisenhower's reluctance to assert command in a forthright manner. He felt Ike's dissimulation succeeded only in confusing Montgomery. That made it more difficult for SHAEF to control him.[55] Smith felt Ike allowed Bradley to fritter away 12th Army Group's offensive power at Aachen, Metz, Huertgen, and Lorraine.[56] (This is a major issue addressed in chapters 5 and 6.) After World War II, he remained in government service, serving first as ambassador to Moscow and then as head of the CIA under President Eisenhower.

Smith's two deputy chiefs of staff, Lieutenant Generals Sir Frederick E. Morgan and Sir Humfrey M. Gale, were British officers of wide experience. They had served Ike well while he was supreme commander in the Mediterranean. Smith insisted that General Gale become chief administrative officer. Under the British system, the chief administrative officer is one of a senior commander's two principal assistants. He handles both personnel (G1 in the U.S. system) and logistics (G4). Ike's chief of staff described General Gale as "a first class manager, practically a genius." He had an "irreplaceable quality of being able to handle British and American supply problems."[57] This officer ably served in a critical capacity.

General Morgan oversaw both intelligence (G2) and operations (G3). He had commanded an armored brigade group in France in 1940. Before joining SHAEF he had risen to corps command in England. Among Morgan's greatest attributes was his talent to act as a balancing wheel for Smith. Smith had a tendency to shoot from the hip. Morgan had a tactful way of first agreeing with his boss and then pointing out problems and alternatives.[58]

Morgan was not liked by the chief of the Imperial Staff. Field Marshal Brooke made no secret of his lack of confidence in Morgan. General Morgan had drafted the initial three-division plan for Overlord. Montgomery, and many others including Ike, found it wanting. In Morgan's defense one should point out that the planning assumptions provided insufficient landing craft to make a larger initial invasion. From then on he was tainted in the eyes of the Imperial field marshals. In his memoirs, Montgomery wrote: "he [Morgan] considered Eisenhower was a god; since I had discarded many of his plans, he placed me at the other end of the celestial ladder."[59] After the war, Monty became chief of staff. The careers of all the British generals who had served at Ike's headquarters wilted.

Because American interwar intelligence training was woefully deficient, most of the G2 section was British. Before the war, American military intelligence knew very little about Nazi Germany. Bedell made up his mind that only British Major General Kenneth Strong was satisfactory as his G2. Prior to the war Strong had been an attaché in Berlin. During the early war years, he headed the German section in the Imperial War Office. Smith became familiar with General Strong during the Mediterranean campaign, where Strong served as theater G2 under Smith and Ike. Strong had his detractors. While he was technically proficient, some observers found him "gullible."[60] His perception of German capabilities in late August was wide of the mark. He failed to understand the resilience of Nazi Germany in the summer and fall. Ike's perceptions would prove more on point. Despite indirect evidence from ULTRA (i.e., train movement information) backed up by aerial photos, Strong provided no advance warning of Hitler's upcoming Ardennes counteroffensive.

American Major General Harold R. Bull was the SHAEF operations officer, G3. He was intimately involved in many military decisions. For example, he actually wrote FWD13765. Eisenhower respected his judgment; he described this key officer as both careful and energetic.[61] At the beginning of the war Bull was G3, Department of the Army. Prior to that he was secretary, General Staff of the War Department, a very powerful position. For a brief period, he commanded III Corps. SHAEF's war room operated under his supervision. General Bull took special interest in maintaining liaison with the army groups. His deputy, British Major General John Whitley, communicated with Monty's chief of staff, Freddie de Guingand, to work out many operational details.[62]

Five senior officers, two American and three British, had tremendous influence on final plans that emanated from SHAEF. But one shouldn't underestimate Eisenhower's input. Ike was a master at pulling strings while standing in deep shadow out of the limelights. In this manner, he could control events while having a shield against organizational friction and blame. Smith wielded enormous power but did so because he intuitively understood what Ike wanted.

Smith described the planning process. Strong, Bull, Morgan, Gale, and Smith would labor over maps spread on the floor. "As ideas were formed, we took the results to General Eisenhower for decision."[63] "General Eisenhower exercised active command of the European front."[64] In turn, this group of generals was supported by a planning section that contained another forty-one officers. This included a dozen full colonels who were experts in their respective fields.

Ike prided himself on his abilities to work with a group of talented individuals while reserving the final decision himself. Ike described the ideal: "The teams and staffs through which the modern commander absorbs information and exercises his authority must be a beautifully interlocked, smooth-working mechanism. Ideally, the whole should be practically a single mind."[65]

Ike felt best qualified in operational matters and felt less technically prepared in intelligence and logistics. He spent considerable time supervising his field commanders.[66] Some staff papers survive that document Eisenhower's direct input on one of the major decisions made during late August 1944.

During the invasion and the battle for Normandy, Ike insisted on naming Montgomery as the single ground commander. Essentially Monty commanded a combined army group containing British Second and U.S. First Armies and directed a single battle to establish first lodgment in Normandy and then breakout into greater France. At that point, Allied strength would have expanded into two army groups, one British and one American. Ike would then move his HQ to the continent and assume the additional hat of overall ground commander. During June and July Ike received criticism from senior levels in the American government for not taking firm enough charge of the battle. Both Secretary of War Stimson and Under Secretary Lovett commented adversely on this point. Even FDR commented to Marshall that Montgomery seemed to be getting all the press and that it was time for Ike to take a more prominent role. Marshall instructed Ike in very direct terms that it was time for him to take charge of the ground campaign.[67]

NORTH VERSUS SOUTH

Pre-D-Day SHAEF planning identified the two best routes into Germany: the historic invasion route north of the Ardennes referred to as the Aachen Gap north and another well-trod route through Lorraine via Metz or Nancy, Manheim on the Rhine, and Frankfurt, and on to Berlin. Aachen was viewed as the main effort, with the southern the secondary attack.* Planners shuddered at the thought of advancing on a single axis. That would be too easy for the Germans, who had shown in every active theater their tremendous skill at delay and defense. Having two efforts complicated German defensive plans, prevented them from denuding the rest of the front to concentrate against a successful effort in a single center, and provided a basis on which the main effort could be shifted in order to gain leverage or recover from a setback. On 18 May SHAEF G3, Harold Bull summarized the findings of the planning staff, specifically the study led by Brigadier McLean. An advance through the Metz Gap would not lead us directly toward the only vital objective—the Ruhr—and a single axis "would lead us to collisions with the enemy main forces on narrow fronts and with no power of maneuver or surprise."[68] An advance through the Ardennes was possible but would be a difficult passage. Flanders north of Roermond is wet, crossed by many rivers, and is marshy. Therefore Flanders would also be difficult going. The area between Roermond and Duren, that is, the traditional Aachen Gap, is "the easiest approach to the Ruhr."[69] The secondary effort should be via Metz. The upcoming lack of port capacity was noted, and Antwerp was identified as the most likely solution.

From early on, Allied planners recognized that logistical constraints would be the Allies' most binding problem. Attack through the Aachen Gap by a large force undoubtedly would be supplied through one of the large northwest ports, Antwerp or Rotterdam. A secondary attack through Lorraine could draw its succor from ports in the south, especially Marseilles. More supplies meant more Allied divisions in the fight and more opportunities to rip open German defenses and destroy the Wehrmacht.

Right from the beginning, with Ike's hearty endorsement, all SHAEF plans included two axes of advance, one north of the Ruhr and the other one south of the Ardennes. The official British military historian, L. F. Ellis, lists

---

*Montgomery told Chester Wilmot in early 1946 that, had he been overall ground commander, he would have made his main effort north of Aachen with British Second and U.S. First Armies.

several reasons for wanting two thrusts. "The estimate of German capacity to resist was largely a matter of speculation, while various factors which would affect Allied strategy could not yet be appreciated."[70] In Normandy and Italy, German defenders had repeatedly conducted long, drawn-out defenses. Why simplify the Wehrmacht's problem by advancing only on a single narrow front?

On August 17th, Hitler replaced Kluge with Model, marking the acknowledgement of the disaster in the Falaise pocket and the desperate German need to reconstitute something resembling a coherent defense in the west. Montgomery observed, "The whole area is covered with burning tanks and motor transport. One column of 3000 plus was caught head to tail and almost totally destroyed. I would say that any German formations or units that escape over the Seine will be quite unfit to fight for months to come."[71] With this important observation about the enemy, Montgomery first laid out to Brooke his concept of operations beyond the Seine. Most senior officers recognized the value of the Ruhr to sustaining German war-making capability. With the Wehrmacht prostrate, Montgomery felt a final thrust deep into Germany, all the way to Berlin if necessary, would cause the Nazi war machine to collapse. Instead of splitting Allied forces north and south of the Ruhr, Montgomery envisioned sending the bulk of both Allied army groups north of the Ruhr. The Allies simply did not have the logistical capability to support two deep thrusts. Keeping one supplied would stress the quartermasters and ordnance men to their breaking points.

The lower panel of map 3.2 presents Montgomery's plan as displayed in the official history *Victory in the West*. Each one of the arrows represents the advance of one corps. Note how British Second Army, making the main effort, traverses Germany. Montgomery's plan has Second Army ignoring the Ruhr and heading directly toward Berlin. There will be much subsequent talk about taking the Ruhr. In Montgomery's plan, the bulk of Bradley's 12th Army Group would advance in support of Second Army, from Brussels, through a narrow band of good ground known as the Aachen Gap and on to the Rhine at Cologne at the northern edge of the Ruhr. This promised to be the main axis of attack. To Bradley's left, British 21st Army Group "[s]hould clear the Channel coast and Pas De Calais and west Flanders and secure Antwerp."[72] Notice the two corps in Canadian Second Army. One extends up through the Channel ports and then to the Scheldt. The second goes to Rotterdam. Montgomery wanted to shut everything south of the Ardennes down at the Moselle and concentrate all logistical resources in a single drive to Berlin in the north.

Under Monty's proposal, the Dragoon force landing in the south of France would move north toward Nancy. But the two American forces, 6th and 12th Army Groups, would *not* link up. Instead of a continuous front, which would draw more American forces south, there would be a gap between Nancy and Orleans on the Loire. The line from Paris to Orleans would be very lightly out-posted to retain the tremendous mass north of the Ardennes.[73] Montgomery reasoned that the Germans were in no position to launch a counterattack in a less than critical area. Especially in early September, he had a point. The bulk of 12th Army Group, all of First Army, and most of Third would advance north of the Ardennes and parallel to 21st Army Group as it reached toward Berlin. Of course, there should be one commander for this thrust. While Montgomery stated he would serve under Bradley, the only logical choice for this post was the field marshal.

Montgomery compared his plan with the German Von Schlieffen Plan of World War I, which called for the Germans to strip their forces from the entire length of the French border and concentrate them on a massive thrust through Belgium. Except, in Montgomery's words, "it would be executed against a shattered and disorganized enemy."[74]

Monty had been to see Bradley and sought the American general's concurrence. Initially Montgomery thought he had an ally in Bradley. The field marshal did not understand that Bradley despised serving under him and would do almost anything to avoid returning to that subservience. Under SHAEF's initial plan, Patton's Third Army would lead the secondary attack toward the Saar. Patton was making outstanding progress in his advance. As early as mid-August Bradley and Patton had been discussing a main attack by three corps that would cross the Rhine at Wiesbaden, Mannheim, and Karlsruhe.[75] Bradley concocted what he called the American Plan. The upper panel of map 3.2 depicts how Bradley had it drawn for his first biography, *A Soldier's Story*.

Two of First Army's three corps would move south of the Ardennes and join Patton in what would now be designated as the main effort. Notice how far south Bradley places the bulk of First Army. It strikes at Mainz while Third Army deals with the Saar. Patton's Third crosses the Rhine between Mainz and Mannheim. Together the American armies would advance first on Frankfurt, then ultimately on Berlin. All of Canadian First Army would be directed to open Antwerp's huge port capacity, which was absolutely essential to support a main effort via the Saar as it advanced east. British Second Army would advance via the Aachen gap and take on the Ruhr.

Bradley's "American Plan"

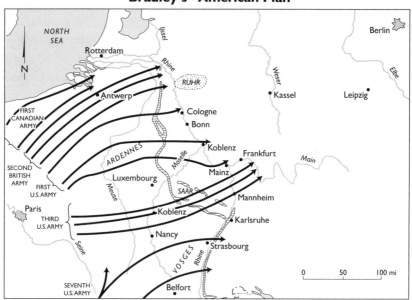

Montgomery's Plan

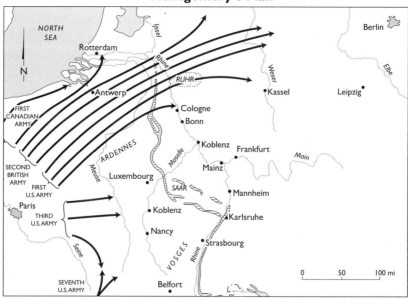

Map 3.2. Bradley's American Plan versus Montgomery's Plan

Patton's thinking paralleled Bradley's, except with a single army, his, instead of two making the main effort. Patton maintained he could cross the Rhine and make it to Berlin via Frankfurt with Third Army alone. That was even more aggressive than Montgomery.

WEST VERSUS EAST

"Narrow" versus "Broad," north of the Ardennes and Ruhr versus Saar, has received a great deal of attention. Most accounts depict the great late August strategic debate as a major donnybrook between Monty and Ike over whether there would be a single thrust north of the Ardennes or a "broad front" more aptly viewed as a primary attack in the north and a secondary attack on Lorraine. Montgomery wanted the largest force possible moving on the northern axis. Bradley thought he could do it with two armies (20–25 divisions) in the south. Patton was so exuberant he boasted he could get over the Rhine with nothing more than his own army. Much less has been said of a far more important difference in what was required in late August to move from west to east.

Since the breakout at Saint-Lô Eisenhower had admonished his commanders to finish the Germans as close to the coast (and its ports) as possible. Don't just chase them back into Germany—finish them in France. Since the beginning of the campaign, Eisenhower anticipated drawing the Germans into a big battle *west* of the Rhine, where Allied supplies would ensure Allied materiel superiority. For Eisenhower, the destruction of the Wehrmacht's ability to take to the field and fight was the key objective. On this point Eisenhower and Marshall were in complete agreement. (Read the mission statement Marshall issued Eisenhower that is the preamble to chapter 1.) Bradley was of exactly the same mind, and he repeatedly said so. Taking some geography, like Berlin, but leaving the German Army in the field with the ability to counterattack, was a recipe for disaster. If a substantial German army was still effective in the field, having the bulk of Allied divisions deep in Germany and far from its logistical base would be a far worse situation than an Allied army coiled up near the Rhine itching for a fight. The resulting campaign plan can be called the "two phase [decisive fight west of the Rhine, then advance into Germany], two thrust [main attack against Germans defending the Ruhr, secondary attack against Germans defending the Saar]" campaign design.

Had the collapse of the German Army in France so altered conditions? Should Eisenhower now throw out his plan to develop Antwerp as a logistics hub and ignite a conflagration west of the Rhine, and join the rush to Berlin?

REMAINING GERMAN STRENGTH

The noted British military historian J. F. C. Fuller is blunt in his assessment of Ike and the fall campaign. "A second Jena had been won and the western road to Berlin opened; as Napoleon had done in 1806. But unfortunately for the allies, through force of circumstances, Eisenhower was neither a Montgomery nor a Napoleon."[76]

Perhaps a relevant question was the nature of that road. Did it, in fact look like the one to Berlin in 1806 or the one to Moscow in 1812? Could the Allies win with a single great thrust, or did they need to lay a better logistical base and defeat a large portion of the German army in the field before marching into the interior of the Reich? Maybe it was well that Ike was neither a Montgomery nor a Napoleon. His armies would not starve and crumble after reaching a geographic objective that proved to be indecisive.

So how big was the German army that remained?

In order to answer the question, should the Allies attempt to win the war in one leap, or alternatively, should they pause at the Rhine and secure a solid logistical base, the strategist had to determine which of three alternative assessments of German strength best reflected the state of the Wehrmacht at the end of August:

1. If the Germans could muster only small delaying forces, then the Allies must pursue to their absolute limit. If necessary, immobilize less important movements to keep the spearheads moving. Generals since the beginning of military history agree on this. If the attack required only a single fight to initiate a blitzkrieg all the way to Germany, the Allies might choose to advance on the fastest route into Germany. A single phase, single thrust campaign that enveloped the initial defending force and then struck deep into Germany would be a bold course of action.

2. If the Germans could emplace only corps-sized units in front of each Allied advancing field army, the Allies might advance after a stiff fight. Small Allied pursuing columns needed to be recombined into attack formations with sufficient combat power to overcome the expected resistance. Bouncing uncoordinated and unsupported

attacks against prepared positions held with some strength would only make the enemy stronger. Supply tonnage for that fight would have to be available. A well-positioned defending corps can be overcome only by heavy fighting on the part of a field army. Attacking on a single axis would be risky, especially if the Germans, otherwise not pressed on other fronts, could reinforce the corps being attacked. The most prudent Allied response would be to destroy as much German force west of the Rhine while building a firm logistical base, that is, a *two phase, two thrust campaign design*. Unlike Hitler, Ike did not have to gamble to win the war.

3. If the Germans could gain time during the first defensive battles east of the Meuse and use that time to generate a defense in depth, the Allies were in for hard fighting. Nothing could be accomplished without a strong logistical base from which fresh divisions and mountains of artillery shells could be hurled at the Germans. Before entering deep into Germany, sufficient logistical capacity (a combination of ports, including Antwerp, and inland transport) had to be in place. Nothing less than the two phase, two thrust campaign had any chance of success. More than likely a major campaign would be needed to defeat the Wehrmacht either just west or just east of the Rhine. Organized and continuous defenses would be best defeated by a penetration attack with enough power to penetrate to the depth of German defenses. Attacking frontally or simply smashing ahead would be an ill-considered, costly strategy. Rapier-like thrusts by even army-sized units were likely to be counterattacked and repulsed, with heavy Allied losses. Even the two phase, two thrust plan would find tough going. Logistical buildup was an absolute necessity.

In early September, tactical commanders saw a disorganized, running enemy to their immediate front. It looked like paradigm 1 to them, and they railed at the logistical constraints that shackled their efforts.

The collapse of German Seventh Army in France after Falaise led many to believe that all the Wehrmacht was kaput. Some remembered how Germany seemed to come apart after the Allies began to crack their defense line in November 1918. SHAEF G2 estimates supported this notion. SHAEF intelligence summary of 23 August stated, "The August battles have done it and the enemy in the West has had it." The London-based Combined Intelligence Committee opined that Germany's position had so deteriorated "that no recovery is now possible." Eisenhower's pivotal order FWD13765 started with "Enemy resistance on the entire front shows signs of collapse." Victory disease even crossed the ocean and entered the Pentagon office of the chief of staff. Marshall issued a communiqué that assumed the war with Germany would terminate between 1 September and 1 November 1944.[77]

Churchill strongly disagreed with the optimists and said so in writing to the British chiefs on September 8th: "Generally speaking I, think it [the Joint Intelligence Committee report] errs on the side of optimism." The British history states flatly, "Neither the President nor the Prime Minister, however, was convinced that the Germans were about to give up."[78] The prime minister felt that "if Germany did not collapse in 1944, the Western Allies, given the wrong strategy, might be badly placed in 1945." Churchill felt the war would extend into 1946.[79]

In the September document, Churchill also pointed to Antwerp and the logistical constraints:

> The Germans intend to defend the mouth of the Scheldt and are still resisting in the Northern suburbs of Antwerp.
> It is difficult to see how the 21st Army Group can advance in force to the German frontier until it has cleared up the stubborn resistance at the Channel ports and dealt with the Germans to the North at Walcheren and to the North of Antwerp.[80]

If Churchill had enough information to understand Antwerp's importance, then one can be sure that both Brooke and Montgomery understood it as well. Churchill's views assumed something like paradigm 3.

In addition to having been run out of France, the Wehrmacht had suffered a major collapse in the heart of the U.S.S.R. During the period 20–29 August, 2nd and 3rd Ukrainian Fronts, containing 886,000 Soviet soldiers, conducted a double envelopment and a battle of annihilation. Much of the Romanian field army was destroyed in this operation. Romania dropped from the Axis and sued for peace. German losses on the eastern front exceeded 400,000 dead and 150,000 POWs. Compare this to 65,000 dead and captured at Falaise.

Military collapse both east and west would have brought down most regimes. As heinous as the Nazi regime was, it was nothing if not strong willed. With enemy armies entering its borders from both east and west, a heroic nation might understandably collapse after losses of this magnitude. Perhaps the Devil has more fortitude than any human can understand. This is what Churchill sensed.

Actual German divisions available 5 September on the western front according to German records:[81]

Table 3.1.

	Offensive capable	Partially fit	Reorganizing	Not fit
Infantry	13	12	9	14
Panzer	3	—	1	7*

Source: Ellis, Brute Force, p. 394.

While they were two of the most despicable creatures of the twentieth century, any rational observer must admit that Hitler and Himmler did create the "Miracle of the West." They pulled together a 135,000-man force by stripping the Wehrmacht's intra-Germany infrastructure and leavening it with returnees from Normandy. This is twice the manpower that was lost in the Falaise pocket. Four army district headquarters were ordered to transform themselves into tactical division headquarters. Splinters and fragments of units congealed around them, and these ersatz divisions went off to stop the Allies. During the second half of 1944, thirty-five ground-down divisions were brought back to strength. From regimental level and below, much had been shredded. Virtually all higher headquarters withdrew intact. Officered by veterans who had experienced defenses reassembled from chaos on the eastern front and other theaters, these divisions provided the framework on which remnants could be sorted out and rewoven into combat units capable of stout defense.

Fifty newly raised "Volks" divisions reached either the eastern or the western front. From this incredible reconstitution effort thirty divisions were massed behind the Roer or in the Eifel.[82] This was double the number of U.S. divisions facing them (although an American division and its associated corps and field army troops were twice the strength of its German counterpart).

Despite the disasters below the Seine and the 175-kilometer German bugout across northern France, the Wehrmacht began to form a continuous front of its own. OKW* finally directed that someone find the keys for the old pillboxes. The brush was cleared from West Wall bunkers and grazing cows removed from atop their overhead cover. These fortifications

*Oberkommando der Wehrmacht, which, despite its title, was reduced to supervising the Western Front only at this stage of the war.

had been neglected since the end of the "Sitzkrieg" of 1940. Hitler had prevented Organization Todt from improving them during the summer, lest his generals begin to look back on them as a safe haven.

Montgomery's concept of ending the war was very different from Eisenhower's. What many observers don't catch is the difference in the amount of resistance the two leaders expected from the Germans. Despite having succumbed for a time to victory disease (the Germans are finished and the Allies can do anything), Eisenhower believed the German armed forces would reconstitute themselves within Germany and that it would take at least one large final battle to defeat them. The official British history denotes the differences in estimates of enemy strength made by Ike and Monty: "General Montgomery believed that the Germans might well collapse, provided the current pressure could be maintained continuously. He *therefore* [emphasis added] favored a concentrated offensive in one sector."[83] Montgomery assumed paradigm 1 and certainly thought one strong "full-blooded thrust" would bring the Germans to collapse. However, his Chief of Staff, General Guingand, who increasingly was on the outs with his commander, doubted that German morale would collapse and they would have to be bludgeoned until the bitter end.[84]

In late August, Eisenhower began to succumb to victory disease. The Germans might be all but finished. However, as the month turned, his estimate of German strength had substantially increased. When he met with his American subordinates on 3 September, he talked at length about a large battle of Germany to finish the Wehrmacht. His estimate was closer to paradigm 2 above. Stated the British official history, "General Eisenhower, from a different position reached a different conclusion. He was not so sure that a concentrated offensive could be maintained or that the enemy was so near to collapse."[85]

Eisenhower did not want to fight this battle deep within Germany, not until he had a close-in secure port—Antwerp. Instead, he wanted to threaten important German industrial capacity and force the Germans to commit major forces west of the Rhine to prevent Allied attacks from approaching the Ruhr and the Saar. Then the Allies could destroy these forces without extending their already overstretched supply lines. During that effort the quartermasters could move their depots forward to support a thrust deep into Germany.

In all of his notes and arguments, Montgomery never acknowledged the existence of this two-phased strategy focused on destroying the Wehrmacht in the field. Instead he implicitly assumed that a massive Allied army that penetrated to Berlin would cause the Wehrmacht to fall apart. Brooke generally agreed with the "imminent collapse" scenario. "On 6th September, the C.I.G.S. informed his colleagues that, although he considered the Joint Intelligence Committee's report to be slightly optimistic, he saw no reason to disagree with it."[86]

ULTRA was identifying corps-sized units forming before each advancing Allied army. Some, like Student's parachutists, came from training and depot troops. Others, like the panzer grenadiers forming in front of Patton, arrived from other theaters. More would come from the German interior and be formed into Volks Grenadiers. Adding evidence of a forming German strategic reserve to the immediate presence of corps-sized units in the field, ULTRA pointed toward something worse than paradigm 2.

Among the military leaders, only Eisenhower (and perhaps Patton's G2, Colonel Dick Monk) pointed toward paradigm 2 or maybe something a little worse. Eisenhower understood that the Germans were far from finished and that Hitler's will contained a lot more iron than had the kaiser's. Stephen Ambrose states, "Eisenhower knew the Germans would not quit until they were incapable of resistance. . . . This theme appears again and again."[87] When reporters asked him on 15 August how many weeks the war would last, Ike vehemently castigated such speculation. He told his aid, Butcher, "such people are crazy." What Ike probably didn't know in late August was that paradigm 3 would become reality.

Recognition that Germany was not yet beaten ruled out a range of strategies based on paradigm 1. Since the time of Sun Tsu, strategists have admonished generals to attack their enemy's will to resist. Frequently this is the enemy's weakest point. In the summer of 1944, this was not Hitler's Achilles heal. Nor was it the Wehrmacht's. The disasters in France and the Soviet Union in 1944 might have brought about the collapse of a less resolute enemy. But the Wehrmacht, although gasping, was resetting in a posture to continue the struggle. There would be no silver bullet hitting the enemy's vital organ, taking him out. The Allies were going to have to destroy the German Army in the field. This was pure Clausewitz: "The strategic offensive pursues the aim of the war directly, aiming straight at the destruction of the enemy's forces."[88]

If the Wehrmacht truly was in irreparable tatters, then maybe a "full-blooded drive" to Berlin might make sense. However, if they had enough recuperative power to assemble a twenty-division force, then a deep thrust on a narrow front with insufficient logistical support could get cut off in the interior of Germany and badly mangled. In this case, Ike's long-term intention to eliminate any such capability near the German border before plunging into central Germany made a lot of sense. Again, it came down to the proper objective. Was it Berlin, or the combat capability of the German Army in the field? This was the essence of the east-west question.

The Allies were at the end of their logistical tether. Even if closer-in ports such as Le Havre and Antwerp were captured immediately, it would take a month or two to recondition them. During that time, some sort of pause was almost inevitable. Granted, every day army engineers repaired more tracks, which freed more trucks. But every move into the interior required more trucks to move the same tonnage a greater distance. Undoubtedly, the Germans would find the means to reconstitute shattered formations and ready another battle. Eisenhower saw this with far better clarity than any of his enthusiastic subordinates. That is why he wanted to finish the German Army along the Rhine instead of chasing it into the interior of Germany. It is the point Montgomery refused to see.

Hitler understood that the Allies had outrun their supply lines. The best way to keep the tether stretched was to deny the use of ports closer to the German frontier. He designated the Brittany and Channel ports to be fortresses. Retreating Germans with little transport were directed to find shelter there.

Hitler and his military machine was not about to surrender. From seemingly paltry resources, it assembled a meaningful capability to resist. A combination of astounding regeneration efforts and shortened lines of communications transformed the Germans from a beaten stream of stragglers to a force capable of cohesive defense. These were still German soldiers defending the frontiers of the Fatherland. They were ready to be counted. Veterans, many of them returning from hospital, were well represented in the ranks of tactical leadership.

Hitler was not alone in perceiving that salvation would arrive the late fall. Jodl, chief of Hitler's immediate staff, told his fuehrer that, if Rundstedt could hold on until winter, "fog, night and snow" would give Germany the advantage.[89]

By falling back toward Germany, the Wehrmacht shortened its supply lines. This both eased supply problems and released personnel from service units required to maintain line of communications. Longer nights and poor weather gave respite from Allied aerial interdiction. Another benefit unknown to the Germans also was gained. Secure teleprinter landlines existed within greater Germany. Ultra only read radio transmissions. More and more operational communications traffic would be shielded from Allied eavesdroppers. As August turned into September, a major intelligence dis-connect had developed within the Allied camp. During late August, forward units chased beaten, disorganized shreds of former German units back toward their homeland. From corps and below, this experience dominated impressions of continued enemy capability.

There was a lot of optimism among senior Allied leaders on the first of September. Almost all of them would have been astonished to learn that twice as many American casualties lay ahead of the Armies before Germany surrendered than the Germans had already inflicted.

THE DECISIONS OF LATE AUGUST

The period between 20 and 3 September was one of the most important in deciding the direction of the European campaign. The Falaise pocket had just been closed. While 60,000 Germans had been killed or captured, almost everyone was disappointed that 40,0000 had escaped. Instead of the methodical advance across France that had been envisioned, post Cobra had brought on a great cavalry charge. Many critical decisions had to be made on the fly.

Despite the protests of his logisticians, on 19 August Ike decided to cancel the planned pause and cross the Seine. That River had been the final D+90 phase line of Overlord. Instead of a methodical buildup to that point, no railroads linked secure ports to the front. Instead deteriorating trucks linked invasion beaches to mostly empty field army level depots. And Paris had to be fed. There simply wasn't enough transport to carry required tonnage forward. If there had been heavy fighting, armies would have been screaming for ammunition. Because of the pursuit, they howled for gas instead.

Eisenhower was extremely concerned about Allied logistical limitations. In order to throw some water on overly optimistic reporters he told them that the inability of supply columns to keep pace with the spearheads that "further movement in large parts of the front even against very weak opposition is almost impossible."[90] In his 24 August cable to Marshall Eisenhower expressed concerns about his logistical capability to support the advance.[91] He wrote General Behon Somervell of his need for additional ammunition, tanks mortars, field wire and above all "heavy duty trucks."[92] In the words of Beetle Smith "By August, our spectacular advance was slowing down and transfusions were not enough. . . . At Supreme Headquarters, with General Eisenhower impatient to give the Germans no time to rest and re-organize, we reached the reluctant certainty that delay was imperative to future success. The advance would simply have to wait until supply caught up. Antwerp was now the key to the situation."[93]

In the field GIs felt the tonnage pinch in their daily lives. Reserve K rations were being issued instead of better fare. In First Army, captured German rations were used. A monotonous diet of North Sea canned fish replaced the humdrum of K rations. Cigarettes became unobtainable. Spare parts and replacements for worn-out equipment were nonexistent.

As early as 19 August, Eisenhower signaled Montgomery: "We are promised greatly accelerated shipments of American divisions from the U.S. and it is mandatory that we capture and prepare ports and communications to receive them. This had an importance second only to the destruction of the remaining enemy forces on our front." There is nothing about penetration up to, let alone over the Rhine or onto Berlin.[94] This is what so maddened Montgomery.

It wasn't as if Ike had a single problem he could contemplate while sitting under an apple tree in an orchard near Granville. Marshall was incensed that Montgomery was lording over everyone and insisted Eisenhower publicly pick up the mantle of direct command of fighting on the continent. His principal commanders wanted to attack in diverging directives. The logistical plan didn't work. To ease that the Americans and British wanted to delay the capture of Paris and all its hungry mouths. The French were not to be denied and were in the process of being insubordinate in order to liberate their capital. Command relationships between SHAEF and the southern invasion force were both unsettled and a major irritant. The bomber barons wanted their freedom from Eisenhower's temporary control.

The proponents of three competing plans jockeyed for position. A logical question Eisenhower asked was, what could the logisticians support?[95]

In late August, assuming no Antwerp, SHAEF logisticians estimated that in the north five corps (fifteen divisions) could be sustained over the Rhine, and three of these could be sustained as far as Berlin. Calculations demonstrated this would take 489 truck companies. But only 347 would be available. Airlift could pinch hit for 60 companies. The remaining 82 companies would have to be scrounged from other units. One can easily see this calculation has stretched everything to the limit. To raise the provisional truck companies required to fill the breach, ten divisions would have to be grounded. Another twelve divisions would be hobbled for lack of supplies.[96] These numbers also validated the calculation of Montgomery and his administrative officers that British Second Army could be supported all the way into Central Germany without Antwerp's support. Similar calculation predicted that if the main thrust was made in Patton's area, massing all transportation might get ten to twelve divisions to the Rhine, but they would run out of support at Frankfurt

The northern route via the much larger and economically more important Ruhr appeared to offer the greatest military opportunity. Threatening this area should bring on the largest German defensive force, to its destruction. Analysis by the staff of the Combined Chiefs reached the same conclusion. Field Marshal Brooke was so adamant about this issue, he wanted the Combined Chiefs to *order* Eisenhower to use it.

On the 20th Eisenhower consulted his staff. Montgomery elected not to go but was represented by his chief of staff, Major General Francis "Freddie" de Guingand. Ike's initial concept had each army group on separate, essentially co-equal, axes toward the Ruhr and the Saar. On 22 August, Eisenhower met with his American commanders. Eisenhower had thought it might be best to move First Army in tandem with Third Army south of the Ardennes. It would then swing north and become the southern pincer that would surround the Ruhr.[97] However, he recognized Montgomery's group would need additional reinforcement to carry out its dual mission of first taking Antwerp, then heading toward the Rhine north of the Ruhr. He intended to give Montgomery the four-plus airborne divisions of newly formed First Allied Airborne Army. De Guingand knew his boss had a very different plan in mind but had been unsuccessful in budging Eisenhower. At the meeting's conclusion he asked the supreme commander not to finalize his thoughts before meeting with the field marshal.

The next day, the 23rd, Ike drove north with Smith to meet with Monty at Conde. Rather intensely, Montgomery insisted that Eisenhower's chief of staff be excluded from the meeting. Monty knew Beetle was becoming increasingly vocal in his criticism of Montgomery's intransigence. Monty knew he could extract more from Ike in a "one on one."[98] In his map trailer, Montgomery began lecturing his boss. While Monty meant to be tactful, his tone was condescending. The field marshal emphasized the need for a firm plan. A single thrust north of the Ruhr by both 21 and 12th Army Groups was the best way to finish the war.

Despite all the emotion, Eisenhower had listened to the content of Monty's criticisms. Montgomery had made a good case that he couldn't open Antwerp and then move toward the Rhine without at least another twelve-division army. Both leaders implicitly understood that would mean U.S. First Army. Ike realized the logistical data militated against the effort south of the Ardennes.[99] Eisenhower personally made a major alteration to the post-Overlord plan. Instead of two co-equal thrusts, the main effort, consisting of the bulk of British Second and U.S. First Armies, would head toward the Ruhr. Canadian First Army would open the Channel ports, Antwerp, and its approaches. By the 24th Eisenhower had changed U.S. First Army's path to north of the Ardennes in support of Montgomery. Instead of a single American corps advancing north of the Ardennes, the bulk of U.S. First Army would attack through the Aachen Gap. The northern wing would receive priority for supplies and support.

During his conversation with Montgomery, Eisenhower pointed out that port capacity was more important at this stage than some of the more glamorous objectives to the east.[100] Ike looked to develop the plan to build Allied strength to sixty divisions.[101] He would need deep-water quays to bring the arriving divisions ashore and port capacity to keep them supplied. He also pointed to German Fifteenth Army, the last major formation west of the German frontier. Destroying it would eliminate a major German capability to resist subsequent operations. The field marshal explicitly acknowledged that capturing Antwerp, including a usable port, was an important objective.[102]

With the movement of First Army's attack north of the Ardennes and through the Aachen Gap, the difference between Monty's and SHAEF's strategies in the north-south dimension narrowed. The modification, induced both by Monty and the SHAEF logisticians, improved Eisenhower's plan. It created a clear main effort on a very important axis of advance. However, Eisenhower remained steadfast in his desire for a continuous Allied line from the North Sea to Switzerland. To keep the Germans stretched, he still wanted two thrusts, albeit now of unequal weight. In the east-west dimension, Eisenhower remained firmly wedded to the destruction of the German Army in a major battle on the Rhine plain. Monty's gaze remained fixed on Berlin.

Montgomery misinterpreted Ike's conciliatory and consensus-seeking language as agreement with the field marshal's position. Countering the centripetal forces among the independent-minded senior officers of the Allied effort was an almost impossible task. To keep the team together, Ike avoided issuing direct orders the way a division commander might issue them to the team he had trained up and was the undisputed single source of authority for. He may have missed the ideal balance point between commander and consensus maker. However, there was no one else who could have come even remotely as close to doing the job.

To ensure their understanding, Eisenhower wrote to Montgomery the next day:

TO: BERNARD LAW MONTGOMERY
AUGUST 24, 1944—TOP SECRET

Dear Monty.

Confirming our conversation of yesterday, the necessary directive will soon be issued to outline the general missions of the two army groups. It will be very brief, giving the Army Group of the North [Monty's 21st Army Group] the task of operating northeast, in the area generally to the westward of Amiens-Lille, destroying the enemy forces on its front, seizing the Pas de Calais area and the airfields in Belgium, and pushing forward to get a secure base at Antwerp. Its eventual mission will be to advance eastward on the Ruhr. By the time Antwerp is reached the general strength and composition of the forces needed for the latter task will have been determined.[103]

The note is clear, if polite. First Antwerp, then the Ruhr. There can be no other interpretation. Note the date. It is six days earlier than Montgomery's decision about use of the Channel ports to support his advance to the Rhine, which will be discussed in the next chapter. Given the heated meeting of the 23rd, Ike's letter of the 24th is unequivocal. After much argument, Ike laid out the priority in words that no participant could have misunderstood.

Montgomery was very unhappy with this missive. He thought he had scored more points with Ike than appeared in this letter. That night he signaled to Field Marshal Brooke: "Ike has now decided on his course of action I do not agree with what he proposed to do and have said so quite plainly."[104] On the 26th Eisenhower passed through Montgomery's forward HQ. The field marshal declined to have much conversation with his boss and instead directed him to a good place to see wreckage left behind by Germans fleeing the Allied onslaught.

Initially, Eisenhower leaned to transferring U.S. First Army to Montgomery's 21st Army Group. When he returned to his headquarters, all of his senior officers, British and American alike, strongly recommended this not occur. Montgomery was too hard to handle. Communications between him and SHAEF, always stunted and stiff, would hinder Eisenhower's control and could lead to Montgomery charging off on his own and becoming his own supreme commander, answering only to Brooke directly. As it was, Montgomery had communicated with SHAEF directly only a few times since June 6th, but he cabled Brooke almost every night. In addition, Ike knew Bradley would balk at losing control over his first love, U.S. First Army.

In a 29 August letter addressed to his component and army group commanders, Eisenhower repeated his clear instructions:

> It is my intention to complete the destruction of the enemy forces in the West and then advance against the heart of the enemy homeland.
>
> The Northern Group of Armies [Montgomery's 21st Army Group] will operate in a zone of action generally west of the line Amiens Lillie . . . destroy the enemy forces south of the Somme. . . . seize the Pas de Calais and secure a base at Antwerp.
>
> The Central Group of Armies [Bradley's 12th Army Group] will operate generally east of the line Ameins-Lille in conjunction with the Northern Group of armies. On its right it will eventually gain contact with Seventh Army advancing from the south from Marseilles, thereby forming a continuous front. . . .
>
> In addition to its principal offensive mission, The Central Group of Armies will complete the elimination of enemy resistance in the Brittany Peninsula. . . .
>
> [12th Army Group] will prepare to strike rapidly eastwards towards the Saar valley.[105]

The priorities are unmistakable. Montgomery's first job is to secure the channel ports and the *port* of Antwerp. No mention is made of the Rhine. Bradley's first job is to advance to the northeast in conjunction with Montgomery's forces. It was to *prepare* for the secondary thrust at the Saar but *not to execute it*. While not a single thrust, the northern attack is a heavily weighted main effort. The secondary effort would commence, *on order*, once the supreme commander could evaluate how the northern attack was unfolding. The logistical data coming from the SHAEF staff that supported this adjustment was simply overwhelming. In the north-south dimension, Ike had shifted about as close as he could to Montgomery's position without giving up altogether on a secondary effort by Patton in Lorraine. However, he remained adamant about not shifting from the two-phase* east-west dimension.

SHAEF staff, apparently General Bull, initially crafted the 21–12th Army Group border to pinch Montgomery out before he reached the Rhine. Until he cleared Antwerp, he had neither orders nor zone of advance on which to approach the Rhine. That emplaced strong control measures to prevent Monty from attempting to run away with the ball. De facto, Bradley and First Army would control the main effort to reach the Rhine until

*Destroy the Wehrmacht along the Rhine, then move into Germany.

Montgomery cleared Antwerp and its approaches and rejoined the eastward attack.

At the time, Montgomery told the director of military operations at the British War Office that "if we make the right decision, we can be in Berlin in three weeks and the war would be over."[106] He told Dempsey that 21st Army Group would be in Berlin in two or three weeks.[107] If that were true, there was insufficient time for even an intact Antwerp to contribute to victory.

General Eisenhower had listened to Montgomery, Bradley, and Marshall as well as his staff planners. The field marshal stated that his army group couldn't both capture Antwerp and leap the Rhine. Marshall indicated it was about time American forces were in the lead. Bradley clearly did not want to serve under Montgomery.

Without waving a big flag that would have incensed the British, Eisenhower had accommodated the views of all three senior leaders. Ike focused Montgomery on Antwerp alone. When Monty secured that objective, he could join the fight for Germany, which is what he wanted to do. Bradley's main effort was shifted north of the Ardennes and into the Aachen Corridor, which had been taken away from Montgomery so that he focused on Antwerp. This gave the Americans a major slice of the main effort and the initial crack at the Rhine.

Perhaps Montgomery wasn't so incensed. Recall that in his initial single-thrust proposal, he programmed Second Army to head toward Berlin while First Army took on the Ruhr.

On 2 September, Eisenhower, Bradley, Hodges, and Patton met at Chartres to discuss strategy. By this point, Eisenhower's thinking was already set. "While Ike leaned to a two thrust strategy, I [Bradley] cannot say that he leaped to embrace my ['American'] plan."[108] The alteration in taskings was clearly communicated by Eisenhower to Bradley. In the words of Bradley, "The northern thrust would go due east from Brussels on a line Liege-Aachen-Cologne, establishing a beachhead over the Rhine. It would consist of three corps: Horrocks' XXX [British], Corlett's XIX [U.S. First Army], and Collins' VII [U.S. First Army]."[109] By the 2nd Eisenhower had lost any notion that the Allies would be able to tramp through Germany at will against minimal opposition. He outlined his expectation about "a great battle of Germany.[110] He wanted to fight this as far west, that is, as close to Allied ports, as possible.

When Bradley and Patton learned of Eisenhower's intent of throwing added weight to the north, they were appalled. American generals would, at best, play supporting or subsidiary roles to that pompous field marshal.

In the words of the official American history, "it was as if Montgomery had stolen their birthrights."[111] Only half in jest, Patton suggested to Bradley that they both resign in protest. Both of these leaders knew that Marshall and Stimson, the secretary of war, were very sensitive about command issues.

Although he grumbled at the time, Bradley generally agreed with Eisenhower's modification. He believed the northern route showed more promise.[112] "On analysis, Ike's' decision to substantially reinforce Monty in a pursuit without pause was a correct one. . . . It was in fact, a single thrust strategy toward the Ruhr, with Patton's army reduced, in reality, to little more than a supporting force."[113]

Eisenhower had told Bradley to reign Patton in. This the 12th Army Group commander did not do. With more than a wink from Bradley, Patton had pushed 140 miles east of Paris and crossed the Meuse River at Verdun. The Saar was less than seventy miles away. Eisenhower had entered the meeting determined to chastise Patton for taking liberty with the freedom of action granted him. This the supreme commander did do. However, there was little point in not continuing the secondary attack, *except to conserve supply tonnage*. With little data to back up their statements, Lee and his Services of Supply said they could support both the main effort to the north and Patton's reduced drive in the south. Patton secured Eisenhower's permission to strike toward Mannheim and Frankfurt—subject to severe supply limitations. By the end of the conference a simultaneous two-thrust operational plan had been restarted. The northern thrust was clearly defined as the main effort. Patton's Lorraine effort was reduced to a spoiling attack designed to hold German forces in place.

At the Chartres meeting, Patton and Bradley wheedled permission to move one of First Army's three corps onto an axis of attack farther south to support Patton. Under pressure and in the spirit of compromise, Eisenhower reluctantly agreed. As will be expanded on in chapter 5, this was a major error. That corps would advance through the Ardennes. Early in their planning SHAEF planners had identified the Ardennes as one of four avenues of approach into Germany—and rejected it because its rough topography wouldn't support high-speed advance of highly mechanized Allied forces. Ike was aware of this.

One hundred fifty kilometers, principally the Ardennes, separated First Army concentrations in the Aachen Gap from Third Army's attack, which would orient on Metz. Most of Third Army's effort would occur along the Moselle River in the 50-kilometer stretch between Metz in the north and Nancy to the south. Eisenhower's initial plan left a lot of passive front between the two 12th Army Group attacks. This clearly wasn't "broad front." It was tightly focused main and supporting attacks.

A second major issue was that SHAEF staff had very skillfully delineated the inter–army group boundary to keep Montgomery's group hugging the Channel coast and away from any opportunity to make off toward the Rhine. However, General Bradley was concerned about the total length and area of responsibility of 12th Army Group's zone. He, like Montgomery, looked east. Bradley was still advocating his American Plan, a two-army thrust south of the Ardennes toward the Saar. He wanted nothing from Belgium except port capacity. On the 29th, at Bradley's request, 21st Army Group 's boundary was moved south to include Brussels. Although Bradley's front was narrowed, the boundary change also gave 21st Army Group enough ground to slide around the Scheldt and reach toward the Rhine. "Thereafter Brussels rather than Antwerp seems to have occupied first place in the minds of the British command."[114] Intelligence reports began revealing the size of a hole opening east of Antwerp that so concerned von Rundstedt. The 21st Army Group commander rechecked the calculation of his logistical sums.

These two seemingly small adjustments, moving a First Army corps south and moving the 21st–12th Army Group boundary so that Monty had an approach to the Rhine from Brussels to Roermond, became the nubs of offshoots that would wreck SHAEF's plan (this will be taken up in some detail in the next two chapters).

The biographer who actually spent the most time interviewing Eisenhower observed, "Eisenhower's great weakness in this situation was not that he wavered, but rather his eagerness to be well liked, coupled with his desire to keep everyone happy. Because of these characteristics, he would not end a meeting until at least verbal agreement had been found."[115] Brooke was more emphatic on this point: Eisenhower acted as "an arbitrator balancing the requirements of competing allies and subordinates rather than a master of the field making a decisive choice."[116] The characteristic that made Eisenhower such a skilled master of keeping his disparate brood moving in the same direction detracted from his aura of being a decisive and "in control" commander. They were opposite sides of the same coin.

Hodges participated little in the heated debate. When the meeting concluded, he understood his primary mission was to get through to Antwerp.

Eisenhower was injured when his small plane made a forced landing, and he was unable to meet face to face with Montgomery. So Bradley personally met with the 21st Army Group commander on the 3rd to relay the decision made on the 2nd. The field marshal was unpleasantly surprised at what he heard.

As a group, the SHAEF planners were less than impressed with the single-thrust arguments of Patton and Montgomery. Planners "labeled them castles of theory built on sand."[117] Montgomery might have been surprised if he had heard those planners remark that even if Patton's proposal reached the Rhine, it was unlikely to force any decisive result. Montgomery's plan might capture the Ruhr, but it was neither tactically nor logistically feasible. In their opinion, neither plan held any promise of becoming reality.[118]

THE PLAN

The final SHAEF plans are laconically communicated:

CABLE FWD13765
SEPTEMBER 4, 1944—TOP SECRET

(Addressed to Ramsay, Montgomery, Bradley, Leigh Mallory, Bereton, Spaatz, and Harris)

. . . 3. Our best opportunity of defeating the enemy in the west lies in striking at the Ruhr and at the Saar, confident that he [the Germans] will concentrate the remainder of his available forces in defense of these essential areas.

4. Present plans contemplate assumption of operational control of DRA-GOON force [the forces landed in southern France] about 15th September. DRAGOON force is now directed on Besancon-Dijon and then on Belfort-Epinal.

5. My intention continues to be the destruction of the enemy forces and this will be the primary task of all elements of the Allied Expeditionary Force.

6. The mission of the Northern Group of Armies [Montgomery's 21st Army Group] and the part of the Central Group of armies [Bradley's 12AG] operating north-west of the Ardennes [i.e., U.S. First Army] is to secure Antwerp, breach the sector of the Siegfried line covering the Ruhr and then seize the Ruhr.

7. The mission of Central Group of Armies, exclusive of that portion operating north-west of the Ardennes are:

a. To capture Brest

b. To protect the southern flank of the Allied Expeditionary Force.

c. To occupy the sector of the Siegfried Line covering the Saar and then to seize Frankfurt. It is important that this operation should start as soon as possible, in order to forestall the enemy in this sector, but troops of Central Group of Armies operation against the Ruhr north-west of the Ardennes must first be adequately supported.

d. To take any opportunity of destroying enemy forces withdrawing from south-west and southern France.

8. Boundary between Northern and Central Groups of Armies subject to adjustment in detail by agreement of the Commanders in Chie, Groups of Armies; Amiens-Brussels-Krefield [Germany] all to the Northern Group of Armies.[119]

This order has implications that are not readily apparent. In this published version, Northern Group of Armies has access to Germany via Flanders. In the map of Montgomery's single thrust, Flanders is where he wanted to take Second Army. Northern Group of Armies plus U.S. First Army were lumped together in paragraph 6 and given the mission of seizing the Ruhr. If the boundary defined in paragraph 8 would have excluded Montgomery's army group from crossing the Rhine, it would have better communicated Ike's intent. The final version of the plan does not. Two corps of the U.S. First Army were to make the initial move to the Rhine north of the Ardennes. As Eisenhower wrote to Montgomery on 29 August, 21st Army Group forces that would add to this effort would be identified and tasked *after* Antwerp port was secure. Switch to an American-led attack to the Rhine north of the Ardennes with British follow-up is clearly in the order, but the change from earlier plans is not made explicit. The intent stated explicitly in Eisenhower's 29 August letter directed First Army to the Rhine via Aachen, while 21st Army Group opened the ports, including Antwerp. After the ports were opened 21st Army Group could then join the Rhine attack already in progress. The published plan muddles Montgomery's priority of Antwerp first, then the Rhine.

Woe be the leader who has headstrong errant subordinates who *think* they are the sole True Believers.

Eminent British historian B. H. Liddell Hart observed that "none of Eisenhower's executives liked the compromise [embodied in FWD13765] but their complaints were not so loud at the time as they became in later months and years."[120]

Beetle Smith expanded on the sparse words of FWD13765. Notice the two objectives he lists are *not* the thrusts north and south of the Ardennes. Instead he emphasizes the east-west dimension of the plan:

> But we still had two major objectives in the strategic plan. One was to mass in the north for the crossing of the Rhine to encircle the Ruhr. The other was to destroy Germans west of the Rhine and move all our forces up to the river barrier to take advantage of such opportunity for a crossing as might be offered.[121] . . . His (Ike's) proposal was a series of interlocking campaigns to split up the German defenders and defeat them in detail.[122] . . . If we achieved the Supreme Commander's full objective, these battles would destroy most of the enemy troops west of the Rhine. Sound military judgment would not justify a determined stand by major enemy forces west of the Rhine once our armies were well through the Rhine. There was always by one inflexible rule, "Destroy the German forces speedily and completely."[123]

Ike had reiterated his strategy of a two phase, two thrust advance. Notice the boundary through Krefeld precluded Montgomery's forces from reaching the Rhine anywhere south of Roermond, which lies on the northern boundary of the Ruhr. The main effort through the Aachen Gap was now assigned to 12th Army Group. Bradley acknowledged he understood that two corps were to attack via Aachen. But specific language stating that instruction is not included in paragraph 6. Nevertheless, elements of not one but two army groups were to capture the most promising objectives—Antwerp and the Aachen Gap. Ensure these efforts get priority by directing that the secondary attack in the south not be supported until the requirements north of the Ardennes are met.

Departures from Ike's intent in the 29 August letter indicate that FWD13765 was not the best-written document of the European campaign.*

---

*In order to reduce the complexities of following September's events, the actions of 21st Army Group will be recounted in chapter 4, U.S. First Army and Bradley's HQ in chapter 5, and Patton's Third Army in chapter 6. Each is easier to follow sequentially through the month. Cross-references to what is going on with the other two are inserted in each chapter as needed.

4

It Wasn't Arnhem versus Antwerp

"The more I considered what we were setting out to
do, the more certain I was that it was wrong."
"I was determined to play my full part in the business; the British forces
would show and did show, that when it came to the mobile battle they
were just as good as the next man. But I had great misgivings."

Montgomery, Memoirs

MONTGOMERY'S CRITICISMS

Of all of Ike's lieutenants, Montgomery was his most severe critic. Monty's style was to maintain a "firm grip" over a battle. "It was always very clear to me that Ike and I were poles apart when it came to the conduct of the war. . . . I planned always to make the enemy commit his reserves on a wide front in order to plug holes in his defenses; having forced him to do this, I then committed my own reserves on a narrow front in a hard blow." In Montgomery's view "Eisenhower's creed appeared to me to be that there must be aggressive action on the part of everyone at all times. Everybody must attack all the time."[1]

In a letter to Field Marshal Brooke on 14 August, about the time the events being described occur, Montgomery was more candid; "His [Eisenhower's] ignorance as to how to run a war are [*sic*] absolute and complete."[2] Arthur Bryant, the editor of Brooke's diary, and a fan of Monty, stated, "I believe that in August, 1944 a Supreme Allied Commander . . . could have ended the war by decisively backing *either* Montgomery or Bradley. But there was . . . no strong hand at the helm, no man in command. There was only . . . a chairman—a shrewd, intelligent tactful careful Chairman."[3]

21ST ARMY GROUP JOINS THE PURSUIT

After the breakout at Saint-Lô, the Americans had run amuck across France. Now it was the British turn. Second Army crossed the Seine on 25–27 August. 30 Corps led with 8 Corps advancing in echelon on the left flank.

Patton is often quoted as ordering his exploiting forces to ignore their flanks. Montgomery's order to his exploiting forces:

> 17. The [Second British] Army will move with its armored strength deployed well forward; its passage northwards must be swift and relentless . . . quite irrespective of the progress of armies on its flanks.
> 24. The enemy has not the troops to hold any strong position. The proper tactics are for strong armored and mobile columns to by-pass enemy centers of resistance and move boldly ahead.
> 24. I rely on commanders of every rank and grade to "drive" ahead with the utmost energy; any tendency to be "sticky" or cautious must be stamped on ruthlessly.[4]

General Dempsey, Second Army commander, demonstrated that he could run an army hard in a pursuit. One of Monty's loyal men who eschewed publicity in any form, he was known as a resolute, self-confident commander who was much liked by his subordinates. An ardent student of war with an uncanny ability to visualize complex features of a battlefield from intense inspection of a topographic map, he retained a good grasp of a fluid battle.[5]

Lieutenant General Sir Brian Horrocks's (commander, 30 Corps) dash into the Low Countries rivaled Patton's sweep from Paris to the Moselle. Horrocks, a legendary commander still recovering from severe wounds, had been brought in to give the British advance more zip. A pair of 30 Corps armored divisions spearheaded his advance. With Household Cavalry scout cars leading the way, the highly regarded (although not by Montgomery) Guards Armored Division rumbled into Brussels amid great cheers. In the style of the best blitzkrieg, the Guards simply bypassed roadblocks and pockets of heavy resistance.

In six days, Second Army had advanced over 400 kilometers. Occasionally an antitank gun sited to cover a defile would slow the British tankers up. But not for long. Mobs came out to heap flowers on British tanks as they sped by. At many villages church bells announced the arrival of smiling Tommies who were already pumped up by the chase.

Perhaps intent on showing his best Allied face, Patton told reporters, "Field Marshal Montgomery has just completely buggered the whole

[German] show. I think that is a magnificent show and as a result of that, it would seem to me that the German plan of defense is completely dissipated. The advance of the Guards Division and the other divisions up there has been something magnificent."[6]

Before Allied shipping could nourish supply starved armies via Antwerp, the 100-kilometer long Scheldt estuary (see map 3.1) had to be cleared of the Wehrmacht. *The Germans had yet to mine the estuary.* In order to clear the north side of the Scheldt, the Allies would have to seize the South Breveland isthmus. Any appreciation of the assignment to secure Antwerp had to recognize this obvious requirement. From invasion planning, Monty knew the importance of the deep-water docks at Antwerp.

Eisenhower and Montgomery met on 23 August. Ike followed up with a letter on the 24th, unequivocally stating that Montgomery was to first capture the Channel ports and "Antwerp as a base." When that was completed, 21st Army Group would head toward the Rhine. On 26 August, Montgomery issued M520, 21st Army Group General Operational Situation and Directive, which complied with the supreme commander's intent. The critical excerpts:

> 3. The tasks now confronting 21st Army Group are:
>   a. To operate northwards and to destroy the enemy in N.E. France and Belgium
>   b. To secure the PAS DE CALAIS area and the airfields in Belgium
>   c. To secure Antwerp as a base.
> 4. Having completed these tasks, the eventual mission of the Army Group will to be to advance eastwards on the RUHR.
> 5. Speed of action and of movement is now vital. I cannot emphasize this enough; what we have to do must be done quickly. Every officer and man must understand that by a stupendous effort now we shall . . . hasten the end of the war.
>   Intention
> 6. To destroy all enemy forces in the PAS DE CALAIS and FLANDERS, and to capture ANTWERP.
> 7. (Canadian Army boundary through Bruges)
> 8. (Boundary between 21 and 12th Army Groups, all inclusive to Second Army) TOURNAI-RENAIX-ALOST-ANTWERP.[7]

Montgomery's order was clear. He understood Ike's very specific concept of maneuver and ordered his army group into compliance. Note that Antwerp is to be "secured for use as a base." For it to be a base, the Scheldt River, the channel from Antwerp to the sea, would have to be controlled by the British. The meaning is unmistakable. Detailed paragraphs of M520

Table 4.1. Capacity of Ports Assigned 21 Army Group
(Short Tons per Day)

	Date opened	Capacity
Dieppe	7 Sep	6–7,000
Le Havre	9 Oct	3,650 in Oct
		5,000 by Nov
Boulogne	12 Oct	11,000 + Pluto pipeline
Calais	Nov	personnel + LST only
Dunkirk	not developed in fall	
Ostend	25 Sep	1,000 by 30 Sep
		5,000 + POL by 30 Oct
Antwerp	26 Nov	19,000 by 7 Dec
		80–100,000 later

Source: *Moulton,* Battle for Antwerp, *p. 77.*

direct First Canadian Army to quickly clear Dieppe and Bruges and then move onto Le Havre and Pas de Calais. "No more forces will be employed in this task than are necessary" so that the Canadian Army can concentrate on "the main business to the north."[8] The main business of the Canadian Army was clearing of the Scheldt. The boundary Montgomery designated more closely followed Eisenhower's intent than did FWD 146375.

Montgomery knew he could not support a reach for the Rhine from his Normandy logistical base. British logisticians planned on trucking supplies no more than 200 miles. Bayeux to Brussels is already 400 road miles. Available supply tonnage and transportation capacity would not allow this eastward movement of Second Army. Recall from chapter 2, a division requires about 500 tons a day to meet its immediate needs. Twenty-First Army Group had fourteen divisions.

Shortening the transit for several thousand tons per day would provide the relief that Monty needed. If the field marshal wanted to head for the Rhine, the immediate requirement was to capture the Channel ports. Their modest quays could not offload the tens of thousands of tons Ike and Bradley needed. Only Antwerp could meet Bradley's needs. But the Channel ports could make the difference for Dempsey.

Analysis of channel port capacity and the opening dates for each shows what was possible. Le Havre had already been allocated to the Americans.

As his army group advanced up the coast and into Belgium, Montgomery made some important calculations. Monty knew Dieppe had the capacity to handle "between 6000 and 7000 tons a day."[9] Monty relates that he calculated that 7,000 tons would be sufficient in the near term.[10] In his words: "On 30 August a decision was made to rely on the early capture of a Channel port such as Dieppe or Boulogne. It was decided to cut down our imports from an average of some 16,000 tons per day to 7,000 tons per day."[11]

This decision had a genesis. In his 26 August M520 directive, in the intention paragraph, Montgomery states his intention was "to destroy all enemy forces in the Pas de Calais and Flanders, and to capture Antwerp." At first Monty felt the Channel ports would not provide enough support to begin British operations east of the Rhine. This is what he told Sir Anthony Eden.[12] Twenty-First Army Group had fourteen divisions, hence a figure of 7,000 tons is sufficient to maintain combat operations in the near term. Monty's chief of administration, General Miles, concluded that the Channel ports could support 21st Army Group.[13] Monty saw the light.

General Simonds's biographer, Dominick Graham, concurs: "Montgomery appeared to think the Channel Ports were more important opening than the Scheldt, perhaps even a greater priority than destroying the Fifteenth Army. He needed the ports to supply his advance."[14] In effect, the field marshal had created an objective that *superseded* the two SHAEF-designated objectives. In the words of Chester Wilmot, "It was now apparent, however, that he [Montgomery] would not need to open the port of Antwerp before advancing to the Ruhr."[15] Be it Montgomery's best professional opinion, his strong belief did NOT give him the right to ignore his commander's direct orders or to operate outside his commander's intent. And there can be no question that Montgomery did not misunderstand Eisenhower's intent.

Dieppe was taken intact in a virtually unopposed operation by 1st Canadian Division on 1 September. It was 175 kilometers closer to Montgomery's forward elements than Normandy. Dieppe met the minimum requirements to propel Dempsey over the Rhine, but it could not sustain additional buildup. Still it added trump to Montgomery's hand as it went into operation within a week. By itself, Dieppe made a forward lunge by Second Army possible. The other ports could begin offloading buildup forces within thirty-five days. Ostend's capabilities provided an additional margin and could have been developed a little faster if absolutely necessary. Landing craft did run up on the beaches there when required. Before the war, Channel ferries plied between Dover and Ostend. If one adds Boulogne's potential to that of Dieppe, Monty would not have needed additional discharge capacity at Antwerp to sustain 21st Army Group. Double track rail lines led from Dieppe, Ostend, and Boulogne and had not been extensively bombed. Boulogne was 150 kilometers closer to the front than was Le Havre. It is on the Straits of

Dover and accessible to England by Channel ferry. This is a critical point to understand. When 30 Corps entered Antwerp on 4 September, 21st Army Group already had in hand sufficient port capacity to alleviate its short-run logistic problems. There was a long term "21st Army Group only" alternative to Antwerp along the Channel coast if either Ostend or Boulogne was secured.

Monty faced two alternative operational designs for his army group. One alternative was to pin German Fifteenth Army to the coast and clear the Scheldt. The second was to create a small logistical base among the Channel ports and use it to support a strike over the Rhine.

Events were moving rapidly. Montgomery thought his tutoring of Eisenhower was having a positive impact. Then Bradley arrived on 3 September to relate the conclusions of the meeting among American generals at Chartres. Despite the fact that Eisenhower had been injured in a forced landing of his small plane and was unable to travel in person, Montgomery was incensed that Ike had not communicated the seemingly new orders in person. When he learned that Patton would continue to get gasoline and that U.S. First Army would not be attached to his army group, he simply exploded.[16] He determined he was not going to sit still.

That day, Montgomery cabled Field Marshal Brooke: "I have not seen Eisenhower since 26 August and have had no orders from him, so I am making my own plans for advancing against the RUHR and am getting Bradley to lend a hand."[17] Montgomery's cable is, to say the least, breathtaking.

Not heard from Ike? What was the message communicated in person by Bradley? Then why not initiate communications with Ike instead of Brooke? This statement underscores that the 30 August decision anchoring logistics on the Channel ports was entirely a 21st Army Group one.

As far as Montgomery was concerned, Allied strategy had unraveled. Patton was going to continue toward the Saar. While 21st Army Group busied itself along the Channel coast, Bradley was going to head for the Aachen Gap, the traditional invasion route from northern France into Germany. That very day, Montgomery issued new instructions not at all consistent with Ike's intentions:

TOP SECRET

M523—3-9-44

General Situation

1. Second Army is advancing to secure the area BRUSSELS-GHENT-ANTWERP. Its left Corps (12 Corps) is echeloned back to watch the left flank until the Canadian Army can get forward to the BRUGHES area.

2. Canadian Army is moving forward, across the SOMME at ABBE-VILLE to its task of clearing the coastal bank.

Intention

3. (a) to advance eastwards and destroy all enemy forces encountered.
   (b) to occupy the RUHR, and get astride the communications leading from it into Germany and to the sea ports.

Forward Boundaries

4. All inclusive 12th Army Group:
   WAVRE TIRELEMONT-HASSELT-SITTARD—GARZWEILER-LEVERKUSEN (On the Rhine)
   All inclusive 21st Army Group
   OPLADEN (on the Rhine) WARBURG BRUNSWICK

Canadian Army

5. Canadian Army will clear the coastal belt and then will remain in the general area BRUGES-CALAIS until the maintenance situation allows of its employment further forward.

Second Army

6. On 6 September, the Army will advance eastwards with its main bodies from the general line BRUSSELS-ANTWERP. Before that date light forces will operate as far afield as desired.

7. The western face of the RUHR between DUSSELDORF and DUIS-BERG will be threatened frontal.

8. The main weight of the Army will be directed on the RHINE between WESEL and ARNHEM.

9. One division, or if necessary, a corps will be turned northwards towards ROTTERDAM and AMSTERDAM.

10. Having crossed the RHINE, the Army will deal with the RUHR and will be directed on the general area OSNABRUCK, HAMM, MUNSTER, RHEINE.[18]

Note how that boundary change of late August became so critical. Without it, 21st Army Group would have been pinched out at Antwerp. M524, which directed Second Army to advance on the Rhine and Ruhr, could not have been written. Montgomery would have had no way to head for the Rhine without additional overt permission from SHAEF. Perhaps all of the apparent mistakes around Antwerp could have been avoided. The course of the war would have been far different.

In a lecture right after the war, Montgomery admitted to the change in priority of objective: "In view of the time factor it was agreed that 21st Army Group should launch its thrust to the Rhine before completing the clearance of the Scheldt Estuary."[19] "Agreed" by Montgomery and himself, but no one at SHAEF. This is straight-out admission that Montgomery changed the priority set by Ike without approval from anyone.

This order was issued on the 3rd. At the time the closest 21st Army Group unit, 11th Armored, was 30 kilometers from the Antwerp. No one yet knew what condition the docks would be in when they arrived. Note that in M523, *no unit is assigned to clear the Scheldt and secure Antwerp as a base.* Second Army is directed to move to the Rhine. The Canadians are stopped near Calais 300 kilometers from Antwerp. Montgomery had altered his M520, which had closely followed Eisenhower's intent. With the logistical base for Second Army securely anchored in the Channel ports, Montgomery had no need for Antwerp. Instead he redirected Second Army to lead a charge to the Rhine. But it is directed far north to Wesel-Arnhem. This is 120 kilometers north of U.S. First Army's advance through the Aachen gap. That is out of range of mutual support. In effect Montgomery, without orders, was forcing Eisenhower's hand. With eighteen divisions (including a portion of U.S. First Army) up along the Rhine, Montgomery reasoned that Eisenhower would have to reinforce a successful assault across that mighty river.

In the British Army the statement of commander's intent is extremely important. Normally the commander's intent is communicated down two levels. In M523, Montgomery had not seen fit to mention, let alone emphasize, the supreme commander's intent to open Antwerp and its approaches. Monty directed Dempsey toward the Rhine. Reference the date on the order. It's one full week before Market Garden is born and two weeks before parachutes begin to open over Arnhem. It is also ten days after Ike underscored the need to secure Antwerp as a working port.

Notice Second Army is directed toward Osnabrück, Hamm, Munster, and Rheine. This takes Dempsey's forces past the Ruhr and on the road to Berlin. Certainly they are not intending to deploy against German forces defending the Ruhr. Their objective is to encircle the industrial area or to open the road to Berlin, not destroy the units defending the Ruhr.

M523 was neither a fluke nor imprecise drafting. It is a concise product of a set of integrated plans formulated by Montgomery during the last days of August and the initial ones of September. Those plans are at complete odds with what Ike intended. Look at the level at which Monty was addressing the problem. Instead of solving the operational problem in a manner consistent with theater strategy, he pursued his own alternative strategy. Thus, a clear violation of his commander's intent.

On the 6th, Montgomery signaled General Crerar, commander of First Canadian Army, the following clarification: "It looks as if the port of Antwerp may be unusable for some time as the Germans are holding the islands at the mouth of the Scheldt. Immediate opening of some port north of Dieppe is essential for development of my plan and I want Boulogne badly. What do you think the chances of getting it soon?"[20]

This signal summarizes the changes to the SHAEF plan Montgomery wrote into M523. He had no intention of immediately opening Antwerp but wanted to ensure his alternate plan for supplying Second Army was intact. Apparently, Montgomery felt a rapid dash to Berlin would end the war quickly, before Antwerp would either be opened or its capacity really missed by the Allies.

Much has been made about possible lack of clarity in the formal order FWD13765 (see the previous chapter). In his memoirs Montgomery states:

> Some have argued that I ignored Eisenhower's orders to give priority to open-ing up the port of Antwerp and that I should not have attempted the Arnhem operation until it was done. There were no such orders about Antwerp and Eisenhower had agreed about Arnhem. Indeed, up to the 8th October, 1944 inclusive my orders were to gain the line of the Rhine "as quickly as humanly possible." On 9 October, Montgomery gave Antwerp was given priority for the first time.[21]

Going back through the communications beginning 23 August between Eisenhower and Montgomery, add all the port capacity planning since the beginning of the invasion plans, and Montgomery's postwar statement has, at best, the smell of mendacity. The excuse about poor communica-tions between Eisenhower's HQ and the rest of Allied headquarters is also overblown. Figure 4.1 is a copy of a memo listing "Signal Situation SHAEF Forward HQS 31 August 1944." It lists the installed line and wireless links between Shell Burst (Eisenhower's forward HQ at Granville) and other com-munications nodes. Note there are both completed telephone and wireless circuits to 21st Army Group main headquarters, lines to 12th Army Group main, and circuits back to England, where Brooke would have immediate

COPY

SIGNAL SITUATION SHAEF FORWARD HQs 1800 B 11 AUGUST 1944.

LINE COMMUNICATION

1. TELEPHONE

Speech available to :-

(a) 12 Army Group Main at LAVAL, but not beyond as the lines are not yet completed to VERSAILLES.

(b) 21 Army Group Main at LE TRONQUAY, but not beyond as lines are not complete to General Montgomery's Tac HQ.

(c) To the UK via BAYEUX, CHERBOURG, PORTSMOUTH CHQ.

(d) To the UK direct by 0200 1 Sept 1944 to Main SHAEF and Goodge Street for the Ministries in LONDON.

(e) Direct or via Switching centres in France to Com. Zone, L of C HQs.

II. WIRELESS COMMUNICATIONS

2. Complete wireless communications are available as follows, some circuits will open at the date given, the others are working now :-

(a) To 12 Army Group Main

(b) To 12 Army Group Advance, set moving up net working.

(c) To 21 Army Group Main, two circuits.

(d) To Main HQs in UK various hand speed and high speed circuits. From Main HQs messages are sent on to Washington and AFHQ.

(e) To General Koenig in PARIS.

S 1333

CLASSIFICATION CHANGED
RESTRICTED
By authority of CALA
By ....
Date 7 AUG 1945

COPY

access. While there are no direct links with 21st Army Group TAC HQ where Montgomery resided, it is inconceivable that a highest priority signal from the supreme commander to Montgomery would not have been immediately forwarded to Monty via British channels, had this been Monty's priority. Communications between 21st Army Group main and TAC HQ were a British responsibility. On the other hand, if someone wanted not to receive the latest orders . . .

In his memoirs Montgomery states that in the early days of September, "he [Eisenhower] was, in fact, completely out of touch with the land battle as far as I could see. There were no telephone lines and not even a radio-telephone between his HQ and Bradley and myself."[22] Later he complains that reply to his 5 September signal was received in two parts on the 7th and 9th.[23] Given the document in figure 4.1, Monty's statements implying American communication trouble also have an air of mendacity about them.

On the 6th Monty did cable Ike: "Received your order FWD 13765 at 0730 hrs today 6 September. You can rely on 21st Army Group to go all out 100% to further your intention to destroy enemy forces."[24]

Both Hamilton and Wilmot understand that M523 was not consistent with SHAEF's instructions but seem to imply that Montgomery's own conclusions were sufficient cause for the field marshal to engage in insubordinate behavior. That Eisenhower subsequently made the best of the existing situation that he found on the 10th has led many American writers away from an analysis of the impact of Montgomery's behavior on SHAEF strategy, with no comment on ex poste explanations and rationalizations proffered from the other side of the Atlantic.

On the 3rd, Horrocks ordered his lead divisions to make a rare night run into what had been German-held territory. Eleventh Armored Division under Major General "Pip" Roberts took to the back roads to Antwerp. (Map 4.1 displays the approach to Antwerp and Comet.) Many thought Pip was Britain's best tank commander. This division had repeatedly distinguished itself since the landing in Normandy.

Tactical surprise was complete. Members of the Resistance showed the Brits ways around German roadblocks on the main routes and bridges. The first Germans that British tankers encountered the next morning were lounging in Antwerp's outdoor cafes. They didn't even bother to look up to see whose tanks were making the racket. Although dockside cranes were wired for destruction, the demolition parties that were supposed to destroy them were nowhere near their duty stations. Ten square miles of docklands were captured intact. Even the cargo cranes remained in good working order.

At the time, Antwerp was a city of 2.5 million. How was a 12,000-man armored division supposed to secure something this large? And complete this job before the 6th, when as of the 3rd they hadn't entered the city? The docks themselves extended six miles down the Scheldt. No one had thought much about how to capture and control them. Roberts and his officers looked at a map and consulted the locals. Lots of roads emanated from a

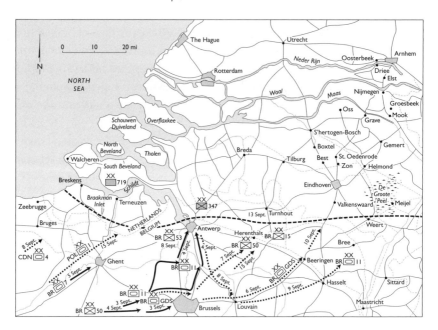

Map 4.1. Advance to Antwerp and Comet

large downtown park. Tommies headed there and to a couple of bridges that spanned the Albert Canal. When they approached the bridges, 20mm and 88mm guns, probably anti-aircraft, took them under fire. With no specific orders and facing stiff fire and with few friendly troops in sight, the tankers demurred crossing the Scheldt. The Germans would not blow the important bridge for another twelve hours.

Deliriously happy civilians were the greatest impediment. Meantime, firefights broke out between resistance fighters eager to liberate their city and confused German detachments. On the downstream end of the city German units moved around with little difficulty. Who was going to attack down the far bank of the Scheldt and cut off six static Fifteenth Army divisions caught on the wrong side of the waterway? At least a full corps was required. Again, M523 assigned *no one*.

On the 4th, ULTRA informed Monty that Germans intended to withdraw via South Breveland and hold both banks of Scheldt and that Hitler was determined that use of Antwerp port must be denied to the Allies.[25] The German high command recognized that the ring around Fifteenth Army was about to close and that an attack at Breda at the neck of the Scheldt must be expected. A single German division, the 719th, guarded the

Breveland isthmus. This low-grade "static formation was composed entirely of elderly gentlemen who had been guarding the North coast and had never heard a shot fired in anger."[26] Model had little on Walcheren except coastal and anti-aircraft on 4th. The 719th had been ordered into Antwerp and its approaches but had not arrived by the 4th. Thirty Corps could have sealed off the isthmus without incurring heavy casualties. Elements of the 347th Infantry division, being evacuated from below the Seine by rail, were diverted into a rail station seven miles north of Antwerp.[27] These were the principal reinforcements to the stragglers and anti-aircraft gunners who were in the city when 11th Armored came calling.

Cornelius Ryan called Monty's failure to immediately seize the seaward approach to Antwerp "the Great Mistake." An examination of a map of the Belgian coast demonstrates why Antwerp is useless as a port until the banks of this narrow inlet of water, including Walcheren Island, is cleared of enemy forces. Conventional historical wisdom is that Market Garden was pursued at the expense of clearing the approaches to Antwerp.

Instead of tending to the Scheldt, Montgomery was arguing with Eisenhower about theater strategy via radiogram. Montgomery signaled: "1. I consider we have now reached a stage where one really powerful and full blooded Thrust towards Berlin is likely to get there and thus end the German war." He went to say that Allied logistics could support but a single thrust and that the northern thrust via the Ruhr is "likely to give the best and quickest results."[28] As early as the 26th Montgomery had told Horrocks: "All risks are justified—I intend to get a bridgehead over the Rhine before they [the Germans] have time to recover."[29] These communications indicate Monty's focus and frame of mind. It clearly was on a single-phase operation, not on Ike's two phases. Neither was it on Antwerp.

Eisenhower signaled Montgomery again on the 5th of the necessity of opening the ports of Le Havre and Antwerp, which were required to sustain 12th Army Group east of the Rhine. Apparently this message incensed Montgomery.[30]

Student's paratroopers began digging in along Waal on the afternoon of 5th. First Parachute Army gained control of 719ID and 176ID, which was made up of hospital returnees. Anti-aircraft troops added a lot of firepower. In the Antwerp area Goring transferred twenty heavy and ten light AA batteries as well as 20,000 Luftwaffe ground personnel, which were used to flesh out depleted infantry formations. The line was thickening. Fifteenth Army was on the wrong side of the Scheldt. Canceling Model's earlier orders for an ill-conceived counterattack against British strength, Rundstedt directed that the bulk of Fifteenth Army be ferried across the Scheldt and that Walcheren be fortified. He left intact Model's orders to fortify the Channel ports and the southern bank of the Scheldt around Breskins. In two days, the Germans had accumulated enough combat power to eject the small British bridgehead across the Albert Canal. Initial troop deployments began on the first day Student's headquarters became operational. On the 6th the Kriegsmarine started to drop enormous quantities of mines into the Scheldt. Had that been prevented or interrupted, Antwerp would have been open as soon as German artillery was cleared from the banks of the waterway.

Montgomery ceded to his opponent an opportunity to get inside his "decision-reaction" loop. Hitler didn't pass it up. When time was most critical, Monty lost a move. Ike's two-pronged strategy, and Patton's aggressive advance, had produced a tremendous opportunity. Monty squandered it in the three-day administrative halt.

South Breveland isthmus is barely 25 kilometers from Antwerp. But the tankers hadn't seized its bridges leading to the far side of the Scheldt. From Montgomery on down, there were no orders to do so. Given M523, there was no reason for anyone to do so. Soon Germans sent them crashing into the water. By the morning of the 5th German engineers had dropped all the bridges, and heavy weapons covered all of the sites with fire.[31] Eleventh Armored's engineers had some assault boats. All but one had been damaged during the pursuit. Nevertheless, a small bridgehead was established on the 6th by the 159th Brigade. There were neither supplies nor additional troops to expand it.

Some historians (e.g., Weigley) fault 11th Armored for not seizing bridges in Antwerp across the Albert Canal. In retrospect, Roberts, 11AD commander, feels he should have pushed on. He stated, "Monty's failure at Antwerp is evidence again that he was not a good general at seizing opportunities. . . . If briefed before, I would have crossed the Albert Canal with tanks to the east of Antwerp and closed the German's route into Breveland and Walcheren."[32] Pip stated the correct qualifier: "If I had been briefed." The fault lay above Roberts. Roberts reported that fuel was reaching him regularly: "I had enough petrol to continue my advance."[33] Horrocks concurs. In his memoirs he states that had he kept 11th Armored out of Antwerp and instead sent it around the city and down to seal off the Breveland isthmus and trap Fifteenth Army on the wrong side of the Scheldt, securing that waterway could have been accomplished quickly.

Dempsey's actions on the 4th were completely consistent with Montgomery's intent. As Dempsey candidly states, "I completely forgot about

Antwerp."[34] Given the orders from his boss, there is little reason to wonder why. From that point in the chain of command down, no one can be found at fault. Failure to exploit the opportunity at Antwerp in the early days of September falls solely on Montgomery.

Horrocks criticizes himself for not sending 11th Armored around Antwerp and onto the Breveland isthmus. In his opinion, the 4th or 5th was the critical period. Had he gone north on either of those dates with a single division, he could have blocked egress from the isthmus. "To my mind, 4th September was the key date in the battle for the Rhine. Had we been able to advance that day we could have smashed through this screen and advanced northwards, with little or nothing to stop us. We might even have succeeded in bouncing a crossing over the Rhine. But we halted."[35] German First Parachute Army commander, General Student, couldn't understand why British armor didn't seal the Breveland peninsula and then slice north into Holland.[36]

Horrocks was too hard on himself. Antwerp's docks were wired with explosives. While the Underground worked feverishly to prevent demolition, no one could have predicted how long they could keep important installations from destruction. Dockland covered ten square miles and contained twenty-six miles of quays. German engineers had thoroughly wrecked virtually every other port. When would the explosives detonate?

Fiftieth Infantry Division, the Northumbrians, was the follow-on force behind 11th Armored. At this time it tagged up in Alost, only a 50-kilometer administrative march from Antwerp. Infantry was required to secure the docklands and get across the narrow, concrete-lined canal that impeded an advance to South Breveland.

If Antwerp was designated the primary objective for Second Army and subsequently 30 Corps, the logical move was to speed 50ID, en masse to Antwerp. Fifteenth Division was on road behind the 50th. If Dempsey did not want to divert the Northumbrians, he had more force to chose from than the three divisions assigned to Horrocks. In fact, most of Second Army paraded by on its way northeast. Eleventh Armored should have been directed to cross the Albert Canal and move down the far bank of the Scheldt. Roberts and his men could have executed a single focused attack while British infantry jointed the Resistance in clearing and securing critical assets in the docklands.

Had Monty directed Dempsey's main effort northward on the 5th, a major coup could still have been achieved. No orders from higher headquarters directed Horrocks to South Breveland. There was the fault. Instead of moving troops to secure the Scheldt on the 6th Horrocks, consistent with Second Army's order, moved east per Montgomery's M523. Guards Armored was to move via Nijmegen to the Rhine at Arnhem. Eleventh Armored was to move to the south of the Guards. One brigade of 50ID went to Brussels, another to Antwerp, and the third was assigned to protect the 30 Corps's left flank.[37] Elements of 50ID didn't enter the port until midnight on the 7th. By that date, Dempsey had lost his race with Student for other bridges over the Albert Canal east of Antwerp. First Parachute Army stood in the way of a cross-Albert thrust toward the Rhine. German paratroopers had taken up their positions on the canal.

Because of heavier resistance, 12 Corps, on 30 Corps's left flank, had moved more slowly than 30 Corps. Lieutenant General N. M. Ritchie, a veteran of the desert, commanded 12 Corps. While Rommel had bested him under very difficult conditions early in North Africa, Montgomery felt "Ritchie did very well in the campaign in North West Europe."[38] Seventh Armored Division and 15th "Scots" Infantry Division were relatively unengaged and within sixty-five kilometers of Antwerp. While 53rd Division ran into some tough resistance along the coast, 7AD, the "Desert Rats," entered Ghent on the evening of the 5th. Twelve Corps took over responsibility for Antwerp on the 7th.

As we will see, British 11th Armored Division played no major part in Market Garden. Yet no one ordered it north into Breveland. Before Dempsey reshuffled his forces, he would have to look to his chief. What were Monty's orders? What was his intent? What did Monty want done? As we shall see, there were no instructions for Dempsey to further secure Antwerp in Montgomery's current operations order: M523.

Monty was not in the habit of revealing his thought process. Certainly not to Eisenhower, for whom he had no regard. Great controversy and quite different recollections have obscured what actually happened. In a lecture given at the Royal United Service Institute on 3 October 1945, Monty did open a window. Montgomery recounted what happened during the critical days: "In view of the time factor it was agreed that 21st Army Group should launch its thrust to the Rhine before clearing the Scheldt Estuary." This is the second time the field marshal revealed this fact. He went on to state that administrative as well as tactical risks had to be taken. He decided he would base his operation on the Channel ports, particularly Dieppe.[39] Agreed by whom? Certainly not anyone at SHAEF.

Why wasn't Monty worried about bagging German Fifteenth Army? Paragraph 9. of M523 provides the answer. Monty envisioned a swing north to Rotterdam or Amsterdam (see map 4.1) that would cut off not only the Belgian port but most of Holland as well. And this might be done with "one division, or if necessary, a corps"! Instead these cities remained in German hands until VE Day. In a formal order, Monty has British Second Army racing 175 kilometers to the Rhine and then splitting itself north to the Zuider Zee and east to the Ruhr. What an incredible disconnect between plans and capabilities. Monty knew better. This mistake truly reveals the paucity of resistance he thought lay ahead of him. The ability to do great things with small forces—because Montgomery believed there were few coherent German defenses—is what made disobeying Ike worth the gamble for Monty.

BLUNDER COMPOUNDED

Patton called it the "unforgiving minute." Never, never allow a disorganized enemy any rest as long as you have an ounce of strength remaining. Formal American doctrine echoed the sentiment. On the 4th, Roberts and his 11th Armored handed Montgomery an opportunity he hadn't expected. Between the 4th and the 6th a determined drive across the Albert Canal and then from Antwerp down the far bank of the Scheldt to the sea would have cut off six-plus divisions of Fifteenth Army and sealed Antwerp's fate for the Allies. If British forces had placed the length of the Scheldt under observed fire at any time during that period, their gunners could have prevented the mining of the waters and the three-week delay while they were swept. Montgomery could have reinstated a plan that complied with what he clearly understood was Eisenhower's theater strategy. But Montgomery had already altered his plans. Instead he coiled British Second Army, which had paused only five days earlier. He intended to skip clearing Antwerp port and ride to the Rhine on a Comet.

Can anyone imagine Patton wasting so many unforgiving minutes? Despite his proclivity to complain, can anyone imagine the American cavalryman swinging so far afield of his commander's intent? If Montgomery and Eisenhower wore the uniform of the same army, what would a general court-martial have concluded?

Even worse, Montgomery knew that the Germans were racing to correct their glaring deficiency at South Breveland. On 4 September, ULTRA intercepted and deciphered Hitler's orders declaring the Scheldt a fortress area.[40] Despite this warning, Montgomery did not move.

As Roberts, Horrocks, and Student indicated, the window of opportunity at Antwerp was three days wide. Thirty Corps reported his tanks still had 100 miles of fuel on board.[41] Horrocks felt he could have "smashed through . . . and advanced northward with little to stop us."[42] Admittedly, Monty's troops were tired. Eleventh Armored tankers were falling asleep in their machines. But the Germans were even more tired and distraught. Victory often goes to the side that finds a final scintilla of strength when his opponent cannot.

Eisenhower did not let a minute of pause pass at the Seine, even though he knew he was headed for logistical trouble within ten days. Monty paused before Antwerp because he feared logistical constraint, not because he reached the end of his logistical tether. As a result, he lost a second opportunity to destroy a numbered German army in western Europe. Comparison to Eisenhower does not make the field marshal look good.

Montgomery stated: "I ordered Second Army to the Rhine as quickly as possible."[43] That is not what M523 says. Monty decided to take a breather. M523 directs Second Army to halt for three days (paragraph 6 states Second Army jumps off on 6 September) to get ready. Missing the opportunity to thrust forward when virtually nothing was in front of Second Army was an unforgivable blunder entirely of Montgomery's making. Patton would have sacrificed his right arm for fuel in his tanks and scattered resistance between him and the Rhine.

Let's review the critical dates:

23 August	Ike and Monty talk in detail.
24 August	Ike's letter clearly states his intent: first Antwerp then Rhine.
24 August	Montgomery's M520 regurgitates Eisenhower's intent verbatim and adds operational instructions to Canadian First and British Second Armies.
25 August	Montgomery's letter regurgitates Eisenhower's intentions; Monty understood Ike.
26 August	21st Army Group's boundary changed to allow advance on the Rhine without getting embroiled in Antwerp.

This gives Montgomery the opportunity to head for the Rhine on his own. Monty tells Horrocks that 21st Army Group must get a bridge across the Rhine before the Germans get set.

30 August	Montgomery decides to base his army group's logistics on Channel ports.

3 September	Montgomery learns from Bradley that Patton is little constrained and Ike intends to push two corps of First Army into the Aachen Gap with first crack at the Rhine.
3 September	Montgomery's M523 directs Dempsey's army to the Rhine instead of clearing the Scheldt.
3 September	Admiral Ramsay signals Eisenhower and Montgomery, underscoring the need to clear the 65-mile-long Scheldt and to prevent mining.
4 September	One of Dempsey's divisions enters Antwerp. There is no follow-up to clear the Scheldt.
4–6 September	Second Army coils up west of Antwerp, readying for the advance to the Rhine at Arnhem that Montgomery had ordered.

This pause is taken despite ULTRA reports that Hitler is reinforcing defenses along the Scheldt.

| 6 September | The German Navy begins to heavily lace the Scheldt with mines. |

GERMAN REACTIONS

On the day 11th Armored entered Antwerp, Hitler reinstated Field Marshal Gerd von Rundstedt as commander in the west. Generally regarded as on of the two or three best senior commanders, he had been CinC (commander in chief) West when the Allies invaded on D-Day. Hitler had removed him in July for being defeatist. But the old field marshal had proved his loyalty to the fuehrer by lending his stature to the tribunal that judged and punished participants in the plot to assassinate Hitler. Besides, Hitler desperately needed the best military talent to lead the recovery of the German collapse in the west. Sometimes referred to as "the Last Prussian," Rundstedt commanded almost universal respect from the German officer corps. Model, who had been temporarily CinC, willingly moved down to army group command.[44]

German commanders could not have been given a greater present than Montgomery's pause. Rundstedt had been a close student of British tactics and Montgomery. He surmised from the pause that Monty would not move forward until all preparations were to his liking.[45] The Last Prussian took the opportunity to shuffle forces to solidify what had been the weakest sector of his front.

Hitler had forbidden earlier attempts to rehabilitate and man the West Wall (Siegfried Line) as he thought the Allies would be stopped along the Somme and Marne.[46] While his stature might be seen to have been diminished, the very energetic Model, as commander of Army Group B, which defended against the Allied thrusts from the Low Countries, remained very engaged and influential in the battles to halt the Allied advance. One biographer states, "Model was by far the deadlier foe. He possessed a virtuosity in the field that Rundstedt could not have matched and self confidence in dealing with Hitler that Rundstedt did not have."[47] The official U. S. Army historian called Model "the Master of improvisation."[48] In early September, Hitler was deep in the Soviet Union, directing frantic attempts to recover from a disastrous summer and somewhat out of touch with the western front. By 3 September, because his headquarters were so far out of communication with the remnants withdrawing pell-mell toward Germany, Model saw little alternative but to rely on the initiative of local commanders to fight the best rear guard actions possible while he attempted to build a coherent defense along the West Wall.[49] This general characterization applied to the resistance U.S. First Army would also encounter north of the Ardennes.

On the 4th the most pressing problem facing the Germans was the gaping hole between the Channel coast and the Neder Rhine. General Student stated, "The sudden penetration of British tank forces into Antwerp took the Fuerher's headquarters completely by surprise. At the time we had no disposable reserves worth mentioning."[50] An 80-kilometer gap had developed between Fifteenth Army moving north along the coast and Seventh Army retreating toward the west. And there was virtually nothing available to hold even the most important crossroads. British tanks had already entered Antwerp. If Montgomery pushed through it before something could be done, 21st Army Group might simply motor to the Rhine and drive through Northern Germany. History told the grizzled German field marshal that he who controlled northern Germany controlled Germany. However, Rundstedt found Montgomery "overly cautious, habit ridden and systematic."[51] In the German commander's opinion Montgomery was likely to give the Germans a few days to pull something together while he put his exploiting forces into good order.

To add to the threats on the ground directly before him, Rundstedt noticed that Allied airborne divisions had disappeared from the operations map. Obviously, they had been withdrawn to prepare a major strike. In a fluid situation against flimsy defenses, airdrops are an ideal method of seizing critical terrain and speeding the passage of armored columns deep into Germany.

Initially Rundstedt didn't appreciate the strategic value of denying the Scheldt to Allied shipping. Hitler had to remind him. During the first crucial week of First Parachute Army's existence, it focused on preventing Montgomery's northeastward advance. Defense of the route north to South Breveland, the north shore of the Scheldt estuary, received scant attention. Only remnants of a low-grade static division barred the way. A strong divisional thrust likely could have pierced their defense and closed the neck of the isthmus.[52]

To the surprise of both Rundstedt and Hitler, German First Parachute Army seemingly precipitated out of the ether. On 4 September, Goering informed a very surprised high command that six airborne regiments were in training and available for assignment and that an additional two could be formed from convalescents and depot troops. German airborne forces were part of the Luftwaffe, not das Heers—the army. Despite constant bombing, the German Rail Service had not lost its marshaling ability. Equipment drawn from depots awaited the troops as they detrained at stations in the Low Countries. This capability, repeated up and down the line, markedly changed the nature of resistance advancing Allied columns met. That afternoon CinC Parachutists, General Kurt Student, received a call from Hitler. He immediately became commander of First Parachute Army. These "paratroopers," few of them actually jump qualified, were rammed into the line along the Albert Canal. The gaping hole that so worried Rundstedt was closed, if only by barrel-bottom scrapings. Two low-grade coast defense divisions ware added to the instant army. Student's HQ moved near the town of Arnhem.

CANADIANS ON THE COAST

Why not use the Canadian Army to secure Antwerp? The second-ranking Canadian, Lieutenant General Guy Simonds, saw the real opportunity. He suggested to his boss that 2 Canadian Corps should continue to pursue Fifteenth Army and cut off its escape across the Scheldt.[53] By winning the race to Breskens, the Canadians might be able to cross over and capture Walcheren before the Germans could fully organize its defense. Someone within 21st Army Group had the right answer. Simonds suggested the move could be supplied by landing craft delivering the necessary tonnage directly across open beach so there would be no impact on the logistics of British Second Army's drive. Seemingly he had hit the magic solution—forward progress without draining tonnage.

Simonds was highly regarded by all. However, Canadian First Army commander Lieutenant General Henry Crerar declined to communicate the idea upward. Crerar and Montgomery were barely on speaking terms. There was no way he was going to question one of Montgomery's direct orders.

"Crerar had not impressed Monty as Commander of 1st Canadian Army."[54] On the first day Canadian First Army became operational, 23 July, Crerar had a big fight with the seasoned commander of British 1 Corps, Lieutenant General Crocker, and Crerar sought to sack Crocker. Monty had written to Brooke, "He seemed to have gained the idea that all you want is a good initial fire plan, and then the Germans all run away!"[55]

In addition to being Monty's subordinate, Crerar was the national commander for Canadian forces. While Montgomery regularly exercised his prerogatives as the British national commander (*nightly* communiqués with Brooke but only irregular cables to Eisenhower), he did not seem to understand Crerar's duties as such. While they responded to different prime ministers, both ministers paid ceremonial homage to the same king, didn't they?

Many Canadians had died in the abortive raid on Dieppe in 1942. Instead of going directly to the orders meeting where M523 was issued, Crerar had delayed to attend the previously scheduled and very emotional memorial service at Dieppe. Fuming, Monty wanted him cashiered for insubordination.

After the war, Simonds told the official Canadian historian, Colonel Stacy, that "Crerar was hypnotized by Dieppe. . . . I pointed out that we should be giving attention to operations farther North. . . . Crerar was just not minding the shop at the time. In consequence we delayed to capture the Channel ports when we should have masked them, pushed on north to Breskens and dealt with the Channel ports later."[56]

It's clear Ike wasn't the only ally Monty had trouble with. Again this incident underscored the difficulty of commanding within the framework of an alliance when subordinates are also responsible to their own governments.

The day after Roberts entered Antwerp, 3rd Canadian Division reached the defenses of Boulogne and Calais. The two armored divisions of Canadian 2 Corps were diverted to secondary objectives around Ghent and Bruges. Here was tremendous combat power within easy marching distance of Antwerp. On 5 September Ostend was captured intact and ready to receive shipping. With a second channel port in hand, why did Monty want Crerar to mount an attack on more minor channel ports instead of the Scheldt? He had already secured enough capacity in the Channel ports to meet Second Army's essential needs while it crossed the Rhine.

One Corps reached Le Havre on 1 September. Probing on 3 September showed defenses were strong. For seven days, Crocker's corps cooled its engines before the fortress port. The attack did not commence until the afternoon of the 10th. Preceded by bombardment from the Royal Navy and a 5,000-ton strike from Bomber Command, 49 Division penetrated Le Havre's defensive works. Fifty-First Division was not far behind. The port was reduced in forty-eight hours of heavy fighting. This port, assigned to support the Americans, would reduce the strain on transportation originating back in Normandy.

COMET

Monty's initial operation to penetrate the gap and head for the Rhine was dubbed Comet (see map 4.1). After talking with Bradley on the 3rd, Montgomery began assembling his outline of British Second Army's advance across the Rhine. A single British airborne division would capture a Rhine bridge, perhaps at Arnhem. All of Second Army would link up with the airborne and speed across the Reich's last great moat. Despite the transportation shortage the RAF moved eleven wings of tactical fighters onto Belgian airfields to support Montgomery's forward movement.[57]

Second Army began its advance to the northeast on the 6th. Dempsey sought Albert Canal crossings closer to the Rhine. His maneuver moved the entire army away from Antwerp and the Scheldt. Again 30 Corps led, with 8 Corps in van. Guards Armored Division moved up the road from Brussels toward the Canal. Eleventh Armored pulled back from Antwerp, moved behind the British line along the Albert, and reappeared on Guards Armored's right flank. Its move resembled that of a pulling tackle in American football. Attempts to secure a crossing of the Albert Canal failed. German defenses had been significantly strengthened. No unit moved north to seal the isthmus to South Breveland. Instead the next two follow-up formations, British 15th and 50th Infantry Divisions, advanced to the left of the twin armored thrust. Their northeastward advances were over 40 kilometers east of Breveland and Antwerp.

Montgomery needed to keep a rival's eye on the advance of First Army, which was tasked to breach the Aachen Gap and make for the Rhine (Hodges actually entered the Stolberg Gap just to the south). (First Army's September will be recounted in chapter 5.) First Army had leaped forward to close a bag around 25,000 Germans at Mons, Belgium, on the 3rd. Its lead VII Corps remained busy around Mons on the 4th. Despite having priority, elements of VII Corps had trouble getting gas on the 4–5th. Upon approaching the Meuse, they ran into heavy German resistance. Due to lack of priority, the other corps designated to attack via Aachen, XIX, was grounded for lack of fuel. VII Corps was over 200 kilometers from the Rhine. Thirty Corps, Montgomery's lead element, was 125 kilometers, so Monty was in good shape.

By 7 September, Montgomery recognized that German resistance was increasing. In his nightly telegram to Brooke he stated that Second Army was encountering determined resistance in the northern outskirts of Antwerp and along the Albert Canal from Antwerp to Maastricht.[58] There was no variable in the field marshal's calculations to absorb the impact of First Parachute Army in Montgomery's plans. Simple correlation of forces demonstrated that Dempsey's men would have to fight long and hard to dislodge Student's paratroopers. And First Parachute Army got larger as retreating remnants of German divisions received hasty infusions of equipment and soldiers from interior depots and returned into the line. This is what Eisenhower correctly feared and what Montgomery refused to take into consideration. M523 remained the plan.

PLAUSIBLE ALTERNATIVES

Where was Monty's vaunted "firm grip of the battle"? Even Nigel Hamilton, a Monty supporter, states, "It is in retrospect incredible that Monty should have allowed himself to be enticed by the idea of a unilateral British drive onto Germany to the exclusion of the vital need to secure quickly the Channel ports, open Antwerp and ensure the capture of the German forces corseted between Second Army and the sea."[59] Perhaps 21st Army Group was too busy plotting Comet's path to see what was directly to their front.

ULTRA provided additional evidence that the Germans were emplacing corps-sized forces in front of each Allied thrust. Any analyst could see no one was about to motor into Germany without a major fight. Rapid advance might push the battleground east. But a major fight was inevitable. That fight would provide enough time for the Germans to pull together additional troops and weapons from depots within the Fatherland. At least one more subsequent fight would have to be fought. Ike was right. Antwerp was absolutely necessary to prepare for this extended campaign. Eisenhower and his staff were looking smarter by the day.

Shame is, Monty could have complied with his boss's order without impacting his drive for the Rhine. A little more audacity and a little less concern about having reserve logistical capacity above what his plan needed would have done the trick. Compared to Bradley, Montgomery had an embarrassment of resources with which to both seize the north bank of the Scheldt and prepare for a Rhine crossing. At least two alternative operational plans would have allowed 21st Army Group to secure the Scheldt while emplacing a corps-size force under a good commander into the spot that was to be filled by 30 Corps when the Rhine offensive kicked off on 7 September.

The first alternative would be as follows: Instead of shifting Horrocks, 11AD, and 50ID in their "tackle pull" to join Guards Armored in the east to claw out a bridgehead over the Albert Canal, send Ritchie and 7AD to reinforce the Guards. Fifty-Third Infantry Division disengages and provides the backup division. In the actual campaign, this role was provided by 15ID, which did not attack through the forward lines achieved by 50ID along the Albert Canal near Gheel until 13 September. In this alternative, 15ID becomes a tactical reserve held just behind Antwerp. Depending on requirements, the Scots could either reinforce the attack into Breveland or move east to aid the drive on the Rhine.

Need more infantry? Look to Canadian First Army. In early September, General Crerar's Army contained:

2 Cdn Corps	1 Br Corps
2 Cdn Inf Div	49 Inf Div
3 Cdn Inf Div	51 Inf Div
4 Cdn Arm Div	
1 Pol Arm Div	

Recall M523 directs Canadian First Army to take the area Bruges to Calais and then to sit. The second alternative plan would be to send at least a reinforced corps from Canadian First Army to clear Antwerp and the Scheldt *beginning 3 September by assigning this mission in M523*. In his postwar description of his actions of 3 September, Monty slips in that one of the tasks of the Canadian Army was to "develop operations for the clearance of the Scheldt estuary, in order to give access to Antwerp form the North Sea."[60] That is not what M523 says. As one Canadian historian observes, M523 "was hardly an order, in the aftermath of three months hard fighting, to spur an army to relentless pursuit."[61]

Let's step away from the problem to gain a little perspective. Three objectives had been identified. Both SHAEF and Montgomery agreed the ultimate objective was a crossing of the Rhine in force. To achieve this, SHAEF concluded that Antwerp was needed to achieve this final objective. The third objective, the Channel ports, was, in fact, tertiary.

The Canadians delivered Montgomery's minimum requirement, 7,000 tons of port capacity, by capturing Dieppe on the 1st. Dieppe began receiving ships on the 8th. About this time, First Army was receiving only 5,000 tons per day and Third Army only 2,000 tons per day.

Despite his calculation that Dieppe's 7,000-ton capacity was sufficient to sustain British Second Army during its leap over the Rhine, Monty wanted more. He constantly badgered SHAEF for more logistical support. Beetle responded by giving 21st Army Group additional American trucking and virtually all of Allied air transport.

Monty remained nervous about the tonnage flowing into his army group. On 6 September he signaled Crerar: "It looks as if the port of Antwerp may be unusable for some time as the Germans are holding islands at the mouth of the Scheldt. Immediate opening of some port north of Dieppe essential for rapid deployment of my plan and I want Boulogne badly. What do you think the chances are of getting it soon."[62] Again Monty reveals he understands the implications of the Scheldt. He also records that, without SHAEF sanction, he is eschewing a working Antwerp for the Rhine. On the 6th, a concerted effort across the Scheldt to Breveland was well within the field marshal's reach.

Crerar's signal to his corps commanders on 9 September reiterates Monty's point:

> 6. In view of the necessity to give first priority to the capture of the Channel ports mentioned above, the capture or destruction of the enemy remaining NORTH and EAST of the GHENT-BRUGES Canal becomes secondary in importance. While constant and close contact with the enemy, now withdrawing NORTH of the R SCHELDT, will be maintained, important forces will not be committed to offensive action.[63]

Now Montgomery's secondary objective became the return to 16,000 tons of throughput to his army group. In M523, Montgomery sets the Channel ports as the sole objective for Canadian First Army. With Dieppe firmly in Canadian hands, Montgomery could have diverted all of Canadian First Army to bypass further engagement along the Channel coast, except at Le Havre, and sent it to clear the Scheldt. During the critical period of 4–6 September a reinforced infantry heavy corps could have achieved the needed tasks to open Antwerp without impinging on the minimum port capacity that Second Army needed to cross the Rhine. With Antwerp intact and subsequently becoming operational, the docks allocated to the British could have supported further exploitation into Germany.

Unlike Falaise, the German withdrawal across the Scheldt was an excruciatingly strung-out affair. Twenty days would elapse before von Zangen completed the withdrawal of Fifteenth Army. Yet on the 9th, six days after 30 Corps spearheads had entered Antwerp, two days after British Second Army had turned east to execute Comet, Monty was frittering away uncommitted elements of his other army in low-payoff tasks.

10 SEPTEMBER, BRUSSELS AIRPORT

Eisenhower's already bad knee was severely injured when his light plane was forced down after the meeting in Chartres. The doctor ordered him to bed, and then, when the swelling subsided, encased the knee in a plaster cast. On the 7th Montgomery, worried about his supplies and feeling the Americans were giving Patton too much tonnage and diverting too little to 21st Army Group, requested a meeting about logistics with Ike. Despite the supreme commander being bedridden, Montgomery declined to make the trip back to SHAEF forward. Medics trundled Ike into a twin-engine B-25 light bomber and strapped his litter in. As there was almost no way for Eisenhower to deplane without medical help, Monty came aboard the B-25 at Brussels airport. Eisenhower's chief logistical and administrative officer, British Lieutenant General Gale, accompanied the supreme commander. As he had done with Smith back on August 22nd, Montgomery required Gale to deplane so Monty could talk to Ike. But Monty's chief administrative officer remained on board.

Pulling Eisenhower's latest directive from his pocket and waving his arms, Montgomery damned the plan in "language that was far from parliamentary," accused the supreme commander of double-crossing him, implied that Patton, not Eisenhower, was running the war, demanded that control of the land battle be returned to him, and asserted that the double thrust would result in certain failure. When he paused to catch his breath Eisenhower leaned forward, put a hand on Montgomery's knee, and said, "Steady, Monty! You can't speak to me like that. I'm your boss." Montgomery mumbled, "I am sorry, Ike."[64]

If Montgomery had operated within Eisenhower's intent during the first days of September, Ike's choice on the 10th did not have to be either Antwerp or Arnhem. A pair of infantry divisions applied early to the Breveland isthmus would have contributed impressively to both operational endeavors. If Fifteenth Army had remained bottled up on the coast, Model would not have been able to concentrate so much force in the counterattacks on Market Garden. Montgomery, who among the three army group commanders best obeyed the principles of mass and objective, missed a very important solution. Montgomery was a very competent operational-level commander, so one can only surmise that his fixation on the Rhine had blinded him.

By the 10th the SHAEF plan of 4 September was in tatters. The opportunity to bag the low-grade divisions of Fifteenth Army and open the port of Antwerp quickly had been squandered by Montgomery's improper action 4–7 September. As we shall see in the next chapter, the combination of increasing German resistance and lack of supply hobbled U.S. First Army's efforts to reach Aachen. On the 10th lead American efforts were halfway between Liege and Aachen and some 60 miles from the Rhine. Bradley had grounded the other formation, XIX Corps, which was supposed to attack into the Aachen Gap. Essentially this operation had not gotten off the ground. VII Corps will not make its first real assault into the Gap until 12 September. Down in Lorraine, Patton also had run into heavier resistance than he anticipated, resistance that ULTRA had warned about. Montgomery's Comet was being similarly buffeted. But British Second Army was across the Albert Canal at Beeringen and had just found a path that led to an intact bridge over the Meuse-Escaut Canal.

To breathe life into his obsession with sending a large force over the Rhine and on to Berlin, Montgomery proposed one of the boldest Allied plans of the war. He would employ three airborne divisions to take a series of bridges over the Maas (Meuse), Waal, and Rhine rivers and then push 30 Corps in a column of divisions over the Rhine. (See map 4.2.) Such a high-risk plan would have been proposed only by commanders "who were convinced that the enemy was routed."[65] When Montgomery sprung his plan, "Market-Garden," to push Horrocks's 30 Corps over the Rhine on a carpet of airborne troops, Montgomery's axis of attack ran through soggy polder that canalized British armor to the few good roads atop elevated embankments. Earlier SHAEF planners had rejected this ground as a major avenue of approach because of the streams and marshes. This should have given Ike some pause. So should the acknowledged increase in German resistance, which "is stiffening somewhat."[66] Instead Eisenhower readily grabbed onto Montgomery's plan. As he would later say, "I not only approved it, I insisted on it. What we needed was a bridgehead over the Rhine."[67] It was a desperate, faulted last chance to grab victory from the jaws of defeat.

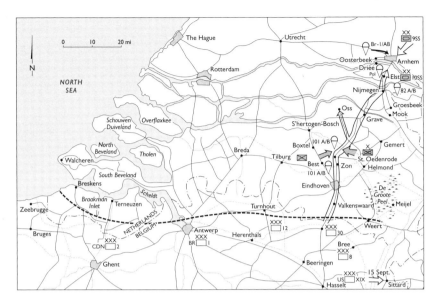

Map 4.2. Market Garden

Montgomery opined that his plan could still thrust all the way to Berlin.[68] He touted an unrealistic projection that additional tonnage could be brought in over the beaches of northwest France. Later Eisenhower penned in his diary, "Monty seems unimpressed by the necessity for taking Antwerp approaches.[69] By mid-September French railroads were sufficiently repaired to push 2,850 tons a day onto the undamaged Belgian railroads.[70] A standard truck company could move 200 tons 100 miles per day. Second Army might have gotten as far as the Ruhr, but not to Berlin, on their 140 truck companies. At the time Hodges was receiving only half what he needed to get First Army to the Rhine.[71]

Some writers have suggested that Eisenhower sacrificed opening the Scheldt by approving Market Garden. An examination of the timeline and Ike's orders does not support this contention. Montgomery had already thrown away the easy ticket to clear the port three days to a week before the Brussels airport meeting. While Eisenhower recognized Market Garden might temporarily reduce British 30 Corps's efforts to clear the Scheldt during Market Garden's execution, he insisted that every other effort to clear the Scheldt would be taken. He convinced Montgomery to concentrate Canadian First Army against the Scheldt. At this late date, this was about the best one could expect. Eisenhower followed up this point on Antwerp in a letter to Montgomery on 13 September:

I understand you will now launch Operation Market on the 17th. I also understand that you are pushing hard for the opening of the Scheldt Estuary and
that your plans for reducing Walcheren Island [at the mouth of the Scheldt]
contemplate airborne support [U.S. 17th Airborne Division was available in
England]. . . . I consider the use of Antwerp so important to future operations
that we are prepared to go a long way in making the attack a success.[72]

Montgomery replied the next day, promising "to develop as early as possible
operations designed to enable the Port of Antwerp to be used."[73] From the
Quebec conference, Brooke cabled Montgomery that if Brooke was CinC
for Western Europe, he would order Monty to cease attempting to seize the
Ruhr until Antwerp port was secure.[74] Montgomery's M525 of 14 September
does not equivocate:

> 10. The whole energies of the [Canadian] Army will be directed towards
>   operations designed to enable full use to be made of the port of Antwerp.
>   . . .
> 12. Canadian Army will take over Antwerp area from Second Army beginning
>   on 17th September.[75]

Of course, Monty's Channel port base was already secure.

Essentially, Eisenhower accepted Montgomery's assurances that the
Scheldt would be cleared as soon as possible. Twenty-First Army Group's
reports in early October that it did not have the power to open the Scheldt
were a rude awakening. Ike was "furious" about the unpleasant surprise and
felt that Montgomery had "pulled the wool over his eyes."[76] While Ike would
subsequently take responsibility for approving Market Garden's impact on
opening Antwerp, he did not think it a major problem on board that B-25
on 10 September.

On the 13th Eisenhower issued a formal directive to his army group
and component commanders, rejecting "a single knife like and narrow
thrust" and reiterating the existing two phase, two thrust campaign plan.[77]
Twenty-First Army Group, U.S. First Army, and First Allied Airborne Army
were specifically tasked to fighting to gain the Rhine and then spanning
that river north of the Ardennes. Third Army was to hold bridgeheads over
the Moselle that threatened an attack, but Patton was not to undertake a
major offensive until the main effort in the north was over the Rhine. This
was a major departure from FWD 13765, which had Patton going all the
way to Frankfurt. Again Ike had moved closer to Monty's point of view. At
the same time Montgomery's army group was to action "my [Eisenhower's]
previously expressed conviction that the early winning of deep water ports
[Antwerp, Le Havre, and possibly Amsterdam] and improve maintenance

facilities in our rear areas are prerequisites to a final all out assault on Germany Proper."[78]

MARKET GARDEN

The concept of a massive airborne operation didn't originate in Monty's HQ. Hap Arnold, commander of the American Army Air Forces, advocated the use of massed airborne divisions at strategic depth rather than a tactical drop just behind enemy positions as at Normandy. Under Arnold's direction, the air staff outlined plans that were presented to Marshall. The chief of staff directed them to be forwarded to Eisenhower's headquarters.[79]

Earlier on the 10th, before the Brussels airport meeting, Dempsey had arrived at Montgomery's HQ with a different concept under his arm. Like his commander, he was obsessed with jumping the Rhine. But he felt increasing German opposition made Comet's planned drop of one division at Arnhem too risky. Instead of Arnhem, he wanted to cross in the vicinity of Wesel, about 60 kilometers closer to U.S. First Army (map 5.3, displays Arnhem, Wesel, and First Army). Without concerted effort from both armies, Dempsey did not believe an operationally significant impact would be achieved against the defenses the Germans had now emplaced.

Monty rejected Dempsey's recommendation of an airborne assault that more closely paralleled First Army's eastward axis of advance through Aachen. Instead of two armies paralleling each other, Second Army would advance almost due north to reach Arnhem.

The 10th of September was the first time Dempsey had seen the Market Garden plan. Dempsey's first reaction to Market Garden was that he could not advance the required 110 kilometers along elevated roads through soggy ground that restricted cross-country movement to Arnhem in the time allotted (two days in the initial plan).[80] But this is where Montgomery, the expert, planned to go.

Later, Monty would paraphrase Dempsey's point about lack of coordinated purpose of coordinated effort between British Second and U.S. First Armies to Eisenhower. One could easily predict his conclusion. Instead of inter-army group coordination, he wanted U.S. First Army attached to his army group to create a two-army thrust. Without that support, the field marshal maintained, he could not make a successful push to the Ruhr. However, his initial planning eschewed any attempt to concentrate the efforts of British Second and U.S. First Armies.

Monty proposed the specifics for Market Garden to Ike during their 10 September meeting at Brussels airport. Recall that this meeting began with a very heated confrontation. After tempers cooled a little, Monty brought up his idea to cross the Rhine on an airborne carpet. It was an expansion of Comet, which had been canceled only that morning. Market Garden dropped three airborne divisions, instead of the one that was to have been part of Comet, to clear a corridor to the Rhine. Given the exchange of strong words with Monty only moments before, Ike looked for reconciliation. By 10 September he was acutely sensitive about the loss of Allied momentum.[81] Eisenhower recognized Market Garden's potential. Here was a proactive step that might smooth very ruffled feathers and restore momentum to the *Allied* offensive.

Initiative is always an important consideration. However, Eisenhower should have pondered Market Garden's opportunity costs and its integration with Bradley's efforts before giving his approval. In other words, he should have replicated Dempsey's reasoning. Rush to judgment in what became a large error doesn't speak well of Eisenhower's operational perspective while lying in a B-25 at Brussels airport.

Virtually no one who was acquainted with the proposal thought Market Garden would succeed. The senior British officers at SHAEF, Morgan, Strong, and Whitley, stated flatly that Montgomery did not possess the drive to carry off the bold offensive, even if the logistical situation had been favorable.[82] Before the operation commenced Smith predicted failure.[83] Ike demurred from ordering Monty not to take an imprudent risk because he felt it was not his place to overrule a British army group commander. Instead he relied on Smith's power of persuasion. This act was forged from something less than sterling moral courage.

That evening, Montgomery's intelligence officer, Brigadier Williams, argued in vain against Market Garden because of all its risks. He also argued that opening the Scheldt should receive priority and that the waterway would not be opened without committing additional divisions.[84]

Monty's initial proposal called for advance beyond the Rhine first to the Ruhr and then all the way to Berlin. To his credit, Eisenhower recognized that Monty's extensions went far beyond 21st Army Group's capability. Ike warned Monty that he would have to throw off division after division to defend his flanks all the way to Berlin. The whole operation would depend on a single bridge over the Rhine. Ike derided an advance to Berlin as "fantastic." A few days later he reported to Marshall, dismissing Montgomery's notion of an attack to Berlin emanating from Market Garden and reiterating the two phase, two thrust strategy.[85] The Germans had sufficient remaining strength to cut off and defeat such an attempted penetration. "Lets get over the Rhine first and we will discuss everything else."[86] Ike's deputy, Air Chief Marshal Tedder, stated categorically that "without Antwerp, we could not get to Berlin."[87] Monty believed that, once over the Rhine, Eisenhower would not stop 21st Army Group's advance on the enemy's capital.[88]

As a good Allied commander, Ike was quick to seal the rift with the field CinC of British land forces. He signaled Monty: "Your M525 has arrived here and I must say that it is not only designed to carry out most effectively my basic conception with respect to this campaign but is in exact accordance with all understandings that we now have."[89]

However 10 September, let alone 14 September, was too late to win an easy victory for the Scheldt. German defenses in Breveland were now well developed, and the Scheldt was full of mines. Monty's greatest error was before 10 September, not after.

Detailed planning for the corps-sized Market Garden airdrop began with a conference between Montgomery and General Browning of I British Airborne Corps on the same day of Ike's visit. Lieutenant General F. A. M. "Boy" Browning, an affable Guards officer, had been decorated with the Distinguished Service Order for action with the Grenadier Guards in World War I. He was popular with his contemporaries but struck some Americans as too "British." He was a perfectionist and always impeccably groomed. Some described him as fastidious, possessing self-confidence that bordered on arrogance and somewhat temperamental. "Boy" Browning had been prominent in raising Airborne in the British Army. He instituted the Airborne's red beret that both British and American paratroopers wear to this day. Browning burned with desire to prove the validity of airborne assault. But he had not commanded them in action.

Monty asked "Boy" Browning if he could hold Arnhem for two days before linkup. He responded that paratroopers could hold it for four. On that occasion, Browning made the famous quip, "I think we may be going a bridge too far." He had serious reservations about the operation's chances.[90] The operation was to commence on the 17th, only a week later. Before proposing Market Garden, Monty hadn't consulted anyone at First Allied Airborne Army. Browning would take the news back to the airborne army commander, Lewis Brereton.

First Allied Airborne Army, the parent organization of Browning's Corps, had become accustomed to short-notice assignments. During August, the airborne army had begun planning on six completely different drops, only to see ground troops overrun their objectives before paratroopers could board their transports. Fortunately, some of the basic work had been done. In preparation for Comet, British 1st Airborne Division (1st Para Division) and the Polish Airborne Brigade had made a thorough study of Arnhem. The airborne army commander was confident his staff could ready the massive operation in a week. To do so, however, required that the principal decisions about the operation be made early, then set in concrete. There was no time to make changes.

Planning for the Market Garden airdrop suffered from flaws due to inexperience, lack of coordination, blind reliance on experts, and lack of unity of command. Lieutenant General Brereton was an American Air Corps officer who had been MacArthur's air commander in the Philippines on December 7, 1941. Prior to First Airborne Army, he commanded 9th Air Force that controlled American tactical airpower in the theater. This was one of the most powerful baronies in the Allied Air Forces. Brereton had been an instructor at Leavenworth in the thirties—a rare credential for an Air Corps officer.

Despite being one of America's senior airmen, Brereton had fallen out of favor by the spring of 1944. Senior American air commanders felt he wasn't up to leading the American tactical air force. Ground commanders did not think he was the right man for the job either. Bradley stated Brereton "did not realize full use that could be made of air effort in assistance to ground operations." He made "no effort to work out the problems of air coopera-tion."[91] Eisenhower expressed some concern about Brereton to Marshall in March 1944.[92] During the major briefing of D-Day plans, Brereton deferred to Pete Quesada to provide Ninth Air Forces' presentation. Quesada and many others thought Brereton was over his head. Moving him to command First Airborne Army was a polite way of moving him aside. Externally, Brereton beamed supreme confidence about Market. Staff officers noticed he had begun chain smoking.

Browning and Brereton had recently come to blows. The dapper Guards officer disliked Brereton and regarded him as a weak commander. Browning had complained to his commander that insufficient time had been given for a proposed drop around Aachen to even distribute maps. Brereton responded he would replace the English officer with Ridgeway. Browning promptly tendered his resignation as Deputy commander First Allied Airborne Army.

In his book on Arnhem, Major General Roy E. Urquhart, 1st Para Divi-sion's commander at Arnhem, states: "[W]e were all becoming increasingly aware of a certain naiveté in upper level planning of airborne operations, particularly at the headquarters of First Allied Airborne Army."[93] Airborne planning tended to emphasize the mechanics of the drop but little else after the parachutes were rolled up. Consideration of German reaction on the ground frequently was not taken into account. At one planning presentation, General Sosabowski, commander of the Polish airborne brigade, was heard to mutter, "But the Germans, General . . . The Germans!"[94]

The final plan laid the three airborne divisions end to end to create the corridor to the Rhine. One Hundred First Airborne Division would drop closest to British lines to seize 25 kilometers of road and bridges over the Wilhelma and Williems Canals. Eighty-Second Airborne would seize a 16-kilometer segment in the middle of the corridor. British 1st Airborne Division, in its first combat in western Europe, would drop on the far (north) side of the Neder Rhine. Ostensibly, the Red Devils had the easiest assignment—securing a bridge across a single river—the one they would be pinned to. However, it was the most exposed to German counterattack and would have to hold out the longest. In what has been regarded as a major tactical mistake, British 1st Airborne dropped on zones 9 to 13 kilometers from the bridges it was to secure.

Commander, IX Troop Carrier Command was concerned that flak sited to protect the Ruhr would make the sky over Wesel too dangerous. Wesel is on the northwest edge of the Ruhr and that industrial area's dense anti-aircraft defenses. The airman's opinion reinforced Monty's.

The impact of flak was a constant bugaboo. Airmen repeatedly used the anti-aircraft threat to veto plans of airborne commanders. Air Vice Marshal Hollinghurst, the British air transport commander, flatly stated that there was too much flak at the Luftwaffe base at Deelen, about 11 kilometers north of Arnhem bridge. If flak muzzles were turned south, it could have disastrous results for transports making their run in to the drop zones. The air vice marshal made his decision on the 11th. But RAF bombers had hit Deelan hard on the 3rd, and much of the flak had been destroyed. As a result of the raid, the airfield became unusable. The reminder of the flak had been removed. Photo recon confirmed this on 6 September.

Given the facts, Hollinghurst's decision was wrong. In any event, how does one allow the air commander veto power regardless of the risk to the ground commander? Urquhart had no authority over the RAF decision. He resigned himself to the distant drop zones. First Airborne Division's combat power would have to be stretched between the DZs and the bridges. This dispersal created serious tactical weakness. It was a major reason for the disaster that befell British 1st Airborne.

Another way to increase the weight of the airborne attack was to schedule two drops for the first day. Air Vice Marshal Hollinghurst was willing to have a go of it. But Major General Paul Williams, commanding general U.S. IX Troop Carrier Command, overruled him. He claimed crew fatigue would be excessive. Brereton backed him up. What an incredible statement! The round trip England–Arnhem is about five hours. Transports returning from a second trip would have to land in darkness. Day in, day out, two sorties might have been excessive. But for a preplanned main effort? Aircrews frequently put in fourteen-hour days on long-range flights. What about the wear and tear on the paratroopers being hacked to pieces by German fire? More importantly, where was the joint commander to evaluate risk from crew fatigue versus the risk of insufficient combat power on the ground? If this was not Brereton, it was Montgomery. He was given command of the airborne army. IX Troop Carrier Command was subordinate to First Airborne Army.

To Brereton's credit, he did order a daylight drop to aid the airborne. He disregarded the threat of fighter interception. The Luftwaffe did make a major attempt to intercept. Not a single transport was brought down by German fighters during the initial drops.

British 1st Airborne Division had no radio equipment with which to communicate with Horrocks, Dempsey, or Monty. At the last minute some American radios and operators were added. However, no one ensured they were trained in British operation. Frequency interference became a problem. For the first three days, no communication was established with 1st Airborne. In frustration, the Red Devils resorted to carrier pigeons. In the end only chance intrusion on an artillery fire control net provided any radio communication whatsoever.

No senior staff officer from 21st Army Group, Second Army, or 30 Corps attended 1 Airborne Corps initial planning sessions that detailed planning of its drops. No aerial photos of 30 Corps route of advance were provided.[95] Despite the critical need for air support, no air-ground parties had been established. Monty seems to have remained remarkably out of touch with day-to-day operations and singularly incapable of controlling events. During the operation, he never visited 30 Corps HQ. Monty did not travel to Second Army until 23 September.

When Monty read the Market plan, he also identified some of its weaknesses. He sent his acting chief of staff, Brigadier Belcham, to convince Brereton to ensure that British 1st Airborne be dropped in a maximum of two lifts. It is hard to imagine that the field marshal would have taken "no" from an English general. But Brereton said, rather foolishly, that it was too late to make even critical changes. The plan went unmodified.

Dempsey's Second Army provided the ground, or "Garden," effort of the operation. Second Army's order of battle included:

8 Corps	30 Corps	12 Corps	1 A/B Corps
11 Arm Div	Gds Arm Div	7 Arm Div	1 A/B/ Div
3 Inf Div	43 Inf Div	15 Inf Div	82 A/B Div(US)
50 Inf Div	53 Inf Div	52 Inf Div (airlanding)	
8 Arm Bde	4 Arm Bde		
101 A/B Div(US)			

Twelve Corps was busy down in Belgium consolidating the gains of 30 Corps. Second Army shuffled units to reinforce 30 Corps up to the strength listed above by the 17th. Forty-Third Division, which had been immobilized with 8 Corps, was brought all the way up to flesh out Horrocks's corps.

In concept, Market Garden was a classic penetration attack. Monty's choice of penetration as his form of maneuver was clearly appropriate for attacking the hardening crust Model was emplacing. Deep penetrations, violently executed, are the best way to shatter a newly formed continuous defensive line that has yet to develop depth. If successful, a series of penetrations might have restarted pursuit warfare, which had brought the Allies so much success in August. Montgomery directed that the ground advance must be "rapid and violent without regard to what is happening on the flanks."[96] During their meeting on 12 September, Monty had underscored for Horrocks the need for speed.

According to the plan, Guards Armored would lead the column of divisions in the attack. It ultimate objective was the Zuider Zee.[97] The second division, 43rd Infantry, was assigned the task of replacing any bridges that were blown. It was to drop off units to hold open a path from 1 Airborne Corps position around Arnhem and the rear of Guards Armored. Forty-Third Division's final objective was to secure a corridor from Arnhem to Apeldoorn, 20 kilometers beyond the Rhine. Guards Armored would hold a stretch of road of similar length north of Apeldoorn. This was an incredibly small force to advance 70 kilometers from a Rhine bridgehead at the end of a 110-kilometer penetration that just arrived at the Rhine's west bank.

As it had specific assignments, 43ID might be understood as a second echelon. Fiftieth Infantry Division was designated corps reserve. Its subsequent assignment was to hold the high ground north of Arnhem. Eight Armored Brigade would drop off to provide armor support to 101st Airborne. All of this was designed to keep Guards Armored focused and moving forward as the cutting spearhead of this corps-sized formation. This is a good example of what a 1944 corps configured for deep penetration looked like. Twelve Corps, west of the penetration, was to widen the corridor. Eight Corps to the east had a similar mission once it closed up to the line of departure.

Officers below division commander did not learn of the plan until Horrocks's primary briefing, only the day before the operation commenced. The white-haired general was in good form as he described the operation step by step. It would be "no pause, no stop." A massive thirty-five-minute bombardment would precede the assault. The corps commander predicted the Guards breakthrough of the defensive crust would be "almost immediate." They would have to continue to "go like Hell." Horrocks expected them to reach Eindhoven within two or three hours. "This attack could end the War."[98]

It had taken Guards Armored four days to advance the 16 kilometers and capture the bridge over the Meuse-Escaut Canal, which was Market Garden's line of departure. To some in the audience, the planned 40 kilometers a day advance to Arnhem over a set of causeways and bridges, even with airborne assaults, sounded incredibly optimistic, to say the least. This rate of advance is normally achieved only during a pursuit against cursory opposition when the attacker has overwhelming combat strength. This was not an accurate description of the combat power Model would bring to bear against Horrocks. One Dutch officer familiar with the ground ahead thought the British were leaving 75 percent to chance. No one was enthusiastic about advancing on a one-tank front up a causeway spanning soggy ground. One engineer thought the plan's requirement to cross so many waterways was like "threading seven needles with one piece of cotton." General Alan Adair, Guards Division commander, thought executing the plan "might be tricky." Breaking through the initial defenses would be tough. But once his division got past the initial defenses, further advance "would not be difficult."[99]

Nine thousand engineers mounted on 2,200 vehicles supported the operation. In preparation for Market Garden, 2,000 tons of bridging were brought forward. For all of Monty's complaints about supply shortages, that's a lot of steel sections.

Horrocks personally watched the beginning of the ground assault embark on its trek up the straight white concrete highway to Eindhoven.

The initial stretch of road was atop a causeway one to two meters above the surrounding flat terrain. Soft, damp ground that restricted tank movement lay to either side. This route of advance was a natural for ambush by small enemy ambush forces armed with anti-tank weapons. German defenders didn't miss their cue. Heavy bombardment initially suppressed the defenders, allowing the first tank squadron company through without loss. German gunners, recovering their senses, quickly hit eight tanks of the second squadron in line. Guards infantry jumped from the backs of the stricken armor and began rooting German ambushers from along the causeway. Horrocks had his work cut out. Twenty thousand vehicles were going to try to go up a single road that an anti-tank company could cork up.

The basic structure of Market Garden's plan compounded risk. A number of risky operations were laid end to end. Each airborne division had to secure its bridges or the armor couldn't advance to relieve the next airborne unit. A roadblock at the head of the advancing column stopped everyone in its tracks even if upline river crossings were secure.

The operational plan for Market Garden contained no branches to accommodate a failure. Alternative routes around possibly blown bridges had not been mapped. Therefore the risks were multiplicative—the inverse of "combat multipliers" that contemporary authors are so fond of. The largest risk was the bridge over the Waal at Nijmegen. An alternative highway or rail bridge spanned every other stream. But not the Waal. Had it not been for the incredibly heroic river assault in canvas boats under direct automatic fire by the U.S. 504th Parachute Infantry of the 82nd Airborne Division, Market Garden would have been two bridges too far. This exposure by itself was more than enough to classify the entire operation as overly high risk.

Speaking to General Gavin, CG 82nd Airborne Division, Horrocks summarized the point succinctly. "Jim, never try to fight an entire corps off one road."[100]

Horrocks demanded a "no pause, no stop" attack until 30 Corps linked up with the gallant paratroopers at Arnhem bridge. That isn't what he got. Guards Armored bedded down for the night when they discovered the Zon bridge blown. Engineers didn't move forward on that bridge at night as the infantry hadn't secured the site before turning in. At Nijmegen, after American paratroopers braved a daylight river assault in flimsy boats against German gunners, a similar stop for the night was made. Americans threw their helmets in disgust and reportedly had to be restrained from attacking the tankers. In the words of one British historian, "Poor local leadership dissipated whatever slight chance there have been" of getting to Arnhem on time.[101]

ARNHEM VERSUS WESEL

Market Garden contained yet another operational flaw. As map 4.2 illustrates, the advance to Arnhem opened a gap between two fully committed armies that invited (and would later receive) counterattack. Market Garden in no way resembled the forty-division "full-blooded thrust" Monty initially advocated. It wasn't even the twenty-division thrust he continued to lobby for. On 17 September, coiling the eight-division British Second Army was beyond 21st Army Group's capability. Two armies advancing in parallel, as initially proposed by Montgomery, made a lot of operational sense. Attacks at a right angle away from each other with a 100-kilometer intervening gap did not.

Brigadier Richardson, 21st Army Group's chief planner, wanted Monty to advance as close to the Aachen Gap as possible. Dempsey was so convinced that Wesel, that is, a parallel advance with the Americans, was the right direction that he was ready to carry on without the airborne. He doubted the extended set of airborne drops was feasible.[102] As with Market Garden, he should have been able to gain the west bank of the Rhine. In a French television interview, former Generals Westphal, chief of staff to Rundstedt, and Manteuffel, commander, Fifth Panzer Army, agreed that 21st Army Group could have "bicycled to Wesel."[103] While clearly an overstatement, resistance along that axis would have been no worse than toward Arnhem. II SS Panzer Corps would have had to motor 50 kilometers to engage Allied paratroopers at Wesel.

An attack toward Wesel would have crossed fewer water obstacles than Garden. However, it is unlikely that Second Army would have jumped the Rhine without intact bridges secured by friendly paratroopers. Was the greater probability of crossing the Rhine really Montgomery's prime determinant? If so, we have an important case of a tactical objective (securing any Rhine crossing) completely obscuring an operational-level one (placing the army group's mass in the proper position to achieve a strategic objective). It is the avoidance of this type of confusion that makes the recognition of the operational level of war so crucial.

If Second Army had been stopped on the Rhine in front of Wesel, it nevertheless would have solved a major problem for U.S. First Army. Concern over the Roer River and its flood-control dams would vex the American army for much of the fall campaign. The Roer flows into the Maas. Second Army would have been on the far side of this system in position to give great support. A strip of land critical to the security of the German buildup for the Bulge would have been wrenched free, and the Allies would have a credible, concentrated threat to the Ruhr.

Two of Eisenhower's strategic objectives would have been achieved by an attack toward Wesel. First, his armies would have achieved strong positions along the Rhine. Second, their presence on especially critical terrain along the Rhine likely would have precipitated the major battle Ike sought. He wanted to chew up German combat power at the place of Allied choosing, away from their logistical sources and before they had time to complete their own concentration and entrenchment.

Had Montgomery attained the Zuider Zee he would have accomplished an even greater dispersion of Allied strength than any permutation of Eisenhower's initial "broad front" strategy. Arnhem is 130 kilometers from Aachen. The Zuider Zee is over 200. As it was, Second Army's lunge toward Arnhem opened a large, wedge-shaped opening between British Second and U.S. First Armies in the vicinity of the Peel marshes. Montgomery was concerned enough about this ever-widening wedge to complain about First Army's protection of his flank.

Brigadier Williams, Monty's chief of intelligence, suggests an alternative explanation for the field marshal's rejection of Wesel. In Williams's opinion, Monty didn't want to share a major advance from the Rhine to Berlin with the Americans.[104] Expansion from Arnhem would clearly be within 21st Army Group's zone.

If Williams is correct, Monty placed ahead of executing the best operation to achieve his assigned objective. Whether for personal or national pride, Montgomery did not obey his commander's (i.e., Eisenhower's) intent. The field marshal violated one of the most basic principles of war—unity of command.

In January 1945, after the Battle of the Bulge, Montgomery would mount a massive attack across the Rhine. The crossing site he chose wasn't Arnhem, it was Wesel.

SCHELDT FINALLY CLEARED

On 14 September, most of 21st Army Group was feverously preparing for Market Garden. M525 handed the problem of the Scheldt to Crerar. He finally decided to concentrate 2 Canadian Corps for the job.

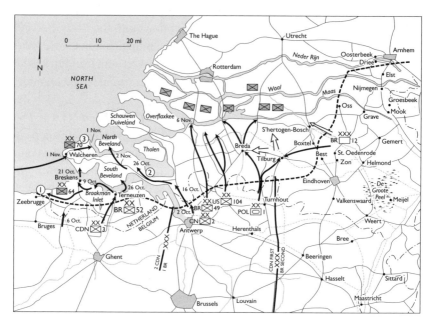

Map 4.3. Securing the Scheldt

In order to clear the Scheldt, three tasks had to be accomplished. (See map 4.3.) First the south bank of the watercourse, the Breskens pocket, had to be cleared. After evacuating the bulk of Fifteenth Army, the Germans had left behind a polyglot force of 10,000 under command of 64th Infantry Division. This force deployed behind an almost continuous water barrier formed by two canals and the Braakman inlet. The Scheldt has two outlets to the sea. In order to place Antwerp's port in operation, only the west Scheldt needed to be cleared. Two bodies of land form the west Scheldt's north bank. The second task was to seal the isthmus and take South Breveland. Finally Walcheren Island, which guards the Scheldt's mouth to the North Sea, had to be secured. A month after British armor had captured Antwerp, not one of these tasks had been completed.

We will not follow the tactical developments of this operation. Canadians, British marines, and regular Tommies fought with ardor and distinction. Unfortunately, their efforts were not matched by speed of decision and support from army and army group level.

Supposedly due to lack of infantry, little was done to reduce the Breskens pocket on the south bank of the Scheldt before the end of September. If resources were needed in addition to Canadian First Army, which remained engaged around the Channel ports, one only need look at the pair of infantry divisions in 12 Corps (above), which did little during the period.

In the meantime Fifteenth Army completed its withdrawal across the Scheldt on the 26th; 86,100 men, 616 guns, and 6,200 vehicles had been extracted. Instead of being cut off and cut up in early September, this force would frustrate 21st Army Group's efforts throughout the fall.[105]

Admiral Ramsay diverted five LCTs (landing craft, tank) from the Ostend ferry to prepare for the Canadian assault on Walcheren Island. Montgomery objected, stating these craft were needed to deliver supplies for more important objectives. Even though they were operating along the coast where landing craft dispatched from England could drop supplies, the Canadian assaults were held up for lack of ammunition.

Eisenhower scheduled a senior commanders meeting in his Versailles HQ for 5 October. As the chief of the Imperial Staff, Sir Alan Brooke, was to attend, Monty knew his own appearance was mandatory. During the fall campaign, it was the only meeting at Ike's headquarters on the continent that Montgomery was to attend.

Montgomery fell back into a pattern the reader is now familiar with. He maintained that his army group could still take the Ruhr without taking Antwerp. In the words of Admiral Ramsay's diary:

> This afforded me the cue I needed to lambaste him for not having made the capture of Antwerp the immediate objective at highest priority and let fly with all my guns at the faulty strategy we had allowed. Our large forces were practically grounded for lack of supply and had we now got Antwerp and the rest of the [Scheldt] Corridor we should be in a far better position for launching the knockout blow.[106]

Montgomery reacted to the criticism of his countrymen. On the 6th he drove to Canadian First Army HQ. Because Crerar was in the hospital, General Simonds was in temporary command. Simonds and Montgomery went over current operations in detail. Too bad Monty hadn't focused in this fashion in early September, before Market Garden. However, Monty continued to designate the Canadian effort as 21st Army Group's second priority.

At the end of Market Garden, Montgomery shifted elements of Second Army into supporting attacks in order to retrieve at least something from the decimation of British 1st Airborne at Arnhem. Supplies and reinforcements were diverted from Canadian First Army. On 9 October, officers from the British Navy reported to SHAEF that the Canadians would be unable to attack until 1 November due to a shortage of ammunition.[107] Eisenhower blew his stack and cabled Montgomery to fix the problem immediately. Still

Montgomery dallied, preferring to give Second Army all it needed at the expense of Canadian First. General Smith personally called Montgomery about the matter. After a heated exchange, Smith, in a rage, thrust the phone upon his subordinate, British General Morgan, and barked, "You tell your countryman what to do." Realizing it might be the end of his career, Morgan told Montgomery that unless the Scheldt was secured, 21st Army Group's supplies would be cut off.[108]

On 16 October, Montgomery finally capitulated and made Antwerp the unquestioned army group priority. In addition to the Canadian Army, the focus of Second Army would be added to the campaign for the Scheldt. Monty's directive of that date stated:

1. The free use of the port of Antwerp is vital to the Allied cause, and we must be able to use the port soon.
2. Operations designed to open the port will therefore be given complete priority over all offensive operations in 21st Army Group, without any quali-fication whatsoever.
3. The immediate task of opening the approaches to the port of Antwerp is already being undertaken by the Canadian Army and good progress has been made. The whole of the available offensive power of the Second Army will now be brought to bear also.[109]

Had this order been issued a month and a half earlier, as it should have been, the entire course of the fall campaign would have been radically altered. In his memoirs, Field Marshal Montgomery takes responsibility for underestimating the difficulty of opening Antwerp: "I must admit a bad mistake on my part—I underestimated the difficulties of opening the approaches to Antwerp. I reckoned that the Canadian Army could do it while were going for the Ruhr. I was wrong."[110]

Twelve Corps, which had been protecting the army's left flank, now became the main effort of a westward attack from the Albert Canal toward the North Sea coast. This corps was reinforced to the strength of three infan-try divisions, one armored division, and three armored brigades. It was given the support of the bulk of army group artillery. 12 Corps now exceeded the strength of 30 Corps on the eve of Market Garden. 8 and 30 Corps, which had been preparing further offensive action north and east to the Ruhr, assumed defensive dispositions.

Now both armies of 21st Army Group had powerful corps engaged in offensive action to dislodge Germans north of Antwerp. The attack appeared reverse L-shaped, with 12 Corps attacking west and 1 Corps attacking north (map 4.3). 12 Corps's westward attack allowed 1 Corps to concentrate its efforts on Breveland isthmus. Its attack into the Breveland Peninsula didn't commence until 24 October. General Crocker dreaded the assault against the isthmus, made more narrow by extensive German flooding. However, 3rd Canadian Division made good initial progress, advancing 4 kilometers on the first day.

Meanwhile Canadian First Army, in Chester Wilmot's words "the Cinderella of the Western Front,"[111] soldiered on. Approximately 50,000 Germans defended South Breveland, with another 7,000 on Walcheren Island. Fifteenth Army was ready for a stiff, bloody fight. Polder is muddy, treeless, and flat. Canadians were forced to advance through an ideal killing ground against machine gunners who had a month to prepare. Resistance within the pocket was not completely eliminated until 2 November.

General Simonds's solution to Walcheren Island was nothing less than brilliant. Walcheren is saucer shaped, with most of its interior below sea level. Back in early October, Simonds had concluded that the sea should be let in. While most fixed German positions were above sea level, flooding would restrict German maneuvers. Halloween evening 4th Special Service Brigade, Royal Marines, mounted in track-laying Buffaloes (LVTs), sailed into the interior of the flooded saucer. They took the Germans from "landward." Two 15-inch gun monitors, led by the veteran battleship *Warsprite*, dueled with Walcheren's seaward defenses. British Marine No. 4 Commando supported the main assault with a cross-Scheldt amphibious landing at Flushing. A third amphibious assault carried out against the east end of the island by 52nd Division was required to eradicate final German resistance. On the 4th, Walcheren—and the Scheldt—was clear of the German Army.

Even Field Marshal Brooke criticized Montgomery on this one. "I feel that Monty's strategy for once is at fault. Instead of carrying out the advance on Arnhem he ought to have made certain of Antwerp in the first place."[112]

Mine-sweeping operations began even before the land battle tapered off. Ramsay lost no time sending in his sweepers on the 1st. Three were hit by enemy fire that day. Sweeping operations took several weeks. Not until 26 November would the first ship dock at Antwerp. The first convoy did not arrive until the 28th.

Securing the Scheldt cost First Canadian Army 13,000 casualties. Chester Wilmot states that this long bloody campaign could have been avoided if an amphibious assault had been made in early September without great difficulty.[113] This is what Simonds had recommended at the time.

5

Concentrate, General Bradley

September was the month of the Big Bust.

Omar Bradley

Still in pursuit mode during the last days of August, most American tactical commanders viewed the West Wall as the last major obstacle before the Rhine. If only the Americans could beat the Germans to its fortifications! But First Army was creaking for lack of maintenance and was running out of gas. And it was about to hit some speed bumps few thought the Wehrmacht capable of emplacing. Bradley's overarching directive, "go as far as practicable," kept adrenaline-filled officers plowing ahead around each successive bend in the road.[1]

Virtually nothing except cheering Europeans hindered First Army's advance during the last week of August. By the end of September's first week "the enemy began to resist the progress with some stubbornness."[2] Beginning the 1st another pocket of Germans began to form due north of Hodges's army's northeast advance. Army documents demonstrate that the army staff "aimed at our enemy, not at the terrain."[3]

On 3 September, VII Corps was held up for lack of gas. When it did get under way, lead elements ran into retreating German columns. In one case, 160 horse drawn vehicles were smashed, leaving the putrid smell of burning animal flesh. Thousands of additional prisoners were rounded up. VII Corps alone counted 7,093 POWs that day. That evening, the Americans left the killing grounds around Mons and headed toward the Meuse. (See map 1.2.) But Germans cut off elements of 3rd Armored Division, further delaying the delivery of gas.[4] Germans still had teeth and the will to use them. Collins had instructions to move via Liege and Aachen toward a Rhine crossing in the vicinity of Bonn, south of the Ruhr. The corps commander expected to cross the Meuse within twenty-four hours. But a large number of roadblocks slowed the advance. Intelligence officers should have read the omen. On the 4th, while Pip Roberts was leading his armor into Antwerp, VII Corps ran into small groups of German tanks. Ten were destroyed. Resistance was described as "moderately heavy."[5]

VII Corps reached the Meuse on the 5th. 3rd Armored ("Spearhead") crossed at Namur to the cheers of a large Belgian crowd. Tankers had little trouble advancing down both banks of the Meuse to Liege. East of Namur, CCA (Combat Command A) found themselves "fighting a sharp battle." Dog faces experienced "stiff resistance" while cleaning out defenders bypassed by Spearhead's lead elements. Third Armored continued to roll forward, "but with new caution."[6] At Liege self propelled guns of the 67th Armored Field Artillery won a duel with 88mm flak pieces attempting to bar the way. Both 1st and 9th Infantry Divisions encountered heavy resistance as they attempted to cross the Meuse. Germans mounted several counterattacks. More than 10,000 prisoners entered First Army cages that day. Prisoners reported reinforcements from within Germany were headed toward Aachen.[7] Spot shortages of fuel plagued American efforts to maneuver.

Moving east of Liege, CCB met "organized and heavy resistance" around 1100 on 9 September.[8] As the tankers approached the German border, town names sounded more German. The civilian population became noticeably more sullen. No more cheering crowds. Intermittent gas deliveries remained a primary problem. All VII Corps divisions had elements that ran out of gas. March serials became strung out along the line of advance from Mons to the Meuse.

To the south, 9ID met quite a different reception when it crossed the Meuse at Dinat. Elements of 2SS and 12SS Panzer Divisions bottled up 9th Infantry's crossing for thirty-six hours. It was VII Corps's toughest fight since the Seine. Again, astute observers recognized that the Nazis weren't giving up. Finally Collins had a task force from 3rd Armored move south on the east bank of the river to break 9th Infantry free. If First Army needed a wake-up call, this was it. For the first time since the Seine, Americans encountered defensive positions strong enough to stall a division cold for more than a day. German resistance was increasing. Here was clear evidence the Germans had a lot of fight left in them and were not about to collapse. Now the military forecast was unmistakable: More fighting ahead.

BRADLEY'S TASK

In early September, Bradley's task was the most intricate of the three army group commanders. FWD 13765 designated three tasks for Bradley. The bulk of First Army was to move north of the Ardennes, reach the Rhine, and then, in conjunction with 21st Army Group, seize the Ruhr. Since late August, Bradley had been aiming to cross the Rhine south of the Ardennes and circle the southern rim of the Ruhr.[9] Now First Army was essentially going to lead the Allies across the Rhine on ground around Aachen that had not been in 12th Army Group plan. Third Army was to make a secondary attack toward the Saar. As a tertiary goal, Brest was to be secured. Bradley would not find the correct balance among these competing priorities.

From north of Maastricht on the Albert Canal to Epinal at the foot of the Vosges mountains, Bradley's front extended over 325 kilometers. More importantly, his 12th Army Group stood astride three of the four axes of advance into Germany: the Aachen Gap, the Ardennes, and a southern axis from Metz or Nancy northeast through Lorraine, over the Rhine, and onto the industrial Saar and Frankfurt. In addition, he was supposed to clean up Brest and then redeploy what was to become Ninth Army to the German border.

While Bradley had a large canvas, his stock of paint was limited. In early September First Army had three corps and eight divisions in total. Patton's Third Army had but two corps and seven divisions in eastern France. VIII Corps of five divisions, nominally a part of Patton's army, was back in Brittany. Formulating and executing a campaign plan on this terrain and with severe resource constraints was a tricky undertaking. As actions of commanders are critiqued, one must remember the extreme level of difficulty of the task.

Essentially, Eisenhower placed Bradley in charge of both the primary and the secondary attacks during September. Montgomery would join the primary attack soon thereafter, but there was no indication that he would be in sole command of this thrust.

Only Bradley didn't get it. Bradley admitted he feared that either he or his beloved First Army would fall back under Montgomery's command.[10] Patton wrote in his diary that "Brad told Ike that if Monty takes control of the XIX and VII Corps Bradley will ask to be relieved."[11] Instead of embracing the de facto assumption of the main effort by employing First Army's best efforts forward to getting past Aachen and the Roer River and onto the open Cologne plain that ran astride the Rhine, Bradley did everything possible to evade Eisenhower's intent and instead march First Army into Patton's secondary attack through Lorraine in a feeble attempt to revive the American Plan. Later in the operation, Bradley's aide recorded in his diary: "Ike was anxious that Brad put the main effort with the First Army and push it to the north . . . concentrating the bulk of his effort on the left flank of the group. Brad was opposed to this, sensing the possibility of a breakthrough in the V Corps sector where sharp penetration had already been made."[12]

ULTRA intelligence readily available to army and army group commanders indicated that getting to the Rhine would require a carefully planned major operation. During the opening days of September, Bradley thought German resistance would remain light—something like paradigm 1. German tenacity at Brest changed Bradley's mind: "If the enemy could command such stubborn resistance in so hopeless a situation as the one at Brest, I was disinclined to believe any predication of collapse until we had reached the Rhine."[13] Bradley came to believe the Germans could generate a lot of combat power. In his later memoir, he stated: "I was sure the Germans could organize at least twenty to thirty crack divisions to defend their homeland."[14] That is closer to paradigm 3.

While Patton and Hodges drained the last of their gas, Bradley's most important task was to concentrate his forces and ensure they had enough depth and staying power to penetrate to the Rhine on carefully selected axes. Remember what British 30 Corps looked like at the beginning of Market Garden? Instead, Bradley's forward divisions were in exploitation mode. Units were strung out along the roads, unable to concentrate much combat power. Artillery was out of position. During the race across France, no one had time to synchronize various arms and supporting troops. With no need to overcome strong resistance, there was little reason to slow down and reorganize. Now was the time to downshift to a slower, more powerful gear. Bradley used his army group staff less intensely than any other major commander in Europe.[15] A recent Office of Military History study on headquarters operations commented on Bradley's "alleged lack of originality as a battlefield commander, his frequent inability to concentrate his forces, and his interest in tactical details at the occasional expense of the bigger picture."[16]

In early September, First Army found itself in ideal positions in which to reconfigure its advance (see final arrowheads, map 1.2). The maneuvers that created the Mons pocket effectively pinched V Corps out of the line. Gerow's troops coiled in assembly areas in the general vicinity of Montcornet, west of both Sedan and the Meuse. XIX Corps, grounded three days in early September for lack of fuel, would have to maneuver through ground already in Allied control in order to regain contact. VII Corps readied itself to enter the Aachen Gap but was not in significant contact. It had sufficient maneuver room to allow higher headquarters to alter the specific portion of the corridor the corps would advance over.

It was not necessary to sweep every square kilometer west of the Rhine to achieve the goals set forth in SHAEF's theater strategy. "Broad front" improperly seems to imply this as an objective. Ike wanted a large American force positioned on the Rhine and threatening to cross. If Eisenhower's original concept of a First Army attack north of the Ardennes had not been modified by Bradley's/Patton's insistence on moving a corps into or south of the Ardennes, the area from Aachen south to Thionville could have been thinly screened by security forces made up from cavalry and anti-tank groups. In September, the Germans had nothing to counterattack with and would have hit nothing in this sector had they attempted to do so. That is 100 miles of front with no offensive action. Bradley had to ensure his main effort, *via the Aachen Corridor,* had enough combat power to pierce through whatever the Germans placed in front of it. His primary attack formation needed enough staying power to advance the full depth from the West Wall to the Rhine. If he had enough strength, Patton's secondary attack could do likewise. But the main effort had to reach the Rhine in force near Cologne on the southern rim of the Ruhr. Ground in between need not be entered for, as Smith stated, the Germans would have to withdraw as soon as a Rhine breach was threatened.

MALDEPLOYMENT OF FIRST ARMY

A major difference between the operational plans of Montgomery, Bradley, and Eisenhower was the number of corps from First Army that was to be committed north of the Ardennes. Monty wanted all three (and then some more). Bradley wanted to allocate but a single corps. He would route the remainder south to support Patton's Third Army as part of Bradley's American Plan. Eisenhower said two. A corps is a large organization, often 80,000 men. The difference between the generals on this point was not small.

When they got together, which was frequently, Ike and Bradley would extensively discuss tactics and operational deployments.[17] Informal face-to-face communication with little documentation was the way Ike preferred to counsel and instruct his subordinates. On 2 September at a meeting with Bradley, Hodges, and Patton, Ike issued his very specific guidance.

Ike's initial concept was unmistakable. Two corps were to enter the Aachen Gap as First Army's main effort. Ike recognized the third corps would have to accumulate gas before moving. When it was refueled, that corps would maneuver to support Patton down in Lorraine.[18] Monty wanted Patton halted indefinitely. Ike ensured the main effort in the north received priority of supply. As logistics sorted themselves out, Eisenhower would free Patton to resume the secondary attack.

The proper way to solve the problem of First Army's deployment was straightforward. Determine the amount of force required to achieve the main objective, reaching through the Aachen Gap all the way to the Rhine, against the resistance likely to be encountered. The remaining forces could be assigned to secondary objectives—Patton's secondary attack and opening Brest. Ultra revealed enemy divisions were assembling in the area around Aachen. Expecting a single corps of three divisions to break through a fortified zone, plunge 75 kilometers into enemy territory and across a river, while fighting a corps-sized opponent, is obviously not the right answer. Without a great deal of analysis it is clear that would take at least two corps and some time. Maybe three corps should be allocated. But certainly not one. Frankly Bradley should have seen this with little coaching from Ike. However, he was transfixed by the American Plan.

First Army did not have to take the enormous risks associated with Market Garden in order to gain the Rhine. Two corps moving together with another corps in trail wasn't anything the Germans were about to attack in early September. An open right flank would have been of little concern. The greater problem was penetrating the West Wall with enough power to make an operational difference.

Altogether Ike's initial decisions made a lot of sense. Like many major operational or strategic decisions, a few words describe a simple-to-grasp action. Recognizing that course of action through all the fog surrounding a fluid situation, as well as the flak from subordinates on your own side who are filled with self importance rather than commitment to the final Allied team goal, takes considerable skill.

Terrain along Germany's western border is far more restrictive than that of northern France and the Low Countries Eisenhower's forces had exploited across. West Wall fortifications were mutually supporting concrete pillboxes covering bands of minefields, "dragon's teeth," and other barriers. In critical areas, the fortifications reached 5 kilometers in depth. In easily defended terrain, the fortified band might narrow to 500 meters. From north of Aachen down into the Ardennes two separate bands were constructed to guard the best strategic avenue of approach into the Reich. The West Wall well reinforced ground that contained naturally strong defensive positions. Despite Patton's often-quoted derision of the barrier, West Wall concrete and steel substantially multiplied the defensive power of its German defenders.

Unlike French commanders behind the Maginot Line, the Germans did not expect their fortifications to be impenetrable. Rather, they were a well thought out addition to a classical mobile defense. The fortifications were intended to ensnare attacking formations and hold them exposed while reserves maneuvered to counterattack and eject what was left.

Staffs at SHAEF and 12th Army Group agreed that the Aachen Gap (the path of XIX and VII Corps on map 5.3) promised to be the best doorway to Germany. Cologne and the Rhine river lie 100 kilometers to the east across level ground. An advance just south of that city leads around the Ruhr Valley's southern rim.

The Roer River lies 20 kilometers to the east of Aachen. Most of the year it's a modest stream. In 1944, fall rains caused it to swell. The Roer Valley is shallow and flood prone. Dams had been constructed upstream to control this tendency. If the Germans opened these control dams in the eastern end of Huertgen forest, a flooded Roer would become a major military obstacle. In September neither the Germans nor the Americans were quick to recognize the tremendous obstacle that could be created if the dammed water was released.

Aachen's prewar population was 165,000, making it a mid-sized metropolis. This ancient city was not fortified to anywhere near the level of Brest or Metz. It was a maze of meandering narrow cobbled streets lined with solid stone houses that made good defensive positions. The city lies in a saucer-shaped dip in the ground. From a tactical point of view, it is not the best of defensive positions. Aachen's rail yards had been considered a key target. Much of the city had been bombed into ruins by the strategic air forces before land battle reached this unfortunate town. In September, only 20,000 wretched civilians clung to its cellars. Aachen guarded the gap between the dense Huertgen forest to the south and the Peel marshes to the north.

South of Aachen lies rugged wooded terrain of the Huertgen forest (map 5.2). A 15-by-30-kilometer swatch of deep draws and steep hillsides covered with pines measuring 20 to 30 meters tall, the Huertgen does not dominate a map of the area the way it came to dominate First Army's efforts during the fall of 1944. The tall pines restricted the limited sunlight that emerged from overcast fall skies. Much of the forest is so dense a soldier can't see more than 20 meters in any direction. Moving cross-county was far more difficult than in the Ardennes to the south or just about anywhere in 12th Army Group area. Much of the pine-needle-carpeted ground was spongy moor. Any movement immediately created mud. A group of men traveling together had a tough time. Even jeeps found the going all but impossible. Dank, wet, and dreary, it was no place to camp, let alone fight.

Sandwiched between Aachen and the Huertgen forest is a narrow piece of ground dubbed the "Stolberg Corridor." It extends from Aachen 30 kilometers east to the town of Düren on the Roer River. It is but 10 kilometers wide at the narrowest point. "Corridor" is something of a misnomer. It is cut by three streams and contains some very rough ground. Patches of firs are interspersed with small industrial towns that draw on large lignite deposits in the area. Map 5.2 gives a sense of the restrictive nature of the Stolberg Corridor. With little engineer work, this terrain became a series of tough interlocking defensive strong points. The Hamich ridge that lies within the Huertgen forest provided the Germans with observation. In a heavy fight, it was almost inevitable the Allies would have to send infantry to take it.

General Patton once said that to find the best routes through Europe, look at the old Roman highways. The Roman road runs north of Aachen. The real "Aachen Gap" lies between Aachen and Geilenkirchen 20 kilometers to the north. The ground is relatively open farm land studded with stout, defensible villages and nasty slag heaps from mines and factories that dotted the area in 1944. The inter-army group boundary gave Bradley a 45-kilometer corridor north of Aachen. A ridgeline that extends northeast from Geilenkirchen merits tactical consideration. But it is nothing like the Hamich ridge in the Huertgen forest. The Aachen-Geilenkirchen gateway, instead of the narrow and constricted Stolberg Corridor, was the better avenue of approach. Sufficient room existed to deploy two corps, each with a division in either second echelon or reserve. A pathway free of direct observation and field artillery fire could have been opened. In early September, there were even fewer defenders here than there were around Stolberg.

Bradley's operation order leaves a lot to be desired. Twelfth Army Group Letter of Instruction 8 (10 September 1944) directs:

3.a.First Army
Continue to advance to the east to crossings of the Rhine river in the vicinity of Koblenz, Bonn, and Klon (Cologne).[19]

The implication was that a corps would move toward each of these cities. Notice they are listed from south to north, although Ike's intention is to heavily weight the north. From their existing positions, this would send First

Army corps through the Stolberg Corridor, the Huertgen forest, and the Ardennes. Ike envisioned a concentrated effort in the Aachen Gap. Instead of a concentrated main effort, these assignments committed First Army to three unsupported efforts splattered over a 100-kilometer front. To cover this much front, First Army would essentially have to advance with all divisions abreast. This is little more than an army-wide frontal attack. No focus, no concentration, no maneuver except motoring straight ahead. It is hard to imagine a less imaginative plan. No army- or army-group-level reserve is designated. The broad sectors militate against the corps commanders' forming any meaningful reserve as well. Instead of concentrating to create the threat on the Rhine that Smith describes, Bradley is pushing everything in front of him in a broad sweep. Ike's strategy did not dictate this diffusion of effort.

FWD13765 clearly weights the attack north of the Ardennes. By now the reader must appreciate the importance of logistical priority. First Army continued to slow up for lack of supplies. Below we shall witness a severe First Army ammunition shortage. Nevertheless, Bradley's Letter of Instruction 8 (12th Army Group's attack order)[20] formally states: "4. Armies will have equal priorities of supply." Instead of attempting to meet Eisenhower's intent to emphasize the north, Bradley did everything he could to facilitate Patton's effort to execute the American Plan.

The logical two corps to lead the Aachen Gap attack were Corlett's XIX and Collins's VII. XIX Corps was already the northernmost corps and up along the Albert Canal. However, Bradley didn't place much stock in Corlett. Despite his good record in the Pacific, he tended to be the odd general out in Europe. Bradley would find reason to relieve him of command within eight weeks. Lightning Joe Collins was Bradley's fair-haired boy and, by all objective measures, the best American corps commander in Europe.

It turned out that First Army did not have enough gas to move all three corps simultaneously. Leaving XIX Corps in place and attacking with the two wheel-horses since they each assaulted Normandy beaches on the 6th of June, V and VII Corps would have done just as well if they had been directed north of Aachen and closely coordinated.

But Bradley was more afraid of losing his beloved First Army (especially V and VII Corps) to Montgomery's clutches than he was interested in supporting Eisenhower's main effort. He was far more interested in adding to Patton's thrust toward the Saar, which was the core of Bradley's American Plan, than in executing operations to achieve his commander's intent. On this score, Bradley shares the podium with Montgomery.

Map 5.1 depicts Bradley's operational design for First Army. Gasoline was still a problem. First Army received only enough to move two corps.

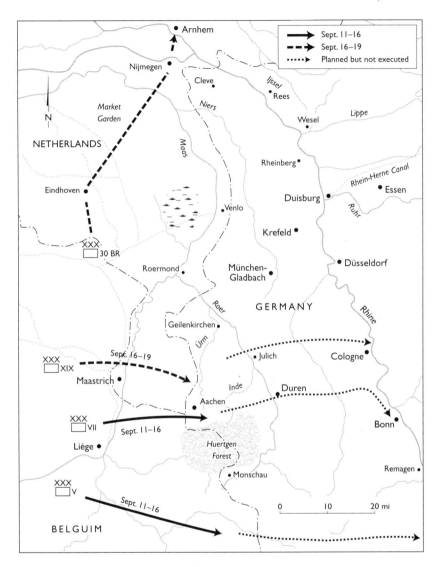

Map 5.1. Bradley's Deployment of First Army

The logical course of action would have deployed two corps in the Aachen Gap in a combination that would insure rapid, deep penetration to the Rhine. Ike's order clearly states that the two northern corps received priority.[21] Bradley improvised a horrific modification to Ike's plan. He ordered Hodges to immobilize XIX Corps.[22] Then he took away roughly a third of its combat power by transferring 79ID down to Third Army, burning gas all the way.

VII and V Corps got the gas. Instead of moving through the more northerly Aachen Gap, VII Corps made the main effort in the constricted Stolberg Corridor south of Aachen and farther from Montgomery. However, V Corps did not head for Aachen to fulfill the plan. Neither did Bradley send it down to Patton. Instead Bradley deployed V Corps into the Ardennes. Recall he and Patton had extracted permission to move the third corps southward to add further weight to the secondary attack. But Eisenhower did not expect this concession to detract from the two corps' operation in the Aachen Gap. Paragraph 7c of FWD 13675 expressly prohibits that: "but troops of Central Group of Armies operation against the Ruhr north-west of the Ardennes must first be adequately supported."

Bradley clearly violated Eisenhower's intent. At Bradley's direction, V Corps generated a small offensive of its own into the Ardennes, focused on the West Wall east of Bastogne. Weakening the main effort to go gallivanting into the Ardennes was the antithesis of theater strategy.

Under Bradley's plan, XIX Corps moved several days after the other two. The time lost in relation to German counter-moves loomed large, especially in relation to the movement of 183VGD as described below. An even bigger problem was that the attacks of VII and XIX Corps were not meshed into a single attack. XIX Corps would not begin its movement east of the Maas until VII Corps had already stalled before Stolberg. Instead of a single concentrated blow, the actions of these two corps were completely un coordinated. As will be recounted below, VII Corps could not continue to advance because it did not have access to the combat power contained in XIX Corps, which was sitting on the side lines. With V Corps off on its own and the movements of VII and XIX Corps uncoordinated, 12th Army Group operations took on the characteristics of an unfocused "broad front" that was nowhere strong enough to reach the Rhine. This is what Montgomery correctly feared. Eisenhower can be roundly criticized for not being firmer with Bradley and Patton. But Bradley must take the greatest share of the blame for not controlling and concentrating his army group better.

Bradley tended to think in very linear terms. Units would continue to strike ahead at the ground immediately in front of them. No one at any level above division constituted a meaningful reserve. Maneuver at corps or army levels, common in the Wehrmacht, is little seen. Operational-level maneuver, which the mechanization and communication capabilities should have allowed the Allies to excel at, is little used. Therefore Allied offensives become very predictable.

There is also a pattern of "layer caking" corps sectors that will repeat itself during the fall. Each corps moves ahead in a sector that tends to be a linear projection of the sector it had advanced over. The theater map begins to look like a series of layers of one corps sector laid atop another, like layers of a cake. From September to November, First, and later Ninth, Army maps take on this characteristic, with the layers expanding or contracting a little over time.

Bradley's order was the antithesis of a concentrated thrust designed to penetrate deeply into the enemy's territory. As we shall see in the next chapter, Third Army was assigned a front almost as dispersed. Almost single-handedly, Bradley transformed a strategy designed to have two concentrated attacks, a main one north of the Ardennes and a secondary one toward the Saar, into a weak, essentially "broad front" frontal attack that had little chance of penetrating the German defenses that were coagulating. One might suspect a little "Monday morning quarterbacking" crept into Bradley's postwar description of the strength of German resistance he expected in early September. If he is held to his words, his attack plan was woefully inadequate to achieve the desired objectives.

As the official historian stated, "General Hodges, in turn had ordered what might appear at first glance to have been a contradiction of General Eisenhower's assignment of priority to the two Corps alongside the British. Instead of the V Corps on the right wing, the corps which he had halted for want of gasoline was the XIX Corps closest to the British."[23] He did so under Bradley's specific direction. The official history goes on to place a fig leaf on the decision, claiming a worry about the large open area from VII Corps, which didn't extend south of Huertgen to Third Army down on the Moselle. But what German threat was going to materialize in the Ardennes during mid-September?

In early September, the Germans weren't strong enough to conjure a bogeyman up in the Ardennes. They were barely holding on. The cavalry group from the unengaged corps could have been given a guard mission in the Ardennes. A couple of towed anti-tank battalions that nobody else really wanted plus the separate 99th Infantry Battalion that had been used for little save a palace guard would have provided strength to roadblock the principal junctions in this rough terrain. Thirtieth Infantry Division had contained the attack at Mortain from such positions. The cavalry would provide mounted patrols to link them together and a reserve to extricate anyone that got in trouble. To keep the corps focused on its primary missions, the cavalry group could have reported directly to First Army.

Twelfth Army Group plans did not take into account the problems that would occur after the initial tactical clashes of a restarted offensive against the West Wall. Because none of the initial engagements had sufficient concentration to force a decision, events did not reveal the horrible lack of proper follow-on plans to cross the Roer and reach the Rhine. The Roer, normally an unassuming stream, is fed from some very impressive reservoirs that pose a significant problem in military engineering: blow the dams, and a raging torrent of water would cascade down the normally docile Roer Valley. Virtually no river-crossing preparation was done. Twelfth Army Group should have been addressing the problems of the follow-on operation while Hodges attended to tactical preparations for the next assault. There were resources available that could have been assembled. Yet 12th Army Group did nothing of the sort. It was not generating the campaign plan and leadership that would place First Army on the Rhine after Hodges had broken through the West Wall.

Eisenhower and SHAEF intended three focused attacks in the theater, the previously mentioned two attacks eastward plus the opening of Antwerp port. If Ike's initial concept had been carried out, he would have 21st Army Group's eighteen divisions concentrating on Antwerp and the Channel ports, eight divisions of First Army opening a corridor to the Rhine and the Ruhr, Third Army's five divisions carrying out the theater secondary attack toward the Saar, and five divisions fooling with Brest. Only the last allocation is a bone of contention. Bradley completely unfocused First Army's effort. Now the size of the mistake of allowing a corps of First Army to slip down into the Ardennes becomes apparent.

Bradley could not possibly have missed Eisenhower's intent to make the operations in the Aachen Gap the main effort or the black-letter meaning of 7C. A less understanding boss than Eisenhower might have summarily relieved his army group commander for this insubordination.* But Eisenhower, working hard to keep his herd of prima donnas working as some semblance of a team, persevered and did not officially mention it.

Both army group commanders consciously disregarded Ike's intent. Bradley's improper deployment of First Army, along with Montgomery's failure to seize the Scheldt early, because he concentrated on a lunge to the Rhine,

---

*Likely command changes would have been to elevate Patton, now redeemed by his brilliant exploitation, to army group and to place either Truscott (another cavalryman and Marshall's pick for next army command) or Gee Gerow, who had also been an Eisenhower pick for army command. See also Eisenhower to Bradley 25 September 1944, SHAEF files, which mentions Truscott and Gerow for army command.

doomed SHAEF's carefully crafted and possibly winning strategy of early September.

FIRST ARMY RESUMES THE ATTACK

First Army was confident of victory. After the slaughter around Mons, Army G2 predicted little but vacuum lay to the front. As late as the last week in September, Hodges believed that, given two good weeks of good weather, Allied air and ground forces could bring the enemy to their knees.[24]

Courtney Hodges was a gentleman. He had heroically commanded an infantry battalion in the First World War, was an excellent trainer of troops, and genuinely cared for his men. Charles MacDonald, the official historian for the Siegfried Line campaign, also commanded an infantry company in First Army during the Huertgen fighting. In his unofficial writings, MacDonald states: "No American commander on the western front had more concern for the men serving under him than Courtney Hodges."[25] But he was no tactical or operational genius.

No one who knew him well would expect him to correct weaknesses in plans that were handed down from command echelons above him. Hodges was a soldier who saluted when given orders and expected exactly that and nothing else from his subordinates. He had entered West Point in 1904 but washed out in mathematics (the subject Bradley would teach) during his plebe year. Entering the Army as a private, he received a field commission. "A natural soldier and leader"[26] who had earned the Distinguished Service Cross, the Silver Star, and the Bronze Star, he was a crack shot and had led the Army marksmanship team.

Marshall thought highly of Courtney—quiet, self effacing and with a thorough understanding of ground fighting.[27] Bradley praised him as "a military technician whose faultless techniques and tactical knowledge made him one of the most skilled craftsmen of my entire command . . . of all of my army commanders, he required the least supervision. . . . I had implicit faith in his judgment."[28]

Most of Bradley's subordinates would have wondered whom their former Army commander was talking about.[29] In their eyes, Hodges lacked Bradley's intelligence, communicative ability, and energy. They described him as "intemperate, unforgiving and brittle."[30] Many found him cautious to a fault. Patton said "even [Bradley] admits that Courtney is dumb."[31] Hodges eschewed plans that relied on complex maneuvers for simple, straight-on attacks. Once he confided to his aide, "Too many of these battalions and regiments of ours have tried to flank and skirt and never meet the enemy head on."[32]

While very experienced, First Army staff also had a tendency toward, in the words of an Office of Military History study, "piecemeal employment of armor and an inability to concentrate available forces."[33] Layering a tactical headquarters (First Army) that had difficulty concentrating forces under an operational level headquarters (12th Army Group) with a similar problem onto topography that was often site for SHAEF's main efforts was a constant source of frustration in the fall of 1944.

Ike worried that Hodges might not show enough drive as an army commander.[34] Even Bradley thought his protégé was conservative and sometimes indecisive. He counted on Bill Kean, his old Chief of Staff, "to keep a fire under him."[35] Hodges thought it "safer, sounder, and in the end quicker to keep smashing ahead than to risk all in a campaign of maneuver."[36]

First Army HQ wasn't very efficient. "When you did a situation report for the Third Army, you showed the positions of the regiments. When your did one for the First Army, you showed platoons."[37] Excessive immersion in detail blinded both Hodges and Bradley to opportunities and requirements at higher levels. They continued to choose the wrong battles in the wrong place for the wrong objectives. First Army staff had the reputation of being "proud, stubborn and demanding." Everyone, including Eisenhower, knew First Army was a "prima Donna."[38]

Hodges's "dogged adherence to book-learned tactics said little for his imagination."[39] He tended toward broad front advances. As the fall campaign wore on, Hodges's actions became increasingly slow and less than decisive. Second Armored Division's commander described First Army as "slow, cautious and without much zip."[40] By the end of the fall campaign, the pressure clearly showed. Pete Quesada, who worked closely with Hodges in order to provide air support, recalled about this period, "As I listened to him, I noticed a kind of panic, that a kind of operational paralysis was setting in him." Signs of frustration and nervous exhaustion became unmistakable.[41]

In a postwar interview, the First Army G3 (operations officer) stated that Hodges "was pretty slow making the big decisions. He would study them for a long time and I often have to press him before I got a decision."[42] The official historian adds, "the conduct of operation of the Siegfried Line Campaign was disconcertingly and even unnecessarily slow and conservative."[43] This is hardly the picture of a leader with a confident grasp of the battle, ready to adapt his plan to changing developments.

Bedell Smith considered Hodges "the weakest commander we had."[44] Later in the war, the Ardennes counterattack stunned the First Army commander. Senior commanders, including Eisenhower, considered his relief.[45]

Major General Bill Kean, Hodges's chief of staff, took up much of the slack. Many First Army officers felt he exercised de facto command. Kean had been well brought up by Bradley and knew the value of completed staff work. A British brigadier on Monty's staff described Kean as "resolute, steady and an excellent soldier"[46] who badgered subordinates in his name.[47] Kean was a less than amiable taskmaster who was much resented by those who worked for him. "We called him old Sam Bly."[48]

Ike formally rated Major General J. Lawton "Lightning Joe" Collins the best corps commander in the theater.[49] A veteran of Guadalcanal, where he commanded the 25th "Tropic Lightning" Division (hence the sobriquet "Lightning Joe"), he was an experienced, aggressive, capable commander. Bradley called him more a man of action than deep thinker or strategist.[50] Brad trusted Lightning Joe's judgment. After the war, Collins's star would continue to rise. In 1949, he would succeed Bradley as chief of staff. Hodges relied heavily on his VII corps commander. Collins worked almost as a co-equal to Hodges. Collins made Hodges look good, and Hodges chose not to interfere with his star player.[51]

Major General "Gee" Gerow led V Corps. An honor graduate of Virginia Military Institute, 1911, he had excelled throughout his career. Gee finished the Advanced Infantry School number one. At Leavenworth he finished number two, missing his long-time friend and study mate Ike's score by a few tenths of a point. Bradley described him as "an outstanding gentlemen and soldier—cool, hard working, intelligent, well organized, competitive,"[52] and Marshall thought highly of him. Gerow had commanded War Plans Division in the War Department when Lieutenant Colonel Eisenhower arrived to serve on his staff. Gerow had always been a good planner with an eye to detail.

Gerow chafed under the First Army regime that seemed to listen to Collins but no one else. But he was not about to buck his commander. Like Hodges, Gerow believed in meticulous planning. Unfortunately, like his boss, Gee was prone to micromanaging that bordered on the dictatorial.

Major General Charles ("Cowboy Pete") Corlett, XIX Corps commander, did not get along with Hodges. Bradley intensely disliked Corlett.[53] Hodges gave him little encouragement and rarely visited XIX Corps headquarters. Bradley said, "Corlett was not one of my favorite people. He was abrasive, short fused and arrived [from the Pacific] with a chip on his shoulder."[54] Corlett was West Point, 1911. From his Pacific experience, Cowboy Pete was a believer in massive artillery support. When he arrived in England, Corlett felt no one wanted to listen to his advice. Unlike Collins and Patch, who were to command amphibious assaults in Europe, Corlett was not included in the primary planning. When his advice about fire support was given short shrift, Pete became cynical.

GERMAN DISPOSITIONS

If there was any time when the reconstituted German line could have been broken, it was mid-September. Market Garden strained First Parachute Army. One hundred forty kilometers to the south, German Seventh Army was locked in a major fight for Aachen. While by no means solved, the worst of Allied logistical shortages had passed prior to 11 September.

Initially the Germans wanted to create a cohesive defense along the Meuse. But Army Group B did not have sufficient control over retreating elements. On 3 September, the same day American forces were chewing up retreating elements of Fifth Panzer Army around Mons, Model decided he had to withdraw into the West Wall if he was going to create anything resembling a continuous defensive front.

In early September German Seventh Army held defensive positions from the Eifel just south of Bitburg to the northern edge of the Aachen Gap at Maastricht. Bald, bespectacled General Brandenberger led this formation. He had a reputation for being unflappable. Brandenberger paid close attention to the military details of an operation. Some said a crisis brought out the best in him.[55] He was a tough, cagey combat commander and very capable at army level command. The Seventh Army Commander favored withdrawing behind the Rhine. Despite his steady hand, Brandenberger was appalled at the confusion and chaos that beset the Wehrmacht as it stumbled back onto the German border. But his fuehrer dictated that Aachen, the sacred seat of the First Reich, must be held.

I SS Panzer Corps held Seventh Army's southernmost sector. It contained headquarters of some tough divisions, 2 Panzer, 2 SS Panzer, and Panzer Lehr among them. However, they could muster only a few thousand combat effectives and a handful of tanks. Initially the corps commander organized them under control of 2 and 2 SS Panzer Divisions. The two divisions had three nominal panzer grenadier regiments that were little more than reinforced battalions. Between them the two divisions contained less than the normal complement for one divisional artillery. With replacements and time this skeleton could be fleshed out. In its current state, I SS Panzer Corps had limited combat ability.

To its north lay a pair of shells of former infantry divisions commanded by LXXIV Corps. Replacement and fortress units were being integrated into them. The ratio of recruits to veterans was 10 to 1. This was the "threat" from the Huertgen: the weakest corps in Seventh Army.

LXXXI Corps defended the Aachen Gap. While its four divisions were stronger than their counterparts to the south, they had been badly mauled (a fifth divisional headquarters was assigned but had no subordinate units). Two infantry divisions opposite U.S. XIX Corps had a breather while Corlett was out of the line waiting for gas. One Hundred Sixteenth Panzer Division was in Aachen. Its panzer regiment had ceased to exist. The German corps commander anticipated the American main effort to hit against Aachen instead of the corridors to the north or south.[56]

Rundstedt understood the critical nature of the Aachen Gap. He grabbed 9th Panzer Division, the only reserve available, and sent it off to bolster LXXXI Corps. Only lead companies would arrive near Aachen by 11 September. Fragments of units that coagulated around 9th Panzer would be the principal defenders of the Stolberg Corridor. Before they were in place a few battalions of 353 Infantry Division held West Wall positions south of Aachen.

Hitler understood the need for immediate reinforcement at Aachen. On the 12th, after U.S. V and VII Corps had begun their reconnaissances, but before the coordinated attacks were scheduled to begin, two infantry divisions in the interior of Germany were ordered to entrain for Model's army group. Model allocated both to Brandenberger. The first should detrain near Aachen around 16 September. With concrete reinforcement plans in motion, the Seventh Army commander energetically set about the task of creating a defense that would hold until they arrived.

Hodges wanted a two-day halt to gather in his strength as an absolute imperative. A thousand tons of ammunition would move forward on a higher priority even than gasoline. The pause would allow time to position artillery. V and VII Corps were to coil order to launch coordinated attacks, but not before 14 September.[57] Bradley thought Hodges had grown overly cautious.[58]

First Army understood the promise that lay before them. First Army G2 "Monk" Dickson wrote:

> A breakthrough in the sector of V and VII Corps of the West Wall offers the possibility of a swift advance to the Rhine. This would force the enemy to

evacuate the Rhineland because he would then occupy a compromised line with an obstacle at his back. . . . Having pierced the first belt of the West Wall south of Aachen the VII Corps has the glittering possibility of rapidly piercing the second, and proceeding via Stolberg-Duren to Cologne. The V Corps has the possibility of continuing its advance north of the Moselle along the valley of the Ahr to Andernacht.[59]

Colonel Dickson said that First Army also knew German strength was coagulating in their sector. He went on to state that the Germans were now resolved to throw everything on the present line to prevent an American breakthrough. Even Bradley was becoming worried that V Corps had been committed on too wide a front.[60]

VII CORPS ATTEMPTS TO SCALE THE WEST WALL

By the time they reached the entrance to the Stolberg Corridor, both Bradley and Hodges understood German resistance was increasing. During his star role in Cobra, Collins demonstrated he could control a five-division–two-echelon force. Why not move one or two divisions to VII Corps and assign Gerow a defensive mission in a wide sector connecting the two attacks? Bradley could have easily sold this solution to Ike. Better yet, hold Gerow's HQ in reserve and let a reinforced cavalry group perform an economy of force role. Fifty kilometers is a lot for a 3,000-man force to screen. But there weren't any Germans out there who wanted to move west.

Increased resistance in VII Corps sector indicated Collins was likely to face a stiff fight. The most important resource First Army could gather was sufficient reserves to reinforce VII Corps and exploit any opening punched through the Aachen Gap. First Army's objective was on the Rhine.

Tasking VII Corps with the main effort but leaving it with only three divisions didn't make a lot of sense. First Army's operations order instructed the Corps to be ready to continue its advance all the way to the Rhine. However, no special engineer arrangements had been provided to cross the Roer, let alone take on the mighty Rhine. Collins, like the other First Army corps commanders, recognized that his corps's zone of action, 35 miles wide, was far too large a frontage to attack on.[61] At corps level, commanders could not correct the overly wide attack frontages dictated by army group and army. But Collins attempted to compensate: he concentrated his three divisions (3AD, 1ID, 9ID) on the northern third of his sector. Fourth Cavalry Group guarded the remaining two-thirds, most of which was opposite the Huertgen.

Collins was very irritated at the delay imposed by higher headquarters. He viewed movement to occupy the West wall as a race between two armies. From a tactical perspective, Collins reasoned that an early start might penetrate into the West Wall before the Germans could form a coherent defense. He wanted to get there first, even if he had little supporting artillery and almost no ammunition at forward supply points.

The Battle of Mons had left a big hole in German lines. VII Corps had been advancing through it, running astride the Vesdre River. On the 11th, resistance markedly increased. By stuffing into the hole whatever troops that were available, the Germans were sealing it. But VII Corps intelligence detected another gap developing south of Aachen.[62]

Collins requested permission to conduct a reconnaissance in force beginning the 12th. Hodges "somewhat reluctantly" granted permission.[63] He cautioned Collins to pull up and await artillery ammunition resupply if serious resistance was encountered. But there would be no two-day halt. Map 5.3 depicts VII Corps's fight up the Stolberg Corridor.

Collins really planned his 12 September "reconnaissance" to be a surprise attack. He faced an interesting tactical question: should he invest Aachen or drive for the Roer?

Collins stated that Aachen had no military significance to either the Americans or the Germans. He concluded his corps could bypass the city.[64] Lightning Joe was ready to bypass the city and head for the deeper, decisive objective. Even though his artillery ammunition was limited and 3rd Armored still had one third of its medium tanks deadlined for lack of maintenance and spare parts, Collins was game. He wanted to blow through the length of the Stolberg Corridor, jump the Roer, and establish a position in Düren, just over the Roer.[65] Collins did not lack for audacity. Again, good tactical instinct.

Recall that corps commanders did not receive ULTRA. First Army was not warning about approaching German reinforcements. VII Corps G2 estimated perhaps 7,000 disorganized defenders faced the attackers.[66] The Germans had a lot of artillery and the guns were well supplied with shells. For the next week VII Corps forward units were constantly bombarded. Against even moderate resistance, a single three-division corps would have had a difficult time getting to the Roer. Speed was everything.

The 116th Panzer Division's commander, General von Schwerin, was no fan of National Socialism. He wanted to make Aachen an open city. Had Collins known, he could have motored into the town unopposed. But he did not. The SS arrested von Schwerin before the Americans realized the opportunity. The price for Aachen was to become very dear.

Collins worried about something materializing out of the Huertgen forest. Ninth Infantry Division protected the corps's right flank by advancing through the Huertgen forest southwest of the West Wall fortifications in the Stolberg Corridor. The narrow width of the corridor almost mandated that he put some troops in the woods. However, VII Corps's troop strength in relation to its mission was limited. Every man committed to a security task meant one less to push up the corridor.

Collins hoped quick, violently executed action would rupture incomplete German defenses.[67] He chose Rose and his 3rd Armored Division to lead the corps's main effort up the corridor all the way to Stolberg. This would take the division right through both bands of the West Wall. Initially, two regiments of 1ID would be in trail. If a major fight developed, 1ID would seize high ground on 3AD's left flank that dominated Aachen down in the "bowl" below.

Rose and Collins were in a hurry. This wasn't always true of the rank and file. GIs sensed the end of combat was near. The country ahead was dark, German, and foreboding. Despite their general's agenda, they were not anxious to be killed in what might be the war's last major fight. Initially First Army thought it had detected a gap in German defenses in the Stolberg Corridor. By the 11th, the Germans had essentially closed any gap that had existed.[68]

The reconnaissance in force advanced on the 12th. CCA entered Germany and the dragon's teeth of the West Wall. CCB stopped near the Belgian border short of the first band of the West Wall for the night. First Infantry Division met heavy resistance, including tanks as it advanced through the woods west of Aachen. Not an auspicious start. German forward elements fought aggressively. The generals might be racing, but the GIs weren't. Elements of 116 Panzer Division entered Aachen; the Germans perceived that this city was the American objective.

At dawn on the 13th, 3rd Armored cautiously moved forward. Ten kilometers and two bands of the West Wall lay between the American tankers and Stolberg. Detachments of 9th Panzer Division, Model's last mobile reserve, entered the Stolberg Corridor from the opposite end. Third Armored stalled in front of the first band of obstacles. A number of pillboxes were not manned, but intense fire from the remainder made it a slugfest. Engineers moving forward to blast a path through dragon's teeth were hit by concentrated artillery and machine-gun fire. Back in Germany, 12 Volks

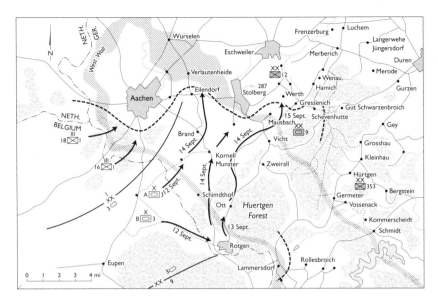

Map 5.2. VII Corps Initial Attack in the Stolberg Corridor

Grenadier Division (VGD), one of the two ordered west by Hitler, prepared to entrain that evening.

On the 14th, VII Corps picked up some speed, as German resistance was not heavy. On the left, 1st Infantry Division penetrated the first band of the Wall and made progress seizing the hills south of Aachen. During the night, the Germans manning the pillboxes in front of 3AD, members of a local security battalion, melted away into the darkness. They left behind several 88mm pieces well stocked with ammunition. Not every German wanted to die this late in the war either. On the 15th, 3rd Armored Division pushed through the West Wall's final band virtually unopposed. A second Landesschuetzen battalion had fled. However, a group of camouflaged assault guns ambushed CCA. The weather was lousy, so few American fighter bombers were in the air. Cumulative tank losses severely whittled down a 3rd Armored that had started the fight seriously under-strength.

With an assist from 1ID, assault guns that had stalled the tankers were routed. The Big Red 1 secured the high ground around Aachen. It had advanced deeper into Germany than any VII Corps unit. As a measure of the intensity of combat, each American division in contact was firing several thousand rounds a day. Self-propelled 155mm guns were put to good use firing at pillboxes over open sights. Even when a round didn't penetrate the concrete, the resulting concussion often killed or maimed the fortification's occupants. VII Corps's attack broke the contact between 116PzD and 9PzD. LXXXI Corps was in a dire position. On its right the lead regiment of 9ID made good progress with the aid of a captured map. But the 9th did not penetrate the second band of West Wall fortifications, so had no way to make out to its final assigned objective, Düren on the Roer. German 89th Division held firm.

Third Armored had been bled badly. Defenders had laid many anti-tank ambushes using everything from panzerfausts to 88mm armed self-propelled Ferdinands. The lead task force was down to thirteen medium tanks. It strained to advance further against 9th Panzer Division. Weather had become so bad that most close air support missions were canceled. Tankers advancing into unfamiliar territory were denied a valuable method of detecting and smashing ambushes.

By the 16th, senior German commanders did not understand why the American attack in the Aachen sector was so timid. Brandenberger wondered when an all-out attack would be launched.[69] He could not understand why more Americans hadn't joined the effort to push through the corridor.

The 9ID moved into the woods to the south of the Stolberg Corridor on a 13-kilometer front—too broad for rapid movement. The bulk of 9ID became involved in fighting for a relatively un-wooded corridor that runs from Monschau to Rollesbroich. Observation and direct fire into the lower portion of the Stolberg Corridor were denied the Germans. Now the priority was to get past Stolberg and Eschweiler. Collins retained "high hopes" of taking Düren.[70] Most days, the weather was too bad for much American air support. However, the Luftwaffe made an occasional appearance, allowing the anti-aircraft gunners to fire their weapons skyward.

VII Corps stood only 11 kilometers from the Roer. That evening a patrol from 1ID reported an approaching German column stretching as far as the eye could see. A 9ID outpost captured a colonel from a unit no one at G2 could identify. It was 12 Volks Grenadier Division.

With 14,800 men and full complements of artillery and anti-tank guns, 12VGD represented a significant addition to LXXXI Corps's combat power. While far from the Wehrmacht's best, it was better than the poor-quality splinters that 353ID had vainly used to hold 3rd Armored back. Hitler himself had directed this division be sent to the Aachen front. Its arrival heartened Germans opposing VII Corps in the Stolberg Corridor.

At dawn on the 17th, under an intense artillery preparation, elements of 12VGD spearheaded an attack on CCA. German attackers became silhouetted in the early morning light. American artillery and mortars blew them to pieces. CCB's planned attack was met headlong by another attack of two battalions from 12VGD. Neither side could move the other. In another action men of 9ID hacked down another 12VGD attack with concentrated rifle and machine-gun fire.

The 12VGD lost the equivalent of one of its regiments that day. Its commander became unnerved. However, these counterattacks convinced Collins his advance was about over. The Germans had reserves; he had none. VII Corps divisions held solidly to their forward positions. But they did not have the strength to push forward. Logistical constraints, especially a shortage of 105mm ammunition, prohibited additional major offensive action. Corridor combat furthered reduced the weakened 3rd Armored. The division counted only one hundred of its authorized four hundred tanks as fully operational. First Army recorded no advance by VII Corps on the 17th.[71] It would not have taken much more to unhinge 12VGD and gained access to Düren. But Collins didn't have it.

By the 18th, VII Corps advance was over. The proud GI author of the unofficial 3rd Armored Division history summed it up: After breaking into Stolberg and becoming entangled in its defenses, "[l]ike an athlete who has breached the tape of victory and stands exhausted, the Spearhead paused."[72] Tactical competence could not overcome American operational error—lack of concentration. Only 7 kilometers of corridor lay between VII Corps and relatively open country along the Roer. But Collins's troops were punched out. As long as the Germans had reserves and he had none, Collins reasoned he could not break through.[73] Recognizing that VII Corps wasn't going to break open the West Wall by itself, on 19 September Hodges ordered VII Corps to consolidate while XIX Corps moved into attack position.[74]

How could this be? A supposedly collapsing Wehrmacht could find reserve divisions, but the huge, triumphant American Army could not? The answer is poor generalship on the part of Hodges and Bradley. Had Bradley followed Eisenhower's guidance, another First Army corps would have been available just as the last German reserves had been committed. The campaign plan was sound, but Eisenhower's most trusted lieutenant, Bradley, defied his commander and botched its execution.

In six days Model and Brandenberger and his subordinate commanders had accomplished a task none of them had believed possible. Supposedly driven into the ground, the German Army had produced more reserves at the decisive point than the American Army could muster. Incredibly, the Germans won the fight in the Stolberg Corridor because they could throw in another division when the Americans could not. Stuck in the obstacles of the West Wall, the main effort of Bradley's 12th Army Group had been brought to a halt.

By not achieving their objective of closing to the Rhine, the Americans had lost a major engagement, though not for want of tactical prowess. The American soldiers had fought at least as well as the Germans. In the end, German generals, with a great inferiority in overall strength, concentrated more force at the decisive point than did Hodges and Bradley. The difference in operational skill between the opponents could not be more obvious. Despite some weakness in his hand, Bradley held more cards. He was simply outplayed.

As recounted in chapter 4, the 1944 edition of FM100-5 admonished commanders to retain a large reserve in the offense. Clausewitz was even more emphatic: "we should never have so many forces in the front line as we have none in reserve. That would be a very great error which would lead to defeat."[75] Introduction of a fresh unit either to continue an attack or to conduct a counterattack has an effect all out of proportion to the number of troops committed. Napoleon instinctively knew this. Victory often has gone to the commander who had the last uncommitted reserve. To begin a battle without one is the height of folly.

Charles MacDonald states in the official history that "the [First] Army faced a handicap both at the start and all the way through the Siegfried line Campaign in a lack of a reserve combat force. On occasion a separate infantry battalion or Combat Command . . . would be called a reserve, but no one would accept these designations as other than nominal."[76] First Army G3 stated, "You can't take chances without a reserve. The situation was that we had many times played our last card. All we could do was sit back and pray to God that nothing would happen."[77] If Bradley had concentrated better on the critical battle to break through to the Cologne plain and ignored the Ardennes, he could have created that reserve.

German commanders had even fewer resources. Yet they always formed a reserve at first opportunity. The principal reason for the lack of American reserves was the American commander's consistent inability to focus the troops available onto the most important task. Throughout the campaign, First Army was deployed in a manner that resulted in few reserves. Some security task, be it in the Huertgen or the Ardennes, always siphoned off troop strength. Lack of reserve is the single best index of the poor operational handling of First Army.

It could have been worse for the Americans. The Germans intended to consolidate the two SS panzer divisions assembling near Arnhem into a single strong formation and counterattack 3rd Armored Division with it. Instead the panzers shredded British 1st Airborne, which valiantly attempted to defend the Rhine bridges at Arnhem.

Of the three senior officers who estimated the size of the American force required north of the Ardennes (Bradley: one corps; Eisenhower: two corps; Montgomery: a three-corps field army), Montgomery appears to be most accurate. Another corps attacking in team with Collins probably would have made it over the Roer, obviating the subsequent bloodbaths in Aachen and the Huertgen forest. But it would have taken a full field army to break out on the Cologne plain and taken on Rundstedt's best, which was Eisenhower's intent all along. By the 19th the Market Garden offensive to Arnhem was under way. The result of that failure validates that it would take a full field army just to make it to the Rhine. Montgomery's idea of taking a two-army thrust all the way to Berlin is not validated by the actual events north of the Rhine and west of the Rhine in September. Eisenhower's judgment appears to be the correct one. The Allies would have to destroy the bulk of the German Army west of or near the Rhine and operate from a solid logistical base before they could entertain a deep incursion to the interior of Germany.

FOLLY IN THE ARDENNES

While VII Corps battered its head against a segment of the West Wall too thick for it to move, V Corps, under orders to do so, wasted its time and gasoline motoring through the Ardennes. We need only touch on the highlights of this ill-conceived operation.

In conformity with Hodges's instructions, V Corps dispatched patrols. None of the division commanders expected these to challenge the West Wall. Gerow concentrated his efforts on a full-scale attack to be launched on the 14th. This was in line with both Hodges and the logisticians. V Corps's G2 estimated fewer than 6,000 defenders. Intelligence officers noted that no enemy formation of divisional size had been encountered by V Corps during the last week.[78]

Bradley's plan envisioned V Corps attacking through the Ardennes in conjunction with Patton down in Lorraine. Gerow thought this to be impractical. Like Collins, Gerow attempted to weight the northern portion of his attack—the one closest to VII Corps and the theater's main effort. Both infantry divisions were concentrated in the north on about a 25-kilometer front. Fifth Armored would sweep through the center with an on-order mission to exploit any West Wall breach created by the infantry. A small riverhead across the Our River was carved out, but there were insufficient troops to hold it. One Hundred Twelfth Cavalry Group screened the southern half of the zone.

Gerow's plan was a sensible adaptation to a very difficult assignment. He sensed the lack of concentration on the main effort and attempted to compensate. But Hodges objected. Bradley had emphasized the need for a strong right wing down near Patton. After "a rather tempestuous discussion" between corps and army commander, an infantry regiment was transferred from the north to 5th Armored, and that division received an assignment to also assault the West Wall.[79] Even the First Army War Journal commented on the extreme width of V Corps zone.[80]

With the revisions dictated by Hodges, Gee recognized that his corps no longer had a point of concentration. If Gerow's plan had been carried out, the main effort made by V Corps might have achieved a better result. This attack might have gained ground along the Monschau Corridor leading to the Roer dams. If First Army had looked beyond the piece of paper coming down from 12th Army Group, they would have seen how critical the dams were to VII Corps's attack. VII Corps was 12th Army Group's main effort. But Hodges was forcing Gerow to comply with Bradley's desire to go gallivanting into the Ardennes. Twelfth Army Group orders stated V Corps was to help Third Army. An unsupported advance in the Ardennes could not possibly help Patton. One might have hoped Hodges would have pointed out the disconnect to Bradley. But Hodges performed as instructed. Gerow grumbled about his army commander. The real problem was at 12th Army Group.

Gerow's three divisions swept forward in a 50-kilometer-wide zone that approximated the battleground of the Bulge. When the Germans came the other way in December, they employed two panzer armies. V Corps achieved great tactical success. German defenders reached West Wall fortifications just ahead of the attackers. But the Americans quickly ejected them in several places. By 16 September, 5th Armored Division had achieved a clean penetration of mostly unmanned block houses of the West Wall east of Diekirch. The hole was 5 kilometers wide. Forward elements penetrated 8 kilometers beyond the fortifications. That was half way to Bitburg. The northernmost division ripped a 10-kilometer hole east of Saint Vith and uncovered the road to Prüm. Twenty-Eighth Division, in the center, bit most of the way through the Wall.

But there were no troops to follow up these shallow penetrations. Initially the Germans had only eight combat battalions in the Ardennes. Perhaps a large, multi-corps thrust might have accomplished more. SHAEF planners had considered this as an option. However, the Germans moved quickly to counter Gerow's thrusts. Battle groups from 2nd Panzer, 2 SS Panzer, and Panzer Lehr scrambled to block the gaps. Germans infiltrated back into pillboxes 5th Armored had already cleared. The armor did not have enough infantry to hold on to what it had seized. By the 18th, the offensive was over. German armor ejected 5th Armored and made local counterattacks to ensure the integrity of the West Wall. All Gerow succeeded in doing was to burn up gas and ammunition badly needed for higher-priority tasks. He didn't have the troop strength to do more.

The Ardennes was operationally a blind alley. In September it could have been lightly screened with a cavalry group reinforced with some towed anti-tank battalions that nobody else wanted, to create roadblocks on the highways that traversed the woods. Bradley and Patton should never have asked Eisenhower to split off V Corps from the attack on the Aachen Gap. Even more so, Ike should have been resolute in resisting diminution of his main effort. Strategists often are pressed to reduce the main effort in order to fund someone else's pet project. The institutional pressure to do so can be overwhelming. If V Corps had been yoked with VII Corps in the Aachen Gap, First Army probably would have gotten over the Roer around the 17th. The Germans would have to face two threats to the Rhine, even though the threats wouldn't have been well-coordinated. Twelfth Army Group probably would have avoided the enormous casualty lists from the assault on Aachen city and the horror of the Huertgen. Bradley absolutely wasted V Corps when it was more needed than at any other time since D-Day.

The opportunity cost of wasting gas to move V Corps into the Ardennes was enormous. From a distance moving one corps or the other four days shouldn't have been overwhelming. But lack of coordinated movement of a six-division mass over more open terrain versus smaller advancing forces was the difference between breaking through a band of tough terrain with little resistance and failing to achieve an operationally meaningful objective. Had XIX Corps received the fuel and had it been maneuvered to support VII Corps, First Army would have almost undoubtedly jumped the Roer in mid-September.

HOW SHOULD FIRST ARMY HAVE BEEN DEPLOYED?

If there was ever a time to avoid "layer cake" corps deployment, it was September 1944. Advance guards would not have enough strength to push through the way they had against scattered roadblocks encountered in late August. The multiple columns that characterized the final stages of the pursuit would have to be replaced with carefully selected fully supported formations capable of generating enough combat power to shatter the ever-hardening German crust. But this must be done only at points selected to unhinge the defense, not all up and down the line. Instead of attacks on everything, tactical thrusts had to be carefully chosen to fit an operational design that achieved the campaign's objective—destruction of the gathering German forces west of the Rhine.

Any competent tactician could identify the ground north of Aachen as the best approach to the Rhine. Given the weak defenses in place along the West Wall, especially to the north, why not take the fastest avenue of approach? That same tactician would also warn against what would amount to a pencil-like thrust of sending only three divisions through 75 kilometers of Germany to engage in a big battle on the near bank of the Rhine. This is especially true when German reinforcements were constantly arriving. Eisenhower had already dismissed Montgomery's "pencil-like thrust" toward Berlin.

The obvious solution was to push two corps north of Aachen, jump the Roer before any one could react, and make for the Rhine bridges, possibly at Cologne. Map 5.4 depicts a possible advance that is consistent with Eisenhower's intent. If successful, such a move would force Rundstedt to commit any reserve he could marshal in order to stop this threat to the Rhine and the Ruhr. Six American divisions (those in two corps) would have had a field day chewing up German armor in open ground along the Rhine. If the airmen could penetrate the lousy weather, they could have wreaked havoc on columns moving to cordon off such an American offensive. Having the third corps of First Army in van as a reserve would have given Hodges additional flexibility and combat power to complete the destruction of German reinforcements west of the Rhine. That was Eisenhower's overarching intent.

Notice how a British Second Army subsequent attack to Wesel would have complemented a successful First Army drive on Cologne. Two Allied armies would have been on the Rhine 80 kilometers apart, daring Rundstedt and Model to attempt to place something on the west bank between them. The British would be poised to threaten to encircle the Ruhr from the north

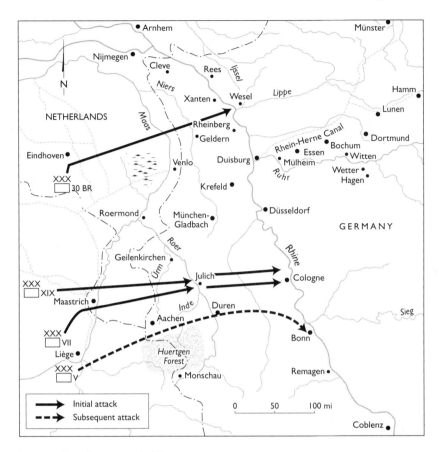

Map 5.3. Eisenhower's Initial Concept

while the Americans closed the circle with a pincer from the south of that industrial jungle.

Punching through the defensive crust the Germans were establishing was best done on a narrow front. American doctrine of the 1940s recognized this. Overwhelming force must be brought to bear. Deep columns with lots of reserves would be needed to maintain momentum. In order to create those reserves, Bradley could not afford to attack everywhere.

The more overwhelming the Americans at the initial point of penetration, the faster they could return to the type of mobile warfare that played to American strengths. Commanders at every level expected rapid movement to resume. The faster attacking formations penetrated, the less time the Germans would have to reassemble defenses. But the advancing armies had to reach each subsequent obstacle with enough combat power to smash through. The situation begged for large units arrayed in deep columns to penetrate on narrow fronts. Reserves would pass through the penetrations and head east.

To cover the distance to the Rhine, Bradley could not expect his lead regiments to continuously enter pitched combat day after day for 100 kilometers and prevail. The men can make an attempt day after day. As they become exhausted, their will to push forward falters. If German commanders throw fresh reserves against them, the likelihood of culmination skyrockets. Even if Bradley's memoirs overstate his actual estimate of German capability at the time, Brad would have to face reserves from the interior of Germany racing to stop what would become the most dangerous penetration toward the Ruhr.

The deeper the penetration, the more exposed American flanks would become. Instead of slowing to allow friendly units to catch up, each attacking force needed sufficient uncommitted combat power to crush the inevitable counterattacks and then continue toward the Rhine. The huge advantage in Allied mobile combat power allowed this kind of risk to be taken. Those counterattacks would have been opportunities to chew up the division-sized mobile formations the Germans had. Their loss would leave the defenders even more helpless to counter further American thrusts. If parried properly, division-sized counterattacks would be too small to threaten compact American armies in attack formation.

More so than a successful Market Garden, a thrust through Aachen threatening the Rhine and the Ruhr would have shattered Rundstedt's efforts. Rundstedt assumed the main Allied effort would come here.[81] Bradley had difficulty in creating the required reserve in echelons above division to prevent culmination. He had some resources, but he did not concentrate them. Give him more divisions and Bradley took on more tasks. Instead of thinking the main effort through to its operational depth, he began tackling another tactical problem close to his immediate front. By concentrating on tactics he missed the fundamental change in the operational level requirement.

The American Army in Europe contained engineers with a great deal of amphibious experience. First Engineer Special Brigade solved the problems associated with the D-Day landings. They had conducted the landings in North Africa, Sicily, and Italy as well. Securing the services of these veteran specialists would have been a prudent step. Instead they were employed as port engineers, a task other units could have accomplished. A lot of expertise in river crossing and amphibious efforts was embodied in 1106th Engineer Group, which soldiered with First Army. It might have been tasked to make special preparations. A hundred LVTs (landing vehicle, tracked—ocean capable amphibians) were made available to cross the Rhine. These and DUKWs (ocean capable amphibian 2½-ton trucks) demonstrated good handling qualities in fast water. DUKWs even bucked typhoon-driven seas in the Marianas that caused oceangoing landing craft to founder. Their amphibian nature was suited to crossing flooded ground. In the south, the Seventh Army engineer, General Davidson, created a special river-crossing school at Camp de Valbonne on the Rhone to teach his engineers how to deal with rapid water. Davidson wanted to be prepared for eight-to-ten-mile-an-hour currents that sometimes appear in the upper Rhine during the winter.[82] This was the same range Bradley's engineers would later predict as the peak of a major Roer flood.

In September, Montgomery made two critical errors. He put the Rhine ahead of Antwerp and he chose to split Allied army group efforts by selection of Arnhem as the objective instead of Wesel. Bradley also went o for 2. While the Aachen Gap was the correct main objective, the campaign plan to achieve this objective was faulty. First Army never had a proper solution to the operational problem before it. Tactical concerns rather than operational objectives governed decisions. Instead of a tight tactical formation with sufficient depth to penetrate the coalescing German defense, Bradley splattered Hodges's First Army against the West Wall like so much Silly Putty. In the second round, First Army picked the least favorable axis to advance on and paid dearly.

Tactics constantly overshadowed operational considerations at First Army. A firmer hand from above might have averted the most egregious errors. If Bradley had worried less about Monty's attempt to purloin his troops and concentrated on a better operational design, the northern half of 12th Army Group might have been the fall's decisive sector.

Even Bradley later admitted he reached the wrong answer. "Looking back," Bradley stated, "I was forced to concede that Eisenhower was probably right in his allotment of those two additional [sic] corps for I had underestimated the resistance that confronted Monty."[83] More accurately, he underestimated the resistance that could and did appear in the Aachen Gap.

MID-MONTH STATUS CHECK

Two days after Eisenhower's meeting in a B-25 with Montgomery at Brussels airport, Bradley sent the supreme commander a very optimistic letter.[84] Having met with the commanders and supply officers (G4) of First and Third Armies, Bradley reported that both armies, at current delivery rates, had enough fuel to fight to the Rhine. Against a norm of an ammunition reserve to supply five days of heavy combat, First Army had five days and Third Army four.

Ike showed pleasant surprise at Bradley's missive. He responded, "The picture you paint is brighter than we thought." Eisenhower gently nudged his friend about getting "our main bodies concentrated across the Rhine." Specifically, he sought to correct the erroneous employment of V Corps, which he had mistakenly approved, "I am much in favor of shifting Gerow [V Corps] to the left to get First Army well concentrated."[85]

Logistical records of First Army demonstrate that Bradley's communication was wide of the mark. While gas deliveries on the 10th and 11th did temporarily improve, they fell back to unacceptable levels the next day. First Army was so short of rations, it couldn't feed its troops without captured rations.[86] VII Corps, the only one about to enter heavy combat, was so short of 105mm ammunition that Hodges wanted to postpone the attack another two days in hope that some could be trucked up from Normandy.

On the 13th Eisenhower had issued the formal amendment to SHAEF plans authorizing Market Garden, reiterating the need for Antwerp, focusing First Army on a drive toward Cologne and Bonn only, and restraining Patton along the Moselle. Clearly his intent was "to push hard over the Rhine on our northern flank with Northern Group of Armies [21st Army Group], First Army and First Allied Airborne Army" as the undisputed main effort.[87] Undoubtedly influenced by Bradley's report on his prospects and having confidence in the upcoming Market Garden operation, Eisenhower wrote a very upbeat letter to Montgomery on the 15th. He assumed the German Army was on the verge of losing very big battles, unsuccessfully defending both the Ruhr and the Saar, and he talked about a subsequent advance on Berlin.[88] This was the last time Eisenhower would be so effusive. Montgomery interpreted Ike's letter as acceptance of his often-expressed need for a "full-blooded" thrust to Berlin and renewed his efforts to ram the British attack on Arnhem forward. He was mistaken. FWD 14784 stated that "a single knife like" thrust into Germany must be avoided. In a letter to Marshall, Eisenhower labeled Montgomery's proposal to "rush right into Berlin" as an impractical "fantastic idea," "based merely on wishful thinking."[89]

Montgomery remained adamant that a single thrust in the north was the only viable strategy and said so in an emphatic letter to Ike.[90] Bradley maintained a thrust through Lorraine to Frankfurt was absolutely necessary.[91] Eisenhower clearly wanted Bradley to pay more attention to the northern route, which was the main attack, but wanted to retain Patton's Lorraine drive as a viable alternative.

After the war Bradley wrote about the 15th, "We did not realize it yet, but the long, long pursuit was over." The quick advance had turned "into a war of position."[92]

Hitler was making incredible mid-course corrections of his own. On 16 September Collins was threatening to break through the Stolberg Corridor, Gerow was punching holes in the West Wall, and Patton was attacking Nancy. Within twenty-four hours, Market Garden would begin. Nevertheless, on that date, Hitler began massing strength for his planned Ardennes counterattack. Hitler's plan displayed both his unbroken will and his refusal to be cowed by the military facts before him. Thirty divisions would be gathered east of the Roer and in the Eifel opposite the Ardennes. Allied intelligence identified elements that would become part of the main striking force—Sixth Panzer Army.

A SECOND ATTEMPT AT THE AACHEN GAP

VII Corps had just lost its race with 12VGD. XIX Corps was about to experience a similar contest with the arriving 183VGD.

XIX Corps had been stranded without gas for three days. Despite being part of the army group's main effort, Bradley chose to expend a great deal of gas to detach the 79th Division from Corlett and send it down to Patton. When fuel finally arrived, Corlett was ordered up to the West Wall. Instead of mounting his own Meuse crossing, Corlett arranged to use bridges erected by British 30 Corps to the north and VII Corps to the south.

Model was very concerned about the advance of Corlett's 2nd Armored. The sector from Aachen north to Geilenkirchen was the *real* Aachen Gap, the high-speed approach to the Rhine. Model informed Student's First Parachute Army that "it is of decisive importance" that they keep Hell on Wheels out of the West Wall.[93] This was the 18th, the second day of Market Garden, a battle both Model and Student were personally straining to contain. Guards Armored had just reached 101st Airborne at Eindhoven. His ordering

Student's forces to counter 2nd Armored while they were so heavily engaged to the north underscores the field marshal's concern. A small *Kampf* group of 10 SS PzD, one of the units pounding the 1st British Airborne at Arnhem, was dispatched to counterattack the Americans at Sittard.

While XIX Corps belatedly wheeled into place, Model moved the full-strength 183rd Volks Grenadier Division into the West Wall. Had XIX Corps got the gas given to V Corps and arrived a day or two earlier, it would have found little besides alarm battalions in the pillboxes. As it had been refitting in Austria, 183VGD did not arrive for several days after 12VGD.[94] With 12th VG Division in Stolberg, 116 Panzers in Aachen, and 183VGD holding the pillboxes to the north of that city, Model now had a continuously manned West Wall directly in front of First Army. However, there was precious little in the line from the West Wall town of Geilenkirchen and 40 kilometers northwest, where the battle to contain Market Garden raged.

On the 19th Corlett ordered his corps to ready an assault on the West Wall the next day. He was confident his infantry could penetrate German defenses. But stretch marks had already appeared in Allied dispositions. The assault toward Arnhem had pulled British 8th Corps north, opening a large gap between them and XIX Corps's left. Lack of progress by VII Corps, which was just breaking into Stolberg, would make the right flank of a successful attack exposed as well. Corlett had but two divisions. In the Stolberg Corridor, the Germans had already demonstrated their ability to chew into overly exposed flanks. Despite what Bradley told Ike, XIX Corps was almost out of artillery ammunition. Poor weather interfered with the last source of additional combat power, the air force. For lack of supplies and troops, Corlett had to postpone the attack. Grenadiers of German 183rd Division began improving their positions in the West Wall. It rained on the 21st. On the 22nd, when VII Corps suspended his offensive, Hodges ordered XIX Corps to indefinitely postpone its assault on the West Wall. Mishandling and mistiming had sidelined a second First Army corps. While this delay dragged on, U.S. 7th Armored Division, then attached to British 8th Corps, was kicked out of the Peel marshes by XLVII Panzer Corps. The Germans were indeed recovering.

THEATER STRATEGY DEBATE CONTINUES

On 22 September, Ike held a meeting with his subordinates at Versailles. As usual, Montgomery did not attend. However on the 21st, he did send another radiogram continuing his long-distance presentation of his single-thrust strategy. Montgomery wrote, "I would say that the right flank of 12th Army

Group [i.e., Patton's attack in Lorraine] should be given a very direct order to halt . . . if you want to get to the Ruhr, you will have to put everything into the left hook and stop everything else.[95]

Over the previous week, the Allied picture had darkened considerably. First Army's attack to the Roer had ended. While there was still some hope of rescuing British 1 Para at Arnhem, it was apparent that Market Garden was not going to be successful. Estimates of German strength recorded continuing recovery. Previously SHAEF had been talking of total German strength in the west of sixteen Infantry and four panzer divisions. Now the published estimate ran as high as thirty infantry and four panzer divisions.[96] This is within the range of paradigm 3.

At the meeting, Eisenhower reiterated his two phase, two thrust strategy in even stronger terms. However, he underscored that the northern thrust was the main effort: "The envelopment of the Ruhr from the north by 21st Army Group, supported by First Army, is the main effort of the present phase of operations."[97] By requiring a clear distinction between requirements necessary to breach the West Wall and to seize the Ruhr from subsequent need to advance on Berlin, he underscored the two phases. SHAEF staff, in studying the logistics of subsequent phase stated that the Allies should "withhold further advance of our troops into Germany until late October."[98] Assuming a functioning Antwerp, the staff estimated five corps (fifteen divisions) could be supported at Berlin as well as another ten divisions between the Rhine and the German capital by early November. Eisenhower repeatedly underscored the need for "21st Army Group to open the port of Antwerp as a matter of urgency."[99]

Eisenhower reiterated the need of First Army to get to the Rhine at Cologne. As a sign of improving First Army's focus, no one mentioned Coblenz. After crossing the Rhine, 21st Army Group would envelop the Ruhr from the north, while First Army would envelop that industrial region from the south. Patton's southern thrust was to be held back until "the full requirement of the main effort have been met."[100]

AACHEN "GAP"—ROUND 3. AACHEN ITSELF

During September the Germans in the west tripled their effective strength in the field. Now seventy divisional flags, including fifteen panzer (eight fitted with Panthers and Tigers), dotted intelligence maps.[101] Many were woefully under strength. But any chance to blow through a paper-thin defense and resume the pursuit had passed.

Belatedly, First Army recognized it would need greater concentration to effect a deliberate attack in its sector.[102] Bradley reduced First Army's front by eliminating its responsibility for the Ardennes. V Corps side slipped northward from the Ardennes. It took over the southern half of VII Corps's sector, including Huertgen forest. VII Corps's front line was reduced from about 60 kilometers to 33. XIX Corps zone remained at 27 kilometers. Seventh Armored was nominally added to Corlett's corps, but it spent its time up in the Peel marshes watching a portion of 21st Army Group's sector. Seventh Armored Division was not available for the upcoming fight around Aachen. VIII Corps, under the supervision of Ninth Army, took over this sector. Eddy's corps finally was freed from Brest. Sixth Armored Division was directed to Patton and 29ID to Corlett. VIII Corps retained but two divisions.

Finally First Army focused on the Aachen Gap. If only this had been done at the beginning of the month as Eisenhower instructed, when Model's defenses were attempting to get into place! Hodges also narrowed the focus of First Army on the Rhine. XIX Corps now was directed on Düsseldorf, within the Ruhr. VII Corps oriented on Cologne and V Corps on Bonn. This was much closer to what should have been done in early September. While an improvement, it was not enough at this late date. By the end of the month this sector narrowing had become insufficient to adapt to increasing German strength. After the stall along the West Wall, First Army objectives set along the Rhine were wishful thinking anyway.

VII Corps had been shut down in the Stolberg Corridor. With 12VGD firmly ensconced in pillboxes and defenders occupying both Aachen city and the Huertgen forest, renewing this advance was not the best course of action. In order to make the corridor safe for follow-on forces, either Aachen or the Hamich ridge (or both) would need to be cleared. However, that tactical observation begged the larger operational question. What was the best way to break onto the Cologne plain? At the beginning of October, a staff officer writing in the First Army War Journal made this admission: "[T]wo divisions [9ID and 3AD fighting in the Stolberg Corridor] were, however, fighting in what was quite obviously readily defensible terrain. Prospects of substantial and rapid advances in this part of the area were slight."[103] The Aachen corridor to the north beckoned.

But First Army was not thinking on anywhere near that operational scale. Instead of looking at the larger picture, Hodges began to pick apart the tactical terrain problems to his immediate front. He identified four pieces of critical ground:

1) Hamich Ridge in the Huertgen forest
2) Aachen city
3) Gaining a breach through the West Wall for XIX Corps [north of Aachen]
4) Clearing the Peel marshes to the north.[104]

Each objective was the result of analysis with a technician's eye. Each involved a separate sector of First Army front. Again the problem was lack of prioritization. If First Army simultaneously focused on all these objectives, it would be committing to frontal attack along its entire front. Hodges should have determined that pushing a reinforced XIX Corps to the Roer would crack any defenses west of that stream and obviate the need to tackle 1, 2, and 4. Instead First Army looked to solve each tactical problem to its immediate front. Preparation for a Roer crossing didn't make the list. Hodges thought on a smaller scale. He felt clearing the Peel marshes and getting XIX Corps through the West Wall were the priorities.[105]

Renewed attack and successful penetration of the West Wall north of Aachen promised a large tank duel on open ground somewhere northeast of Aachen. Such a contest would have been far more preferable than an infantry brawl among the tangled trees and industrial towns to the south of that ancient city. A rapid jump across the Roer would make virtually every dug-in German position west of that river untenable. With VIII Corps relieving V Corps in the Ardennes, Hodges had the ideal force to swing around Aachen and place in team with XIX Corps in the Aachen Gap north of that city and belatedly execute what Eisenhower had outlined three weeks prior. That didn't happen. Fortunately, 29th Division, freed from Brittany, brought XIX Corps back up to strength. However, it was tasked to hold the line from Geilenkirchen north toward 7AD, which was still in the Peel marshes, and, like that division, the 29th would not be available for offensive action.

Time had worked against Hodges. He could not build up combat power as quickly as Model raised his by reshuffling units into the West Wall. Speedy penetration was imperative. Market Garden had failed, reducing the defensive problem and substantially improving the Germans' ability to counter-concentrate. In late September Patton's assaults along the Moselle had also petered out. Model had more than enough time to improve his positions and gain maximum advantage from the West Wall. Now that the British no longer pressured him, he could move infantry into the line and create an operational armored reserve from the panzers that were released. Given a week or two, repair crews could substantially increase the number of German tanks ready for combat.

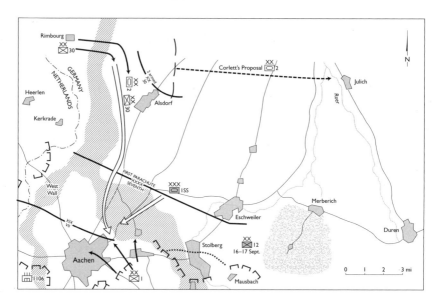

Map 5.4. XIX Corps Encircles Aachen

Model and his commanders understood that the Aachen Gap was the major priority. German staffs had completed their decision loop and were ready for exactly what First Army was about to try. The only hope Hodges had was a well-supported attack on a narrow front and a slow German response. Anything he could do to deceive the Germans would pay handsome dividends. Unfortunately, the First Army commander did little that wasn't expected by his enemies.

First Army staff officers had been thinking about the proper way to capture Aachen ever since First Army began its approach to the West Wall. No one was anxious to engage in urban warfare. First Army intended to encircle Aachen. One might have expected a double envelopment that included VII Corps coming up from the south (map 5.4). In the upcoming fight, Army staff left the heavy lifting to XIX Corps.[106] Second Armored was to stack up behind 30ID as an exploitation force. For a change, an American corps formation would have some depth. Thirtieth Infantry Division would assault on frontage of only a single mile. Corlett believed in massive fire support. A total of twenty-eight artillery battalions, including monstrous 240mm howitzers of army artillery, would fire in support of the assault. Concentrating firepower and attacking on the smallest possible front were key. At the division and corps level, American commanders had learned the value of concentration.

The tasks now assigned to XIX Corps exceeded what a reinforced two-division operation could achieve. As soon as 30ID broke through the West Wall, 2AD was to motor the nine miles to the Roer. Meanwhile 30ID was to turn right and encircle Aachen from the north. VII Corps 1ID would assist with an attack to link up with 30ID. Thirtieth Infantry Division would have to attack through 10 kilometers of heavily defended terrain. First Infantry Division was required to advance less than three.

German artillery increased its bombardment of VII Corps, holding that division to short creeping advances in the Stolberg corridor during the last days of September.

Target date for the attack was 1 October. Instead of a multi-corps offensive, 30ID would be the army's main effort. It would have to blast through the West Wall on its own. Second Armored would hold itself ready to exploit any gap torn open by Old Hickory.

The objectives were commendable. However, Corlett was allocated nowhere near enough combat power to achieve them. If a much stronger VII Corps couldn't reach the Roer on the 22nd, why did First Army believe a two-division attack against much better prepared and concentrated defenders succeed? Given the ten-day hiatus, why not trundle a pair of V Corps divisions around behind VII Corps and reinforce Corlett? That made more sense than sending them into the Huertgen. If Aachen was the key to forward movement and the attack would run both north and south of the city, no further advance into the Huertgen was required. Again, ensure the main effort had the power to succeed before taking on additional tasks. Assigning Corlett's small corps to worry about both Aachen and the Roer made little sense. Why not task Collins with a major push south of Aachen to encircle the city? If XIX Corps was to have any chance of crossing the Roer, it did not need to be worrying about encircling Aachen as well.

Fortunately, German intelligence officers were busy confusing themselves. They anticipated the major effort to come up the Stolberg Corridor south of Aachen. The logical counterpoint was a diversionary attack in the sector that First Army chose for its main effort.[107] Perhaps as an afterglow of Market Garden, German intelligence speculated that a ground offensive would be linked with a large airborne assault designed to carry the Americans over the Roer and onto the Rhine. Even threats on two axes create advantages.

General Hobbs used the ten-day interlude to retrain his division on the assault of fortified positions—sign of a good commander. Engineers practiced assault crossing techniques and combined arms teams rehearsed extensively. Four thousand replacements were integrated into 30ID.

Four hundred fifty fighters and medium bombers were supposed to lay a carpet à la the breakout from Normandy in front of 30ID. Unfortunately, 30ID had suffered heavily from that effort, which unleashed Cobra, and was very nervous about the aim of the air corps. A day before the attack, the weather changed to rain mixed with snow. On 1 October, an overcast sky brought forth a downpour. Due to the weather, close air strikes were out of the question. Tankers looked at the deepening mud with great foreboding. Corlett had to delay a day.

When the assault kicked off on the 2nd, 30th Division assaulted on its narrow front. While they had wider zones of advance, each regiment attacked in a sector only 1,000 yards wide. Hobbs guided Old Hickory onto ground north of Aachen's suburbs and about 5 kilometers south of Geilenkirchen. This avoided much of the built-up area around Aachen and the thicker West Wall fortifications that defended approaches to Geilenkirchen to the north. He correctly reasoned it was more important to get through the Wall and out into the open than to shorten the run around Aachen by a few kilometers. Still the first wave had to negotiate large wire obstacles and climb a steep ridge.

American artillery put in an outstanding performance.[108] Throughout the fight, sound and flash detection devices quickly identified German artillery positions, which were immediately shelled and shut down. Heavy artillery ranged deep, hitting communications sites, HQ, and supply installations. Up front, dogfaces received a lot of direct support artillery. Ammunition supply remained a problem. Mortar rounds in 81mm were in particularly short supply throughout First Army. Corlett, a big advocate of the heavy use of artillery, decided it was better to save lives than hold back an artillery ammunition reserve. He consigned virtually his entire allotment to supporting the initial assault. Even with this allocation, XIX Corps artillery ran short of shells to run the entire desired counter-battery mission. Hodges reprimanded Corlett for his ammunition expenditure. Corlett's reply was less than diplomatic.[109]

In order to penetrate through the depth of the first defensive belt, both assault regiments chose to attack in a column of battalions. Thirtieth Infantry Division hit the weakest enemy point with the greatest possible friendly concentration. Indirect fire had little effect on the pillboxes. Nevertheless, assaulting infantry, heavily reinforced with tanks and self-propelled tank destroyers and using recently practiced tactics to assault fortified positions, made steady progress. Dogfaces worked to within 10 meters of the pillboxes and assaulted with flamethrowers, grenades, and finally demolition charges.

The regimental columns were very fortuitous. When lead battalions stalled, regimental commanders committed follow-on battalions to the assault. Gutsy infantry action carried 30ID forward.

Despite the forebodings of intelligence officers, Hobbs's assault achieved complete surprise. The Germans expected an attack, but not where 30ID hit. Surprise markedly slowed the German response.[110] The first counterattack did not come until midnight. American artillery fire smashed it about so badly that only a brace of assault guns and a trickle of infantry splattered into 30ID.

However, by the end of first day of the attack, Rundstedt recognized that the XIX Corps effort was more than defenders in the area could handle. Ever since the attack began, German commanders had attempted to create a tactical reserve. They wanted to assemble enough combat power to eject XIX Corps from the West Wall. Model understood that local reserves were insufficient and scraped around for more.

On the second morning Old Hickory continued its advance. The forward regiments were up against block houses situated on that steep, long ridge. It proved a tough position to crack. German commanders assembled sufficient power to generate a serious counterattack—yet another sign of increasing German strength. Elements of 116 and 1st Panzer Divisions ripped into the long, exposed flank of the division the Germans dubbed "Roosevelt's Butchers." Hobbs was stopped in Übach.

Old Hickory had not scooped out a large enough bridgehead to allow 2AD to enter. In Normandy Hobbs and Corlett had seen how the premature entry of armor into a constricted battlefield can create chaos. Early commitment during the crossing of the Vire River had created a horrible mess. Nevertheless, the corps commander committed CCB, which entered Übach on the 3rd in order to add its weight to 30ID's attack. If he lost the gamble, columns of vehicles would bunch up, creating another inviting target. Passage of lines is always a difficult maneuver. Commanders can lose control if units become entangled with each other in a close-in furball with the enemy. As it attempted to advance through Old Hickory, 2AD found itself fighting a meeting engagement with one of the attacking German formations. Notice the armor, instead of heading for the Roer, was needed just to break into forward German defenses. The entire attack was "underfunded."

General Bradley had come forward to witness the attack. After spending time with Hodges and Collins he went forward by jeep to Corlett's HQ. Just as he arrived a pair of Messerschmitts came by, guns winking, only to be chased away by a bevy of American machine-gun fire. Seventy-five Luftwaffe fighters attacked First Army that day. American AAA claimed an unreasonable number of them shot down.

The German commander had set his counterattack for 0215 of the 4th. But he had control problems of his own. At the appointed hour, only an engineer battalion was ready. The main attack was delayed until dawn. One prong of the German effort bit into 30ID positions in Ubach. Short rounds from their own artillery caused problems. A second attack force ran into CCB as it attempted to emerge from Erbach. American armor smashed the attackers. One German battalion was reduced to twenty-five men.

Because of the heavy fighting, the Americans did not begin to take ground until late afternoon. For the next two days the armor eked out an additional 3 kilometers by employing similar tactics. German-speaking Americans found an operative field phone in one bunker. They called the next pillbox. "We've just taken your comrades and now we are coming after you." Twenty-five Germans emerged from the next position, their hands held high.[111] Second Armored followed 30ID in van. Corlett knew that additional German armor had reinforced the defense. But 2AD was pulling free from the German positions. The shelling was so bad that a single armored infantry battalion lost two commanders that day. By nightfall the armor had advanced about 800 meters. They were still short of the Geilenkirchen-Aachen highway.

The Germans were unable to get a line of tanks and anti-tank guns in position to oppose 2AD until the morning of the 6th. Another large-scale counterattack was mounted. This time Americans took to the pillboxes. Now German infantry had to assault these tough fortifications. They took at least four, capturing one hundred Americans. Other American manned pillboxes held out. The Germans were stopped by concrete of their own making. The initiative returned to American hands, and CCA crossed into the bridgehead.

XIX Corps plans had 2AD moving north to cross the Roer while 30ID moved east to complete the encirclement of Aachen. Second Armored's planned mission was so independent that a three-battalion artillery group from corps was to be attached instead of simply being placed in direct support. Corlett wanted to unleash the armor and send it to the Roer. However, Hodges became very concerned about the intensity of the fighting. He ordered Corlett to confine operations to the vicinity of the West Wall and not to make for the Roer.[112] Instead of giving him an exploitation mission, Hodges directed Corlett to have 2nd Armored Division follow in the path of 30ID. This essentially eliminated any chance of exploitation to the Roer and focused the attack on encirclement of Aachen.

As ordered, Corlett redirected the main effort to linking up with 1ID and thus encircling Aachen. Instead of heading to the river, 2AD stayed close to Old Hickory's left flank. CCB assumed defensive positions on the outer arc of the corps advance. Second Armored's commander, General Harmon, protested First Army's modifications to the plan. Harmon, an old cavalryman and armor pioneer, had commanded 2nd Armored as far back as North Africa. Slashing offensive action toward the Roer, not defending 30ID's encirclement of Aachen, was the proper task for Hell on Wheels. Another protesting voice from within XIX Corps did not bring further endearment from First Army staff.[113]

German resistance to 30ID's attack began to waver. It is questionable whether CCA was needed to support the attack. The 30ID picked up speed. By the 7th the American attack was cleanly through West Wall fortifications. The Germans were unable to react. On the 7th General Hobbs signaled, "I entertain no doubts that this line is cracked wide open. . . . We have a hole in this thing big enough to drive two divisions though."[114] However, those two divisions were not available.

XIX Corps had carved an arc over the northern approaches to Aachen. First Army became increasingly impatient with the progress of XIX Corps. Hodges continuously called Corlett, demanding more speed. A First Army staff officer remarked that low causality figures indicated XIX Corps wasn't fighting hard enough. When Corlett heard about this, he was outraged. He mounted his jeep and sped off to First Army HQ. Fortuitously, Hodges wasn't there.

Only 6 kilometers between 30ID and VII Corps remained to be closed. Hobbs recommended that 1ID begin to move to close the gap from their end. Both Corlett and Hodges concurred. However, all VII Corps divisions were committed. To allow 1st Infantry Division to coil up a regiment for the attack, Collins inserted a corps engineer group into the line. Big Red One's pincer attack kicked off on the morning of the 8th.

Rundstedt attempted to move his final reserve forward. However, ISS Panzer Corps, consisting of 116 Panzer and 3 Panzer Grenadier Divisions, had trouble assembling. It was constantly hounded by Allied air. Torn-up railroad tracks impeded their movement. Advance elements did not reach the Aachen battlefield until the 10th. Rundstedt commanded that these divisions be committed as concentrated formations and not piecemeal. Model fretted that no counterattack could be mounted before the 12th. Declaring an emergency, he sidestepped Rundstedt's orders and committed 116 Panzer in dribbles. Model feared he couldn't hold together his splitting seams without their help.

Both a gap in the line and a time window had opened before the Americans. Lack of both reserves and the vision to cross the Roer instead of worrying about a pile of rubble cost the Americans any chance of operational success. Between the 7th and the 12th or 15th of October, a multi-divisional exploitation force might have leaped the small river and created a mass too difficult for the Germans to move. It was the Stolberg Corridor mistake all over again.

Nevertheless, 3PGD's attack caused 1ID's commander, General Huebner, consternation. In two days of fighting, 3PGD lost one third of its combat effectives. Additional days of tough fighting by both Old Hickory and the Big Red One were required to close the last few kilometers. XIX Corps became increasingly stretched to defend both the hook that surrounded most of Aachen and the remainder of its sector. All three of its divisions, including 29ID, became heavily involved. Regimental-sized attacks repeatedly hit first one American unit and then another. Deflecting them sapped strength and temporarily prevented 30ID from closing the gap. Corlett asked for reinforcement. Hodges had none to send but exhorted him to close the gap. Corlett gave 30ID a 2nd Armored tank battalion and a separate infantry battalion. Like Collins, Corlett placed an engineer group in the line to free infantry. First Infantry Division was now moving. On the 16th, almost two weeks after XIX Corps's offensive started, 30ID linked with 1ID.

Even before the encirclement had been completed, First Infantry began to systematically clear the city. Another five thousand shells re-stirred its rubble. After the expiry of a demand to surrender on the 11th, 1ID infantry entered the city. On the 13th fighting in northeastern Aachen was described as "from attic to attic and from sewer to sewer."[115] Flamethrowers were used close in to reduce fortified buildings. This was urban combat at its worst. Some Germans infiltrated through the rubble to attack from sectors already thought cleared. Perhaps only two thousand combat-effective Germans remained within the city's limits. German artillery east of town rained as many as five thousand shells a day on 1ID units. Fighters repeatedly raked this ancient site of empire. Scarcely a roof remained intact. On the 15th elements of 3PGD mounted a stiff counterattack against 1ID in order to break into what was now called the Aachen pocket.

By the time First Army finally closed the ring around Aachen, 30ID had suffered 3,100 casualties. First Infantry Division endured almost as many.

The last German remnants in Aachen surrendered on 21 October. Neither division had the strength for further offensive action. The three-week operation to capture Aachen achieved little for the Americans. At the operational level, it was a German victory. Crucial time had been gained to continue their efforts at regenerating their force. Allied initiative had been almost completely dissipated.

On the 18th, Bradley relieved Corlett. Upon hearing the news, Hobbs broke down and wept. This good division commander felt he had let his boss down. Corlett said leaving his beloved corps "was just plain heartbreak."[116] Earlier Ike had told Marshall both Gerow and Corlett were capable of army command.[117] Relief of Corlett after his successful fight around Aachen poisoned the command climate in First Army.[118] Many officers thought he had been badly treated. However, Collins remarked that it was easier to deal with his successor, General McLain.[119]

Since the beginning of the campaign, Corlett had pressed to advance in the north. He had wanted to strike for the Roer instead of fooling with Aachen. While Corlett might have made First Army staff mad, his military reasoning surpassed that of his superior headquarters.

Corlett had been given a no-win assignment. The objectives were contradictory and far beyond the capability of the forces assigned to him. Bradley stated that Corlett was "unable to control a red hot temper." The poor handling of XIX Corps by First Army had given him reason to get that way. Assigning a subordinate inadequate resources, heckling him as he attempts to accomplish the mission, and then relieving him when the tasks are finally completed are not the marks of a good leader. Bradley recommended Corlett be sent back to the States for a rest and a complete physical checkup. Ike wrote that he would have him back as a corps commander after his rest. That never happened. Corlett commanded a corps in the U.S. for the rest of the war.

General Ray McLain became the new XIX Corps commander. He was the National Guard officer who had turned the faltering 90ID into an outfit worthy of its sobriquet, "Tough Hombres." Marshall took special interest in his selection. The chief of staff wanted all serving National Guard officers to understand that outstanding performance as a divisional commander could lead to higher command.

Logistical support still did not match combat expenditures. Bradley's army group alone needed 20,000 tons a day. From 1 to 15 October, it could get only 12,500 tons/day.[120] The effort to encircle Aachen had consumed a lot of tonnage. Now the bill for the Scheldt came due. Without supplies landing on Antwerp's docks, 12th Army Group would have to husband its meager incoming supply. It would not be able to support another major offensive until the first of November.

On 25 October, General Bradley presented General Hodges with the Bronze Star for successfully capturing Aachen.

BUTCHERY IN THE HUERTGEN

Hodges, veteran of World War I, remembered the threat of German counterattack from the Argonne forest hitting the AEF's flank. The First Army commander had similar concerns about Huertgen. In his memoirs, Collins echoed this fear. Collins compared the potential for German counterattack from Huertgen to the threat from the Argonne forest to Pershing's advance in World War I.[121] Of all his wartime judgments, this might be one of the most ill-considered. The German Army was barely hanging in and in no condition to counterattack in less than the most critical situations. The German corps and army commanders couldn't understand why the Americans didn't simply create roadblocks in the outer fringe of the woods and avoid the Huertgen altogether.[122]

One reason for entering the woods might have been to seize the Roer dams (see below). But there is no evidence that Hodges ever had capture of the dams as a motivation for entering the Huertgen.[123]

Heavy woods strongly favor the defender. In the Huertgen, conifers rise over 75 feet above a spongy, water-logged carpet of pine needles. Even during the day little sunlight penetrates to the ground. The trees cover the steepest slopes of the Ardennes and line deep, gloomy gorges that are impassable to any vehicle. They are extremely difficult to maneuver in. It is very easy to get lost. In the Huertgen, no one could see very far. Where was the enemy sniper? The mines? Attacking infantry stumbles into a machine gun protected with overhead cover. Control breaks down. No rational person is going to move while hot metal is screaming overhead. One tree looks like another, especially when one's chin is pressed into the mud. Calling in artillery or mortars is almost impossible. You are not sure where you are, and the enemy is only a few dozen meters away. Tanks couldn't penetrate through the thick trees. The air corps can't see you because of the overhead canopy. But move you must. You must get around that gun or you'll be there all day.

FM100-5 for 1944 said little about woods except to bypass them. That advice might have been well heeded by Hodges and Collins. In the words of a German general, "There was no use the Americans going through the

Huertgen Forest, as it was easy to see it would be hard to take and easy to defend. Had you gone around it on both sides, you would have had almost no opposition. We did not have enough troops in the area at the time. Also, had you bypassed the area, we could not have launched a big counter-attack there, not with the army of 1944."[124] General Brandenberger, German Seventh Army commander, couldn't believe the Americans would make such a thrust through such inhospitable terrain while committing insufficient forces in the Stolberg Corridor.[125]

A higher-level commander should have recognized that any opportunity that had existed in the Stolberg Corridor had long since closed and chosen a different battle. Hodges, with Bradley's approval, could have reinforced XIX Corps's October attack to have enough maneuver elements to leap the Roer from a penetration north of Aachen.

Instead Hodges ordered attacks that sent division after division into the blackened green hell of Huertgen. No subordinate dared object or ask why.[126] Apparently Hodges gave no serious thought to bypassing the woods.[127] While XIX Corps carved a hole in the West Wall north of Aachen, 9th Infantry Division made another attempt to advance into the Huertgen. Hodges squandered a good division in an attack into the woods for no good operational reason.

Collins states, "I was directed to renew the attack to break through the remainder of the forest and seize the town of Schmidt, north to the upper reaches of the Roer River. No mention was made of the two major dams on the Roer and its Urft tributary south of Schmidt, nor were they assigned as objectives of the VII Corps."[128] Collins goes on to state that the dams were important but neither SHAEF, 12th Army Group, First Army, nor his own usually good G2 and engineer identified the risk the water behind the dams poised for anyone crossing the Roer downstream.

Bradley had been determined to push V Corps into some action down south. Each time the attack into the Stolberg Corridor was renewed, V Corps was trundled a little farther north. By the beginning of November, it was almost entirely employed in the Huertgen. By no means did this effort have anything to do with Patton's effort in Lorraine.

A three-month string of butcheries continued in the Huertgen forest. Tactical considerations repeatedly drove the Americans into the forest. By the time it was over the American Army committed a peak force of 120,000 in the Huertgen. They were opposed by perhaps 80,000 Germans, mostly from second-line formations. American casualty lists exceeded 33,000 names; 24,000 in combat and 9,000 to disease and combat fatigue.

Detailed German records were lost, but the Wehrmacht suffered about the same number.[129]

As Weigley stated, "The Huertgen Forest was a worse American military tragedy than the Wilderness or the Argonne."[130] Even Bradley admitted that he erred in estimating the difficulty of attacking through the Huertgen. "In launching Cota [28ID, second attack on Schmidt], we grossly underestimated both the terrain and the German defenses."[131] Major General Cota commanded 28th Division, which relieved 9th Division in the Huertgen on 25 October. Both divisions suffered horribly. The 28th, a Pennsylvania National Guard Division, used a red keystone as its symbol. After Huertgen, it became known as the "Bloody Bucket."

THE ROER RIVER

The Roer River is normally a quiet, unimpressive waterway. Its headwaters gather in the Eifel. They curl around in a steep ravine before flowing south to north. The Roer meets the Maas (Meuse) 40 kilometers away at the Dutch town of Roermond near the German border. Rarely does its stream exceed 30 meters in width. Normally its slow current is no impediment to a military crossing.

The problem was the huge amount of water stored upstream, principally by two dams, the Urft and the Schwammenauel. Over 123,000 acre feet of water was contained behind them. Enemy-controlled release could create a lake up to several kilometers in width and create currents as high as 10 miles an hour (14.7 ft./sec.) in the more constricted portions of the watercourse. When the Americans prepared to cross the Roer in early 1945 German engineers released a steady flow, which swelled the river and prevented 12th Army Group from crossing it for eleven days.

Both American and German commanders were slow to recognize the impact of the Roer dams on a potential river crossing. In mid-September an American hasty crossing of the Roer driven home with great violence probably would have succeeded brilliantly. If the Germans blew the dams early, they risked trapping many Germans on the west bank.

A historian who has examined American reaction to the Roer dams in the fall of 1944 found, "My research turned up nothing in the records of 12th Army Group, First Army VII Corps or V Corps that notes any discussion during the period from September to early November of attacking the dams."[132] Bradley admits he and his staff did not understand the potential for major flooding until "mid to late October."[133] The first officer who seems to have identified the potential flood risk was Major Jack Houston, G2, 9ID. In his 2 October intelligence summary, he wrote that by regulating outflow from the dams "great destructive waves can be produced which would destroy everything in the populated industrial valley as far as the Meuse and into Holland." First Army G2 discounted this estimate.[134]

The increase of river velocity rather than the size of the flood was the larger engineering problem. Slow-moving boats and rafts get swamped and overturned. Instead of the boats landing in close order, the current scatters them all over the far bank. Pontoons are difficult to launch and assemble. Anchor cables pull loose. Out-of-control rafts crash into floating bridges, breaking them. Fast-moving current twists steel bridge sections into junk. Thirtieth Infantry Division engineers found crossing the fast-moving Roer more difficult than their subsequent crossing of the 350-meter-wide Rhine.[135]

River-crossing technology in 1944 had great difficulty in dealing with 10 mph (14.7 ft./sec.) currents. By comparison, currents in Hell's Gate, where Long Island Sound meets the East River at the north end of Manhattan, run about 10 mph. Amphibious technology of 1950 was able to land in Inch'on harbor, where the current runs 13.5 feet per second (8 knots).[136]

Current speed declined as the river spread out and flooded a wider band of lowland as it moved north. Securing a strong crossing cable against which a bridge or ferry could be anchored was key. At Maastricht on 15 November, the Maas River attained a velocity of 11 feet per second. But a well-anchored pontoon bridge kept accepting traffic at a rate of two thousand vehicles per day. During the course of the flood, the bridge was extended from 470 to 670 feet. A Bailey bridge placed on top of a ruined permanent bridge stayed open continuously.[137]

By late 1944, treadway bridges had been tested in the United States in streams moving 10.4 feet per second.[138] Engineer reference data indicates that "risk" crossings can be made in 11 feet per second currents on both World War II–design float bridges and tactical ferries.[139] Amphibious landing vehicles, DUKWs and LVTs, proved to remain seaworthy in storm tides on the Pacific. Ultimately, LVTs (first used at the invasion of Tarawa) were used to cross the muddy flats that flooding ultimately did create in the Roer Valley.

Pontoon bridges are most susceptible to fast currents. Fixed Bailey bridging, up and out of the water, is immune to current. Using the abutments of a pre-existing destroyed bridge markedly assists their installation. On 25 February, during the actual flooding of the Roer when the Germans opened the dam, 292nd Engineer Battalion installed a Bailey bridge on the abutments of a destroyed Roer bridge that carried the autobahn over the river. Only 67 meters needed to be spanned. The battalion opened the bridge for tank traffic in less than twenty-four hours after installation began.[140]

Concentrated artillery provided tremendous protection against enemy attack. Even if all of the bridging was destroyed, initial assault objectives could have been carefully phased to stay within the firing arcs of artillery emplaced on the west bank. With far less artillery than Hodges could have assembled along the Roer, 101A/B Division withstood the wrath of a panzer army at Bastogne.

Patton faced a similar problem during his November offensive. While it is out of sync with our timeline, the experience of 90ID, which crossed the Moselle north of Metz as part of Third Army's big November push, is instructive. Ninetieth Infantry Division was to cross the Moselle at Thionville and construct a bridge so 10AD could pass through and race to encircle Metz. When crossing operations began on the morning of 9 November, the river was 300–600 feet wide. That in itself was a more formidable barrier than the Roer under normal conditions. By noon, the river had swollen to 2,400 feet[141] with current from 7 to 10 feet per second.[142] None of the available bridging was even close to being able to handle this expansion. To deal with the current, the complement of engineer crews on the assault boats was doubled. In one regiment, sixty of eighty boats were lost after the first wave debarked. Because of the flooding, the Americans floated over flooded German minefields, which was an unexpected benefit. While crossing sites were positioned to minimize enemy observation, some of the assaulting force had to directly attack some of the outermost defensive forts of Metz. Yet the Tough Hombres got eight infantry battalions across. That evening, a local German counterattack pushed back one of the assaulting American battalions.

The Germans did not strongly defend the river line. Troops in the area were not Germany's best. XII Corps's attack south of Metz threatened and absorbed Balck's only real reserve, 11PGD. A regiment of 25PGD infantry, reinforced by tanks and assault guns, hit 90ID hard just as a bridge had been completed. German gunners dismantled the bridge. American infantry fought hard during the night. At daylight twenty-eight battalions of American artillery devastated the panzer grenadiers. Over four hundred dead Germans marked the battlefield. Even though not a single bridge supported 90ID's "bridgehead" for three days and ammunition ran low, the Tough Hombres held on to their positions and expanded them eastward.

The floods washed out bridges the length of the Moselle, stranding 5ID and all of XII Corps as well. Patton wrote, "I had seven divisions across an unfordable river and no bridges."[143] While rains and mud slowed XII Corps spearheads, the supply problems from the severed bridges did not impact its rate of advance. While difficult, the problem of Roer flooding was not insurmountable.

In the alternative, the dams could have been targeted for destruction. A glider-borne raid might have been the easiest way to capture and disable the dams. The Germans at Eben Emael and the British at Pegasus Bridge demonstrated how effective this tactic could be. Well-placed demolitions would open the flood gates and drain the water in a few days. The risk to the raiding party would have been high. But far fewer people would have been lost than in the grinding fall campaign that ensued. Only six German attackers were lost at Eben Emael. The earlier the raid the better. Again, the beginning of October appears to have been the best time. Let the waters recede while Bradley scrounged for artillery shells. A relative handful of transports and gliders would have been needed.

In early December, at the request of General Hodges, RAF 617 Squadron, "The Dam Busters," made a run on the Roer dams with Lancasters modified to carry outsized basketball-shaped bombs designed to skip across the water and slam into the concrete structures. Airmen felt the size and strength of the dams and the resulting pinpoint accuracy required made them poor bombing targets. Initially they rejected the operation as impractical.[144] After much argument, bombers dropped ordnance on two days, with very disappointing results. Only twenty hits were made on the two big dams, and they caused little apparent damage. Hodges felt the dams should have been hit by one thousand bombers a day until the dams failed.[145]

Heavy artillery might have been emplaced within range of the dams, say at Rotgen or even Kalterherberg. A 240mm howitzer could throw a concrete-piercing 360-lb. shell 25 kilometers. One 240mm round would not break a dam. However, heavy artillery was both very accurate and very destructive of fixed targets. In the Ninth Army area heavy artillery destroyed two bridges over the Roer. One was dropped with nine rounds; the other fell after twenty-two.[146] Available artillery within 12th Army Group could hit the dams with perhaps forty rounds per hour around the clock. Multi-battalion TOTs* hitting the concrete-clad earth-filled structures would have been

*Time on Target: all shots carefully timed to arrive exactly at the same second, with devastating impact.

very exciting. Watching large chunks of concrete leap from the dams day after day would do little to settle Germans responsible for deploying forces east of the River. Harassing fire from 155mm Long Toms would keep German engineers from inspecting or repairing the damage in between heavy salvos.

BREST—A SUPERSEDED OBJECTIVE

Initial Overlord plans had required the Breton ports be secured. Deep-water facilities at Brest that could receive transatlantic ships were especially prized. During World War II, crated equipment of divisions arriving directly from America needed the large cranes and deep water of Brest, Le Havre, or Antwerp. The only reason why the Overlord plan tasked a corps to attack into Brittany was pressure from logisticians to seize Brest.[147]

The Canadians pulled up before Le Havre on 1 September. By that time, the Americans knew the port of Brest had been heavily damaged by the Germans. Le Havre was 400 kilometers closer to the Allied front line. On the 3rd American supply planners recommended that Lorient, Saint-Nazaire, Nantes, and the artificial port intended for Quiberon Bay not be developed. They would have scratched Brest as well "had the Battle of Brest not been in progress."[148] Le Havre fell on 10 September. From that date, there was no reason to continue combat operations in Brittany.

On 10 September, while both First and Third Armies were stalled for lack of supply, Bradley made VIII Corps in Brittany the number-one supply priority. Most of the enormous ammunition tonnages used to bombard Brest arrived via truck from the Normandy.

Ultimately, 25,000 tons of ammunition would be shipped for the operation. Almost since D-Day, the U.S. Army had faced an ammunition shortage. Had this squandered tonnage been available later in September in Lorraine and the Aachen Gap, the Allies might not have ceded the initiative. Using the data from table 2.3, 25,000 tons equates to 40 division-days in full attack. What could this effort have achieved in the Aachen Gap? A big logistical chip had been wasted when the probability of gain was zero. This is generalship at its second-worst.*

In addition, Ninth Air Force flew more than 6,200 sorties against Brest between 25 August and 19 September. As one air historian put it: "Brest remained a battered monument to the uneconomical use of airpower. A

---

*Squandering human life, like in the Huertgen, eclipses it.

vast number of aircraft had been used to clear a besieged area while forces plunging deep into the heartland of the enemy were without their services."[149]

Clearly Ike dragged his heels about eliminating Brest as an objective. As late as 13 September, he was talking about its deep-water quays. This was a major error on his part. If he wasn't familiar with the numbers, someone like Gale should have laid them out for him.

Why did Americans continue the fight at Brest? Patton provides an answer. In his diary he records Bradley as saying, "I would not say this to anyone but you, and have given excuses to my staff and higher echelons, but we must take Brest in order to maintain the illusion of the fact that the U.S. Army cannot be beaten." Of Omar's sentiment, Patton writes, "More emotion than I thought he had. I fully concur in this view."[150] Patton echoed these sentiments in his book: "We both felt that the taking of Brest at that time was useless . . . when the American Army put its hand to the plow, it should not let go."[151]

Any perception of American invincibility existed only in the minds of a few American commanders. Certainly, it had little impact on Rundstedt or Hitler. Pride clouded operational judgment, with enormous implications. What would have been the impact of a fully supplied infantry corps in September's Scheldt battle? Another corps, even with diminished supply, might have been decisive in Market Garden or in the Aachen Corridor operation.

Brest cost the American Army 9,831 casualties. Not a single division would enter via this port. Its development was abandoned. In his later biography Bradley said, "We might have been well advised at this point to give up the good fight and let Brest remain in German hands."[152] In the end Bradley found the correct answer.

6

Patton's Lorraine Campaign

The 29th of August was one of the most important days of the war. . . .
I presented my case for a rapid advance to the east for the purpose of cutting
the Siegfried line before it could be manned. Bradley was very sympathetic
but Bull (General Bull, Eisenhower's G3) and, I gather, the rest of SHAEF's
staff did not concur.

It was my opinion then that this was the momentous event of the war.

George Patton

At the end of August, virtually no organized resistance impeded American
columns as they sped eastward. Patton believed that in another ten days
he could breach the West Wall, enter Germany, and maybe end the war.
"Now is the moment, Hap [General "Hap" Gay, Third Army assistant chief
of staff]. They are ours for the taking. If we delay, the price will be written
in blood." Patton added, "It is such a sure thing, that I fear someone will
stop it."[1]

PATTON

Sixty years after the events in Western Europe, the stars of many American
commanders have faded. Patton's flag, bright and colorful as ever, still snaps
smartly in the breeze. Patton, the caricature of a rough talking, hard-charg-
ing general, captures the imagination of a legion of admirers. His strident
"war face" attracts many who seek the quintessential warrior. Others, put off
by his bellicose, profane, and crude histrionics, say he bordered on madness.

No other commander in World War II more deeply impressed his
personality on his command than George Patton.[2] Some say Patton transformed Third Army into his own image. Many believed Third Army began
to exhibit the mannerisms and idiosyncrasies of its colorful commander.

Another American general summed up the consensus opinion of the Third Army's commander's point of view: "He gave one the impression that he considered World War II, so far, to be Patton vs. the Wehrmacht."[3]

And colorful he was. Patton had the kind of personality that humans warm to and admire—and large organizations abhor. Only through the intervention of Marshall and Eisenhower was Patton saved from repeated efforts at self-immolation—the "slapping" incidents in Sicily, where Patton struck hospitalized GIs the general thought were malingering. That process cost Patton his close friendship with Ike.

Despite his brusque demeanor, Patton cared deeply for his own troops. Like the better-advertised actions of Eisenhower, Bradley, and Hodges, Patton saw to the welfare of his men. Remembering his own World War I experience, he saw to it that drying rooms were established for frontline troops caught in the incessant Lorraine rain of fall 1944. He personally wrote and distributed detailed instructions on the prevention of trench foot. To his subordinates, he stressed the individual officers' responsibility for the health and well-being of their troops at all times.[4]

Behind the tough image stood a towering intellect self-taught in the operational art. While he struck an anti-intellectual tone popular with the culture that produced him, here was an officer who had spent a lifetime thinking deeply about his profession. "The source of his genius was in his library and on the job learning, rather than in the Army schooling system."[5] Patton read extensively on strategy and the operational art, glossing many of the works as he read. British General Essame, who wrote a book analyzing Patton as a military commander, stated, "In the hours of peace time reading and reflection which he had spent in his study lies part of the explanation of his speed of decision when these very problems arise again in a new form."[6] Patton was the master of mechanized warfare in exploitation. Once on the move he made decisions quickly and maneuvered his units with speed and confidence. Von Rundstedt considered him a far more dangerous opponent than Montgomery.[7] *Patton simply moved faster than the Germans could react. As much as his tanks, Patton's mental agility created the speed of his maneuvers.*[8]

Patton was also influenced by his belief that he was a warrior continuously reincarnated through the long march of time. History influenced him heavily, as we shall see in discussing Metz. Patton felt it was his destiny to attack through Lorraine and conquer Germany. This was the same route where his revered World War I commander, General Pershing, intended to win that war.[9]

Much of Patton's focus was on leadership and the human element of combat. Why do men fight? During the fall 1944 campaign he stated that the principal job of an army commander is "telling somebody who thinks he is beaten that he is not beaten."[10] Patton reflected, "It is really amazing what the determination on the part of one man can do to many thousands."[11] A man of action, Patton wrote early in his career that "execution is to planning as 5:1." By 1944 he changed the proportion in his combat notes to 90/10. He understood the value of face-to-face communication with subordinate commanders and the importance of overseeing the execution of orders. Despite his tough reputation, Patton constantly praised good performance and was very slow to remove a subordinate having a tough go of it.

Patton and Eisenhower shared a mentor—Fox Conner. General Conner was Patton's commanding officer in Hawaii during the mid-twenties. Clausewitz was one of many books George worked through under the elder officer's guidance. In the margins beside the German author's passage "if the object of combat is not the destruction of the enemy force but merely shaking the enemy's feeling of security, we go only so far in the destruction of his forces as is sufficient" George wrote, "BUNK always go the limit."[12] Conner wrote in Patton's efficiency report, "I have known him for fifteen years in both peace and war. I know of no one who I would prefer as a subordinate officer."[13]

Bradley had always been ambivalent about his old boss. He was horrified to see Patton risk men's lives in Sicily just to beat Monty to Massena. Patton had no American rival in large-scale mobile warfare. However, as Third Army approached the Moselle, Bradley mused, "I was not sure how good a tactician he would be in a tough fight."[14]

As in chapter 5, we back the calendar up to early September. SHAEF's master plan, FWD13765 (chapter 3) has been issued on 4 September. It directed a primary attack on the Ruhr north of the Rhine and a secondary attack toward the Saar. That Saar attack fell almost exclusively to Patton. Recall that Ike, Bradley and Patton had met at Chartres prior to the order's issuance. Patton and Bradley had wheedled permission from Eisenhower to advance in Lorraine when Ike had been determined to place him on a shorter leash.

PATTON'S INITIAL CAMPAIGN PLANNING

Like a good chess player, Patton always thought many moves ahead. He was always thinking about the next campaign as well as the current battle and how they fit together. This is the mark of an operational level thinker.

Patton was familiar with Lorraine from World War I. It was the site of his first tank battles. Before returning to the States he had traveled extensively in this part of France. As early as August 21st, Patton was planning for his advance beyond the Meuse. Even though he contemplated pursuit, unlike Hodges and Bradley, he did not want to advance with all units abreast. He wanted to attack toward a line Metz-Nancy-Epinal with two corps forward and one back to give depth and provide a reserve. When Manton Eddy, the XII Corps commander, asked about flank security, Patton responded, "[T]hat depends on how nervous you are by nature. . . . [B]y advancing in depth—that is one division following the other—that lack of defense is immaterial."[15]

On the 29th, several days before the meeting with Eisenhower and Bradley at Chartres, Patton traveled to that city and buttonholed Ike's operations officer, General Bull, who was visiting Bradley's forward headquarters, Eagle TAC. Patton reiterated his case. This chapter's opening quote records Bull's response. The news got worse. Bradley told Patton that yesterday's zeroing of Third Army's gasoline ration was not a one-day anomaly. Third Army's supply tonnage would be curtailed for several weeks to come.

Patton wanted the ball. When it was given to him, he could run. But the decision on the main effort was made two echelons above him. Patton could, should, and did forward his ideas on strategy. But when the decision was made, Patton's job was to create and execute battle plans that achieved his commander's intent, not to scheme to get the ball back.

Patton's point of view was from the wrong end of a telescope. The important question was how best to defeat the entire German war machine. Running a few unsupported divisions into the Siegfried Line wouldn't do that. Gee Gerow and the 5th Armored proved that in the Ardennes (chapter 5).

Patton repeatedly quoted Kipling: "Fill the unforgiving minute with sixty seconds' worth of distance run." By August 31st, the "minute" for the Moselle was already lost. Three panzer grenadier divisions (3 and 15PGD newly arrived from Italy plus 17SS PGD) barred Patton's way. Had the gas drought never occurred, Third Army would have crossed the Moselle and even entered Metz. But Model had enough in front of Patton's lead elements to cause Third Army to deploy for battle. If gas shortage hadn't stopped him at the Meuse, panzer grenadiers would have repulsed any unsupported attack east of the Moselle. Either way, Patton wasn't going to reach the Rhine in early September with any achievable permeation of supply and transport allocation. To say otherwise is to perpetuate a myth that is not consistent with German capability at the time.

Nevertheless, at the Chartres meeting with Eisenhower on 2 September, Bradley and Patton continued to harangue the supreme commander about moving V Corps south. As his subsequent deployment of Third Army will demonstrate, Patton knew moving a corps into the Ardennes would do nothing to help his advance. He contributed to one of the major errors of early September: insufficient weight and concentration of First Army's attack north of the Ardennes.

Everyone was looking at avenues of approach that extended all the way to the Rhine. The shorter road and rail lines went east from Metz to Saarbrücken on the German border and then northeast to Mannheim. A parallel route via Nancy and Morhange to Saarbrücken wasn't much longer. Saarbrücken lies on the Saar River, which is a barrier to further movement toward the Rhine. The West Wall lines its far bank. Armies moving from the Moselle and the Saar also have to cross the usually small Seille River, which is a tributary of the Moselle. Sixty-five kilometers southeast of Nancy lies another opening in the escarpment protecting the Moselle, known as the Charmes "Gap" or "Trough" (Trouée de Charmes).

Metz, the historic guardian of Lorraine, bristled with deep fortifications. Several rings of stout forts guarded the city. A number of them were sited on high ground west of the Moselle. Their observation and guns dominated the surrounding territory. Despite being old, the fortresses proved almost immune to any weapon short of a direct hit by large-caliber artillery or bombs. The city has a history as citadel that goes back to the Romans. Attila the Hun was the last attacker to successfully sack the city, in AD 54.

By contrast Nancy had been neither capital nor bishopric. No one had fortified the city. While both are transportation nodes, Nancy is the more important of the two. Just west of Nancy the river splits into two streams. The Moselle proper winds 15 kilometers southeast of the city. Nancy is closer to the Mortagne River, which flows northeast. A dense woods, the Forêt de Haye, lies between the Moselle and Nancy. To the east several large buttes and escarpments, known as the Grand-Couronne, canalize and dominate movement toward the Saar and ultimately the Rhine.

Unlike Aachen to the north, neither Lorraine town absolutely corks the path east. Each has a major trunk railroad that converges on Saarbrücken, a fortified link of the West Wall to the east. These two lines delineate the two major axes of advance in Third Army's area. Positions at Metz and Nancy were too distant to provide mutual support. Units in one town could not fire on or intervene in the events around the other. Lack of mutual support is important to understand. An attacking army could advance via one without capturing the other.

While screwing up theater strategy, Patton made some very astute assessments of the upcoming advance into Lorraine. Tacticians pay very close attention to topography. Folds in the ground determine intervisibility—who can see whom in a firefight. In turn that immensely affects the weapons that can get into a given firefight, where to maneuver to bring those weapons to bear, and who ultimately prevails. Patton held that maneuver of large units was dependent on transportation corridors rather than folds in the ground. Study the road net and the rivers to find the best axis of advance. Once that has been determined let your tactical commanders examine the ground on the selected axis. They will pick out the topography that will most facilitate the fire and maneuver required to move up it. In other words, make operational decisions on operational-level considerations and then let tactical commanders do their job in order to achieve the operational design.

Using this approach, Patton identified what he called the "Nancy Gap" as the best approach to the West Wall. "If you find a large number of big roads leading through a place, this is the place to go regardless of enemy resistance. It is useless to capture an easy place that you can't move from."[16] Combining his knowledge of history and a map inspection, he identified the bridge, or *pont*, at Pont à Mousson, about 27 kilometers north of Nancy, as a high-speed ancillary approach within the Nancy axis.

It is difficult to imagine a Patton in command of First Army hitting the Aachen Gap with insufficient power and reserves to finish the job while his subordinate corps wandered off into the Stolberg Corridor and the Ardennes.

Patton identified a possible Rhine crossing at Worms.[17] He identified Nancy was the correct portal. If Patton had only remained concentrated on this objective instead of spreading his initial effort along the Moselle from Nancy to Metz, the history of the Lorraine Campaign would have been a happier story for American arms.

THIRD ARMY

In the rapid exploitation across France, Third Army continuously chased and beat up a crumbling Wehrmacht. Over mile after mile of roads lined with smashed German equipment, Patton's rampaging columns passed through lines of waving mademoiselles, swigged captured champagne, and won many small engagements while suffering few casualties. Few armies were ever in better spirits. Everyone anticipated the opportunity to relieve themselves into the Rhine.

By 29 August the Third had been reduced to a two-corps army. Its third cohort, VIII Corps, was back in Brittany laying siege to Brest. Patton recommended it be removed from Third Army so he could concentrate on the battle to the east. On 5 September VIII Corps was transferred to the newly fielded Ninth Army. On that date Third Army contained:

XII Corps	XX Corps
4th Armored Division	7th Armored Division
35th Infantry Division	5th Infantry Division
80th Infantry Division	90th Infantry Division
2nd Cavalry Group	3rd Cavalry Group

On 25 August, Bradley promised to return XV Corps to Third Army. Initially it consisted of French 2nd Armored Division and 79th Division, already mentioned, that was coming down from First Army. It wouldn't arrive until after Third Army's assault on the Moselle was under way. Until they assembled, 35ID would be engaged in guarding the army group's south flank.

As late as 8 September, Patton continued to ask Bradley to release 6AD and 83ID from their security mission along the Loire. Patton made the critical point. "But Bradley said 'I can't take the risk.' And by so saying takes a much worse risk."[18] In order to concentrate enough force to be successful at the critical point, one must accept risk at noncritical points. Had Bradley accepted more risk in early September with both First and Third Armies, his casualty lists for the final four months of 1944 might have been much shorter.

Third Army included fifty-one non-divisional field artillery battalions, twenty-three antiaircraft battalions, and fifteen tank destroyer battalions. Twenty engineer combat battalions and three engineer general service regiments gave Third Army more engineer capability than First Army, which made the main effort and had the Roer to contend with.

The ever-aggressive, if bombastic, Major General Walton Walker herded XX Corps toward Verdun. Walker was short and on the rotund side. His face was a perpetual scowl, and he always had a head of stream. Walker tended to display a self-important impatience with everything. This had quite the opposite than intended affect on many officers. Walker knew his business, however. He was Patton's favorite. "Walker would accomplish great feats—if he didn't burst first," quipped the Third Army commander.

Walker's admiration of his boss bordered on worship. Patton referred to the XX Corps commander as "a fighting son of a bitch." Walker was always ready to fight and willingly carried out his superior's orders. Walker, USMA 1912, had been cited for gallantry in World War I while commanding a machine gun battalion.

Major General Manton Eddy, only recently elevated to command XII Corps, moved toward Toul. Patton and Bradley agreed that he had done an outstanding job leading 9ID. He had commanded that division under Patton in both Africa and Sicily. Bradley called Eddy's "100 mile drive from Orleans, France to Troyes, one of the most electrifying of the war."[19] Unlike most other corps commanders, Eddy was not a West Pointer. He obtained a commission in the Regulars in 1916. During World War I he served with a machine gun unit that saw a lot of combat. Eddy was wounded in the fighting. Manton was a heavyset man, and his personal chef always set a good table. Despite his comfortable HQ, he was a hard-driving commander with a reputation for excellent tactical execution. Eddy was a nervous sort and tended to worry. On more than one occasion, Patton had to buck him up and steady his nerve. In postwar Leavenworth's classrooms, Eddy's timidity around Nancy has been roundly criticized. Toward the end of September, after Eddy seemed to lose his nerve in the face of a German counterattack Patton mused about relieving him. But he concluded that no one better was available. Instead, after cussing him out, Patton said, "Now I will go home as I know you will win."[20] That act is a measure of Patton's remarkable leadership skill and his courage in delegating to his subordinates.

During the fall, Eddy operated under an additional handicap. "P." (for "Professor") Wood, the high-strung but highly regarded commander of 4th Armored Division, had little respect for his boss. He felt Eddy did not understand proper employment of armor in mobile warfare and was not about to listen to someone who didn't. This interpersonal conflict underscored a major difference between infantry officers schooled in the Benning tradition of smooth coordinated advance and the cavalry tradition of wide sweep and deep penetration that devolved onto the armor branch. Patton described Wood as his best division commander. Unfortunately, Wood's uncurbed insubordinate behavior would ultimately force Patton to relieve him.

Patton thought highly of Major General Wade Haislip and was "delighted" to have him back.[21] Haislip had performed exceptionally well leading XV Corps in the race across France. Wade was at West Point with the two army commanders he would serve under—Patton and Patch. He had brought up XV Corps staff since assuming command in February 1943. They had served together from the Desert Training Center through Northern Ireland and across France. XV Corps staff was considered one of the best in the ETO.[22] By September, XV Corps had compiled an impressive combat record. Haislip showed adaptability in getting along well with Leclerc, the brilliant but very prickly commander of French 2nd Armored Division.

Haislip's relations with Patton and Third Army staff were excellent. But Seventh Army staff thought "Wade was something of a screamer."[23] Haislip would spend a significant part of the fall in Patch's Seventh Army. While they were not close, Patch had great respect for Haislip. Sandy described him as well educated and informed, with an excellent mind, and persuasive. However, he wanted detailed orders from above and was sensitive toward criticism.[24] Like Walker, he had to fight to keep his weight down. His "physique was not impressive."

The popular perception of Patton is that of a lone warrior staring off into the distance while he formulated his strategy. While Patton's will often towered over everyone in his presence, he was a great believer in thoroughly completed staff work. He picked his staff carefully and fought hard to protect them. In private his senior officers could address him as "Georgie." Colonel Brenton Wallace, assistant G3 on Patton's staff observed "The Old man hated show and sham. He was interested in one thing only, efficiency. . . . if you knew your job, you were allowed to perform it in your own way and you were never told how to do a thing, only requested in a quiet gentlemanly way to do it."[25]

There was no question of who was boss. However, Patton believed in building a consensus among his senior commanders. "Patton never launched a campaign without first thoroughly exploring it with his senior commanders. He never jammed an operation down their throats. It was his practice to assemble the corps commanders in the War Room, have the Planning Group outline a proposed operation, and then invite the former to 'work it over.' He encouraged free and frank discussion."[26] Sounds a little like Ike's approach. It was also the antithesis of Hodges's First Army—and Montgomery's army group HQ.

While he felt it necessary to put on his "war face" to motivate the troops, he talked to officers in a different vein. Many were still afraid of this aloof, intense warrior. But staff members were free to voice an independent opinion and be seriously heard out. You could change Georgie's mind. Patton believed in mission-type orders and gave his subordinates freedom to execute his directives by whatever means they saw fit. Patton knew how to build a team and wield it effectively. In return his subordinates were intensely loyal to him.

Much of Third Army's staff had worked together since the Western Task Force in the invasion of North Africa in 1942. Major General Hugh J. Gaffey was chief of staff. Like Patton, he was a tanker. He had been chief of staff to Patton at II Corps in North Africa and commanded 2nd Armored Division in Sicily. He was very reluctant to give up divisional command but did so at Patton's request. Brigadier General Hobart R. "Hap" Gay, assistant chief of staff, was an old cavalry man and fellow polo player. Loyal to a fault, he had served as Patton's chief of staff in both North Africa and Sicily. He did know how to run an efficient staff. Gay was Patton's closest confident and one of his principal tactical advisors. Hap was no great thinker and tended to reflect Patton's ideas instead of identifying weak arguments. Because of his lack of breadth, both Eisenhower and Beetle Smith suggested to Patton that he be replaced. Georgie stubbornly refused but did bring in Gaffey.

Prior to serving with Patton, few Third Army staff officers had much of a reputation. Patton knew how to coax outstanding results from ordinary officers. That is a mark of an outstanding leader.

In Colonel O. W. Koch, Patton did have a crackerjack G2. During the German counterattack at Mortain Patton became deeply impressed with ULTRA. Despite his bombastic statements about disregard for the enemy, Patton wanted all the information ULTRA could provide. He sat with his ULTRA handler every day and listened carefully to what he had to say.[27] Patton felt staff work began with the G2. He never made a move without first consulting with Koch. But the Third Army commander liked to be his own intelligence analyst and do the final intelligence integration himself. He believed he was blessed with a "sixth sense" that allowed him to discern the intentions of his opponent.

Initially Patton did not like to work with logistics and tended to ignore logistical constraints. Sometimes this led him to make some grievous errors. Patton learned and improved in this dimension as the campaign progressed. However, he relied heavily on Colonel Walter Muller, his G4, to handle all logistical matters and keep them away from the CG. While the Third Army commander did not like to acknowledge logistical constraints, he loudly praised the work of his own logistician. Muller was a "can-do man" who produced practical solutions in short order. If Patton had been a general for Caesar in a previous life, then Muller had been Ali Baba of Forty Thieves fame.

Unlike First Army, few of Third Army's units had experienced the frustrating, bloody close-in fighting of Normandy's hedgerows. Only a few of Patton's divisions had seen intense combat. While this may have made them a more optimistic group, the army's tactical leadership tended at the beginning of the Lorraine Campaign to underestimate the difficulty of dislodging determined defenders from good defensive position.

GERMAN DEFENSES

The amount of concentration Third Army would need would primarily be a function of the amount of resistance that lay before them. ULTRA had already detected the panzer grenadier divisions, which were enough of a concern.

Generaloberst Johannes Blaskowitz commanded Army Group G, which controlled First Army, opposing Patton, and Nineteenth Army, which defended the south of France. An east Prussian and member of the old German Officer Corps, he had a reputation of being a solid if nonpolitical commander who had gotten crosswise with Himmler. Hitler sacked Blaskowitz for allowing Patton to establish Third Army across the Moselle; General der Panzertruppen Otto von Knobelsdorff, a Russian front veteran and Hitler favorite, commanded First Army. While brave and steady in times of crisis, he was no towering tactician.[28]

The enemy retreating back from France was in a sorry state. In late August, German First Army mustered nine infantry battalions, two field artillery batteries, three flak batteries, ten anti-tank guns and ten tanks.[29] Nineteenth Army had lost 1,316 of 1,418 artillery pieces in its retreat from Southern France.[30] As General Mellenthin, Army Group G chief of staff (1A), stated, "Those of us who had come from the Russian front, where the German formations were still in tolerable fighting order, were shocked at the condition of our western armies."[31] This was the picture American corps-level intelligence officers saw. Had they the ability to see deeper, they would have been startled at the enemy forces converging on the Moselle.

At the end of August, Hitler recognized two priorities above all others on the western front. Now that Antwerp had fallen, the banks of the Scheldt must be held and the estuary mined. Second, Patton had to be stopped.

Hitler demanded Patton be counterattacked. On 3 September he ordered Model to concentrate his largest armored force on upper the Moselle to strike into Patton and the American flank.[32] ULTRA picked up Hitler's attack orders and informed Patton he was about to be hit.[33] But the general did not take the threat as seriously as he should have.

Several layers of defenders were forming ahead of Third Army. Metz contained large Nazi NCO and OCS schools. Division 462, created from student regiments, would turn in a first-rate performance during the battle for Metz. Ninety-Second Luftwaffe Field Regiment, formed from school troops in Nancy, also fought with distinction. Regardless of the timing of reinforcements from other theaters, these troops would have prevented a *coup de main* in their respective cities.

A bleeding and punched-up 17SS Panzer Grenadier Division assembled in Metz on 31 August. This was the principal mobile formation that had attempted to contain Patton during the last days of the pursuit. The gasoline-induced respite allowed this formation to draw replacements from 49th and 51st SS Panzer Grenadier Brigades. The 49SS had already been chewed up by elements of XX Corps in delaying actions between the Seine and the Marne. With this infusion, 17SS came back up to strength.

The gas-induced pause allowed the two panzer grenadier divisions detraining from Italy time to set up defensive positions. Third and 15th Panzer Grenadier Divisions (less one regiment sent to contain U.S. V Corps to the north) took up positions along the Moselle on 1–2 September.[34] While these veterans of Field Marshal Kesselring's (German commander in Italy) masterly campaign of delay in Italy did not arrive with their organic armor, they represented cohesive, potent combat power. On good defensive terrain, these two divisions by themselves would have given the four to six lead divisions of Patton's army a good fight. There was more. On 1 September less capable volks grenadier divisions, the 553rd and the 559th, detrained in Lorraine. They would fight long and hard. Two other divisions, handpicked by Hitler, were entrained and en route.

With this mosaic in view one can understand Colonel Koch's intelligence summary:

> Despite the crippling factors of shattered communications, disorganization and tremendous losses in personnel and equipment, the enemy nevertheless has been able to maintain a sufficiently cohesive front to exercise an over-all control of his tactical situation. His withdrawal, though continuing, has not been a rout or mass collapse.
>
> Numerous new identifications in contact in recent days have demonstrated clearly, that, despite the enormous difficulties under which he is operating, the enemy is still capable of bringing new elements into the battle area and transferring some from other fronts.
>
> It is clear from all indications that the fixed determination of the Nazis is to wage a last ditch struggle in the field at all costs. It must be constantly kept in mind that fundamentally the enemy is playing for time.[35]

While this is not what he wanted to hear, Patton listened. A lesser staff officer would have not been so courageous. Koch was warning his boss that the general's preconceived "sure thing" was not consistent with German combat power that lay to Third Army's front. For this, Farago has written, Koch deserved the Medal of Honor.

The panzer grenadiers would not be dislodged by recon patrols or unsupported tank columns. Nevertheless, Patton maintained his belief that rapid advance through Lorraine and into the heart of Germany was possible.

Lorraine had changed hands between Germany and France three times in the prior one hundred fifty years. The nationality of the indigenous population began to change at its border. Since 1940, a Germanization campaign had removed 35,000 French-speaking citizens and brought in a large number of ethnic Germans. GIs noticed a sullenness among Lorraine's civilians they had not previously experienced. Patton was not fond of the province. He half jokingly referred to it as a "nasty country where it rains every day and where the whole wealth of the people consists in assorted manure piles."[36] When not mixed with rain and being churned to slop by tank treads, the farmland here was very productive. However, it rained almost constantly during the fall of 1944. Patton observed, "There is about four inches of liquid mud over everything and it rains all the time, not hard but steady. Combining his knowledge of history and a map inspection, he identified the bridge (*pont*) at Pont à Mousson, about 27 kilometers north of Nancy, as a high-speed ancillary approach within the Nancy axis.

PATTON'S PLAN OF ATTACK

Several intelligence sources outlined a coherent defense forming in front of Third Army. But Patton maintained the defenders wouldn't amount to much. He revealed his inner feelings in response to a reporter's question: "You can't have men retreating for 300 or 400 miles and then hold anything—the psychological result of long retreats."[37] Patton always denigrated large fixed fortifications as nothing more than monuments to the stupidity of man. He continued, "As soon as a man gets in a concrete line, he immediately says, "the other man must be damn good, or I wouldn't have to get behind this concrete."[38]

In 1944, the American Army did not use the term "operational level of war." One of the most serious students of war in the service, Patton knew more about campaign planning and the maneuver of large units than any other American officer. His plan, released 5 September, was journeyman

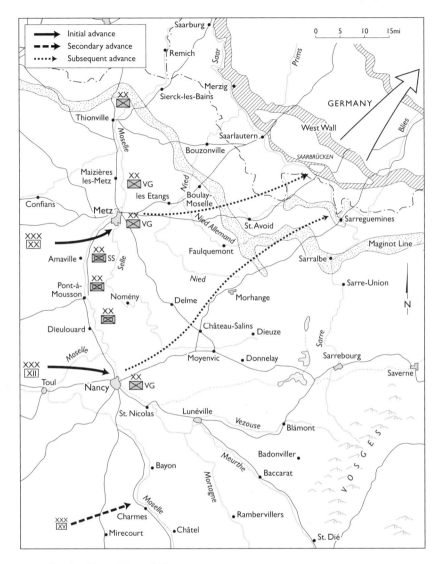

Map 6.1. Third Army's Initial Plan

work. Third Army's area of operation extended north-south through 125 kilometers of rolling terrain. Patton concentrated his troops on about 50 kilometers of it. Pursuant to Bradley's instructions, Patton envisioned a two-part operation to the Rhine.[39] First, his army would achieve a bridgehead over the Moselle. In the second phase Third Army would slice through Lorraine and seize a bridgehead over the Rhine.

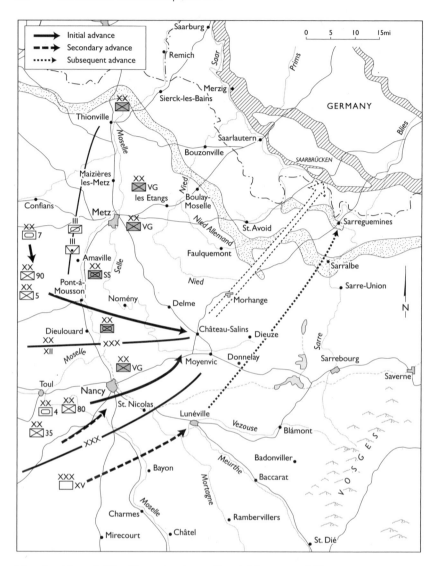

Map 6.2. Alternate Plan Concentrating on Pont à Mousson and Nancy

Tactically, Patton preferred to make assaults on the smallest possible frontage with the largest possible artillery support.[40] Despite his reputation, Patton cared deeply for his troops and employed these methods to keep casualties to a minimum. He frequently pointed out that armored warfare, while hard on the iron beasts, resulted in far shorter casualty lists than infantry combat. He thought siege warfare to be folly.[41]

XX Corps would cross the Moselle near Metz, seize that city, and then subsequently cross the Rhine at Mainz (map 6.1). XII Corps would cross the Moselle and seize Nancy, then cross the Rhine near Manheim. Patton liked some depth in his attack formations. While he didn't quite have control of XV Corps, he planned to echelon it to his right upon its attachment to Third Army and instructed it to be ready to pass through the bridgeheads of either of its lead corps. Of course, the champion of filling the unforgiving minute moved out as soon as he could. Waiting for XV Corps would certainly have been a mistake.

But on the 3rd, Third Army divisions ready for operations equaled the force that Collins commanded in VII Corps at the beginning of the Cobra breakout. Instead of covering both high-speed avenues of advance through Lorraine, why not initially attack the most important one via Nancy? (See map 6.2.) Advance one corps directly toward Nancy and the other against Pont à Mousson, already identified as an important adjunct just north of Nancy. A concentrated Third Army should make short work of the defenders there and blow the road to Mannheim wide open. Subsequently XV Corps could be used to reinforce and widen this attack or to start a second one just north of Metz to surround that city if that proved necessary. The one thing all combat to date had proven is that infantry in prepared positions in the woods or in large towns required extended heavy combat by large numbers of troops and a lot of time to overcome. There was no reason that Patton's fast-moving columns would want to get bogged down in any of that. And a concentrated Third Army would be better prepared to fight through large defending formations, should all the intelligence and ULTRA people be right.

THIRD ARMY TACKLES THE MOSELLE

The Moselle itself is not large, averaging 50 meters across and 2 deep. However, it is a swiftly flowing stream, making assault crossing and pontoon bridging difficult. Its steep-sided valley is as much an impediment to military maneuver as is the river itself. Coming from the west, there is quite a drop to reach the floor of the narrow Moselle Valley. On the opposite side of the river lies a series of heights that allow a defender to dominate any attempted river crossing. There is a break about halfway between the two cities where a major road crosses at Pont à Mousson. Since ancient times this approach has been a favorite of invading armies moving in either direction. As one moves from west to east, the tableland of the Lorraine plain narrows as it approaches the Franco-German border along the Saar River.

Neither American corps had much of a picture of enemy dispositions along the Moselle. Both treated the initial action as a movement to contact. Such operations are best accomplished with the smallest possible unit exposed to first contact with the enemy. A string of broken-down vehicles littered their approach. No unit had done much maintenance in the last month.

On 1 September 3rd Cavalry Group, XX Corps, having captured four thousand gallons of gas from the Luftwaffe, sped a small recon element 120 kilometers from the Meuse to the Moselle. Several mechanized patrols set up observation on the river before being chased away by the Germans. Reaching the river 12 kilometers north of Metz, the scouts reported Germans retreating away from that fortress city.[42]

Planners had some information on the fortress of Metz. The forts extended 15 kilometers north and 30 kilometers south of the city. No one expected the "outdated" Metz fortifications to be much of a problem. Walker had the good sense not to attack the fortified zone directly. He looked for an intact Moselle bridge that could be the target of a *coup de main*. Metz would be bypassed "if it doesn't fall like a ripe plum." XX Corps armor would strike out toward bridges over the Saar 45 kilometers east of Metz. Similar to Collins at Stolberg, XX Corps staff thought in terms of exploitation. After encircling Metz, the corps staff planned a drive that would take XX Corps across the Rhine at Mainz and then straight up the Main River valley from that town was Frankfurt.

On 2 September Walker opened his operation with a diversion. Elements of 7th Armored feinted north toward Sedan. By siphoning gas from many vehicles, the division was able to mobilize enough armor to make the move appear credible. Initially XX Corps had little intelligence about German dispositions along the Moselle. By 5 September XX Corps cavalry probes had identified significant defensive positions in that portion of Metz west of the river. However, corps officers continued to underestimate the defensive strength of Metz and its ring of forts. Even the postwar history described them as "the poorly manned fortifications of Metz."[43]

While XX Corps made its initial advance to contact, Eddy's XII Corps began its assault on the Moselle just north of Nancy. Pont à Mousson, 27 kilometers north of Nancy, immediately attracts a tactician's eyes. It was the fastest way to get free of the Moselle and its escarpment. After all, rapid movement to the Rhine was the mission. Nancy could be assaulted overland from the rear.

As a high-speed avenue of approach, it also attracted defenders. Over time, the best approach for a hasty attack against an unprepared enemy often becomes one of the most heavily prepared defensive sectors. Third PGD elements moved into the area during 1–2 September. Despite FFI* reports of the reinforcement, XII Corps G2 incorrectly advised 80ID there wasn't much across the river to oppose them.[44] The Americans didn't recognize that a major collision was about to occur.

While he attacked with two corps abreast, Patton designated XII Corps at Nancy as the main effort. About 15 kilometers south of Pont à Mousson the river splits. (See map 6.2.) The channel that continues south is called the Meurthe. Nancy is tucked along its east bank. The Moselle runs west-southwest to Toul and then bends southwest. Ground contained in the resulting triangle between the Moselle bend and Nancy is dominated by a heavily wooded and deeply cut high ground known as the Forêt de Haye.

Eddy had two only divisions available for the Moselle crossing. Thirty-Fifth Infantry Division was still tied up in the southern flank guard mission. The jump across the Moselle was only an intermediate operation. Patton had tasked XII Corps to go all the way to Mannheim. He planned to assault on the 5th. Montgomery's 30 Corps had just captured Antwerp, and U.S. First Army was still involved around Mons and was nowhere near the Meuse. Eddy's secondary attack was a week ahead of the movements to the Rhine that the main attack up north would have to make.

Eddy's concept of operations placed his divisions in column, one behind the other. Eightieth Infantry Division would attack with all three regiments abreast. McBride would execute a hasty attack from an approach march. One regiment, after moving from its assembly area 25 kilometers from the river, was to make the assault crossing at Pont à Mousson and prepare for CCA, 4th AD to follow as the exploiting force. A sister regiment would attack at Millery about 14 kilometers south. The third regiment would attack due east from Toul through the Forêt de Haye and advance directly on Nancy. Twenty-two kilometers separated the effort emerging from Toul from the next closest attack at Millery. Eddy hoped this looked like a straightforward main attack toward Nancy. In fact, it was a diversion.

At corps level, the disposition of 4AD provided some depth. Eddy planned to feed 4th Armored through the bridgehead at Pont à Mousson. It would sweep around and encircle Nancy. Against a weak enemy, it was a bold plan. If it could be set free, a concentrated 4AD could lunge deep. That's what Eddy's commander, Patton, was looking for. The subordinate was attempting to meet his commander's intent.

*French Forces of the Interior, or Maquis: French citizens as organized resistance.

Essentially, 80ID was committing itself to a frontal attack across a defended river line along a 30-kilometer front when enemy dispositions were unknown. That breaks just about every tactical rule. Patton always made a distinction between speed and haste. Attacking without proper reconnaissance and not retaining a strong reserve were unforgivable sins. Third Army had a lot of artillery. Eddy and McBride should have secured much stronger support. The overnight delay provided ample emplacement time.

Patton visited XII Corps on the 3rd. He was more interested in discussion about breaching the West Wall than worrying about crossing the Moselle. He must be charged with not sufficiently reviewing and correcting a very faulted plan. Most likely, his prejudgment that the Germans wouldn't put up much of a defense was the source of the error. However his ULTRA-derived information about the dispositions of 3 and 15 PGD, incidentally units from successful operations in Italy, not stragglers from the retreat across France, told him otherwise.

Patton had fought over this ground in 1918. While forward, the emotional Patton visited the huge monument to remember World War I American dead at Montsec. While there, he might have thought a little more of the gambles with his men's lives that he was taking by pushing so hastily into unknown enemy defenses without properly taking into account German strength.

The then current operations manual depicted a stylized river-crossing operation.[45] First attackers cross the river, most likely on assault boats, and establish a beachhead. Second, assault forces capture the high ground to deny enemy observation of the planned bridge site. Finally, heavy bridging is emplaced and reinforcements secure the bridgehead. He knew the World War I rule of thumb that attackers needed 3–1 superiority at the point of contact to prevail against defenders who had gotten set. Six–one against improved positions and river lines would be a better estimate. Did XII Corps have anywhere this combat power against what ULTRA had informed Patton lay east of the Moselle?

The manual emphasizes the attacker must deny enemy observation of the bridge site. Engineers are not likely to get much done if the worksite is swept with machine-gun fire. Not much of their work is likely to remain intact if it is within range of observed artillery fire that can be adjusted on the bridging.

High ground on the far side of the river dominates Pont à Mousson. Germans watched the Americans as they came up the road from Flirey to their final assembly areas on the west bank. Prior to the main column coming down the road, no American had even seen this stretch of the river with his own eyes. The Americans would remain in assembly areas under enemy observation overnight and make a morning crossing. That almost guaranteed the Germans would be well prepared and at peak readiness.

There was no tactical surprise. Elements of 3 PGD on two hills near Pont à Mousson had their crossing sites under observation. Promised American air support never materialized. All XIX TAC sorties were tied up attacking Brittany. Not a single tank supported the crossing. The only artillery fire came from a sole battalion in direct support of the attacking regiment. Even then, there was a critical shortage of 105mm ammunition.

Two assault battalions placed their boats into the water at 0930, well after first light. German artillery and mortars bracketed the attackers before they got near the water. One battalion took to the ground. It did not move again until darkness. Inadequate American fire support could not silence the German guns. The other assault battalion made several attempts but could not close to the river bank; German fire was too intense. Most of the assault boats were smashed. Several night crossings were attempted. Machine-gun fire met the hapless infantrymen and engineers. A single four-platoon beachhead was finally established. Germans counterattacked. Fighting was dominated by bayonets and grenades at close range. The American position was smashed back into the river. One hundred sixty Americans were missing.

Eightieth Infantry Division's diversionary attack from Toul successfully crossed the Moselle. It didn't have strength to push through enemy blocking positions thrown up about 6 kilometers east of the river in the Forêt de Haye. The middle regiment's crossing near Millery was also successful. It too met with tremendous resistance east of the Moselle. Eightieth Infantry Division now had several major fights on its hand. But McBride didn't have sufficient reserves to influence the battle.

On the 6th Eddy called a halt to his main effort at Pont à Mousson. McBride maneuvered to establish a secure bridgehead as heavy combat continued for the better part of six days. While stalled, XII Corps was far from finished.

After the initial attempt to cross the Moselle, Patton had a chance to adjust his plan of attack. XX Corps was not decisively engaged. By the evening of 6 September it was clear that crossing the river would involve a major fight. XII Corps did not have enough strength to do the job. During the 6th only one combat command of 7th Armored was in heavy contact attempting to clear the western approaches in XX Corps's sector to the

Moselle. It was having a lot of trouble, and Patton was ready to goose the division commander, Major General Silvester. From Walker's reconnaissance, it was clear the defenses around Metz were extensive and heavily manned. An intelligent move would have been for some—or most—of XX Corps be sent south to assist in the advance *past* Nancy. Patton, usually an agile warrior ready for such maneuvers, seemed oddly detached from the fight to get over the Moselle. Instead he was still not recognizing the now apparent strong German resistance and instead was focusing on the run to the Rhine. In this manner, he was mimicking Montgomery's unrealistic assessment of German resistance in Holland to an advance to the Rhine.

Patton's attitude came through in his press conference of the 7th. In his opening statement, he said, "I am very proud of the troops of this Army for getting across the goddamn river [Moselle]." Only his army wasn't really across the river. "I hope to go through the Siegfried line like shit through a goose." In response to why he thought so, he retorted, "my natural optimism."[46] Then he made the comment about the fighting quality of soldiers who had retreated 300 miles. Yet the day before, 80th Division's attempt at a Rhine crossing had been repulsed with heavy loss of American life. Of course a wartime press conference is not a venue to explore tactical problems. But Patton showed no concern about the fact that his current attack on the Moselle was far less than successful.

Let's return to the XX Corps attack up near Metz. Fighting around the west bank forts covering the approach to Metz was a lot tougher than anyone anticipated. Several small streams that flow into the Moselle have 80-meter-deep ravines that the Germans stoutly defended. Surprisingly, Germans counterattacked 90ID *west* of the river as the Tough Hombres prepared for their river crossing. While a panzer column penetrated next to the division's HQ, the attack was thrown back with heavy German losses. XX Corps staff had enough information to modify the more rosy projections of immediate enemy withdrawal made only a few days before. Corps G2 had identified 17SS PGD in defensive positions opposing XX Corps and knew of 3 and 15 PGD. Evidence of both Panzer Lehr and 21 Panzers, more of the force being assembled for Fifth Panzer Army's counterattack, had also surfaced. However, these two divisions had moved away from the Metz area in early September during the gas drought.[47]

A platoon from 7AD crossed the river at Dornot, just south of Metz near a pair of its defensive forts on the 7th. Fifth Infantry Division passed through 7AD, reached the river, and made an assault crossing at Dornot, to bail out the armored infantry. This was a poor site selection. The Germans had excellent observation of 5ID operations from Fort Driant on the west bank and Fort Verdun to the east. Both of these forts were part of the defenses of Metz. They proved to be very well engineered.

Rain fell on the morning of the 8th. Infantry and engineers slithered down to the riverbank of the cold, fast-running Moselle. Their small wooden boats bobbled like overloaded bathtubs in the current. General Irwin, 5ID commander, positioned three 105mm artillery battalions to support the crossing. Fifth Infantry Division's attack was no surprise. The defenders repeatedly struck the infantry who made the far shore. Thirty-six separate counterattacks were counted in a sixty-hour period. German flak tanks cruised up and down a parallel road, raking the shallow bridgehead with automatic cannon fire. From this cauldron 5ID infantrymen began whispering their own password: "The wounded don't cry."[48] Members of 17SS PGD, the division that had many delaying skirmishes while retreating "300 miles" before Third Army, pressed home at least thirty counterattacks, screaming obscenities as they looked to throw the small bridgehead into the water.[49]

On the night of the 8th, Irwin concluded that a second assault crossing further south, near Arnaville, would be needed. He wanted to withdraw the men near Dornot. Walker wouldn't let him do so until a second crossing was successful. Careful preparations were made. Nine battalions of corps artillery and an engineer group assembled to support the second attack. Until Arnaville, the 84th Smoke Generator Company had been performing as a Red Ball trucking outfit. For the first time, massed smoke generators were used to cover a crossing site. After Arnaville, this became Third Army river-crossing SOP.

On the 9th and 10th, XX Corps artillery fired forty thousand rounds. Despite that impressive figure, ammunition rationing limited supporting fires. Whenever American artillery stopped, German mortars worked over the crossing site. SS panzer grenadiers on the heights poured fire directly on American infantry sprawled on the ground. About 0200 on the 10th, the second assault crossing began. Initial tactical surprise was achieved.

Forty German batteries fired on the crossing site at Arnaville. Rain added to the misery of the engineers dealing with the cold river. Many bridge sections were demolished by enemy fire, and the two bridging companies sustained 25 percent casualties in twenty-four hours. It was very clear that no one was going to leap the river and rush to the Saar. Irwin's infantry finally stabilized their bridgehead on the 12th. A Class 40 bridge spanned the river. But the fortifications of Metz intervened. On the 13th the fixed batteries of Fort Driant, which covered the western approaches to

Metz, opened up on 5ID's crossing sites. A raft was smashed, and its drifting wreckage broke up the heavy pontoon bridge. 5ID was in for a rough time.

Initially, XX Corps deployed to conduct a double envelopment of Metz. While Irwin struggled to the south, 90ID was up to the river around Thionville, 52 kilometers north of Metz. Given that the bulk of XX Corps attacked south of the fortress and XII Corps was attacking at Pont à Mousson and Nancy even further south, this was an major extension of Third Army's active front. After seeing the resistance that Irwin had encountered, Walker knew a double envelopment of Metz was more than his corps could handle.[50] He repositioned his troops to concentrate on a single envelopment from the south. Remaining Tough Hombres scowled across the river at the 559VG Division.

From the 8th to the 15th, 7AD had accomplished little save observe a few defenders in the western outskirts of Metz. Walker issued orders for elements of 7th Armored to enter Irwin's bridgehead. On the 16th, the armor crossed over the Moselle. Ninetieth Infantry Division moved elements south to cover positions directly west of Metz vacated by the tankers. By the 25th, 5ID, with armored support, had advanced about 6 kilometers from the Moselle to the banks of the Seille. But there was insufficient infantry to tear a hole in the defenders. German defensive positions along the Seille were more than even a reinforced 5ID could handle. The 17SS PGD clung tenaciously and repeatedly counterattacked. Irwin had shot his bolt.

Walker reluctantly informed his boss that he could not take the city. The 17SS Panzer Grenadier Division fought viciously to prevent Walker from establishing a secure bridgehead over the Moselle. Division 462 held the fortress. In open terrain, this formation would have been little more than a crust defense and a series of delaying detachments. Multiplied by the combination of a major river, a large city, and a hundred years of concrete fortifications, Division 462 fought Walker, an able tactician, to a halt.

Patton was bitterly disappointed. Now he was taking heat from Bradley. Based on Third Army's commander's boast, Omar had assured Ike that a major crossing of the Moselle could easily be achieved. On the 7th, 8th, and 9th, Patton, the identifier of the "unforgiving minute," lost a bunch of them. This is about the same length of time as the "gas drought" he railed against.

Bradley, worried that Patton's lead of his attempt to revive the American Plan had stalled, released 35ID to XII Corps's full control. The 12th Army Group commander pushed XV Corps forward. It assumed the flank-protection mission southwest of Nancy.

Eddy's first approach to the Moselle at Pont à Mousson had been a disaster. Like any good tactician, Eddy lost no time in reformulating his plan. Initially he thought of committing CCA, 4th Armored at Pont à Mousson — reinforcing failure. P. Wood didn't like the idea. He was vociferous about his objection. Eddy discarded the concept. On the 7th, Eddy's new plan created a second divisional attack by 35ID south of Nancy. Corps artillery would emplace to support the new effort, while the entire 4th Armored would stand ready to exploit efforts of the new right wing. Again P. Wood didn't like the idea. He balked at striking out from this bridgehead because of the number of small streams on this axes of advance. He preferred to commit his division in the north once 80ID gained success. Eddy continued to prefer committing his armor on the southern axis. He had good reason. Tactical recon finally was producing information. Cavalry reports indicated the enemy giving way in the south. Eddy decided Brigadier General Dager's CCB would follow 35ID. CCA would be held in corps reserve and go either north or south, depending on developments. After a heated exchange between Eddy and Wood, 4th Armored struck out to the east.

On the 10th, two regiments of 35ID assaulted the river south of both Nancy and the Forêt de Haye. Fifteenth Panzer Grenadiers opposed the effort. One of the first crossings was thrown back by a 15PGD counter attack. German artillery destroyed the first bridge assembled by the engineers. Even the Luftwaffe put in an ineffective appearance.

After hard fighting, 35ID achieved a secure crossing. On the evening of the 11th, CCB was ordered to cross into 35ID's bridgehead. Lack of bridging didn't stop 8th Tank Battalion from crossing the Moselle and its associated canal. A platoon of Shermans fired their 75mms into the far bank, breaking it down. Logs were thrown into the mud and tanks roared down into the river. Water surged to turret level. Tanks that bogged were pulled out by others that successfully reached dry ground. Half-tracks and even jeeps were winched across. It wasn't until next afternoon that engineers finally completed a 168-foot floating bridge.[51]

The tankers were bent on developing a breakthrough. They swung further to the east of 35ID, seeking to envelop Nancy. Desperate German counterattacks were repulsed with heavy casualties. By the night of the 14th, CCB had traveled some 20 kilometers east from the Moselle and laggered southeast of Nancy. CCB tankers stood 5 kilometers northwest of Lunéville.

Success in the south opened opportunity in the north. The enemy cannot be strong everywhere. This is a major advantage of attack on two axes. This time General Mc Bride created a fully supported attack at a weak spot in 3PGD positions a few kilometers south of Pont à Mousson (but still 20 kilometers north of Nancy) at Dieulouard, which had been briefly reconnoitered the night before the ill-fated attempt at Pont à Mousson. On the 12th, the Powder River men succeeded in securing a crossing. Nine artillery battalions and fifty massed .50 caliber machine guns manned by engineers and anti-aircraft crews fired in support of the crossing. Divisional engineers manned the boats and readied foot bridges. Corps engineers stood ready to install heavy treadway bridges that would allow tanks to cross.

On the wet heels of 35ID, CCB, 4th Armored division crossed into the bridgehead. They moved forth rapidly to the important crossroads at Château-Salins that led to Sarreguemines and Saarbrücken. Then CCB shifted south to Arracourt, due east of Nancy. CCA moving from the 80ID's crossing north of Nancy at Dieulouard and CCB moving from 35ID's crossing south of the city roared forward to encircle Nancy. It was a textbook double envelopment conducted by a corps. Hitler was outraged.

While Eddy put together his successful Moselle crossing, Haislip closed up on XII Corps's southern flank. Patton ordered XV Corps into the attack on the 11th. Initially, Haislip intended to place his two divisions in column. Instead, Patton widened XV Corps's sector, which forced the divisions to advance shoulder to shoulder. Sidestepping some entrenched Germans, Leclerc's French 2nd Armored Division maneuvered the bulk of his division deep into German positions. The French ran into 112 Panzer Brigade on the 13th. American observers vectored a gaggle of P-47s to help the French Shermans. Jabos worked the Germans over. French armor moved up through apple orchards and stands of pine and caught many Panthers in a narrow valley below them. Newly manufactured panzers were being disassembled by 75mm rounds. Only four of the Panthers limped away. Meanwhile 79ID chewed up disjointed elements of 16 Division. What was left continued to withdraw.

On 14 September, elements of French 2nd Armored Division, Third Army, met elements of French 1st Armored Division, Seventh Army, near Clefmont. Twelfth Army Group had linked up with 6th Army Group. Third Army no longer had an open southern flank. XV Corps reached the Moselle at Charmes, about 30 kilometers south of Nancy, on the 15th and advanced to positions east of Lunéville on the 22nd.

IKE SHUTS THIRD ARMY DOWN

A lot of generals were closely following events east of Nancy. On the 12th Bradley met with his army commanders and senior logistics officers. Based on the improved supply situation, Brad allowed both First and Third Armies to continue their advances.[52]

But Eisenhower had other priorities. Twenty-First Army Group was about to begin Market Garden on the 17th; VII Corps, the army group main effort, was about to attack up the Stolberg Corridor. Even these two operations taxed the supplies available. The Canadians attempted to clear the Scheldt and open Antwerp. Ike had no choice, but, in the words of order FWD 14764 (Third Army), "must push only far enough, for the moment, so as to hold adequate bridgeheads beyond the Moselle and thus create a constant threat to the German forces."

Bradley told Patton his offensive would have to be curtailed if he could not achieve a solid bridgehead by the evening of the 14th. If a bridgehead had not been achieved, part of Third Army would go over to the defensive. The remainder would move north to support V Corps in the southern portion of the Ardennes. However, Bradley "was none too anxious to shift Third Army to the north."[53] Even Montgomery communicated that he thought a "deception plan" causing the Germans to reinforce around Metz-Nancy, would be beneficial to Market Garden.[54]

Patton told Bradley that the Germans had no reserve or defenses in depth. Based on Patton's overoptimistic reports of progress along the Moselle, Brad give Ike an upbeat report on the 14th. He told the supreme commander that the next forty-eight hours would tell the story of how far Third Army would advance. With only three days to Market Garden, Ike was very encouraged. Later Bradley would criticize Patton for his less than candid assessment. Patton was still selling his case for more resources.

Despite the setbacks along the Moselle in both corps sectors, Patton was slow to acknowledge that he was up against a hardened defense. On 12th his staff determined "we had enough supplies to get to the Rhine and force a crossing."[55] Third Army had enough gas to move the 175 kilometers between the Moselle and the Rhine but had enough ammunition for only four days of heavy fighting. Remember, the West Wall sits between the Moselle and the Rhine. Patton had yet to get an exploitation force over the Moselle, let alone cover the 85 kilometers to Saarbrücken's pillboxes. The Rhine was another 100 kilometers beyond Saarbrücken. Patton knew time was running against him.

It was hard for Patton, a man who saw his destiny just 100 kilometers up the road on the banks of the Rhine, to accept that he has been told not to go there. Ex poste, it is difficult for many to accept that this was a proper constraint, as the main effort that Eisenhower was succoring failed. But it is not for a field army commander to question theater strategy once it has been decided on and announced. Patton's job was to salute and carry out his orders: tie up as many mobile German units as possible with the least consumption of supplies. All plans to attack in depth to the Rhine were now moot.

Fourth Armored had drafted almost daily plans for exploiting a Moselle bridgehead. Most drafts pushed the entire division forward as a solid mass. The success of the 80th's attack in the north reopened the 4th's preferred route and raised the possibility of a double envelopment of Nancy. That is what Eddy chose. Wood gave CCA commander Colonel Bruce C. Clarke, one of America's best armor commanders, his head. After a false start Clarke positioned his command to cross at the hotly contested 80ID bridgehead between Pont à Mousson and Nancy. Thirty-Seventh Tank Battalion, led by Creighton Abrams, took the lead. His performance in this exploitation and the upcoming battles around Arracourt would seal his legend.

The remainder of the operation to secure Nancy and move east has many interesting tactical lessons. However, nothing in September impacted decisions at the operational or theater strategic level so we will discontinue following the tactical detail.

PATTON RECONSIDERS HIS CAMPAIGN DESIGN

By the 14th, Patton had begun to recognize the error of not concentrating both his corps at Nancy. Operational commanders choose where to fight and how to concentrate for that fight. Patton's initial concept to attack on two axes (Metz and Nancy) was a major operational fault. In order to advance to the Rhine, Third Army did not need to clear both cities. Nothing but school troops and alarm battalions defended Metz. In the fortifications they were encased in, they stopped Walker's XX Corps cold. Had they been left in Metz, they would have poised no threat to XII Corps, assaulting Nancy 50 kilometers away. Had Patton concentrated two corps on the Nancy axis, we can easily speculate that the near breakthrough that did occur would have become a clean break.

Patton concocted a plan to concentrate 4th, 6th, and 7th Armored Divisions as well as 35ID and 80ID under Eddy.[56] This was solid movement in the right direction. Instead of aiming at Worms, Patton began thinking of crossing the Rhine farther south. On the 14th, he selected Mannheim. Patton directed this massive exploitation force to strike for the Rhine at Darmstadt, a little north of Mannheim. This will not be the last time we hear about this crossing point. Patton wanted to shift to a column of divisions. A reduced XX Corps would contain Metz.

On the 16th Patton issued new orders to his corps commanders. Patton "advised but did not order"[57] that Eddy attack in a column of divisions.* In that deep formation, the first assaulting division blows a hole in the enemy defense and holds it open while the follow-on units race through. The process is repeated until the attacker is completely through the defensive belt. The final division (hopefully armored) is free to enter the exploitation phase, running amuck in the enemy's rear, restoring fluid mobile warfare. The greatest American comparative advantage lay in mobile warfare.

Patton scheduled the attack for 18 September. One XII Corps division would leapfrog from the achievements of another. Fourth Armored Division would lead to the East. Hopefully the armor would seize a passage by *coup de oile*. The 35ID would follow the armor and widen the gap. Sixth Armored Division would add its weight to the forward attack, with 7AD in van. The 80ID would clean up first at Nancy and then around Saarbrücken.[58] Patton was also ready to shut the Metz operation down and concentrate on the main effort by XII Corps. Walker was concerned he could not take Metz. Patton informed him that if Metz had not fallen in a few days, 7AD would be transferred to Eddy and a truncated XX Corps would just contain Metz.[59]

If only Patton would have come to these conclusions ten days earlier at the beginning of the Moselle operations. Had he achieved such concentration of effort at the beginning of the campaign, he just might have made it to the Rhine.

XV Corps would echelon to the south and drive on Mannheim. However, this corps was to be prepared to move over the Rhine on bridges captured by one of the other corps. Patton did not succumb to layer caking. He was ready to maneuver one corps through another in order to maintain the momentum of a deep drive.

Logistics underscored the need for a single Third Army thrust. Patton's tonnage allocation would not support more than a five-division offensive.[60] A

---

*Patton's diary still mentions Worms as the objective. The official history states Darmstadt.

three-division effort at Nancy was not able to break through; a larger operation was required. Therefore two simultaneous independent attacks could not be sustained. Patton recognized the supply problem. On the 18th, he entered in his diary, "We are very short of ammunition."

Finally the correct solution! It was Patton's own. Only Eisenhower had said NO! The order holding Patton along the Moselle so the main effort up north could be fully supported was finally being enforced. Of course this looks idiotic to the commander of a secondary attack that is showing promise. But higher headquarters must make the judgment and rule. That's why they are called *orders*.

On the 20th he penned into his diary: "I was convinced then, and have since discovered I was right, there were no Germans ahead of us except those we were actually fighting. In other words, they had no depth. It was on this day that I definitely decided not to waste capturing Metz, but to contain it with as few troops as possible and drive for the Rhine."[61]

General von Mellenthin, chief of staff to Balck, the German Army Group commander, agrees that Eddy's halt was a mistake. While the Germans had created a tough crust defense along the Moselle, they did not have sufficient in-depth operational reserves. Patton decried the supply constraints that had ended his pursuit. General von Mellenthin believes the golden opportunity was on the 15th, when 4th Armored had nearly achieved breakout: "These operations were successful and Nancy fell on the 15 September, but the Americans failed to exploit a fine opportunity for a rapid advance to the Saar. General Eddy, the commander of XII Corps, turned down a request from the 4th U.S. Armored Division, whose commander, Major General J. S. Wood, realized that our First Army had no reserves and could not resist a bold thrust along the Marne Rhine Canal to Sarrebourg."[62] "At that time the West Wall was still unmanned, and no defense could have been made there."[63] Only the newly formed 113 Panzer Brigade forming along the Saar stood in the way."[64]

Of Patton's new plan to concentrate and break through, Mellenthin comments, "This was the order of a commander who could think on big lines, and who could thoroughly understand the character of armored warfare." "However XIIth Corps postponed the advance until the 18th in order to clear up German pockets near Nancy and thus gave our First Army time to concentrate in the Chateau-Salins sector."[65]

If there had been sufficient supply to allow Patton to continue, it appears likely that he would have made it all the way to the Rhine. The secondary attack might have become successful enough to have become the primary and headed toward the Ruhr, or wherever 12th Army Group could have best engaged and destroyed the Wehrmacht. But remember Market Garden was about to begin, and Bradley was promising to get past Aachen and onto Cologne. Given the severe resource constraint, Ike had little choice but to put Patton back on a leash. To recognize that the primary attack would fail when the secondary attack probably would have succeeded is Monday morning quarterbacking.

FIFTH PANZER ARMY COUNTERATTACKS

Many Allied generals thought the Germans were on the verge of collapse. Instead, Hitler had been planning to counterattack Patton's army since the beginning of September. The fuehrer found "that Cowboy General" to be the most dangerous in the Allied stable. Fifth Panzer Army HQ, with no assigned combat formations, came down from Holland on 9 September to command the effort. That was eight days before Market Garden and eight days after 30 Corps arrived in Antwerp. OKW didn't perceive Monty as the threat. Here is a benefit of Ike's two-pronged strategy. What chance would have 21st Army Group had if the three PGDs and Fifth Panzer Army had been directed to Holland?

Hitler assembled all the offensive power he could under Fifth Panzer Army and tasked them to stave in Patton's right flank. A series of tank battles swirled around Arracourt on the 18th. The 11 Panzer Division, a decimated 21 Panzer Division, and several panzer brigades with many factory-fresh tanks, were assembled for the operation. The 3 and 15th PGDs were also involved. Imagine what this force could have done if it wasn't needed in Lorraine and was available to oppose First Army around Aachen and Montgomery around Arnhem? Fourth Armored Division demonstrated its prowess by shattering newly formed panzer brigades. Patton's troops, especially 4th Armored and French 2nd Armored, destroyed much of what Manteuffel committed to the counterattack. Arracourt demonstrated that veteran American tankers, not retreaded German ones, were now master. Clarke and Abrams continued to demonstrate their skill at killing panzers. Balck learned, in the words of his chief of staff, that "American air power put our panzers at a hopeless disadvantage, and that the normal principles of armored warfare did not apply in this theater."[66] But Eddy and Patton could not feed sufficient combat power into the area to create operational-level breakthrough from tactical success. Patton's September offensive came to a close.

General Mellenthin stated that, because all available reserves had been dispatched to contain First Army at Aachen and nothing was available immediately after the battle at Arracourt, "General Patton might have [reached the Saar and the Rhine] if he had been given a free hand. At that time the West Wall was still unmanned, and no effective defense could have been made there."[67]

In a separate action in the last days of September, 559VGD, reinforced by elements of 15PGD, mounted an attack that ejected forward battalions of 35ID from their positions in Forêt de Grémecey. General Eddy, XII Corps commander, got very nervous. Patton, who was present the day the attack developed, had ordered Eddy to commit his reserve, two combat commands of 6AD, to correct the situation. Eddy hadn't done this. On the 30th, the Germans threatened to cut off two 35ID regiments. General Gaffey, Patton's chief of staff, was visiting XII Corps HQ and heard Eddy issue an order for 35ID to withdraw. Gaffey immediately called Patton, insisting that he come forward. Forty-five minutes later Patton had collected Gaffey and had driven to 6AD HQ, where Eddy and 6AD commander Grow were meeting. General Baade, CG of 35ID (who would subsequently take a bullet in the jaw in the upcoming counterattack), was summoned. Patton chewed out the XII Corps generals, "saying he was disgusted with them" for losing ground and allowing the situation to deteriorate. He instructed 6AD to retake the woods "or not come back." Patton ordered all of the generals to go forward to personally lead their troops "to make up for their [the generals'] shortcomings." Then Patton announced, "Now I will go home, as I know you will win."[68]

Sixth AD recaptured the lost ground. About midnight Patton put in a call to the XII Corps chief of staff. Later Patton recounted, "On being informed that he was asleep, I too went to bed as I knew the situation must be all right."[69] After 3PGD was pulled out to reinforce at Aachen, XII Corps pushed 553VGD back and established a bridgehead across the Seille; 553VGD held the line north of 559VGD.

PATTON ACHIEVED HIS ASSIGNED OBJECTIVE

Subsequent to the logistical problems evidenced by the gas drought, Ike had made a crucial adjustment to his two thrust theater strategy. Third Army was tasked with generating a secondary attack, not one of two co-equal thrusts. We should evaluate Patton's fall campaign against two criteria:

1. Did it materially assist the primary attack?

2. Did it create a position or opportunity to become a primary attack should the need arise?

The record supports an affirmative answer to both questions. Despite Patton's bitter pouting, a case can be made that Third Army should have received even fewer assets with which to achieve his stated operational objectives. XII Corps drew off some of the Wehrmacht's most potent armored counterattack forces and chewed them to pieces. The enemy acted as if the Lorraine threat was one of the main efforts—one cannot ask a secondary attack to achieve more. Patton met his first operational objective.

At Arracourt, American armor opened the road from Nancy to Château-Salins and ultimately Saarbrücken. Had SHAEF decided to shift their main effort, additional supplies given to a two-corps operation on this axis might easily reached the Rhine and threatened the Saar.

Patton achieved the objectives assigned to him by SHAEF strategy. Neither Hodges nor Montgomery and his lieutenants could make that statement. Third Army, as directed, generated a secondary attack, created a credible threat, and drew off significant combat power.

Patton did not violate any direct orders. In his heart, Patton had no intention of fulfilling Ike's intent. He had Bradley's acquiescence at least part of the time. As long as Patton was prosecuting his secondary attack to the hilt according to SHAEF plan, he was on the right track. When he tried to influence SHAEF strategy by attempting to get into fights not called for in order to divert resources, he was guilty of detracting from unity of command. A general of his vast understanding of the military art cannot be excused from this breach of discipline.

Unexpected success of the secondary attack is a major advantage of a two-pronged advantage. In September–October, SHAEF's main effort was not successful. Had Patton moved just a little faster, he might have created a major breakthrough. If SHAEF had modified its theater strategy to take advantage of operational breakthrough in Lorraine, the war might have been foreshortened.

METZ: THE OPERATIONAL EMPTY

Unfortunately, Patton also regressed.

While Third Army was still in England, Patton called Koch into his office. Patton had his finger on a map of France. "Koch," Patton said, "I want all of your G2 planning directed here." He was pointing at Metz.[70] Metz had been a strategic location since ancient times. Patton was very aware it had last been taken by Attila the Hun in 641. He became obsessed with becoming its next conqueror. Over time, Metz became heavily fortified. Some wag dubbed it "the Wonder City of Fortifications." By World War II its defenses included an outer ring of twenty-eight forts about 10 kilometers from city center and an inner ring of thirteen. In 1944, many officers, including Patton, scoffed at the obsolescence of these works. Instead they proved very resistant to high explosives and very tough to crack.

Patton's perception back in England was not altogether unfathomable. Lorraine sits between the Ardennes and the Vosges. It is the traditional southern approach to Germany. After the sound of September's fighting fell away Mellenthin stated: "We anticipated the next American thrust would come through the historic 'Lorraine Gateway' between Metz and the Vosges. . . . [W]e had to consider the Belfort Gap . . . but we had no doubt that the main thrust would be in Lorraine."[71] However, Patton had already identified the axis via Nancy as the best way to transit Lorraine and get over the Rhine.

Humans often grasp sharply defined symbols to represent a more ethereal underlying concept. Lorraine Gateway was the right concept. Metz by itself meant little. However, symbol is often confused for concept. This happened to Patton in October.

Balck and Mellenthin were very competent practitioners of the operational art. After the fall of Nancy, they wanted to fight a withdrawal action from Metz. With U.S. XII Corps firmly ensconced on the east side of the Moselle, there was no reason to expend scarce resources over the city. However, they feared a "stand fast" order from Hitler. So the German generals ensured no first-rate troops were committed to the city proper. The student officer/NCO ranks of Division 462 were increased to ten thousand, but only by adding second-rate troops. Not a single tank was left within the city.

Hitler did not disappoint his Army Group G leadership. Not only were the defenders of Metz to stand fast; Hitler designated the town a fortress and called upon its commander to accept being surrounded rather than retreat.

Supposedly Patton determined that Metz was too dangerous a thorn in his side. But there wasn't anything sharp in the city. Out of artillery range of Nancy and with not a single tank, how was Division 462 going to threaten anyone? Patton knew this. When he really felt he might break out, he was more than ready to have Walker's XX Corps mask Metz and to advance to the Rhine without taking the city.

The real motivation for Patton's behavior shares a common root with Brest. Writing to General Somervell on October 4, Patton said, "Yesterday we started an assault on one of the principal forts south of Metz. . . . So far we have never failed in any operation and I can see that it is desirable to inculcate in the German mind that when the Third Army attacks, it always succeeds."[72] At Metz, as at Brest, Americans got caught up in cracking a hard nut despite the fact that the interior no longer contained any useful nourishment.

Metz became Third Army's primary objective. One author labeled it "the center of gravity of Third Army's campaign." It was exactly the opposite. In Clausewitzian terms, a "center of gravity" is the enemy "hub of all power and movement on which everything depends. That is the point against which all of our energies should be directed."[73] The critical distinction is "center of all power," which if destroyed causes the enemy to fall apart. Patton made what was essentially a "throw away" delaying position his primary objective. It was a fundamental operational error that a general of his caliber never should have committed. Metz was his obsession.

Patton constantly needled Walker, CG XX Corps, about Metz. In September, Walker produced Operation Thunderbolt—a major air-ground effort to reduce the fortifications of Metz. Many American soldiers fought bravely, but to little avail. "All during October lights burned in XX CP plans for destruction of Metz and the drive to the Saar were the foremost preoccupation of all concerned."[74]

In October, when both orders and logistics shut down any serious Third Army offense, Patton began pecking at Fort Driant, one of the stoutest of the forts of Metz. Bradley didn't like this poking around Metz. "For God's sake, lay off," said Bradley.[75] But Patton felt he couldn't restrict an army commander from making small-scale attacks within his own zone.

A lot of senior officers, including Ike and Montgomery, came to observe the proceedings at Metz. Patton became more anxious to complete his victory. Patton ordered Walker "to completely occupy Ft Driant if it took every man in the Corps."[76] Artillery and air bombardment simply couldn't penetrate several feet of reinforced concrete. By the fall every commander in ETO should have understood that attacking determined defenders ensconced under layers of concrete is a very unproductive way to use good infantry.

This battle got out of hand. The commanders on the scene knew the effort was fruitless. General Gay went forward to see what he could do. Finally Gay called a halt to the operation on 12 October. Later Patton admitted that beginning the assault on Driant was a mistake. Patton mused in his diary, "I was over optimistic in Letting 5th Division to start" attacking the fort.[77] That division finally quit hurling itself against all that concrete on 13 October, after suffering eight hundred casualties. Patton was badly shaken by the failure. Walker would remain involved with that fortress until mid-November.

Metz became a contest of operational illogic. Even General Patton recognized the Nancy-Château-Salins axis should be his primary effort. Both Patton and Hitler erred in concluding the city had any value. But the actions of Balck and Mellenthin created conditions that made the fight work strongly in the Germans' favor. In essence, Metz become an oversized expendable combat outpost. It was not part of Germany's main defenses. For the better part of two months second-line troops in an expendable position drained off the energy and ammunition of Third Army. This was a brilliant operational performance—for Balck and his staff. The Germans caused the Americans to fight a major battle at a place that was not critical. They tied Patton down with small numbers of troops that were not necessary to overall theater defense.

7

November Rerun

In effect we are there.

General Bradley, 23 November 1944

As SHAEF's senior officers gathered in Brussels on 18 October, they collectively felt a lot of frustration. The promise of war's early end had been grounded out in unsuccessful operations stretching from the Scheldt to the Ardennes. Montgomery's great diversion toward Arnhem was an operational failure. The combination of Monty's dalliance south of the Maas in early September and Market Garden had prevented the Allies from securing Antwerp. At the meeting, Monty expressed optimism about finally clearing the Scheldt. U.S. First Army had finally surrounded Aachen on the 14th. But Hodges had failed to break through to the Rhine—or even the Roer. First Army suffered twenty thousand casualties in its failed attempt. By design, Patton's secondary attack had not moved beyond Metz. Although he came close, Patton did not break through.

After the war many senior German generals, Rundstedt, Blumentritt (Rundstedt's chief of staff), Student, and Westphal, among others, stated that a strong push from Belgium across the Rhine and into Germany would have easily succeeded.[1] Horrocks led a corps-size assault to Arnhem, as did Collins past Aachen toward Stolberg, but neither broke through. However tumultuous it looked from the German side, there were still a lot of Germans in the field who were ready to defend the Fatherland.

Ike was under a lot of pressure. Marshall had just completed a week-long visit to the European Theater. The chief "made no effort to disguise his unhappiness with the strategic situation, particularly Antwerp."[2] He still sought victory in Europe by New Years and explicitly said so in a cable to Eisenhower.[3] The Combined Chiefs of Staff began a formal study of an all-out offensive to finish off Hitler by year end.[4] Marshall wanted to put it all on the line. Use previously top-secret proximity-fuse artillery shells. Use all the supplies. Commit all Allied troop units, including those that might otherwise be refitted and retrained for 1945 operations.

The British field marshals, Montgomery and Brooke, did little to hide their continuing contempt of Eisenhower's generalship. While at the Combined Chiefs' meeting in Quebec on 22 September, Brooke penned in his diary, "[T]he opportunity for decisive victory at the decisive point before winter had passed." During Marshall's European visit, Monty requested and was granted a private meeting. The field marshal complained that Ike's command of ground operations was "ragged and disjointed," that Ike "lacked a firm grip," and that "operational direction and control were lacking."[5] Marshall barely retained his cool. In his inimical way, Monty completely misread the meeting and wrote that "I gave him [Marshall] my views on the present organization for command. I think it did some good."[6]

Ike understood there would be no silver bullet striking a secret vital organ that would bring the monster to the ground. He confided in FDR's press secretary, Steve Early: "People of the strength and warlike tendencies of the Germans do not give in; they must be beaten into the ground."[7] But Ike couldn't seem to find a flank to turn or a gap to penetrate. The monster held him at bay. As early as 25 September, planners were assuming that Antwerp would not be open before 28 October.

The Germans were getting stronger. Nubs of twenty-five shattered divisions had been rebuilt as volks grenadier divisions. Building from a core of veteran officers and noncoms leveraged the value of new conscripts. It created battle-worthy divisions in the shortest possible time. An additional fifteen divisions were formed up from scratch.[8]

A major effort would be required to overcome the heavy resistance encountered along the German frontier. The Allies needed more troop strength in order to resume the advance. Only Antwerp's docks could support them. Tonnage constraints limited the Allied buildup. Additional divisions entered the continent, but logisticians stated they could support no more than twenty in active combat. Even Brooke agreed the Allies must secure the Scheldt. The Joint Planning Staff of the Combined Chiefs echoed the convention: launching an all-out offensive before the opening of Antwerp "would be to court failure."[9]

Logistical problems remained enormous but had changed their complexion. Recall that the high-tonnage transportation system was a working railroad connected to a port. By the beginning of November, ports assigned to American forces offloaded 47,300 tons a day (table 2.3). Railroads were delivering about 23,000 tons a day to depots east of the Seine, or about half the landed tonnage.[10] Still, trucks had to deliver large tonnages from the beach and had to move everything from depots near the railheads at Liege and Nancy to forward units. Trucks assigned to the field armies were supposed to go no farther back than depots in the advanced communications zone. Instead many went as far back as Paris looking for scarce supplies, which placed added strain on limited transportation assets. The 650 tons per day per division slice* covered expendable supplies. Using that criterion, forward deliveries seem adequate. But movement of replacement equipment, construction materiel, and new units added many thousands of tons to be moved. An armored division that just lost 10 percent of its tank fleet in heavy battle needed a thousand tons of new tanks.

The official history states, "The shortage of ammunition, more than any other factor, determined the character of tactical operations in October."[11] By 9 October the magazines were empty. Ammunition famine hit Third Army hardest. At times firing was restricted to 1.1 rounds/day per 105mm howitzer. In a period when heavy pressure need to be applied to German defenses, large-scale attacks were almost impossible. This transformed September's stall into relinquishment of the initiative to the Germans. In the last week of October, 80 percent of ammunition fired by XX Corps was from captured stocks. During the attack of Aachen, German, Russian, and French pieces delivered much of the artillery support.[12]

To add insult to injury, thirty-five loaded ammunition ships stood in the English Channel. A combination of increased landing of new units, Channel storms, and extremely poor port management had reduced ammo discharge to 1,000 tons a day. There was not enough ammunition on the continent to cover already approved issues. If only Antwerp's quays were available!

Ammunition supply was so balled up that Lee's people declared a moratorium on shipments to field armies effective 9 October to 2 November while COMZ tried to sort out what it had, unload some of the ammunition ships at anchor, and build up stocks in forward depots.[13] The field armies had to subsist for thirty-three days on less than a normal eight-day issue.[14]

Ships backed up in Europe just as a worldwide shortage of seagoing bottoms threatened to slow the buildup in the Pacific as well as in Europe. The shipping crisis was so serious that the president himself had to intervene.

*See chapter 2, "Required Tonnages."

Because of the backlog of ships needing unloading, Army Service Forces back in the United States suspended further shipments lest even more ships become immobilized awaiting a European berth. Antwerp's ample wharves would have eliminated this problem. Better COMZ management could have done a lot to alleviate the problem. After numerous general officer investigations, Somervell remarked, "This [logistical management in Europe] is lousy and I want to send somebody to jail for it."[15] This extended and deepened the problem to extremely dangerous levels. On 20 October, Ike again cabled the Pentagon about the artillery ammunition shortage. This time he communicated with Marshall.[16] Despite Marshall's statement about the impending end of hostilities in Europe, Ike wanted 5.3 million 105mm rounds, two and a half times October's production for all theaters. Marshall responded that Ike would get everything available except minimal needs of other theaters. This gave ETO 3 million 105mm rounds en route. Two and a half million rounds would be expended in November. Then came the Battle of the Bulge. Somervell did what he could to increase production. Some soldiers were furloughed to pick up skilled jobs they previously held at ammunition plants.

Lee's organization had completely lost control of its inventory. Old ammo dump sites were scoured. Four thousand tons of unrecorded inventory was recovered in this manner. This doubled what the ledger said was available. Again, poor record keeping hobbled tactical operations.

From mid-October to mid-November, a massive effort to offload demurred ammunition ships took place. From 19 October to 12 November, American ports in northwestern Europe offloaded an average of 6,614 tons of ammunition a day.[17] The rate of unloading fell off 4–5 November as number of backlogged ships declined. By the beginning of the November offensive, Advanced Section (ADSEC) ammo dumps held 60,000 tons, versus 3,500 a month before.

In mid-October the weather, which hadn't been all that good, worsened markedly. During 1944 Western Europe had some of the worst weather of the century. Right at the height of the ammunition shortage, the air force chalked up day after day of "no fly" weather. Hence a bomb drought accompanied the artillery shell shortage. From mid-October to December, tactical aircraft flew missions on less than half the days.[18] Rain and cold made life miserable for everybody. No one suffered like the dogfaces in water-filled foxholes. Sickness rates skyrocketed. Both infantryman and tanker had difficulty maneuvering in the mud. Restricted ability to move cross-country affected attackers much more than defenders, ensconced in fixed fortifications.

Because of stalled tactical operations, the ammunition shortage, and the horrible weather, SHAEF briefly considered stopping further offensive action and holding in place. This course of action would have ignored the risk that the Combined Chiefs had taken by depriving the Pacific in order to defeat Germany first. A pause in Europe would have renewed the arguments of King and MacArthur to switch the main effort to the Pacific. Ike was very familiar with this pressure from his tour in the War Plans Division during the opening days of the war.[19] That such a plan reached discussion stage is a measure of the problems logistics and increased German resistance were creating.

Any thought of crossing the Rhine and attacking deep into Germany had faded with the summer sun. Grandiose plans of deep penetration into Germany promulgated by every operational headquarters in early September were no more than scrap paper. Ike had no thought of capturing Berlin, or even the Ruhr, with the upcoming November offensive. Allied generals had to focus on a way to get to the Rhine. However, follow-on to the two-army attack to be known as Queen did show Ninth Army encircling the Ruhr from the north and First Army completing the circle from the south. Twenty-First Army Group was eliminated from the projected advance. As Montgomery had yet to clear the Scheldt and the difficult Peel marshes barred Second Army's advance, Montgomery could say little. Maybe that was by his design. He always avoided committing British infantry into deadly urban warfare, as Britain had reached the limits of its available manpower.

Besides, Monty wanted to get to Berlin and not be entangled in heavy fighting in lesser battles.

Eisenhower began to talk in terms of attrition. "During this period we took as a general guide the principle that operations, except in those areas where we had some specific and vital objective, such as in the case of the Roer dams, were profitable to us only where the daily calculations showed that enemy losses were double our own."[20] That was a decision born out of frustration. Good German generalship and bad weather had obviated all the Allied optimism and opportunity that had permeated the first half of September. Eisenhower's move toward attrition also lessened the focus on his primary and secondary attacks. Some of his decisions began to have a "broad front" feel.

The Brussels conference concentrated on "a more modest program" than the final defeat of Nazi Germany.[21] In his conversations with Marshall, Bradley made it clear that the Allies would be lucky to reach the Rhine by Christmas. Berlin was out of the question for 1944.[22]

Monty still wanted Ike to concentrate on a single thrust north of the Ruhr. Ike continued to favor a primary and a secondary attack.[23] "It is going to be very important to us later on to have two strings to our bow. Can't forget that you were very wise in making a provision for this at Mareth and it paid off."[24]

The northern "Ruhr thrust" would continue to be the primary attack. However, this time 12th Army Group would be in exclusive control of the main effort. At least one error in command structure was corrected. Eisenhower directed that First and Ninth Armies would team up and drive toward Rhine crossings south of Cologne. A successful effort would place the two armies on the southern rim of the Ruhr. Twenty-First Army Group would concentrate on opening the Scheldt and then closing on the Rhine in its sector. It would not have the strength to conduct both operations simultaneously.

SHAEF's SGS 381, dated 28 October 1944, superseded FWD 13675.[25] It acknowledged the "enemy's resistance has stiffened" and that logistical limitations had prevented the Allies from overrunning the Siegfried Line. The order now designated three phases: the battle west of the Rhine, crossing the Rhine, and the advance beyond the Rhine. In implicit acknowledgment of how difficult the first two phases were, the third phase was not spelled out. Montgomery's primary task remained opening Antwerp. Then he was supposed to cross the Rhine in Holland. No longer was the Ruhr part of his responsibility. Crossing near the Ruhr was theater main effort and was exclusively Bradley's. Again without waving flags, Ike had finished transferring the main effort from the British to the Americans. Bradley continued to control the secondary effort as well. Devers's group had a subsidiary role to protect Bradley's flank but retained the mission to secure crossings and deploy in strength across the Rhine.

In the initial phase Patton would again make whatever secondary effort logistics would allow. Previously, in private, Ike had told Patton that British manpower problems would continue to shrink Montgomery's forces and that he would limit the size of 6th Army Group. The continuous parade of new American divisions would enlarge 12th Army Group and make it the dominant organization in the final phases of the campaign in Europe.[26]

Excerpts from the 28 October SHAEF Directive outline the new campaign:

> 3. The enemy's dispositions clearly indicate his concern to protect the Ruhr and the Saar, as it is in front of these areas, and particularly of the Ruhr,

that his main concentrations are to be found. He is sensitive also to a threat against the Belfort approaches to the upper Rhine Valley.

4. Limitations of maintenance and transportation prevented our overrunning of Siegfried Line before the enemy's resistance stiffened. We know have to deploy superior forces in the forward area and furnish them adequate resources for intensive fighting. These forces cannot be maintained effectively during the winter months without the use of the port of Antwerp. Consequently the securing and placing in operation of that port is our first and most immediate objective.

5. My intention continues to be the destruction of enemy forces.

6. The General plan, subject always to the capture of the approaches to Antwerp is:

   a. Making the main effort in the north, to defeat decisively the enemy west of the Rhine and secure bridgeheads over the Rhine; then to seize the Ruhr and, subsequently, to advance deep into Germany.

   b. To conduct operations in order to destroy the enemy in the Saar, secure crossings over the Rhine and be prepared for an advance from the Saar, at a later date, in accordance with the situation then prevailing. All these operations are to be so timed as best to support the main effort to which they are subsidiary.

   c. On the southern (right) flank making full use of the maintenance resources available from the Mediterranean to act aggressively with the object, initially of overwhelming the enemy west of the Rhine and, later of advancing into Germany.

8. The mission of the Northern Group of Armies is:
   First Phase
   a. A first priority to open the port of Antwerp.[27]

This straightforward strategy would be no surprise to the Germans. The Allies had been hacking in this general direction for a month and a half. The ammunition-induced October pause allowed the Wehrmacht to dig deeper. A war-winning strike was beyond SHAEF's capabilities in November 1944. The last thing Allied armies wanted to do is to slug toe to toe in close terrain against an enemy fighting from improved positions. SHAEF's lack of imagination played to German strengths.

As Stephen Ambrose described it, "The campaign that resulted was the least glamorous, and the toughest, of the war."[28] It would be characterized by hard slugging against tough positions and a lot of dead and hurt men lying in the cold mud. It was grind-it-out, head-on-attrition war at its worst.

Monty kept looking for a rapier-like thrust that would cause a collapse analogous to France in 1940. Ambrose ruefully points out that the Wehrmacht was nothing like the French Army. The Soviets had already reached this conclusion. They designed their campaigns to kill Germans, not force a dramatic drive on the German capital.

However, recent disagreements over strategy created massive impediments to fresh thinking. Moving the axis of 12th Army Group's main effort risked moving toward Montgomery-dominated operations east of the Rhine. Extend an advance from Aachen to Cologne due east across the Rhine and one advances south of the Ruhr. Move it north and one also goes north of the Ruhr, in parallel with Montgomery in a "single full-blooded thrust." Bradley was so worried about losing out to Montgomery that he moved Ninth Army from south of First Army to north of Hodges's command. Anything to prevent loss of his beloved First Army to that damned Englishman.

In his 1969 work, Stephen Ambrose compares Eisenhower's situation to that of Grant in the Wilderness in 1864.[29] Grant was not going to find an easy way around Lee. Instead, the Federals were going to have to continue smashing the Confederates until they were completely stove in.

Weigley, in the title of his book, has called Grant's smashing *The American Way of War*. He argued that most American military effort in World War II was head-on employment of brute force. This characterization misses the essential element. The legacy is not "smash on," *but in an attempt to achieve an advantage from operational-level maneuver*, keep smashing on. The question becomes, did Ike and Bradley keep on seeking operational advantage?

Ambrose states that the analogy of the Wilderness could be extended. The Confederates were not going to crack. Their army couldn't simply be outmaneuvered. It had to be destroyed in the field.

The strategic parallel is there. Perhaps a second extension down into the operational level can be made. The strategy is to destroy the enemy army in the field. The operational problem is how to destroy it with the least cost in friendly blood, and sooner rather than later. Grant did not simply march down the road from Washington to Richmond and smash away. Grant recognized that Lee's army ensconced in Richmond's prepared defensive fortifications would be his greatest problem. He sought to interpose his army between Lee and Richmond and then crush the Rebels. Grant sought the Confederate flank no fewer than nine times in his maneuvering from the Wilderness to Petersburg. To prevent Lee from maneuvering back to Richmond or to disrupt Sherman's drive to the sea, Grant had to grapple with and hold the Army of Northern Virginia. Several tough assaults, such as the fight at Bloody Angle, stained Virginia's red soil crimson. Some people could see little save a butcher's bill. But Grant had a campaign-winning plan. The more men Lee lost, the more constrained became his freedom to maneuver. The less the Confederate ability to maneuver, the more likely Grant could seek advantage from his own maneuver to crush the Rebel army and win the war.

He continued to seek Lee's flank as the least costly method of destroying him. The attempt led to a semicircle of battles that led around Richmond and all the way to Petersburg. Lee's successful parries did not erase Grant's intent. The Union general wasn't afraid of a head-on battle of attrition. But operational-level maneuver leading to first dislocating, then destroying, the Confederates was his objective.

With no open flank, another approach would have to be created. Either the Allies could engage in a frontal attack or they could "create" an open attack by conducting a penetration. The legacy of Grant was to *seek* an advantage before the battle via maneuver. Lacking an apparent approach, Grant created one at Vicksburg by finding a way to transport his army below the Mississippi bluffs. Several starts ended in frustrating failure. But he prevailed. Grant attempted to repeat this process in the Wilderness. While seeking advantages, Grant was willing to conduct hard fighting. Once engaged on the battlefield he tended to bull ahead rather than to continue to maneuver. Taking casualties while seeking advantage results in fewer deaths overall than not making a solid attempt. This was the reasoning behind the Battle of the Crater.

Concentrating great power in order to penetrate, and enduring long initial casualty lists, was in Grant's tradition. Simply lining up in a frontal attack and flailing away was antithetical to what the Civil War general attempted. Unfortunately, Bradley did not continue this tradition.

Might a more creative solution have been drafted for November 1944? Destruction of the German Army, not encirclement of the Ruhr, was the center of gravity. Loss of the latter would not have ensured the former, but with no defenders, the Ruhr would be the Allies' for the asking.

They key to finishing off the German army was the elimination of its ability to conduct a major counterattack. Destroy that capability, and any operation that successfully pierced the very hard forward defense the Germans had emplaced would ultimately prevail. The critical lynch pin, in Clausewitzian terms, the center of gravity around which all else turned, was Sixth Panzer Army. Destroying this concentration of armor was the real objective in November. The Allies might pick an important geographical objective such as the Ruhr or the Saar to strike toward. But the real objective was to challenge the panzers to a fight and to kill them, preferably on open ground where the Allies could bring their firepower to bear. Ike had said as much. Bradley, the commander charged with creating the main effort, needed to create a campaign plan that drew the panzers out of their lair and then killed them.

It was a job for the ground forces. Allied intelligence had identified the trains bringing the Germans forward. Even with the targeting information, air power did not stop or even seriously impede their emplacement.

One way to force Sixth Panzer Army to engage was to create a breach in the West Wall wide enough to support operations along the Rhine. Once breached in strength, German forward defenses were at risk of being rolled up from the rear. Relatively immobile volks divisions could not hope to win a race to the Rhine with motorized Allied formations. Hitler would have had the choice of attempting to hold forward positions along the West Wall or extracting the infantry required to defend the Rhine in time. Allied commanders had every reason to believe their enemy would choose the latter. Sixth Panzers would have been drawn into the battle to gain time to man the Rhine defenses. Undoubtedly both Model and Rundstedt would have wanted to counterattack with their armor.

ALLIED INTELLIGENCE AND THE GERMAN BUILDUP

Beginning in September, Allied intelligence began to systematically misread German intentions. ULTRA cataloged a massive buildup but did not reveal Hitler's plan to launch a massive counterattack through the Ardennes. G2 officers concluded the buildup portended greater reserves designed to parry Allied attacks rather than to fund a counteroffensive that history recognizes as the Battle of the Bulge. These errors were impounded in impressions of the enemy held at the very highest Allied levels.

SHAEF chief of intelligence, British Major General Strong, opined that November was the month Hitler dreaded most.[30] Strong saw a parallel between the left-right stretching of the cordon that contained Normandy in July and Allied efforts along the West Wall. Keep slugging away and the opportunity for another Cobra would present itself. Many officers in SHAEF felt that somewhere the Germans had to crack.[31]

The accretion of Sixth Panzer Army in the general vicinity of Cologne, which Allied intelligence was aware of, seems to have belied Strong's assessment. Sixth Panzer Army was the strongest and most efficient mobile force in the German order of battle. Apparently it was tasked to counterattack against any crossing of the Roer.[32] Given the placement of the enemy's principal theater reserve and constant improvement of frontline positions in the Aachen-Huertgen sector from two months of combat, it would seem the best place for the Allied main effort was any place other than the Roer plain.

The operational reserve in Bradley's sector was the well-regarded XLVII Panzer Corps, consisting of 15PGD and 9PzD. In order to husband his buildup, Hitler was willing to cede some ground in noncritical sectors. But he was adamant about holding every square centimeter in the Aachen sector. If the Allies breached the Roer, the attack positions for the Ardennes offensive would become compromised.[33] The Allies were up against a tough, motivated opponent who had regenerated a lot of combat power.

Twelfth Army Group had unmistakable firsthand evidence of improving German combat efficiency. During October, German defenders around Aachen had showed renewed vigor. A poorly deployed 28ID was badly trounced at Schmidt in the Huertgen. In the north, a corps-sized force ejected 7th Armored Division from its positions. Between 27 and 29 October the American armor rocked back 5–7 kilometers. British 12 Corps had to be committed to restore the situation. An enemy capable of a corps-sized counterattack was not on the verge of collapse.

Despite evidence to the contrary, the notion that the Germans were about to collapse hung around right to the end of the campaign. On 12 December, 12th Army Group's G2, Brigadier General Siebert, wrote, "It is now certain that attrition is steadily sapping the strength of the German forces on the Western Front and that the crust of defenses is thinner, more brittle and more vulnerable than it appears on our G2 maps or to the troops in the line . . . the breaking point may develop suddenly and without warning."[34] Allied intelligence seriously underestimated the difficulty of advancing from Aachen to the Rhine. Twelfth Army Group never penetrated deep enough to reveal the magnitude of the error. Bradley's armies never came close to engaging Sixth Panzer Army east of the Roer.

GERMAN PERCEPTIONS

As the Allies entered provinces traditionally affiliated with an expanded Germany, Nazi human intelligence capability increased. Not all "liberated" Europeans were inimical to the German cause. American radio discipline was notoriously poor. German intercept stations had little difficulty in locating and identifying Allied formations.[35] German order of battle specialists provided a reasonably accurate picture of their enemy.

The "Last Prussian" anticipated a renewed American thrust to seize the dams and cross the Roer. Rundstedt's principal objective was to prevent the Allies from interrupting the buildup for Wacht am Rhein. Along the Roer, he did not have the luxury of any maneuver room. If the Allies gained the

Roer in strength, the counteroffensive would be jeopardized. While German strength increased, Rundstedt knew most of it would be husbanded for the new offensive. Twenty-five of the rebuilt divisions would become available in November. Two would go to the eastern front. Fifteen were earmarked for the strategic reserve. Rundstedt would receive eight.[36]

Hitler ordered that the Allies must not cross the Roer. Further, Rundstedt had to retain bridgeheads to the east bank at Jülich and Düren. That order, unknown to Allied intelligence, would have made German destruction of the dams very difficult. As long as significant German forces remained west of the river, opening the dams would doom them. It also meant that German field commanders had scant room in which either to form a forward security zone or to back up as tactical conditions might warrant.

At their respective levels, Rundstedt, Model, and von Zangen (commander Fifteenth Army) were very competent commanders. It was folly to assume they wouldn't create a difficult defense in depth. Due to bad weather and General Lee's mismanagement of ammunition resupply, the Wehrmacht had four to six weeks to get ready. That meant frontline positions would be improved. Even German positions outside of the West Wall were well dug in, wired, and mined.

Allied strategy for November was easy for the German high command to discern. It aimed at the hardest surface on the Western front, the area between the Peel marshes and Huertgen that centered on Aachen. If the German infantry withheld for the counteroffensive had been fed into the trenches east of the Roer, Bradley's task would have been even more difficult. Nevertheless, November promised to be just the type of battle the Allies least desired: a frontal assault in miserable weather and terrain against a well-prepared, forewarned, and determined enemy. The "get to the Ruhr" strategy no longer made sense.

BRADLEY'S CHOICE

The first operational task Bradley faced was selecting the point of main effort. It was his most important decision. Staying with the assumption that Rhine crossing sites near Cologne were the proper objective, it was not a given that Bradley had to take the shortest route via Düren on the Roer. Initial guidance had two of Bradley's armies attacking in team from Aachen to Cologne and then one looping north.

Bradley had three options. The first: he could continue to make the Stolberg Corridor the main effort. Knowing the strength of the enemy positions, this meant additional activity in the Huertgen. The Hamich ridge that extended into the Huertgen provided excellent observation of the eastern portion of the corridor. If a deliberate attack was going to pound up the Stolberg Corridor day after day against well-supplied enemy artillery, the ridge would have to be taken. The water behind the Roer dams had to be dealt with. A major buildup of engineer bridging and river-crossing equipment would have been prudent. It would be needed for the Rhine crossing anyway.

Conceivably Bradley could have shifted 40 kilometers south into the Ardennes and begun with a major attack up the Losheim Gap (his second option) to capture and neutralize the Roer dams. This would have the advantage of moving south of the Roer and the dams and opening the offensive on fresh ground. Planners had become increasingly concerned about the potential for flooding. An advance here would debouch on the southern portion of the Cologne plain west of Bonn and. While assigned to the Ardennes, Ninth Army studied an attack from Prüm across rough ground to Coblenz.[37] As the Siegfried Line here had been breached and the axis was south of the Roer, this approach had some advantages.

The third approach traveled on the open ground north of Aachen. XIX Corps had already chewed a hole in the West Wall here. Compared to the other two approaches, this was level, unforested ground. American armor would have to fight the mud but could be deployed. Many slag heaps and small, stout villages created defensible strong points. However, they were readily targeted by artillery.

Fifteenth Army, replacing Fifth Panzer Army HQ, which was coiling up for the Ardennes offensive, controlled most of the German frontline forces from the Huertgen forest to Geilenkirchen. The northern end of the line, including Geilenkirchen, was defended by 183rd VGD. XII SS Corps's 176 Division was north of that town and out of 12th Army Group's area of operations. Ninth Army identified 9th Panzer Division in reserve on the east bank of the Roer on the northern boundary of the army's area of operations. Fifteenth PGD "was known to be in the vicinity 'on call.'"[38] American intelligence had pinpointed Model's operational reserve.

Most of the Ninth Army front was held by LXXXI Corps. Eight kilometers that roughly paralleled the positions of XIX Corps was held by 246VGD. This outfit had been chewed up in the battle for Aachen and was in very poor shape. It was the lowest-rated division on the front. Third PGD, eleven thousand strong, defended 5 kilometers from the woods north of Stolberg northward. Given their strength and narrow frontage, the panzer grenadiers packed quite a punch. Twelfth VGD, with 6,381 men, was the highest-rated division in terms of morale and training.[39] It was earmarked to be withdrawn for the Bulge buildup. However, on the day Queen commenced, it still defended Stolberg and its corridor. Composed of poorly trained scrapings from the Navy, Luftwaffe, and the recent call-up of 17- and 18-year-olds, 47VGD was coming to its relief.

LXXIV Corps of German Seventh Army held most of the Huertgen opposite 4ID of VII Corps and V Corps. From north to south, the Germans deployed 275 and 69 Divisions. Neither the Americans nor Germans rated 275 Division very highly. In addition, two infantry divisions, 340 and 363, would be used to replace and support frontline units. American intelligence was aware the Germans had formed additional volks grenadier divisions and had the capability to effect this reinforcement.

German artillery, especially in the Aachen sector, was very strong. By the end of November Fifteenth Army had one thousand guns (including AA engaging ground targets) and good ammunition stocks. Throughout most of the fall German artillery was the biggest killer of Americans.

None of the frontline divisions were first rate. The Germans were at their weakest in front of XIX Corps north of Aachen. Reinforcements arriving in the Stolberg Corridor made this axis less attractive with each passing day.

Behind this maze lay an expandable moat, the Roer River. Normally it was a docile stream, but dammed reservoirs behind the Huertgen forest contained enough water to create a 2-kilometer-wide flood for two weeks. If Bradley was to gain the Cologne plain, he had to deal with this river. If his main effort was opposite the Roer, he had to plan for a deliberate crossing against the deep reserves the Germans could throw at any attempt. Detailed studies of the Rhine River bank were compiled.[40] However, no similar plans were made for a major effort to cross the Roer. One wonders if anybody seriously expected to deal with a flooded river. If not, and there were no plans to capture the dams, how was Bradley supposed to get to the Rhine? Had somebody shuffled this into the "too hard" pile and left it there? Without a plan to cross the Roer, the upcoming offensive, Queen, did not make a lot of sense.

If closing to the Rhine was the objective, Sixth Panzer Army was the center of gravity. Left unfettered, this force would stop any effort to cross the Roer and advance. A 12th Army Group's intelligence summary just before the November offensive states that "the key to the enemy's essential capabilities and intentions was the disposition of his identified panzer and panzer grenadier divisions."[41] Bradley's memoirs echo the sentiment: "in late November Sixth 'SS' Panzer Army would probably wait to hit us while we were crossing the Roer, for if they should counterattack while we were astride that river, they might seriously embarrass us there. Thus we were resigned ourselves to a knockdown drag out fight between the Roer and the Rhine."[42] In selecting his main effort, Bradley had failed to shape a campaign plan to deal with this threat. The October notion of sending a single division across the Roer could not possibly succeed against the reserves the Germans had assembled. A strong American reserve would be needed to cross the Roer and then take on the panzers.

Initially Ninth Army was inserted south of First Army in the Ardennes. If the main effort was north of Aachen, there would be no need to shuffle it north. Instead it could slide immediately north and relieve V Corps, which could then concentrate where the main attack was planned. XIX Corps was already deployed north of Aachen.

Attacking east through the Ardennes appears to have been the least-promising alternative. As one crosses the Our River going east, the terrain gets even worse. And somewhere out there was a panzer army. By November, no Allied general should have relished fighting large German formations in wooded broken ground.

Repeating the headlong attack from the Stolberg Corridor to Huertgen would be the second-worst campaign plan. German defenses appeared to be stronger south of Aachen than north. The ground to the south was a lot more restrictive. Both Stolberg and the Hamich ridge in the Huertgen had to be taken before a spearhead could pass. Otherwise observed artillery fire would smash it. An operation aimed up the Stolberg Corridor would proceed more slowly, thereby increasing German reaction time. With Sixth Panzer Army nearby, this was a major problem.

QUEEN

On 21 October, three days after the Brussels conference, Bradley issued instructions to his three armies for the upcoming offensive. Instead of a number of creative alternatives, Bradley birthed a very straightforward frontal attack. First Army would make the main effort south of Aachen up the Stolberg Corridor. As might be expected, VII Corps would be its main effort. After securing the corridor, it would force a crossing of the Roer, near Düren. The army group commander hoped "that Collins could duplicate his breakout at Saint Lo and dash to the Rhine."[43] V Corps would attempt to make headway in the Huertgen again. In other words, Hodges's army would attack over the most constricted portion of the terrain around Aachen against a defender that had been much reinforced. Forward defenses would give the Germans sufficient time to react with the largest reserve they had assembled since Mortain—Sixth Panzer Army.

Ninth Army would generate a supporting attack north of Aachen. XIX Corps would move from positions it had held since October and cross the Roer at Linnich. However, its primary mission was to protect First Army's left flank, so it was to heavily weight its right. XIII Corps, newly placed in the line on the northern part of Ninth Army's sector, would seize Geilenkirchen and defend the army group's northern flank. This was exposed to an assault from the now familiar gap between British Second Army and Bradley's forces. Second Army was scheduled to clear ground between the Maas and the Rhine, which would reduce the threat from this quarter.

Effectively, First and Ninth Armies would conduct a broad four-corps-wide frontal attack from the West Wall to the Roer. A huge air bombardment would precede the attacking armies. But it would only superficially resemble the air strike that sprung Cobra.

Down south Patton would prosecute an attack in Lorraine up to the West Wall. The intent was for Third Army's effort to eventually converge with First Army's along the Rhine. There was no thought of Queen and Third Army supporting each other tactically in the opening stages, as the Ardennes created a large gap between the primary and secondary attacks. Devers would conduct an offensive into the Vosges. Montgomery, still trying to clear the Scheldt, would accomplish little along the Rhine. Queen was SHAEF's main operation for the month of November.

Hodges issued the First Army attack order on 25 October. An entry in the war diary: "This field order which set forth the main objectives of the upcoming drive is probably the most important order issued by General Hodges to date. On its successful completion may very well depend the early outcome of this war."

In Bradley's words:

> The plan called for Hodges to ram through to Duren with Simpson on his left flank. There he would force the Roer 15 miles east of Aachen and push on across that barrier to Cologne, 25 miles beyond it. Our primary objective in this offensive was destruction of the enemy's forces west of the Rhine. If we could defeat him there as we had in Normandy, we might hurdle the Rhine on the run as we did the Seine. . . . I anticipated we might reach the Rhine within 30 days after jump off.[44]

Later on Bradley stated the presence of Sixth SS Panzer Army would probably extend the operation beyond thirty days.[45] On 14 November, Chester
Hansen, Bradley's aide, wrote in his diary, "We can push to the Rhine in a
matter of days." That such a large change in German capability induced
such a small change in military plans is hard to understand. The expectations for Queen sounded like the expectations senior commanders had for
Collins as he first entered the Stolberg Corridor in early September.

There was even less to Queen than met the eye. Instead of concentrating forces, these plans diffused First Army along a 75-kilometer stretch of
the Rhine. If this was a weak plan against limited resistance in early September, it was sheer folly against a panzer-army-sized counterattack force.
Little seems to have been learned. Again there was no thought of narrowing
the advance and concentrating combat power for deep penetration. First
Army's order alerted V Corps to drive on Koblenz and VIII Corps on Bonn[46]
while VII Corps focused on Cologne. First Army would continue to batter
against the toughest surface on the western front. Siegfried defenses were
thicker here than in any other sector. The Stolberg Corridor was an in-depth
set of strong points firmly imbedded in an industrial jungle. Two divisions
had already been shattered in the Huertgen. Patton observed Bradley's
contention that if all Allied armies attacked simultaneously, it might win
war.[47] Again, this wasn't Eisenhower's sin. But he did little to correct it. By
November, the Wehrmacht was too strong for this approach to work.

No reserve or follow-on force was designated. Who would exploit a
breakthrough made by the initial assaults? Where was the multi-division
force that would take on Sixth Panzer Army without deviating from the
high tempo required to reach the Cologne plain? Unlike Cobra, it did not
provide the forces to exploit a breakout—certainly not the frontline divisions
that had to bore open a hole in prepared defenses and to make a deliberate
crossing of the Roer.

Planning for the advance beyond the Roer was even more curious. The
letter of instruction states: "After the attack of the First Army has reached the
Rhine, Ninth Army will attack northward between the Rhine and the Meuse
(Maas) Rivers and gain contact with British Second Army. It will then take
over the area west of the Rhine from the Rhine to the Rees, inclusive."[48]
Instead of keeping both armies yoked together on the southern face of the
Ruhr after a Rhine crossing, the armies would split. U.S. Ninth and British
Second Army in a pincers movement west of the Rhine would scoop up
remaining German defenders.

When he traveled to Europe, Marshall reviewed some of the preliminary plans for Queen. After the war Marshall said he had serious reservations about Bradley's prospects for crossing the Rhine in the Queen offensive. He said, "I didn't see how he [Bradley] could do it" (Pogue interviews of Marshall, cited in Cray, p. 484).

Bradley initially indicated to Montgomery that 12th Army Group's multi-army offensive would strike with ten divisions. The actual main effort amounted to the lead divisions of VII and XIX Corps. Monty was appalled to find the initial attack deployed only four divisions. In the field marshal's estimation, this was far too little to push through the defenses arrayed along the Roer. He questioned the wisdom of continuing a secondary attack when the main attack had insufficient strength.[49]

The field marshal made a little-noticed volte-face. Now he agreed with Ike that "the decisive battle for Germany might well be fought west of the Rhine."[50] Monty asked if Bradley had made any plans for shifting divisions from the Metz area to Aachen or vice versa, if such a shift was indicated. In a formal reply, Bradley responded that he did not anticipate any such shift. Bradley estimated his armies would be on the Rhine at Cologne by 15 December.[51] However, SHAEF planners had looked at the possibility of moving a corps from south to north or vice versa. SHAEF and Montgomery had found some common ground. Montgomery wouldn't support the offensive because it didn't have a "hope in Hell of succeeding." While his conclusion was understandable, Montgomery was still part of the same Allied effort.

Given the need for speed and the relatively small size of the primary attack, why not eschew the constricted Stolberg Corridor for better ground between Geilenkirchen and Aachen? As the official history states, "Even a superficial glance at the terrain in front of the Ninth Army as opposed to that facing the First Army would raise the question of why the First instead of the Ninth drew the role of 'main effort'."[52] As this axis was less well defended than the Stolberg Corridor, the observation is correct on two counts. Professor Weigley stated, "The Roer plain was infinitely to be preferred as a battle ground over the Huertgen forest."[53]

Bradley supplied his answer: "You don't make your main effort with your exterior force."[54] This explanation, however, does not stand up to analysis. By the time Queen was ready for execution, XIII Corps was in place as the northernmost corps. In the actual campaign it was the northernmost "outside force" and performed well at its task of securing the northern flank. But Bradley did not want to use the inexperienced Ninth Army to lead his November offensive. As Bradley himself pointed out, Ninth Army was "relatively untried."[55]

First Army headquarters could have controlled a main effort in the Aachen Gap north of Aachen. XIX Corps and either V or VII Corps could have been the main attack force. Ninth Army could have remained in the south where it was initially inserted into the line, controlling American units in the Huertgen forest and the Stolberg corridor south of Aachen. However, expecting Montgomery might gain control of the northernmost American army, Bradley did not want to risk First Army that far north.[56] Thus Bradley's concern about who might control First Army displacement militated against selection of the best axis of advance, the Aachen Gap, as the location of the main effort.

In the actual campaign, Ninth Army conducted an attack designed to support First Army's movement through the Stolberg Corridor. XIX Corps would conduct a major attack north of Aachen. While the sector is narrow, a two-corps (XIX and VII) effort could have been mounted there while XIII Corps performed its assigned mission. On narrow fronts, each corps could have retained the reserves needed to deal with the Roer and the Sixth Panzer Army counterattack that virtually every American commander expected. Why worry about an "outside flank" defended by a corps when no provision was made to counter the primary threat to success of the operation? To be successful, the Americans had to act more quickly than the Germans could react. Two concentrated corps in mutual support, with adequate reserves and advancing over open terrain, had the best chance of generating the tempo required to break through, cross the Roer, and prepare for the inevitable counterattack.

The axis north of Aachen reaches the Roer at Linnich and Jülich, which are about 9 kilometers apart. If Bradley wanted to cross the Roer on a wider front, one army could have veered to the southeast after passing Eschweiler and headed for Düren. This approach would have avoided punching up the Stolberg Corridor and fighting in the Huertgen. Düren was Bradley's intermediate objective on the Roer for First Army. However, the choice between rapid crossing at Jülich versus heading southeast to Düren would be obvious. The greater the number of German troops potentially trapped on the wrong side of the Roer, the slower the Germans would have been in blowing the dams. Once the Americans were across the Roer in strength, flooding the Roer behind them would slow their advance but not threaten their existence.

Remember, Ike's orders were to cross the Rhine, not the Roer. The Roer and the likely fight with Sixth Panzer Army were but intermediate steps. Of course the entire offensive might stop because of blown dams. That was what happened in 1945. But the dams could be blown only once. Had they been destroyed in late November, they would not have remained a threat after the Bulge.

Bradley was very enthusiastic about Queen. In passing, Bradley mentioned to an aide that "it might be the last big offensive necessary to bring Germany to her knees.[57]

TOO MUCH SAFETY

The air strikes that supported Queen were larger than those marshaled for Cobra. All commanders were concerned for the safety of American ground troops. At Saint-Lô, too many bombs that fell short of their targets hit our own troops. During Cobra, the bomb line was set 1,200 yards in front of friendly positions. The Queen bomb line was set at 3,600 yards. An uncovered strip of ground a mile wide can contain a lot of dug-in defenders.

Most of the air strikes were targeted against towns and road junctions to the rear of German front lines. Little effort was made to target specific formations and installations. World War II repeatedly demonstrated the futility of dumping high explosive on nonspecific targets. The noise and dust were impressive but little of substance was hit.

The strategic bombers mounted the maximum effort. In ninety-five minutes 1,204 8th AF bombers dropped 4,120 tons on their targets; 1,188 RAF heavies dropped 5,437 tons. These amounts of explosive rivaled the yield of small tactical nuclear weapons. As usual, crews reported high accuracy.[58] Ninth Air Force mediums were tasked to bomb towns directly in front of VII Corps. Because of poor weather only 150 aircraft dropped ordnance.

Because of the wide safety zone, many frontline defenders were not even aware of the massive bombing preparation. Unlike Panzer Lehr that laid in the path of Cobra, frontline units were not disrupted. Prisoners from 12th VGD in front of VII Corps estimated casualties at 1 to 3 percent. The divisional phone system was knocked out.

In weighing the risks, Allied commanders chose to minimize the risk of friendly fire and the expense of leaving frontline German positions untouched. Does one accept the risk of "Blue on Blue" casualties or leave enough effective enemy weapons intact in the safety zone to make casualty lists even longer? No analysis can capture the intense stress commanders must withstand when forced to make such grisly choices. Put bluntly, commanders could not afford the safety margins they selected. By protecting troops from friendly fire, they left too many enemy guns unbombed. Even American air commanders expressed disappointment with the results.[59]

FIRST ARMY ATTACKS TOWARD THE ROER

By early November, First Army had been considerably reinforced. It contained:

V Corps	VII Corps	VIII Corps
5th Armored Div	3rd Armored Div	9th Armored Div
8th Inf Div	1st Inf Div	2nd Inf Div
28th Inf Div	4th Inf Div	9th Inf Div
99th Inf Div	104th Inf Div	83rd Inf Div
102nd Cav Gp	103rd Cav Gp	14th Cav Gp

The 99ID was new to combat. Non-divisional artillery totaled forty field battalions and thirty AA battalions. Twelve non-engineer combat battalions backed up the frontline divisions. Given the army's size, the engineer complement wasn't particularly strong. Maintaining supply routes through the mud, assaulting fixed enemy positions, and crossing a river subject to flood would require a tremendous engineering effort. Total First Army strength exceeded 318,000 men, 60,000 more than in early September. Except for 28ID suffering from the effects of Huertgen, most combat units were well rested.

VIII Corps and its commander, Major General Middleton, had served under First Army during the heavy fighting in Normandy. On the day he made colonel, Troy Middleton was the youngest one in the AEF. During World War I Marshall called him "the outstanding regimental commander on the battlefield in France." But Middleton left the service in the thirties to take the job of comptroller at Louisiana State University. Although later Ike blocked his promotion to permanent two-star rank because "he left us when the going was tough,"[60] General Gay rated Middleton the best tactician serving under Patton.[61]

Under the Queen plan, First Army would make the main effort to establish a bridgehead across the Rhine south of Cologne (map 7.1). Again 12th Army Group had made a poor call. First Army compounded it by projecting the "layer cake" of corps all the way to the Rhine on a 100-kilometer front. At this late date, each corps was expected to hurtle the Roer and its associated

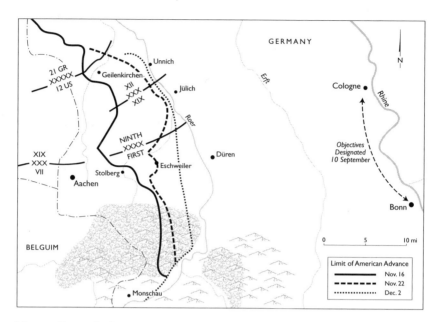

Map 7.1. Rates of Advance in Queen

reservoirs and to advance through 60 kilometers of heavily defended ground that had a panzer army hidden in it. Then they were supposed to seize Rhine bridges! No plans were made for attacking formations more than a division deep. Even though First Army had twelve divisions rather than the usual nine, no army-level reserve was constituted. No plans were made to maneuver a major force through a targeted breach in the well-prepared defenses.

In a 29 October letter to 12th Army Group, Hodges stated, "Present plans of this army do not contemplate capture of these [Roer] dams."[62] If so, Bradley must have planned to cross the river in the face of a flood threat. However, no extraordinary engineering preparations were made. On 7 November, Hodges alerted V Corps to prepare a plan to capture the dams *if* First Army received an order to do so.

All in all, it was an unimaginative frontal attack in very close terrain and against a well-supplied, well-prepared enemy. Except for the heavy bombers, it wasn't much different from First Army's failed assault in September. Back then, Bradley faced a much weaker and disorganized enemy.

VII Corps's plan was predicated on seizing crossings of Roer—only 11 kilometers away. Hodges told Collins to be prepared to cross the Roer and seize the army group objective—Rhine bridges near Cologne. Quite a tall order for a corps that had not gained more then a handful of meters in the last month. Note again crossing plans are not predicated on seizing the dams.

VII Corps's sector again comprised the Stolberg Corridor. VII Corps's G2 had a healthy respect for the enemy opposing him.[63] The corps would duel again with 12VGD as well as 275VGD. During six weeks of relatively static front, American intelligence officers had compiled a very good picture of the opposing force. In headcount, VII Corps had a 5–1 advantage over its enemy. That promised success. However, during those six weeks Germans had dug deep, mined, and wired in. Defenses were organized in depth. Several defensive lines had been given similar treatment. Hodges didn't have a reserve. Model did. His army group reserve, XLVII Panzer Corps, was keyed for counterattacks into the Aachen sector. Rundstedt and Model had a good idea of where Bradley would strike.

Bradley did not create an operational reserve. VII Corps held the bulk of 3rd Armored Division back as an exploitation force. The Spearhead Division would dash toward the Roer through any hole the infantry made that debouched onto open ground. At least at the tactical level, commanders were thinking about the depth required to accomplish the mission.

VII Corps assault troops kicked off at 1245. A midday attack was out of character and did come as a surprise to the Germans. Nine infantry regiments and a combat command composed the front ranks. After the bombers dropped their loads, thirty-two artillery battalions picked up the bombardment. Collins, Hodges, and Bradley were confident VII Corps would smash through behind all this firepower.

For three days infantry on both sides fought bitterly for possession of the high ground that dominated the Stolberg Corridor—the Hamich ridge and Donnerberg Hill, which is situated between Stolberg and Eschweiler and has a commanding view. (Refer back to map 5.2 for terrain detail.) At times five artillery battalions chewed up the ground in front of an attacking infantry battalion. Defenders repeatedly counterattacked.

German artillery was very active. On the 18th, 13,200 rounds hit VII Corps and a portion of XIX Corps. Throughout the battle German artillery continued to punish the Americans. Hitler released some ammunition stockpiled for the Ardennes offensive. It was a slugfest. Following the blow by blow adds little to the analysis of the campaign's pivotal decisions. After clipping off a corner of the Huertgen forest in order to facilitate movement up the corridor, Collins emerged onto the Roer Plain at Merberich west of Düren on the 29th.

Commitment of 4ID and V Corps to the second Battle of the Huert-gen Forest made little sense. Planners thought 4ID could emerge from the woods and take Düren on the Roer. The division never made it out of the woods. Once VII Corps broke onto the Roer plain, the Huertgen lost any tactical value. There weren't enough Germans in the forest to threaten Collins. Again, the dams were not designated as an objective.

During the attack Hodges visited 4ID. He became worked up at their methods of attack. Courtney did not like seeing the way they attacked "running down roads . . . instead of advancing through the woods tightly buttoned up yard by yard."[64] He did not ask the more appropriate question: Why is this division attacking through the woods in the first place? Again we observe senior commanders examining tactical details when larger issues went unattended. Why another frontal attack in the woods? The 9 and 28IDs had already been shattered there. Given the depth First Army and VII Corps needed to advance, 4ID in reserve ready to tackle the Roer would have been a more logical assignment.

In twenty days of campaigning, most First Army attacking divisions advanced 2–5 miles. They still had 2–4 miles to go before reaching the Roer. The Rhine lay another 25 miles away. Only a public affairs officer could call this a success.

NINTH ARMY

Six foot four, raw boned, and bald, Bill Simpson was an impressive man. A strong-willed, quiet Texan, he exuded the aura of a general. Charles Mac-Donald described him as "an infantryman with a fatherly devotion to his troops after the manner of Bradley and Hodges."[65] "Simp" had been Patton's roommate at West Point. Like the other field army commanders in 12th Army Group, he did not distinguish himself academically. Bill graduated second from the bottom.

Many found him a natural soldier and leader. Bradley described Simpson as steady, well-organized, earthy, a great infantryman, and leader of men.[66] He had extensive combat experience—the Moros in the Philippines, Pancho Villa along the Southwestern border, and the kaiser's troops at the Meuse Argonne. During the Great War, Simp had risen to chief of staff of the 33rd Division and won the Silver Star. World War I left him with a respect for the support big guns and tanks could provide the rifleman. Simpson was a graduate of both Leavenworth and the War College. Of the three army commanders under Bradley, "Simp" had the best grasp of logistics.[67] Ike rated the big Texan as a "clear thinker, energetic and balanced."[68]

As in First Army, most of Ninth Army staff were infantrymen. Many had worked together under Simpson as Fourth Army HQ in the United States. They gained the reputation of being solid and reliable. Bradley stated, "Unlike the noisy and bumptious Third and the temperamental First, the Ninth remained uncommonly normal."[69]

By the beginning of Queen Ninth Army controlled:

XIII Corps	XIX Corps
7th Armored Div	2nd Armored Div
84th Inf Div	29th Inf Div
102nd Inf Div	30th Inf Div
113 Cav Group	

XIX Corps retained most of the units that had been involved in the fight around Aachen. It commanded three good, battle-tested divisions. Thirtieth Infantry Division, making the corps's main effort, had made the final linkup around that city in October. XIX Corps artillery contained nineteen firing battalions. Non-divisional artillery in Ninth Army totaled thirty-three battalions.

Major General Alvan Gillem assumed command of XIII Corps in the United States in December 1943. Gillem had come up from the ranks. Prior to taking corps command, he commanded the Desert Training Center in California and the Armored Force at Fort Knox. XIII Corps had become operational only on 8 November. Two of its divisions were new to combat. The 84ID, the Rail Splitters, had landed in Europe only on 1 September. Some of its transport had been stripped for Red Ball duty. Both the 84th and the 102nd would see their first action in the upcoming operation. Seventh Armored, a hard-luck division, was recouping from the drubbing it had taken in the Peel marshes. Its commander had just been replaced. The 113 Cavalry Group had just moved over from XIX Corps. In addition Ninth Army directly controlled a brigade of Belgian fusiliers that Monty had wanted to get rid of. For the most part, they were used as MPs.

Ninth Army had been in its sector barely three weeks before the start of its offensive. It had precious little time to lay down artillery ammunition. Ammunition rationing had to be strictly enforced. There weren't enough intact roofs to keep all of the army's assigned troops out of the rain. Engineers worked constantly to keep the paved roads from disappearing altogether into the mud. There weren't enough hardstands to keep arriving supplies stacked up out of the muck. Other engineers started sawmills that provided 60,000 board feet a day. Locally produced steel I-beams aided in bridge construction. Some of the most critical spare parts were fabricated in local industries. A lot of captured German materiel was used. There were shortages of specialized skills; men capable of installing large telephone switches, printing maps, and operating heavy equipment were in short supply. The logistic situation was precarious but not critical.

Ninth Army wound up concentrated on a narrow front almost by accident. The British took over a sector from Roermond to Geilenkirchen. If anything, Simpson and his subordinate commanders complained of a lack of sufficient room to deploy their troops. The idea of multiple echelons either didn't occur or didn't appeal to them.

The Ninth would attack over open plain that lies immediately north of Aachen. As this is the often-referred-to Aachen Gap, we will follow this advance in some detail. Second Armored officers labeled it good tank country.[70] Unlike the Stolberg Corridor, there was no forested high ground that militated against an attacker. Ninth Army needed to cross an open strip between the tiny Wurm "River" and the Roer. Simpson would have to traverse less than 14 kilometers from the old West Wall breach scooped out by XIX Corps in early October and the Roer. The ground to be covered was studded with about forty small villages consisting of stout stone houses, but the corps was east of the West Wall. Typical villages were one thousand to two thousand in population and situated about 2 kilometers apart from each other. Most had excellent fields of fire. A number of them were mutually supporting. Many houses had been reinforced by military engineers into de facto pillboxes. Some had cellar roofs reinforced with twelve inches of concrete. Ninth Army understood the strength of these positions.[71] Much of the land between them was open and under cultivation. Mine shafts and slag heaps were interspersed.

The official historian stated, "Except for timing, the fighting on the Ninth Army front was as different from that on the First Army Front as, say, Normandy was from Guadalcanal."[72] Flat open terrain made the principal difference. Armor could maneuver. Targets could be detected from a distance and fire power brought to bear. Unlike the Stolberg corridor, this ground favored American strengths.

The road network was good. Two main roads ran through the area of operations, Aachen to Linnich and Aldenhoven to Jülich. Each provided a good supply route to one of XIX Corps's objectives on the Roer. Almost constant rain had softened much of the level ground. Commanders at all levels were very worried about off-road traffic ability, especially for armor. Most of Ninth Army's medium tanks were fitted with 5-inch "duck bills," which extended track width and improved tank maneuverability over muddy ground.

First Army planned to start with carpet bombing behind German forward positions. Ninth Army was more concerned about the potential of all those villages being turned into fortified anti-tank nests. Newly formed XXIX TAC supporting Ninth Army directed four groups of fighter-bombers against villages to the immediate front of Simpson's assault forces. Medium and heavy bombers targeted specific villages behind those to be hit by the fighter-bombers. This deployment of airpower made better use of bombers. They received very specific aim points that could be handled by existing bomb-sight technology. Low-flying fighter-bombers, which could better discern friend from foe, handled close-in targets.

Ninth Army was to attack to the Roer and protect the army group's northern boundary. Two fortified towns, Geilenkirchen in the north and Würselen in the south, constricted the army's zone of advance (see map 7.2). Both towns were embedded in the fortified belt of the West Wall. Most of the West Wall fortifications in the 15 kilometers between Geilenkirchen and Würselen had been cleared by XIX Corps in October. Ninth Army would have to seize these two towns. Then it would advance across the open Roer plain against fire from the small villages to reach the Roer. The consensus view was that Ninth Army faced a five-day fight from line of departure to the Roer—a distance of about 12 kilometers.[73]

XIII Corps was to seize river crossings at Linnich. British 43rd Infantry Division of British XXX Corps concentrated behind XIII Corps and stood ready to fill in the northern part of XIII Corps's sector as the Americans advanced.[74] XIX Corps made Ninth Army's main effort oriented on Jülich with orders to cross the Roer. By comparison First Army had assigned the capture of each of these towns by a single combat command during the October attack. This demonstrates how unrealistic Hodges's orders to Corlett (prior CG, XIX Corps) had been. Ninth Army's subsequent mission was to seize crossings over the Rhine near Düsseldorf at the westernmost tip of the Ruhr. Düsseldorf is 40 kilometers from the bridges south of Cologne that VII Corps of First Army was to head for.

Simpson directed XIX Corps to weight his attack on the south flank near the VII Corps boundary. McLain recognized the urban complex

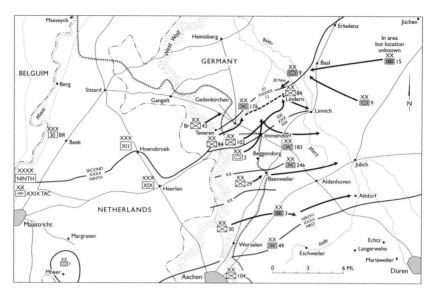

Map 7.2. Ninth Army in Queen

around Eschweiler poised a problem. The 30ID had already run into problems there. Initially McLain placed his main effort in the center. The corps would veer southward when it had advanced beyond the problem area. All three divisions would attack abreast. Simpson ordered that 2nd Armored Division angle north in order to open some of XIII Corps's sector. The plan was to pinch 2nd Armored out of the front line as infantry divisions advanced and allow it to coil up. Hell on Wheels would become a reserve to exploit crossings over the Roer to be made by the infantry in the vicinity of Jülich.

Ninth Army G2 recognized that Germans knew an attack was impending.[75] XIX Corps would strike several days before elements of XIII Corps. Americans habitually attacked at first light. In order to gain some element of tactical surprise all three XIX Corps divisions were to attack at midday. They did so with little artillery preparation. The change in cadence worked. Frontline German units were not prepared for the initial assault. All XIX Corps divisions made good initial progress.

Queen was XIII Corps's first fight. It drew a slightly less difficult assignment than XIX Corps. The 84ID, the northernmost division, would attack the fortified mining town of Geilenkirchen (population 20,000) on the inter-army group boundary. Initially it would operate under British 30 Corps so that both British and American troops assaulted the town under a single commander. By using a British headquarters, the Royal artillery, with its better ammunition supply, could pound the town. XIII Corps was to cross the Roer at Linnich, about 8 kilometers north of Jülich.

The Ninth Army engineer was very worried about the dams.[76] A special intelligence study was made of them. Additional data was requested from the theater engineer. Ninth Army instructed all subordinate units that no Roer crossing (except recon patrols) was to be made without express army approval. Despite recent rains that had swelled the Roer from 60 to 100 meters wide, army group had made few plans to marshal engineer assets for a deliberate crossing of the Roer. If the dams blew, an assault crossing would become a major engineering effort.

Because of all the rain, officers and men alike worried that mud would stop everything bigger than a jeep. General Harmon, 2AD commander, got in a tank and maneuvered in a field near the Wurm River. He could barely make 3 mph in first gear. Concerned, Harmon turned to the sergeant who normally commanded the Sherman. "Can we make it, Sergeant?" "Yes, Sir" came the quick answer. Harmon believed in his men. He informed Simpson that the mud, while a handicap, would not stop his division.[77]

Würselen was a heavily defended town on the German main line of resistance at the southernmost extreme of XIX Corps. Thirtieth Infantry Division orchestrated a well-rehearsed deliberate attack headed southeast to cut the town off. Its three organic regiments attacked abreast. An attached regiment from 84ID was in reserve. Employing good combined-arms tactics, the division made short work of its assignment. Old Hickory's greatest problem was the immense minefields laid by the defenders. Anti-tank mines deterred supporting tanks and tank destroyers, reducing them to a "support by fire only" role. Despite being up against 3PGD, "30th Division's advance was one of the better gains made anywhere during the early days of the November offensive."[78] Hobbs moved much more quickly than did 104ID, under the venerable General Terry Allen, just to its south in VII Corps zone.

Maneuver of the 29th "Blue and Gray" Infantry Division is an interesting example of an infiltration attack. Throughout Hedgerow Hell in Normandy, Major General Charles Gerhardt had commanded the "Blue and Gray." He viewed the open spaces in between the well-defended villages as the soft "edges." He proposed to move his infantry in through them to isolate the strong points from the rear. Gerhardt planned to infiltrate two regiments abreast until the first line of villages had been penetrated. When the key town of Setterich on the Aachen–Linnich highway was reached, his reserve regiment would be committed to attack up the main highway toward the Roer.

The fighter-bomber strikes in 29ID's sector had some impact on the defenders. The mediums cratered many towns, including Jülich and Linnich. The main span over the Roer at Jülich was dropped. German engineers emplaced three pontoon bridges. This might have been taken as a key intelligence indicator of German intentions. One might infer they were not anticipating a flood coming down the river from blown dams.

Infantry began infiltrating under the cover of smoke. As soon as they got between the first village strong points, a huge volume of small arms fire pinned them to the ground. Small folds and some drainage ditches provided a little cover. German mortar and artillery fire sought out these hiding places. Despite what some "maneuver warfare" enthusiasts might advocate, infiltration between mutually supporting strong points did not prove to be a panacea.

The 29th began reducing strong points one at a time. Only the lead battalion of each regiment had been committed during daylight. They had advanced barely 500 meters from their lines of departures. Setterich remained out of reach.

In the northern sector of XIX Corps, 2nd Armored committed a combat command to a more conventional attack. As with the 29th, 2AD smoke screened the midday attack. Fighter-bomber strikes were effective. The armor made good progress, little hindered by the mud. Many defenders were overwhelmed by the sight of so many armored vehicles coming at them en masse. *Feldgrau*-clad soldiers surrendered. German artillery was spotty and tended to impact behind fast-moving attackers. Within two hours the first villages fell under Hell on Wheels. One task force was rocked back by strong anti-tank fire. But CCB attained its objectives by nightfall with relative ease. Solid combined-arms tactics had performed better than infiltration by the Blue and Gray to the south. Bypassing defenders who can't interfere with your further progress is one thing. Attempting to bypass mutually supporting strong points can be suicide.

To the south of the 29th, 30ID coordinated its efforts to clear the fortified area with 104ID of Collins's corps. All in all McLain's corps had put in a good first day. Second Armored had penetrated over three kilometers, and 30ID was well on its way. Twenty-Ninth Infantry Division made less extensive gains.

At the theater level, German reflexes were excellent. Only a few hours after the attack commenced, Rundstedt recognized the combined First-

Ninth Army drive was Eisenhower's main effort.[79] German intelligence officers estimated five armored and seven infantry divisions were involved. This was almost double what Bradley actually committed on the 16th. Rundstedt judged XIX Corps's effort north of Aachen the most dangerous attack. Second Armored Division was on open ground of the Roer Plain. Normally the Americans did not expect a German reaction for twenty-four hours.[80] Rundstedt immediately released his operational reserve, XLVII Panzer Corps (9 Panzer and 15 PGD), to counterattack and destroy 2AD at first light on the 17th. Most other reserves were frozen by Hitler. Rundstedt reached down into Holland and ordered 10SS Panzer Division to move.[81] Warning orders went out to three other divisions in Holland to prepare for movement south. Third Parachute Division and two infantry divisions would also make this trek before Bradley's offensive was finished.

Unfortunately, the British did not mount as much as a feint in support of 12th Army Group's offensive. There was no reason not to move 10SS Panzer. U.S. 104ID had participated in the opening of the Scheldt under Montgomery's command. When this division was identified as part of the American attack, Rundstedt became even more confident of his conclusions. Defend against Bradley and don't worry about an assault toward the Rhine by Montgomery. Reshuffle local reserves and Hitler's offensive preparations can go on undisturbed.

On the morning of the 17th, 9th Panzer Division, supported by thirty-six Tigers from a non-divisional battalion, struck 2nd Armored Division. Panzers rolled out of a heavy mist. American tanks had just moved into their attack positions. A furious tank duel ensued. American tankers shot up their basic loads in and around their open positions. But the heavier guns of the Mark Vs and VIs made their presence felt. Wider German tank tracks gave them a mobility advantage in the muddy ground. The lead 2nd Armored task force withdrew back into the houses of Puffendorf, leaving behind a lot of brightly burning hulks. During the withdrawal, a tanker lieutenant dismounted. He calmly went from foxhole to foxhole informing infantry of the retrograde. Meanwhile his tank stayed in an exposed position to provide cover while the dogfaces moved to safety. This action was credited with creating an orderly withdrawal instead of a panicked bugout.[82]

The Tigers and Panthers did not follow into Puffendorf. The Germans did not want to get caught in close quarters where American infantry and the power-traverse turrets of the Shermans would put them at a disadvantage. Besides, 9th Panzers also had taken a lot of punishment. That day XIX Corps Artillery fired 26,628 rounds. XXIX TAC attempted a few sorties, but misty rain greatly limited their effectiveness. Artillery on both sides stripped away infantry support of the other.

The fight continued to be tank to tank on into the evening. German tankers got the better end of the duel. Hell on Wheels lost more than fifty tanks. Some thought this the worst drubbing 2AD took during the war.[83] Shermans could not stand against Panthers and Tigers when there were long fields of fire in open ground. Superior German tank cannons made the resulting duels death matches for the Americans. Hell on Wheels had to beat off at least four separate German attacks.

While CCB was taking a pounding, CCA managed to take some ground. General Harmon ordered his secondary attack plan into effect. CCA motored along secondary roads south of the tank duel. They moved in the direction of Ederen, another village along the highway to Linnich. German artillery retaliated with a tremendous concentration. A line of anti-tank guns overwatching a 15-foot-wide anti-tank ditch stopped further progress. Armored engineers had prepared a section of treadway bridge to breach the obstacle. No one could move because of the effective anti-tank fire. Harmon realized he had gone as far as he could in the face of 9th Panzer. But 2AD had absorbed the primary impact of the available German operational reserve; Hitler would have to either release panzers from the strategic reserve or accept the threat of a Roer crossing. Harmon speculated that Sixth Panzer Army would soon arrive to cover a withdrawal behind the river.[84]

The Blue and Gray Division was slow to get started the second day of the offensive. American tankers were concerned because their supplies would have to come up the lane from Setterich. 29ID still had not cleared the town. Second Armored continued to push Gerhardt to take Setterich, clear the road up to his CCA ensconced in Puffendorf, and find a way across the anti-tank ditch. These had all been listed in the plans as 29ID objectives. The Blue and Gray continued to make little headway with their all infantry attacks on German strong points. Now McLain also laid pressure on Gerhardt to get moving.

Gerhardt committed to another attack. It commenced just before dawn on the 18th. More conventional tactics were to be employed. The initial appearance of tanks before the defenders of Setterich was less than auspicious. A platoon's worth either mired in mud or fell victim to panzerfausts. But west of the town tank fire smothered riflemen in trenches and allowed American infantry to move against them. By nightfall the 29th was into the town. The anti-tank ditch was not crossed until next morning.

In the remainder of the Blue and Gray sector, combined-arms teams made good progress. Twenty-Ninth Infantry Division artillery maintained concentrated fire on villages until attacking tank-infantry teams moved to within a few hundred meters of the objective. Tanks picked up the suppression mission as the artillery shifted. The division had found "the correct technique for fighting the battle of the Roer Plain: determined infantry accompanied by close tank support and covered by mortars."[85] "The factor most directly affecting operations appeared to be the use of tanks."[86] By the evening of the 18th, the 29th had broken the main defense of the German 246th Division. The Blue and Gray continued its eastward trek toward the Roer.

In XIII Corps sector, the fight for Geilenkirchen was not scheduled to begin until 18 November, two days after XIX Corps had begun its attack. It was hoped the offensive to the south would draw off some of the defenders. That didn't work.

Geilenkirchen lay astride the 21st/12th Army Group boundary. Such junctions were notorious weak spots. To mount a strong attack up this supposedly weak alley, Ninth Army gave temporary operational control of 84ID, the "Rail Splitters," to British 30 Corps. The Brits mounted a double envelopment of the town. At the level of field army and below, relationships between the armies were excellent. Only at the uppermost reaches of command were relations contentious.

The Rail Splitters attacked from the southwest. The Brits supplied several troops of flail tanks. During the early morning darkness they cleared paths through the minefields. Two American assault battalions moved in behind the flails and began rolling up the German defenses. The Brits had ample piles of artillery shells and bestowed them freely on the town. The commander of XII SS Corps was very concerned about Geilenkirchen. He was surprised at the strength of the Allied attack and recognized that attacks from west and south could pinch it off.

After successfully securing the town, continued movement by the 84th to the northeast became mired in mud and increased enemy resistance. Fifteenth Panzer Grenadier Division, which initially had moved in front of 2nd Armored Division to the south, now created a major defensive barrier in front of the Rail Splitters. Rain on the 21st deepened the mud to an impassable quagmire. The division advanced only another 3 kilometers. Still General Horrocks, commander British 30 Corps, complimented 84ID highly on the professionalism and skill the division showed in its first fight.[87] Dogfaces appreciated even more the standard British rum ration he provided to the Americans.

Faced by much of XLVII Panzer Corps, CCA now took up the lead while CCB licked its wounds. Elements of 15 Panzer Grenadier Division reinforced 9 Panzer Division. American tankers felt the presence of the new resistance. A series of small attacks and counterattacks along the anti-tank ditch occupied forces from both sides.

On 18–19 Nov XXIX TAC flew "armored column cover" missions reminiscent of air ground action during the pursuit across France.[88] The Luftwaffe rose to oppose these efforts. One American squadron was bounced by twenty-five FW 190s east of Aachen. The P-38s claimed seven kills with no friendly loss. P-47s encountered twenty aircraft near Heistern and sent eight to earth. On the 21st fifteen P-51s encountered sixty Me109s and claimed ten down, again without friendly loss. Pitting poorly trained replacement pilots against American veterans did nothing to help the Wehrmacht.

An enormous rainstorm hit the night of the 19th. Some 2AD officers wanted to postpone further effort. Disregarding their advice, Harmon pushed on. Both CCA and CCB fought in the morning's driving rain. On the 20th, 2nd Armored attacked behind a barrage laid down by six artillery battalions. American tankers advanced up the road to the next major town—Gereonsweiler. The panzers were too hard-pressed to counterattack. On the 21st Shermans rolled forward to a point where the Roer was plainly visible only 3 kilometers away. German counterattacks finally materialized. A company of attached infantry from 102ID was roughly handled. But mud-strewn tankers and riflemen threw the Germans back. Second Armored now stood on ground assigned to XIII Corps for the final push. The tankers remained there for several days until relieved. In six days Hell on Wheels had advanced through 10 kilometers of heavily defended ground and fought off a major portion of the enemy's operational reserve.

Panzers reappeared on the 20th and began beating up 2nd Armored again. Hell on Wheels slowly ground forward. By the 21st the Blue and Gray was within 3 kilometers of the Roer. Intelligence officers began picking up signs that Germans opposite 29ID were preparing to withdraw behind the Roer.[89] Gerhardt spurred his division on. What he was observing was the withdrawal of 245VGD so that 340VGD could take its place. The 245VGD was little more than a cinder. One regiment had only 350 effectives, another only 120. The Germans threw in another infantry division and two volks artillery corps (each equivalent to a U.S. artillery group). These were units released from the Ardennes buildup. Hitler had to reach into his bag, but he hadn't reached very deeply.

By the 21st, the Germans had a lot of forces at risk west of the Roer. The fight for Geilenkirchen was in progress. The divisions of XLVII Panzer Corps were on the west bank. If the Germans blew the dams, these forces would also be trapped. Efforts to move them eastward would provide Bradley a time window to secure his bridgehead.

XIX Corps stood three divisions abreast on a 12-kilometer front within spitting distance of the Roer. Jülich was less than 3 kilometers away. XIX Corps staff was very optimistic. A quick push to the Roer now seemed at hand.[90] While no breakout was imminent, Americans were in relatively open country facing an enemy executing a passage of lines. Model's operational reserve was already tied down. Down in First Army, forward troops had yet to break out of the Stolberg Corridor or the Huertgen.

Now was the time for army group to switch priorities and spur Ninth Army's XIX Corps on. The Germans were showing signs of exhaustion. Redouble efforts. Attack day and night. Rapid penetration of the remaining defenders would catch many Germans west of the Roer. Most likely, their commanders would delay releasing flood waters until they were retrieved.

Higher headquarters needed to assemble what was needed for a contested crossing of the Roer. The 340VGD was transiting the likely crossing sites. There would be a big fight. If Bradley moved quickly he would not have to face 10SS PzD until he was over the river. Armor, artillery, ammunition, and engineer material needed to get across the 90-meter-wide river as quickly as possible. Combat troops would need to advance far enough forward to shield bridge sites from direct fire but stay close enough to the river to receive the benefit of artillery massed on the west bank. Heavy artillery had to be emplaced for deep counter-battery fire. German artillery remained a potent threat. Radar-directed anti-aircraft guns had to be sited to cover the crossing site. Well-equipped bridging engineers on both banks would make bridge maintenance a lot easier. Drop zones for aerial resupply needed all-weather radio, light, and radar beacons. There was a lot to do.

Capturing existing bridge sites would be important. Even if the Germans dropped the span, its abutments could be used to install a replacement Bailey span. The best way to secure flood-survivable bridging was to get it up off the water.

Ninth Panzer Division and 15PGD had been transferred to XII SS Corps, which desperately tried to keep the northern wing of Ninth Army away from the Roer. Holding German armor in place remained a good mission for 2AD. On the 21st, 3rd Armored down in VII Corps sector had been pinched out. Bradley might have moved it laterally between the armies to exploit across the Roer. Looping 5AD up from V Corps was another alternative. First Infantry Division had already secured the Hamich ridge and moved beyond it. Given no one was tasked with seizing the Roer dams, the efforts of 4ID and V Corps could have been curtailed and used to add weight to a Roer crossing. A successful Roer crossing would eliminate any need to move through the Huertgen. One would expect renewed American effort to burst across the river with enough strength to stand up to Sixth Panzer Army.

BRADLEY SLOWS DOWN

Instead, Bradley ordered the opposite. On 23 November Bradley told Simpson to slow down! Apparently Bradley's reasoning was twofold. Finally he began to worry about the water behind the Roer dams. Second, Bradley did not want Ninth Army to advance until First Army had come even.[91] Gerhardt (29ID) told his regimental commanders not to press their attacks. "Omar says in effect we are there, there is no sense pushing it until the other people [i.e., First Army] get up there."[92]

It was rather late to be thinking about the dams. Pulling units even is the signature of a frontal attack. That is the last thing 12th Army Group wanted to do. Allowing XIX Corps to cross while large German forces opposing other Americans remained west of the Roer was possibly the best method of ensuring against flood. VII Corps was still just east of Eschweiler, and a lot of Germans were west of the river. Given just a few days of being able to work on both sides of the Roer, American engineers could erect treadway bridges on existing abutments that would be up and out of any water surge that might be induced by flooding. In addition to the armor that could have been redirected into the bridgehead, XIII Corps was reorienting away from its flank mission. It could have added weight to the attack by crossing into a XIX Corps bridgehead.

Crossing the Roer was only an intermediate objective. Bradley was supposed to threaten the Rhine. How was he supposed to do this when he had no plan for rapid movement over the Roer?

In response to Bradley's instructions, Ninth Army slowed its advance. XIX Corps began a pattern of attacking one day and consolidating on the next. War on alternate days is no way to execute inside your enemy's decision-reaction loop. In battle, speed is of the essence. Move twice before your enemy moves once and he is doomed. Instead, the Americans gave away this very advantage. Relatively slow advance gave the Germans the most precious of commodities: time to react. Bradley's error was inexcusable. When they became most valuable of all, days, not minutes, were wasted.

On the 24th Ninth Army identified 10SS PzD beginning to arrive.[93] The window began to close. On the 26th, two days after 10SS Panzer arrived, McLain told his division commanders to resume full-court press. In a series of sharp fights, XIX Corps closed up along the Roer on 28 November.

Undersized XIII Corps took over part of Ninth Army's forward sector on the 24th. XIX Corps had finished its movement to the river. Eight artillery battalions were passed from XIX Corps to XIII Corps for the upcoming operation. This brought XIII Corps Artillery up to thirteen firing battalions. An additional three XIX Corps battalions reverted to Army control in general support. One of 7th Armored's tank battalions was attached to the 84th for the upcoming attack. Belatedly General Gillem and his staff began plans to span the stream. Gillem was not able to reassemble his corps until the 28th. Initially the plan envisioned 102ID mounting an assault crossing of the Roer near Linnich. Both 84ID and 7AD, which was still licking wounds incurred in the Peel marshes, would exploit east of the river.

General Bolling, CG 84ID, had learned a lot about frontal attacks on fortified positions in the last ten days. Instead of charging head-on toward the high ground, he planned a night attack. Two regiments in the easternmost section closest to the Roer would be employed. The 335th Regiment had seen little action while attached to 30ID. It got the assignment as main effort. Now the Germans began to furiously attack the Americans in Lindern. The fight went on for several days; Rail Splitters prevailed.

Before the heroic effort at Lindern concluded, Gillem returned to the problem of reaching and forcing the Roer. The 102ID was redesignated XIII Corps main effort and tasked to seize intact bridges near Linnich if at all possible. Remembering the artillery pounding XIX Corps had taken, a massive counter-battery effort was directed at German batteries east of the Roer. Twenty thousand rounds were expended. However, lack of good plots on enemy batteries limited its success. XXIX TAC added some fighter-bombers to the effort. Still, German gunners hit 102ID hard as it approached the Roer. On one occasion, fourteen battalions of German artillery east of the river fired a concentration against the Americans. All through November, German artillery registered quite a kick. "In many respects, the battle of the Roer plain was an artillery show." Germans opposite XIX Corps fired 13,410 rounds a day and estimated American incoming at 27,500 a day.[94]

By 4 December, four days after XIII Corps had started for the Roer, the operation was over. Its two infantry divisions had closed the final few kilometers to the river. Now they stared at SS troops on the far side. Ninth Army, the less-experienced formation, had moved far quicker than First Army and at least met its intermediate objective. (Refer to map 7.1.) One must conclude that operations in the Aachen Gap moved 50 percent faster than for the attacker in the Stolberg Corridor.

Ninth Army suffered 1,133 killed, 6,864 wounded, and 2,059 missing. Simpson's men captured 8,321 and estimated they had killed upward of 6,000. But the defense never showed signs of rupture. Rundstedt had achieved an operational victory. He had held the Americans at bay without dipping into Hitler's strategic reserve.

THIRD ARMY

By 1 October Third Army and Fifth Panzer Army, which opposed it, were both on the defensive.[95] XX Corps conducted limited attacks on the outer forts of Metz. They accomplished little except extending casualty lists and shortening ammunition stockage reports. XII Corps committed 6AD to a limited attack that pushed 555VGD back toward the Seille. Patton was allocated only 3,500 tons of supplies a day. That was barely enough to fund one anemic corps offensive while sustaining the rest of Third Army. As always Patton stretched what he was given.

At SHAEF General Bull drafted plans to resume the offensive. As we have seen, the primary effort remained in the north. Third Army would resume making the secondary effort "from the Nancy salient" toward Frankfurt.[96] Third Army resumed heading northeast rather than east in order to provide additional support for Bradley's effort. Frankfurt became Third Army's objective. Crossing the Rhine between Mainz and Worms was listed as the intermediate goal.[97]

Bradley contemplated a wider encirclement of the Ruhr than did Ike.[98] Bradley was beginning to toy with a plan that ultimately swung Patton from the upper Rhine to encircle the Ruhr. This would swing clear of the rough terrain of the Eifel. First Army was tasked with forming a close-in pincer of the Ruhr after seizing a Rhine bridgehead near Cologne.

But Bradley envisioned Third Army's initial attack to be more modest. The army group commander wanted a limited offensive to gain crossings over the Saar River 50 kilometers from the Moselle. This would position Patton to move against the West Wall in a subsequent operation.

On 19 October Patton had offered to drive to the Rhine in three days,[99] provided he was supplied with 2,000 tons of ammunition a day to do so.* It is doubtful that he meant his boast to be taken seriously. Patton wanted Bradley and Eisenhower to understand he was ready to resume a major offensive. Patton didn't want his superiors to take any of his divisions and wanted as much supply tonnage as possible. By November Bradley felt that Patton's offensive had degenerated into "a ghastly war of attrition."[100]

Patton saw the Rhine riverbank between Worms and Mainz as the best crossing point.[101] That would take his army east from Metz (or northeast from Nancy) to Saarbrücken on the Saar and then northeast to the Rhine. This axis of advance would take Patton just northwest of the Vosges. Mainz, where the Main meets the Rhine, is 60 kilometers (straight line) upstream from where the Moselle joins the Rhine. Patton created his concept for the operation. Gaffey and Gay designed the offensive based around Patton's concept.[102]

Patton lost XV Corps (French 2AD and 79ID), which was transferred to 6th Army Group (Seventh Army). Third Army received three newly landed divisions, 26ID, 95ID, 10AD, and the newly arrived III Corps headquarters, which Major General John Millikin, who had not seen combat, commanded. While Patton knew Millikin and had a good opinion of his skills, he initially objected to placing a corps commander without combat experience over veteran divisional commanders.

First Airborne Army asked how they could support Third Army. Patton stated he'd rather have a single airborne regiment available on twelve hours' notice than to have to go through a longer cycle to get a larger force.[103] No airdrop supported this campaign.

To Patton's south, 6th Army Group would concentrate its offensive on the left of its zone; Seventh Army would attempt to force the Saverne Gap. In effect, Balck would have to parry the offensives of both Third Army in Lorraine and Seventh Army in Alsace. General Bull, SHAEF G3, stated that "the joint Third Army–Seventh Army offensive is not the most important sector of the front."[104] The push through the Saverne Gap is recounted in chapter 8.

---

*From chapter 2, table 2, an army of three armored and six infantry divisions in full-scale attack would expend 3,900 tons of ammunition a day. Patton appears to be modest in his ammunition request. Two thousand tons would require 500 truckloads or fourteen 2½-ton truck companies to move from the railhead, assuming the trucks are 80 percent available and carrying maximum overload.

Patton was itching to resume the offensive. Laying aside some preliminaries, he had two alternative plans. Fort Driant as meat grinder convinced everyone that Metz should be enveloped and not assaulted directly. Plan A had the bulk of XX Corps crossing the Moselle at Thionville, bypassing Metz from the north, and moving on to a crossroads on the highway from Metz east to Saarlautern and the West Wall. XII Corps would attack on a second axis from positions east of Pont à Mousson to Faulquemont and then toward Saarbrücken. XX Corps would bypass Metz and attack east on the road to Saarbrücken. XII Corps would drive northeast toward the XX Corps's axis of advance. The two would converge on Saarbrücken. Under Plan B, the newly arrived III Corps would be fleshed out. It would attack over the Moselle north of Metz, while XII and XX Corps attacked together south of Metz.[105]

However, those initial plans evolved into something less auspicious. Instead of bypassing Metz, XX Corps would make a double envelopment of the fortress. A strong five-division XII Corps would attack northeast toward Saarbrücken. Its subsequent objective was a crossing of the Rhine near Darmstadt. This is north of Worms and just south of Frankfurt.

This time Patton paid very close attention to logistics. His staff carefully drew up tables of tonnages required to support each plan. By the beginning of November, it appeared there would be enough supply to support attacks by all three of Bradley's armies. Patton understood that he was third priority. Artillery ammunition, except for 240mm howitzers and 8-inch guns, was in good supply. However, the offensive would consume far more rounds per day than COMZ could be expected to deliver.

Patton felt most German formations were deployed near his front line. Once he pierced the main defenses, he would be able to race forward. By placing 4th and 6th Armored Division together in XII Corps, Patton created a strong, experienced exploitation force. XII Corps resembled V Corps when it broke out at Saint-Lô, three infantry divisions in the first echelon, with two armored divisions ready to break out. The Rhine flowed northward 225 kilometers to the east, and Patton was confident he could reach it in short order. He believed his armored divisions would slice through a poorly manned West Wall, which snaked through Saarbrücken, and run for the Rhine.[106] His subordinate commanders were far less optimistic. They felt West Wall obstacles would hang tanks up. In their opinion, reducing the West Wall would require a tough infantry fight.

There was concern about water held behind dams flooding the Seille. In an attempt to minimize the river's impact on the upcoming offensive, P-47s purposely opened the Étang de Lindre dams east of Dieuze, inundating the town. The Jabos punched holes on 20 October to allow the water to drain.

General der Panzertruppen Hermann Balck, transferred from command of Fourth Panzer Army on the Russian front, replaced General Blaskowitz as commander, Army Group G. Balck had a reputation of being a solid, tenacious tactician and something of an optimist. During October, OKW had taken Army Group G's primary reserves. The 3 and 15PGDs went north to prepare for the Ardennes offensive. Fifth Panzer Army HQ and its subordinate panzer corps HQs made the same trek. Balck shifted 553VGD, a solid division, down to Nineteenth Army to oppose 6th Army Group. To replace them Army Group G received three low-grade VGDs.

That left General Balck with two armies. Balck concentrated the bulk of his resources in German First Army in front of Patton. It contained nine divisions, five of which were in respectable shape. Balck deployed them to form a continuous front employing "elastic" defensive tactics. Only security forces would hold the first few kilometers of depth. Their role was to deceive the Allies as to the exact location of the main line of resistance. Hopefully, the Americans would expend most of their bombs and artillery shells on the relatively unmanned security zone, leaving the primary positions intact and ready to repel attacking infantry and tanks. Thousands of mines were laid. Balck wanted each division to place a regiment in reserve. Because of their extended front, most divisional commanders had only a battalion held out. Balck held veteran 11PGD, with sixty tanks, ten assault guns, and two panzer grenadier regiments, as his operational reserve in First Army area.

Balck expected Patton to resume his offensive in the first half of November. He expected the Allied main effort to fall against his First Army. Nineteenth Army, ensconced in the Vosges, would oppose Devers's 6th Army Group. German sympathizers behind Patton's lines and radio intercepts of careless American radio traffic gave him a good picture of Patton's dispositions.

Rundstedt suggested some tactical withdrawals in order to form new reserves, including withdrawal from Metz. Balck didn't want to give up any ground. If he did so, Patton would undoubtedly attack at the point of withdrawal. Balck told Rundstedt he would be ready to counterattack the instant Patton made any headway. He was attempting to extricate 21PzD from a place in the line south of Patton's area when the American attack struck.

Patton initially scheduled Third Army's offensive to commence 3 November. Weather refused to cooperate. Torrents of water fell from the sky, engorging streams and creating mud seas. On 7 November Generals Eddy and Grow (6AD commander) wanted to postpone the attack because of the horrendous conditions. Patton recorded in his diary, "I asked them to name their successors. They immediately assented and as usual did great work,"[107] attacking on the 8th as scheduled. If only it would stop raining! The troops called Lorraine "trench foot country." Because the weather just prior to the attack had been horrendous, the Germans were taken by surprise.

XII Corps attack began with a murderous artillery preparation. Seventeen corps and twenty divisional artillery battalions fired almost 22,000 rounds. Forward units had not followed Balck's instructions on thinly held forward positions, and many German gun positions were smashed.[108] Initial American infantry assaults met limited German resistance. XII Corps needed to ascend two hill complexes (Morhange and Dieuze plateaus in the Forêt de Château-Salins and Forêt de Bride). Mud was a greater retardant than German resistance. But stubborn strong points, some ensconced in World War I trenches, and the hilly topography began to canalize and slow American advance. Many officers wished this offensive could have been mounted on the firmer ground of October.[109] XII Corps had a sector that was far too wide. It was arrayed across 50 kilometers of front instead of a sector of attack that should have been less than half that (FM100-5 of 1944, the "book," recommended a division attack on a mile front). This caused Eddy to string his three infantry divisions out in line instead of creating a column of divisions for deep penetration. After all, Patton had decreed XII Corps would cover the 65 kilometers to the West Wall in two days.[110]

By the second day, flooding had taken out all but one of the bridges behind Third Army over the Moselle. The Seille expanded from 200 to 500 feet.[111] At one time Patton had seven divisions (including XX Corps) across the Moselle and no bridges to support them. He continued to attack while his engineers tried everything imaginable to get supplies across the river.

The decision as to when to commit the armored exploitation force is critical. Commit too early and the tanks become enmeshed in the initial fight to break the defensive line (sometimes called the "break in"). Commit too late and the enemy may have emplaced enough reserves to prevent the armor from breaking out. In Lorraine's horrible weather, this problem was further exacerbated by the deep mud that ensured no one would move faster than low gear at best. Most analysts agree with Mellenthin that "Eddy would have done better to wait [to commit the armor] until his infantry had eaten away more of our defense zone."[112] American armor was committed while the infantry was fighting its way onto the two hill masses and got hung up on some of the surviving anti-tank guns covering the roads. Then again, 11PzD did counterattack on the 10th. It was a tough call. German company-sized blocking units of tanks and infantry were large enough to contest a road on which an American tank battalion task force was advancing. The attacker's normal response is to seek a flank on the roadblock. But mud often defeated this tactic. Would larger forces in column have found a way around while the forward task force held the defenders? With the mud, it is difficult to say. The 11PzD fought well, slowed XII Corps to a crawl, and even captured a sizable number of Americans when an unsupported advance retook Rodalbe on the 12th. XII Corps never achieved a breakthrough.

By then Patton knew it would be a grinding slugfest. He recorded in his diary entry of the 12th, "I must get the XII Corps in column of divisions so as to give one division at least a chance to rest, sleep and get hot food and dry out."[113] It is unfortunate that this formation, in lieu of a three-division wide advance, was not adopted from the beginning.

Despite the horrendous rain, XII Corps pressed their attack hard and brought about the collapse of 48th Division in the northern wing of the sector. In a bold dash through the mud, 6AD slithered forward and captured an intact bridge over the River Nied. German commanders scrambled to meet the emergency. Rundstedt released 36VGD from Seventh to First Army. This was a strong unit earmarked for the Ardennes offensive, with a full complement of artillery and officered by eastern front veterans. It was joined by 21PzD. Together they formed a solid block below Faulquemont. This stopped further advance by 80ID and 4AD to the northeast.

Third Army met German tactics similar to those that repeatedly stopped U.S. First Army during September in the Aachen corridor. The Germans moved reserves into secondary defensive positions faster than the Americans could advance. Eddy had armor in depth. But mud and rain slowed his ability to advance. He had no fresh infantry to commit when his lead divisions became exhausted. Weather and perhaps premature deployment of his armor caused the attack to stall. Balck had reserves to commit, while Eddy had only exhausted mud-caked dogfaces pushed to the limit of their endurance. Had the weather been better, the armor might have gained sufficient speed to break through.

On the 14th Eddy issued new orders, slowing XII Corps until XX Corps got beyond Metz. However, 80ID and 6AD, in a fierce attack, dislodged German defenders from the high ground south of Faulquemont.

A pause lasted four days. XII Corps was exhausted and disorganized. Again, a column of divisions would have prevented this unfortunate stoppage. On the 16th, despite a Hitler "no retreat" order, Balck decided to remove his mobile troops from Metz. The mostly elderly gentlemen of Division 462 (the officer candidates had "graduated") would remain behind as a rear guard.

During the night of 17–18 November, German First Army backed up to a line Faulquemont–Benestroff–Bourgaltroff and broke contact with Metz.

When Eddy resumed his advance, mud and rain limited his attacking divisions to a crawl. By the beginning of December, XII Corps had pulled to within sight of Sarre-Union. This town, half way to the West Wall, had been reached in ten days of combat, not the two. Thirty kilometers in ten days versus Patton's boast that 65 kilometers were to be gained in two days. Eddy's three infantry divisions had suffered over 7,000 killed and wounded, enough to take off their combat edge.

XII Corps's maneuver threatening Sarre-Union set off alarms in Balck's HQ. Rundstedt recognized the threat but had nothing to send. Only formations being assembled by OKW for the Ardennes offensive could shore up the situation. At first Keitel, Hitler's long-suffering de facto chief of staff, refused the request emanating from Balck. Finally OKW relented, and Panzer Lehr was released to deal with the problem. It had to march 500 kilometers from Munster to where Balck needed it. The move made Lehr late for the Bulge. What would have happened if Patton could have advanced both XX and XII Corps far enough toward the Rhine to have forced more of Sixth Panzer Army to react?

METZ ENCIRCLED AND XX CORPS ADVANCES

The 90ID's crossing of the Moselle has been recounted in chapter 6. Tenth Armored Division crossed the Moselle into 90ID's bridgehead north of Metz on the afternoon of the 14th. The route assigned to 10AD had little to recommend it. The few roads were in disrepair. Soggy fields would not support the weight of cross-country armored movement. Fortunately, the tankers met with little resistance except the mud. During the first few days the armor took six hundred prisoners. Skies cleared a little. Reminiscent of the race across France, XIX TAC P-47s patrolled over the advancing armor. Progress was rapid on the 17th. On the 18th 10AD reached the Nied River near Bouzonville. The bridges were blown.

The 5ID pushed up from the south. It cut into elements of 17SS PGD, which also held the line against 80ID's efforts on behalf of XII Corps to the south. The 5ID seized crossings across the Nied française. The bulk of the division continued toward Metz. Walker called Irwin to compliment his division's progress.[114]

In order to keep up the pace, Van Fleet leapfrogged his regiments forward. Specific terrain objectives were no longer assigned.[115] The mission was to link up with 5ID. Infantry rode trucks when they could and moved overland when they couldn't. Often American attackers overwhelmed German rearguards before they could detonate pre-set demolitions. From the 17th to the 19th decent flying conditions allowed P-47s to escort the advancing infantry. They plowed the ground only 100 meters in front of the dogfaces with .50 caliber. The 5ID enjoyed similar support.

Walker's infantry divisions completed the encirclement of Metz on the 19th. The American flag would not fly over the city until the 22nd. In order to conserve artillery ammunition, Walker forbade direct assault of the forts that continued to hold out.

The official history states, "This operation [encirclement of Metz] skillfully planned and marked by thorough execution of the plan, may long remain an outstanding example of a prepared battle for the reduction of a fortified position."[116] At the tactical level, this is true. At the operational level one wonders if the time absorbed by this operation would have been better used had the fortress been bypassed and the spearheads headed east. Encirclement of Metz is a good example of the difference between the tactical and operational levels of war. While the divisions performed brilliantly at the tactical level, XX Corps was attacking the wrong objective. It should have been taking the fastest route to the Rhine. That was not a combat assault over the Moselle north of Metz and then encirclement of the fortress. It was a high-speed attack south of Metz from an existing bridgehead.

Moving from 5ID's bridgehead, XX Corps might have concentrated on crossing the Saar and penetrating the West Wall. This was one of the options Patton initially identified. Obliquely, the history goes on to make a similar comment: "However determined enemy resistance, bad weather and attendant floods, plus a general tendency to overestimate the strength of the Metz fortifications, all combined to slow down the American offensive and give opportunity for the right wing of the German First Army to repair the tie between XXXII Corps and XIII SS Corps in time for an organized withdrawal to the Sarre River."[117]

Walker knew his job was only beginning. "With General Patton's injunction that the Sarre must be crossed ringing in his ears," Walker ordered 10AD concentrated and headed toward that stream.[118]

Departing from the initial plans, Patton wanted to shift his attack eastward. Now it would cross the Rhine near its juncture with the Moselle.[119] This was in accordance with Ike's wishes. The move placed XX Corps up against one of the densest portions of West Wall. The Orscholz, or "Siegfried Switch Line," was designed to prevent just such a movement. Unfortunately American intelligence had little information on its defenses, and XX Corps ran headlong into it without proper preparation. This underscored another shortcoming seen throughout Third Army. Given the October pause, tactical intelligence up and down the front was inadequate. Tactical commanders should have had detailed maps of German defenses. In what became known as the Moselle triangle, fortifications were arranged more than 3 kilometers deep. The short hiatus in eastward movement of XX Corps while it sealed the ring around Metz gave the Germans some time to complete their defenses.[120] On the 19th, XX Corps stalled before the switch line.

To the south of this fight the remainder of 90ID plus 95ID advanced to the Saar River from positions along the Nied River. This advance began on 25 November. They attacked against three weak German divisions. Again swollen rivers, blown bridges, and endless mud proved more of a problem than enemy resistance. On the 27th Van Fleet halted his division for a day so that engineers could repair the roads sufficiently to bring up his armor.

Walker told Patton XX Corps would be ready to attack toward Saarlautern on the 29th. Despite the physical condition of his troops, Walton wanted to push the enemy until they broke. However tired the Americans were, the XX Corps commander felt the Germans were in worse shape. Walker ordered 90th and 95th Infantry Divisions to make a coordinated assault on the Saar Heights. They ran into quite a fight. Walker's persistence and willingness to carry the fight were characteristics Patton valued highly.

Patton called Bradley, who said the First/Ninth Army effort was not achieving the desired results. Twenty-First Army Group would secure the bombers to support Walker if Third Army could achieve a breakthrough.[121]

Over the next several days, XX Corps succeeded in pushing through the Saar Heights and to the river. Rundstedt reprimanded General der Panzertruppen Knobelsdorff (German First Army commander) for retreating behind the Saar. However, Balck had ordered him not to risk destruction of his forces west of the river. The 95ID pulled up just before Saarlautern, which lies west of the river, on the 1st of December. Medium bombers plastered the city on the 2nd. The 95ID entered it later in the day. The 90ID gained the riverbank to the north. Walker alerted 5ID, which had been cleaning out resistance around Metz, to be ready to exploit any bridgehead 90 or 95ID made over the Saar.

Both 90 and 95IDs had suffered a lot of casualties since they had crossed the Moselle. Four of 95ID's infantry battalions had been reduced to 55 percent strength. The Division G3 entered an efficiency rating of "very weak," almost an unheard-of admission on official records.[122] Constant battle with mud had also sapped their energy. Even Patton recognized his forward divisions were tired. Neither division advanced more than 200 meters into the West Wall fortifications before the Ardennes counteroffensive brought their attacks to a halt.

NOVEMBER OPERATIONS IN PERSPECTIVE

The strategic objective assigned to Bradley was a crossing of the Rhine just south of Cologne. Ike wanted the main effort in the north, specifically north of the Moselle. That did not dictate the Roer had to be tackled. Conceivably, Bradley could have moved from the toeholds in the Ardennes or even concocted a campaign up the Moselle Valley with First and Third Armies.

Still, the Aachen axis was most likely. Without the dams, the Roer wasn't much of an obstacle. The key terrain was the dams or, more accurately, the water behind them. Once Bradley settled on the Aachen sector as the site of his main effort, he had three options:

— capture the dams by ground assault
— destroy the dams by bombardment or raid prior to his offensive
— prepare to cross the Roer before the water was released and have support ready to hold the bridgehead against a likely flood.

Incredibly, in November he chose "none of the above." The truth is Bradley had no coherent plan to deal with the Roer. What is difficult to understand is that no one formulated one during the October hiatus. No one in 12th Army Group seemed to have entertained a trans-Roer assault before the dams were emptied. "The precluding factors were the Roer River dams, whose capture by First Army had been deemed necessary before launching the attack across the river."[123] With no plan to deal with the Roer, Queen made little sense. It had no way of advancing to its objectives along the Rhine. Closing up the length of the Roer with the dams intact had no value. Yet when Ninth Army approached the stream, Bradley stated, "In effect we are there."[124]

Bradley could have mounted a river crossing under threat of flood. It would have been a calculated risk. With a lot of effort it was doable, especially if a bridgehead could be secured before the water was released. A sharp penetration could have carried to the river in one sector, leaving many Germans west of the river. A window of opportunity would have remained open while German commanders struggled to move their forces back and decided what to do. Ninth Army's success up to November provided such an opportunity. A Ninth Army dash across the Roer while the bulk of German forces opposing First Army were in contact west of the Roer would have presented Model and Rundstedt with a difficult choice: either sacrifice the Germans west of the Roer or allow Ninth Army at least a couple of days to stock supplies and emplace fixed bridges before releasing the water. Again Patton's record demonstrates that holding a riverhead, even with bridges that have been washed out, is not an impossible task. The only effective counter would have been taking a large slice of the divisions Hitler was hoarding for the Ardennes offensive to counterattack Ninth Army's bridgehead. And they would attack into heavily concentrated artillery and be subject to intense air attack if the weather broke.

Some authors have suggested an advance up the Monschau corridor (which extends from the eastern end of the Ardennes, past the Roer dams, and into Germany) as a possible solution. Unlike the situation in September, this option in the late fall had some merit. Perhaps a multi-divisional operation might have worked. While the unfortunate "Bloody Bucket" made an attempt at Schmidt, a second division might have advanced in parallel from Lammersdorf. It could have been the upper pincer, with the lower jaw formed by a multi-divisional attack from Monschau. It would have been a tough, bloody, and large preliminary operation. However, it would have been far preferable to the actual V Corps attack into the woods for nothing but tactical objectives. In either case, Germans would be hard-pressed to prevent the remainder of 12th Army Group from reaching the Roer and then forcing a crossing.

Just before the German Ardennes offensive in December, V Corps did commence an attack toward the dams. Two infantry divisions attempted a double envelopment through six miles of terrain that was "as forbidding militarily as anything that had been encountered during the course of the Siegfried Line campaign."[125] In three days they advanced about three miles to Kesternich, when German infiltrators got in behind the Americans and made their advance positions untenable. About 1,300 battle casualties resulted. The German Ardennes offensive ended any further attempt as V Corps began fighting for its life against the assaulting panzers.

With little departure from SHAEF guidance, the main effort could have been shifted to the Geilenkirchen–Aachen corridor over which Ninth Army advanced. A three-corps army with a strong second echelon focused on operations over the Roer could have concentrated north of Aachen. Aachen was already in American possession. Geilenkirchen would be taken as part of the initial effort. A spearhead between the two towns did not have to become ensnared in either. An attack to first neutralize the dams, followed by a strong thrust in the north, would have crossed the Roer. Hitler would then have the choice of committing Sixth Panzer Army to stopping Simpson or risking a crossing of the Rhine. Only a threat of this magnitude would have wrestled the initiative away from the Germans.

Lorraine contained neither flood-threatening reservoirs nor refitted panzer armies in reserve. Another alternative would have been to shift the main effort into that province. Patton was a proven ground gainer, aggressive in the offense. Adding a second army to the southern attack, or at least reinforcing Patton with a brace of corps, would have been required to shift weight. Ninth Army could have remained south of the First. The Allies could have shifted forces behind the Ardennes much easier and more quickly than a countervailing German move subject to Allied attack. Allied railroads were now in good operating order, and gasoline was no longer a major constraint.

In order to shift the intended axis of attack, Bradley would have needed Ike's concurrence. Ike remained committed to the northern route. The Combined Chiefs had designated it as the preferred route. A lot of the heat generated between the Brits and the Americans was ostensibly over this issue. The Ruhr and Berlin lay beyond SHAEF's reach. The goal of closing on the Rhine and destroying the German army west of that river contained less latitudinal imperative than September's strategy. Both Montgomery and Brooke stated it was more important to pick a main attack and stick to it rather than dissipate Allied strength in broad frontal attacks to the Rhine.

Bradley finally made a choice in early December. He wasn't willing to cross the river while under threat of flood. Neither did he think the dams could be destroyed by bombardment.[126] Bradley concluded he had to take the dams by ground assault from the west and southwest.[127] The Battle of the Bulge interrupted these belated plans.

Montgomery wrote Eisenhower that "[w]e have therefore failed; and we have suffered a strategic reverse."[128] While Ike howled at Montgomery's candid remark, the field marshal was correct. Bradley had not delivered.

BRADLEY AS OPERATIONAL COMMANDER

In his second memoir, Bradley didn't mince words. "To put it candidly, my plan to smash through the Rhine and encircle the Ruhr had failed." The battle "was sheer butchery on both sides."[129] The official historian agreed. The First-Ninth Army offensive "failed to achieve the hoped for successes."[130]

November had been a tough problem. Bradley blew a much easier one in September. He failed to redeem himself during several lesser opportunities, including the XIX Corps attack in early October.

Writing in 1952, the noted Australian historian Chester Wilmot summarized the observations of Bradley's non-American critics: "Bradley was an able tactician, but he was less competent in the realm of strategy [operational art]. In Normandy, commanding First U.S. Army, he had shown himself to be a resourceful leader, but neither then nor later did he seem to appreciate the importance of concentration or balance." "Bradley could deliver the stroke but he was less able to create the opportunity for it." When Bradley created his own campaigns in the fall, "he dispersed his effort."[131] Additional information made available after Wilmot penned those words does not contradict them.

A note in Brooke's files attributed to Montgomery echoes the negative tone about Bradley's operational-level performance in the fall. "It is my impression that Ike thinks Bradley has failed him as an architect of land operations."[132] For his part Bradley states that "Ike never said this to him or anyone else."[133]

Weigley described American generalship as "unimaginative and cautious" and officered by generals who were "competent but addicted to playing it safe."[134] Bradley was an intelligent and personable man. He repeatedly demonstrated his organizational and leadership skills. An able tactician, he demonstrated clear ability at army-level command and below. However, the fall campaign demonstrated that he had difficulty seeing the possibilities of large-scale maneuver and the uses of operational-level reserves. Instead of seeing the whole canvas, he concentrated on improving the shape of each sub-element in the painting. It was as if his understanding of tactics blinded him to the larger scale of the operational art. A large troop list and a wide front meant that there were a lot of tactical problems to be solved. He concentrated on each of them in turn rather than grasping the need to link battles into a campaign that achieved the assigned theater objective. Neither the effort in September nor that in November was a success. In September Bradley did not single out the essential battles from a string of opportunities that were presented. He did not look beyond the next set of engagements to create combinations that penetrated deeply into the enemy's array. Lack of focus prevented 12th Army Group from reaching the Rhine. Instead, Bradley turned what should have been a penetration operation into a frontal attack.

November cried for a creative solution. Bradley had Ike's confidence. Bradley would have gotten a careful hearing on anything he wanted to propose. But he came up with nothing. His plan had no chance of reaching his assigned objective along the Rhine. He had no clue as to how to cross the Roer. Instead, he reached back to the form of his successful Cobra operation: bomb massively and then make a big push. However, conditions were very different. In Normandy there was no floodable moat, no large panzer army in reserve ready to crush any budding penetration.

The current "book" admonishes, when operational art is not properly orchestrated, war devolves to "a set of disconnected engagements, with relative attrition the only measure of success or failure."[135] Unfortunately, this describes much of Bradley's work from September to November.

8

Opportunity in the South

The Allies should advance on more than one axis of advance to keep the Germans guessing as to the direction of our main thrust, cause them to extend their forces, and lay the German forces open to defeat in detail. A single axis would lead us to collisions with the enemy main forces on narrow fronts and with no power of maneuver or surprise.

SHAEF Staff, "Post Overlord Planning," 18 May 1944

On 15 August, the anniversary of Napoleon's birth, Seventh Army landed along the Côte d'Azur in southern France. Seventh Army contained a single U.S. corps composed of veteran divisions of the Italian campaign and an amalgamation of French divisions in varying states of organization and equipment. The landings unfolded textbook-like against limited opposition. *Time* labeled the landings "A Tactician's Dream."[1] The attack up the Rhone valley has been dubbed "the Champagne Campaign." The Germans retreated as rapidly as possible. A procession of feted Allies followed them up the valley. At times, it looked more like a victory procession than a combat maneuver. A great expanse of southern France was liberated at very little Allied expense.

Logistical succor for the Allies was supposed to gush forth from Dragoon. For the first several months that did not happen. Tonnage flowing north was insufficient to support Seventh Army, let alone contribute to Bradley's units that had advanced from the west. No fresh bread or meat was available in Seventh Army until 26 September. At times troops were ordered to subsist on two-thirds of a K ration a day. Again, the problem was a shortage of trucks. To meet the problem, rehabilitation of rail lines up the Rhone was accelerated.[2] The landing of railway units was moved ahead of additional combat units. Until Marseilles was linked to the front with rail service, the southern approach would be of no logistic assistance to Ike.

When Patch issued a new directive on 29 September, available logistics could not support major offensive action.[3] Instead, Seventh Army's supply situation was critical.[4] As in ETO-supported units, there were massive shortages of artillery and mortar ammunition. These constraints were not alleviated until the second week in October. The all-too-familiar story of a supply-induced delay gave German Nineteenth Army time to fortify itself in the woods and mountains of Alsace.

VOSGES, THE BELFORT GAP, AND THE SAVERNE GAP

Two approaches toward Germany led from the tip of the Rhone Valley (see map 8.1). The obvious approach was through the "Belfort Gap" (B on map 8.1) between the Vosges and the west bank of the Rhine. But a jump due east across the Rhine below Strasbourg led into the Black Forest—and nowhere. The second approach (A on map 8.1) enters the Lorraine Gateway where Third Army was struggling. Patton had little force south of Lüneburg, especially when XV Corps was transferred to Seventh Army later in the fall. The Marne-Rhine Canal complicates matters in the eastern portion of Lorraine. But a little work with unit boundaries could have provided room for Seventh Army to advance via Saarburg to the Rhine in the vicinity of Manheim. An attack on this axis could have become either a southern pincer targeted on the Saar or the beginning of an advance on Frankfurt. Recall this is the secondary thrust line outlined in Ike's initial directive (FWD13765—chapter 3). An Epinal–Baccarat–Saarburg approach would encounter some hills. Then again most of Lorraine was hilly.

The Vosges mountains split the Lorraine gateway from the Belfort gap in Alsace. They run from southwest to northeast. The Saverne Gap, which connects the Alsatian plain to the Rhine Valley, bifurcates the range. To the southwest, the mountains are called the High Vosges. Peaks rise to 1,300 meters. The Low Vosges are far more dissected and irregular. They present a far more difficult barrier to military movement. Throughout history, these mountains have been viewed as an impenetrable refuge. Ruins of pre-Christian redoubts remain. No army had ever forced a crossing.

The Vosges road network in 1944 was sparse—barely adequate for division-sized operations. Most roads followed valley floors flanked by forested, sharply rising mountains. Commanders on both sides described fighting in the close terrain of the Vosges as being similar to jungle fighting.[5]

The Saverne Gap itself provides a third axis of advance, C, an offshoot from axis A above. The gap leads to Strasbourg. Turning north, an attacking

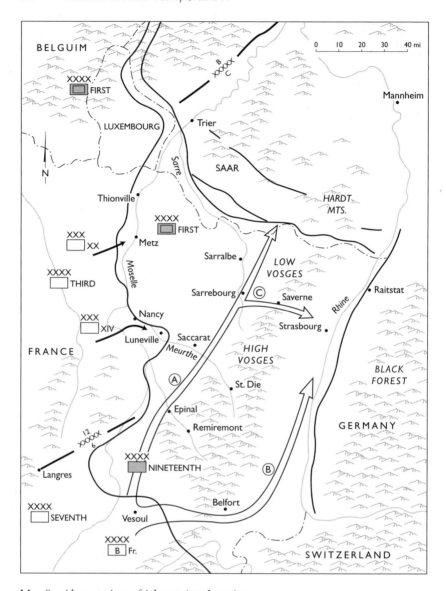

Map 8.1. Alternate Axes of Advance into Lorraine

army could gain access to the Rhine around Manheim, where a crossing could lead to the Saar.

The Meurthe River is a major military obstacle. It originates in the mountains, flows past Saint-Dié and Lunéville and finally empties into the Marne-Rhine Canal, which, in turn, runs into the Moselle. This forms a barrier across the axis that leads into Lorraine. High ground to the north of the stream gave the Germans added advantage against an American attack. The Marne-Rhine Canal, which connects the Moselle and the Rhine, is a second water barrier to a Lorraine advance. The canal runs from the vicinity of Nancy, past Saarburg, and then through the Saverne Gap to the Rhine.

DEVERS AND 6TH ARMY GROUP

The infantry fighting vehicle used in Desert Storm comes in two versions. The infantry vehicle is the M2 Bradley. Armored cavalry use a variant known as the M3 Devers. Externally, they are difficult to distinguish. Most soldiers call both "Bradley." Bradley and Devers were the only two American army group commanders in the ETO. As with the fighting vehicles, everyone recognizes Bradley. Devers is little mentioned.

Lieutenant General Jacob "Jakie" Devers was Marshall's man. He had a reputation for accomplishing every task he was assigned. Devers has been described as a solid, hard, and persistent worker.[6] When it appeared that Marshall would command Overlord, he indicated his principal commanders would be either McNair (army group) and Devers and Bradley (armies) or Devers (army group) and Bradley and Hodges (armies).[7] The implied rank order is obvious.

Devers spent most of his career as an artilleryman. After the untimely death of a real mobile warfare pioneer, General Adna Chaffee, Marshall appointed Devers to command the Armored Force and School. Unlike Bradley, who was busy inculcating the fundamentals of soldering into raw divisions, Devers participated in the change in thinking that discarded outmoded doctrinal notions from the twenties and early thirties.

Based on the results from Louisiana and the German use of kampf-groups (ad hoc combat groupings, usually combining smaller units from several arms—e.g., infantry, artillery, engineers, armor), the notion of the tank-infantry-artillery combined-arms team began to emerge. Devers was a key player in its formulation. He recommended that armored divisions be reorganized to create balanced combined arms forces.[8] Marshall approved. On the other hand, Devers did not think much of the tank destroyer arm that had come into vogue.[9] An artillery man eschewing guns is not what one might expect, but his views proved correct. Devers is largely responsible for creating self-propelled artillery, including the design of the M7 self-propelled 105mm, that so well served the Allies in Western Europe.

Patton knew Devers well. They were 1909 classmates at West Point. Jakie always seemed to be a step ahead. While Devers was chief of armor, Patton served under him, first as commander of the newly activated 2nd Armored Division and later as CG, I Armored Corps. Patton referred to Devers as "a clever man."[10]

Marshall sent Devers to command ETO in May 1943. While in that position he crossed swords several times with the American commander of MTO—Eisenhower. Ike struggled to obtain some bombers for his active campaign, and Devers blocked transfer of four bomb groups. Ike never forgot the arguments and kept something of a grudge.[11] The two quarreled again when Devers complained that Ike was taking too many talented officers from the Mediterranean to staff Overlord.[12] Later, Eisenhower recommended Patton receive his third star ahead of Devers. It was one of the few personnel issues Marshall ever questioned. Ike modified it.[13]

When he was given command of ETO, Eisenhower suggested Devers be given command of the Mediterranean. That was one way to get rid of him. Bradley quoted Patton as saying that Ike had called Devers "22 Caliber."[14] Patton's diary was even more pithy: "Ike hates him [Devers]."[15] Bradley stated he might have been prejudiced by Ike. But Bradley found Devers "egotistical, shallow, intolerant, not very smart, and much too inclined to go off half cocked."[16]

Ike and Beetle Smith became particularly unhappy with Devers's management of the Alsace campaign. Despite 6th Army Group's 2–1 strength advantage, Ike felt Devers's command seemed paralyzed whenever the Germans moved a division. During the German counterattacks in the Bulge and Alsace, Ike considered replacing Devers with Patch. At war's end Eisenhower rated Devers twenty-fourth on a list of general officers under his command. Six corps commanders placed higher.

This analysis didn't take into account the reduced combat power of French divisions, which constituted the bulk of Devers's force. Especially early in the campaign, French forces were short of equipment, trained leaders, and proper logistical support. Seventh Army had but a single corps of three U.S. divisions; they were badly stretched over a lot of terrain. Sixth Army Group divisions held far greater frontages than their 12th Army Group counterparts. Sixth Army Group had but a single fighter bomber group in support; 12th Army Group had more support than that for each of its divisions. Devers operated at some distinct handicaps.

Either Eisenhower or Marshall was wrong about Devers. If it was a vote, Patton liked Devers.

Doctrinally, corps and army groups were supposed to control combat operations only. Logistics and administration flowed from division to numbered army to COMZ. An army group headquarters was supposed to be small. Unlike Bradley's behemoth, which was heavily involved in logistics and administration, Devers ran a small HQ. He rarely interfered with the tactical operations of his subordinate commanders.[17]

Alexander "Sandy" Patch commanded Seventh Army. Termed "the Quiet Hero," General Patch "inspired confidence, admiration and perhaps affection among his men."[18] Sandy helped chase Pancho Villa in 1913 and saw the trenches in World War I. Prior to arriving in ETO, Patch had extensive combat experience in the South Pacific. His background in jungle fighting at the end of a tenuous supply line equipped him well for the upcoming campaign in the wilds of the Vosges. The jungle also taught the great difficulty of, and the absolute necessity for, maneuver in close terrain. Otherwise a small force can stop up a much larger one at terrain bottle necks. New Caledonia, a French possession controlled by some very independent Frenchmen, also taught Patch a little about how to deal with officers like de Lattre.

Truscott described Patch as "keenly intelligent," "a man of outstanding integrity, a courageous and competent leader, and an unselfish comrade in arms."[19] Perhaps there is no higher accolade then the recollection of a grizzled sergeant who served under him: "He never needlessly expended a GI's Life."[20] In many ways the personalities of Patch and Patton were at opposite poles. Patch never used profanity and avoided publicity. Yet the two men were good friends.[21]

Not everyone was enamored with Seventh Army staff. XV Corps commander, General Haislip, who had spent a lot of time under Patton, did not care for them.[22] On the other hand, Haislip was one of Patton's favorites.

Lucian Truscott commanded VI Corps and its three divisions. Truscott had graduated from the Army's first OCS in World War I and commissioned in the cavalry. An outstanding polo player, he had become a protégé of Patton. A graduate of Command and General Staff School, he taught there in the mid-thirties. Truscott commanded a task force in the Torch landings and aggressively sought combat to destroy his enemy. He was made commander of the well-regarded 3rd Infantry division and led it through Sicily, into the beachhead at Salerno, and in the assault at Anzio. He became commander VI Corps there. Bradley tried hard to obtain Lucian's services for the Normandy invasion. When it was thought Patton might be shipped home after a political gaffe in England, Truscott's name was mentioned as potential commander, Third Army. He was widely respected by the senior American commanders in Western Europe for his ability to see what needed to be done and then aggressively execute it. Truscott would rise to command Fifth Army in October 1944. Troops serving under him were fiercely loyal to Truscott's combination of tactical prowess and concern for their well-being. More than one officer turned down promotions in order to remain under Lucian's command. Truscott was a hard-driving leader. He understood the importance in acting faster than the enemy could react. In contemporary terms that is described as operating inside the enemy's decision loop.

Truscott chose three veteran divisions from among those in Italy for VI Corps. The 3, 36, and 45IDs had extensive mountain combat experience in Italy. Back home, two of them had been neighbors. The 36ID was Texas National Guard; 45ID hailed from Oklahoma, Arizona, New Mexico, and Colorado. Both had controversial episodes in Italy but became good divisions. The 3ID, Regular Army, had received its baptism during the landings in North Africa in November 1942. Both the 3rd and the 45th participated in the assault on Sicily. Independent 442 Regimental Combat Team (RCT), famous for its hard-fighting Japanese American Nisei, joined VI Corps on 15 October.

Seventh Army was supported by XII TAC under Brigadier General Saville. During the fighting in the High Vosges, its principal strength was thirty-six P-47 Thunderbolts of 324th Fighter Group in Tavaux. This was by no means an overwhelming amount of air support.

While an army group in name, Devers's command was little more than a small army in September. With the activation of 6th Army Group, French units previously known as Army B were redesignated First French Army. The French formations were in the process of "whitening"—replacing African colonials with residents of metropolitan France. A lot of training and re-equipping would need to be accomplished before they would be capable of offensive action.

The story of First French Army underscores the difficulty of Allied command. Americans wanted to do nothing except defeat Hitler. But the battle for the soul of France also raged. The French government wanted to divert troops to clear German pockets along the estuary of the Gironde and possibly to forestall communist insurrection. Garrison duty along the Italian border (northern Italy was still in German hands) also threatened to sap manpower. Devers had to constantly fend off drains of French manpower to national assignments that did not contribute to the mission of 6th Army Group.

Jean de Lattre de Tassigny, commander, First French Army, "was no shrinking violet."[23] De Lattre has been described as a friendly if somewhat emotional and volatile man with a twinkle in his eye.[24] Some called him Roi (King) Jean because of his high-handedness in dealing with others. He constantly complained that the French were being shorted on supplies by the Americans. Then again, the Americans were just his ordnance masters. Jean's real boss was de Gaulle, who did not appear on SHAEF's organization chart. De Lattre was always sensitive about having French troops shoved aside and assigned unimportant tasks. The French wanted to be in on the final kill, not policing bypassed pockets somewhere in France.

De Lattre didn't impress every Frenchman. Leclerc, commander of the crack French 2nd Armored, viewed him as a turncoat for his complicity with the Vichy government. Marshall visited de Lattre during his October visit to the ETO. He had just come from his chilly visit with Montgomery. The French general pressed his complaints about supply, charging that the American troops in 6th Army Group were doing better than the French because they had diverted supplies destined for his army. Marshall took umbrage and walked out of the meeting.

French First Army contained two corps. Lieutenant General Émile Béthouart commanded I Corps. Prior to being elevated to corps command he was CG 3rd Algerian Division, an outfit that compiled a good record in Italy. He had also served as the chief of staff of National Defense.[25] General Joseph de Goislard de Monsabert commanded II Corps. Both were regarded as experienced, capable officers.[26]

The French Army was improving. But it was far from a fully formed, offensive-capable formation. During late September, French First Army received half the tonnage the one-corps Seventh Army received.[27] Deficiencies in French military service support infrastructure contributed to the problem. Many of the new recruits lacked any training whatsoever. Few had any experience with American equipment. Unlike American replacements, which had gone to basic and advanced training before getting shipped out, these recruits had to learn what they could after being assigned to combat units.

ENEMY FORCES

By the time Dragoon force reached the base of the Vosges, it had swept 89,000 Germans into POW cages. Only 11th Panzers came out of the Rhone Valley looking like a division. However, it was panzer only in name. Only a dozen operational tanks and a pair of self-propelled guns remained.[28] Most of the stubs that sported infantry division flags had two thousand to three thousand men remaining. All in all, Army Group G had lost half its strength.

Nineteenth Army held the Moselle River from Charmes through Epinal and onto Remiremont at the base of the Vosges. The defensive line followed the foothills and then blocked the Belfort Gap, which anchors on the Swiss border. The army-controlled kampfgroups assembled around five infantry divisions (16, 716, 189, 338, 198). SS police, stray sailors, and whoever else evacuated from southern France were added to these formations. Nineteenth Army artillery included about 120 light and medium pieces and 25 dual-purpose 88mm. Balck confessed he had never commanded "such a mixture of badly equipped troops."[29]

Opposite XV Corps was German First Army, now headed by General der Panzertruppen Otto von Knobelsdorff. A decorated WWI infantry officer, Otto had been a panzer corps commander on the eastern front 1942–44. He was awarded the Knights Cross with Oak Leaves and Swords for his efforts. Knobelsdorff was an outstanding combat commander but wasn't very enthusiastic about National Socialism.

General von Mellenthin, chief of staff of Army Group G, recalls the Germans anticipated the next blow would strike in the Lorraine Gateway. "We had also to consider the Belfort gap . . . but we had no doubt that the main thrust would be in Lorraine, for an attack on Alsace was bound to come to a standstill on the banks of the Rhine."[30] Balck and Mellenthin considered the Marne-Rhine Canal, north of Lunéville, as the most threatening axis of advance. This appraisal precipitated the collision between XII Corps and all the armor Hitler and Balck would muster during mid-September. Because Patton had been on the defensive since then, nothing further had erupted from the Nancy bridgehead. However, Army Group G kept a careful watch over the Lorraine Gateway.

German commanders had come to respect American firepower. Army Group G sought to employ an "elastic defense." Small units would hold a security area and trick the Americans into believing forward defenses were the main line of resistance. They hoped the bombs and shells would fall there while the principal defensive positions, emplaced several kilometers to the rear and in depth, would not receive the initial pounding.

AN ARMY GROUP WITHOUT A MISSION

After the junction between Seventh and Third Armies near Dijon, there was little operational reason for 6th Army Group. Its formation rested on two factors, one political, one administrative. As Ike stated in a letter to Bradley, the best way to integrate the French was to keep them within an American army group.[31] Eisenhower had more than his fill of trying to control the French. They had been trouble for him ever since North Africa in 1942. With them firmly ensconced in 6th Army Group, Ike did not have to deal with the French directly. Second, administrative control of 6th Army Group did not transition to the European Theater of Operations until November 20.[32] Until then, Devers drew supplies from the Mediterranean. Much excess stock existed in the Med; Ike would have been foolish not to take advantage of this as much as possible.

What was 6th Army Group supposed to do? Given September theater strategy, the obvious order from SHAEF would move Seventh Army up the northwestward side of the Vosges on Patton's flank. An axis Baccarat–Saarburg–Saarbrücken would have accomplished this. Forget about Metz. Focus Third Army from Nancy to Saarbrücken. While French First Army was assembling, it could hold defensive positions along the High Vosges and the Belfort Gap. As the French gained offensive capability, a limited attack through the Belfort Gap might add to Rundstedt's headache. Any progress through Belfort would make German positions in the High Vosges untenable. They would sit on cold mountain tops between two Allied thrusts. As these German formations possessed little offensive capability, they would be far more threatened than a threat.

SHAEF had no objective to assign to 6th Army Group, so Ike gave Devers an "independent status."[33] The supreme commander decided an advance on the Belfort Gap and to Strasbourg would best satisfy this requirement.[34] The official order read:

FWD 1482714 Sept 1944

3. The mission of Sixth Army Group is: to destroy the enemy in zone west of the Rhine, secure crossings over the Rhine and breach the Siegfried Line.

It is important to note the order to cross the Rhine. It was repeated in all SHAEF general orders through November.

Devers was assigned the usual three missions: destroy German formations in this sector, breach the West Wall, and cross the Rhine. Those instructions can be interpreted as having 6th Army Group form a third effort for the theater. This interpretation was to have damaging repercussions. Ike's decisions about 6th Army Group demonstrate a decided lack of focus. SHAEF did not integrate 6th Army into theater plans. In effect, Eisenhower told Devers, do anything you want as long as your don't expose Bradley's flank. Left to his own devices, Devers came up with his own program.

DEVERS'S OPERATIONAL PLAN

The 6th Army Group commander was disappointed that Ike did not give his formation a larger role in the upcoming September offensive.[35] But he applied creative thought to the mission assigned him. Devers recognized the sterility of attacking through Belfort. Recall that Balck and his staff came to the same conclusion.

Devers produced a nonconventional campaign plan. Instead of attacking up the Belfort Gap, Devers planned movement up the west side of the Vosges to the Saverne Gap. There he would create a strong single envelopment with Seventh Army through the Saverne Gap to Strasbourg. Moving Seventh Army up the western side of the Vosges also kept it close to Patton. It facilitated a change in mission that could send it through the Lorraine Gateway at the southern rim of the Saar. French First Army would threaten the Belfort Gap. Germans remaining on the west bank of the upper Rhine would be pocketed by these two forces. The primary mission of First French Army was to generate itself. As an army-level formation this unit had little offensive capability until this task was complete.

Devers's plan was a doctrinally correct single envelopment a la 1944's FM100-5. And it worked. Wasn't a threatened Rhine crossing that either could envelop the defenders of the Saar or advance east of the river toward Frankfurt the best possible outcome Devers could have achieved? Napoleon's route of advance into Germany had been Frankfurt–Fulda Gap–Berlin. Was Devers very crafty or simply lucky? One thing is certain. Devers' plan was not the "safe" course of action.

As we have seen before, exemplary performance at a lower level of war can seldom correct a fundamental error made at a higher level. Simply put, the higher-level error usually orients the lower-level commander on

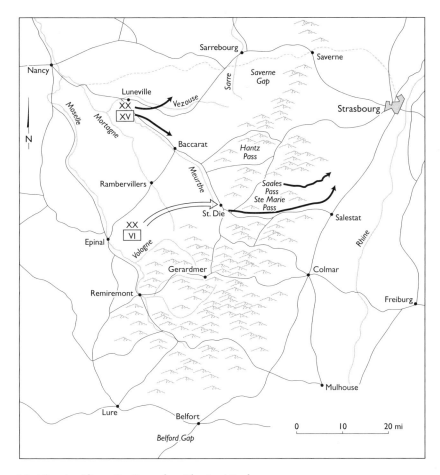

Map 8.2. An Alternative Secondary Theater Attack

the wrong objective. It seldom matters how well one advances in the wrong direction. No operational plan could correct the strategic error embodied in that unfortunate selection of 6th Army Group boundary. Perhaps Ike approved 6th Army Group's planned advance through the Vosges simply because it didn't interfere with SHAEF's primary plans.[36]

ATTACK ACROSS THE VOSGES

Patch had a variation on Devers's theme. Instead of moving directly for the Saverne Gap, he would direct his primary attack through the minor passes just south of Saverne but still in the High Vosges. (See map 8.2.) This took him up the road to Saint-Dié. He would extend via Molsheim and down into Strasbourg. VI Corps would make the main effort. XV Corps would support this attack on the northern (left) flank of VI Corps.

Employing mission-type orders, Patch did little more than designate the attack axis as Saint-Dié–Molsheim–Strasbourg. His two-page directive was issued on 20 September. The corps commanders were left to decide the exact place and formation for the attack.

Truscott dubbed VI Corps's upcoming operation "Dogface." The highest-speed approach to Saint-Dié was the route up from the Moselle that passed through Bruyères. Thirty-Sixth Infantry Division, reinforced by the famous "Go for Broke" 442nd RCT, manned primarily by Japanese Americans, would make the main effort about a week after the operation began. It was Truscott's plan to have 3ID lead the attack the remaining 20 kilometers from Brouvelieures to Saint-Dié. In turn, Truscott gave his divisional commanders wide latitude.[37] Command philosophy in Seventh Army paralleled that of Patton and was near the polar opposite of Hodges's practice in First Army.

Opposing Seventh Army was German Nineteenth Army under General Wiese. Nineteenth Army was weak. Balck rated only three of the "divisions" as divisions. The remainder were regimental-sized kampfgroups.[38] He had concentrated the greater part of his strength in German First Army opposing Patton. The Army Group G commander reasoned that the mountains of the Black Forest, east of the Rhine opposite the High Vosges, led nowhere. This was the best sector on which to take a risk.

Balck recognized the threat against the Saverne Gap that was beginning to form. Once the Parroy Forest had been breached, there were few obstacles between the Americans and Saverne. If Patch and Truscott penetrated through the Gap to the Rhine, it would split Nineteenth Army. Alternatively, a thrust to Saarburg would split German First from Nineteenth Army and create a threat against the Saar. (Fifth Panzer Army was still in a sector between them but would be withdrawn shortly for the coming Ardennes offensive.) Operationally, the threats were about equal. Strategically, there was little comparison. Saarburg was the greater threat. Either relegated both Belfort and the High Vosges to unimportance.

German officers designated the Meurthe River, which flowed down from Saint-Dié in High Vosges and through Baccarat, as the main line of resistance (MLR). German commanders wanted time to fortify it heavily. To give themselves that time, they deployed the bulk of their forces in a 12-15-kilometer-wide security zone in front of the Meurthe downslope from Saint-Dié.

Bruyères is a collection of stone and masonry structures that sits in a bowl in the mountains. It is dominated by the surrounding hills. Men of the less-than-first-class 16VGD defended the town. 36ID concentrated two regiments to conduct an envelopment through the wooded hills west of town. Heavy vegetation shielded the attackers from both artillery observers and the German machine gun pits defending Bruyères. The remaining two regiments (counting 442 RCT) were given very broad frontages to conduct supporting attacks. As a diversion, the division commander massed the 57mm anti-tank guns from all of his regiments on the obvious approach into town on the open ground to either side of the road up from Laval.

The assault kicked off on the morning of 15 October under drizzle and thick fog. Heavy fighting lasted four days. German machine gunners ensconced in stout buildings were difficult to dislodge. Every time the Americans made some progress, German forward observers brought down showers of artillery shells and mortar bombs. The 36ID's enveloping force finally succeeded. The 45ID also succeeded in capturing Brouvelieures 3 kilometers up the road.

To the south 3ID was not heavily engaged. Truscott quietly withdrew two of its regiments and had them attack through 36ID. With this maneuver, the corps commander concentrated five of his ten infantry regiments (two from 36ID, one from 45ID, and two from 3ID) on a 10-kilometer front headed for the Meurthe River crossings at Saint-Dié. The entire maneuver was masked by a deception operation. The 3ID faked an attack toward the Schuluct Pass. Radio traffic of a larger force was simulated, and equipment with 36ID markings was "lost" in the area. The 3ID soldiers sewed 45ID patches on their uniforms.

Per the plan, 3ID continued the attack toward Saint-Dié on 20–21 October. Resistance became spotty and unorganized. The German corps commander did not move major reinforcements against VI Corps main effort until the 28th. Truscott had pulled off a dazzling example of concentrated infantry attack shielded by a deception campaign. Without the help of armor or supporting air, American mud sloggers had displayed tactical brilliance. Despite the difficult terrain, Truscott threatened breakthrough.

To seal the impending breach, the Germans finally threw in four infantry battalions. What was left of 106 Panzer Brigade moved north from in front of French First Army. For eighteen days the two lead regiments of 3ID fought uphill against panzer grenadiers and troops from Austrian alpine battalions. By 3 November, 3ID dogfaces looked out on the Meurthe Valley from the heights opposite Saint-Dié. The 45ID to the north and 36ID to the south fought hard to keep up. The Germans torched every bit of shelter in their path, leaving the Americans exposed to the cold rain. Much of 16VGD and its reinforcements had been destroyed. Five thousand Germans huddled in VI Corps POW enclosures.

Truscott's attack to Saint-Dié is an excellent example of tactical use of mass on a narrow front to effect a penetration. The crossed rifles that signify U.S. Infantry shined. This fight showed experienced American infantry could take on their German counterparts, even in bad weather, and beat them.

The attack to Saint-Dié was Truscott's swan song in the ETO. On 25 October he left to take command of Fifth Army in Italy. Major General Edward H. Brooks, who had compiled an excellent record commanding 2nd Armored Division from Normandy to the German border, moved up to command VI Corps. Recall from chapter 1 that he was in command of 2AD at Mons. Like Truscott, he was not a West Pointer but a proud alumnus of Norwich. Brooks was a soldier of great experience, and he looked the part. Quiet and unflappable, this New Englander was a highly competent leader.[39] Ike rated him as one of his better corps commanders and Ridgway's equal, quite an accolade.

As impressive as the advance to Saint-Dié was, one must remember the Germans were fighting in their security zone. While the bulk of its combat units were engaged, VI Corps had yet to hit the MLR. This was defense in depth.

From Balck's perspective at the operational level, VI Corps's advance into the Vosges was relatively unimportant.[40] Efforts of U.S. Seventh Army from 20 September through the end of October were about as operationally threatening to Army Group G as the repeated assaults on Metz. Only second-rate infantry and formations burned out in the heavy combat against Third Army around Arracourt opposed Seventh Army's efforts. Where was the major threat to Saarburg and the Rhine?

Balck's major operational-level reaction was to shift 21PzD from the Vosges sector to create a reserve in Lorraine. His principal concern remained a breakthrough by Patton's forces. A rebuilt formation, the semi-trained 708VGD replaced the panzers in the Vosges Line.

Better-prepared positions behind the Meurthe now lay before the Americans. German commanders had designated them the "Vosges Foothill Position." Hitler's personal order barred further retreat. After all, they fought on newly reconsecrated "German" soil. OKW planners expected this position to hold out until at least the spring of 1945.

XV Corps had drawn up in front of the Saverne Pass. Three, and in some cases four, lines of prepared fortifications barred the entrance. After clearing the Parroy Forest and assisting VI Corps's 45ID around the Rambervillers–Baccarat highway, Haislip's corps saw little offensive action in October. Leclerc's division had seized the area around Baccarat. Forty-Fourth Infantry Division brought his corps up to customary three-division strength.

South of Seventh Army, II French Corps attacked directly into the High Vosges during October. Initially German intelligence read French administrative shuffling as a buildup for an attack on Belfort. This set off sharp and bloody fighting, principally with 198th Division. But little of significance was accomplished. De Lattre recognized that any worthwhile offensive action in Alsace would have to be down in the Belfort Gap.

NOVEMBER'S STRATEGIC PERMUTATIONS

Bradley and Eisenhower visited Dever's headquarters on 16 October. Ike wanted to know how much logistical support Devers could provide Patton. Devers responded, about 1,000 tons a day starting 15 November.[41] Using the tonnage relationships developed in chapter 2, this amounts to support for two divisions. Ike was not pleased with the answer. He thought that Dragoon should have been able to contribute more than two divisions at this late date.

The operation that advanced VI Corps to Saint-Dié was one of the American Army's better October performances. Despite this, "the results of 6th Army Group operations during October led Eisenhower to doubt that Devers's command could make any major contribution to the Allied advance in November."[42] Granted, First French Army had turned in little that would impress any but local commanders. No one expected it to do otherwise. Given Hodges's performance in the Huertgen and Patton's at Fort Driant, it is difficult to reconcile the performance of VI Corps and Ike's conclusion.

Marshall had visited Europe in early October. Had the Devers-versus-Eisenhower rub surfaced again, there was another back-door way to have removed the 6th Army Group commander. Until mid-October, Devers wore two hats. In addition to 6th Army Group, he commanded the North African Theater of Operations, U.S. Army (NATOUSA). On 22 October, the deputy chief of staff, Lieutenant General McNarney came over to head NATOUSA. If Ike had no confidence in Devers and, as a result, was underutilizing 6th Army Group, then Ike had a duty to so inform Marshall. An honest conversation between Marshall and Ike could have resulted in

Devers being rotated to DCS back in the States. Or Marshall could have banished Devers to North Africa. Attaching Third Army to 6th Army Group and assigning it responsibility for the secondary effort would have been natural outgrowths. Extending a little further, Truscott, a Patton protégé, might have taken over Third Army. Gerow, who had returned to the States to testify about Pearl Harbor, might have gotten the Fifth Army Command Truscott went to. (Gerow became the last corps commander in Europe elevated to army command: the Fifteenth). All of this would have been far preferable to assigning a whole army group a less-than-pressing mission.

Ike liked to quote Clausewitz. The Prussian master must have been frowning down from Valhalla as he read Ike's 23 October directive. Sixth Army Group was to play Cinderella.

Eisenhower's orders for Devers were succinct:

2. . . . Your role would be to protect the Southern flank of the Third Army throughout its operations. This, as I see it, will entail your advance into Germany in the direction of Nurnburg. It may be that the logistical situation will not permit your advance as deep as Nurnburg. . . .
3. An advance to Munich and the clearing up of the Southern portion of your Army Group area I look on as a subsidiary role to be carried out as and when resources permit.[43]

What Eisenhower appears to have had in mind for both November and December was for Devers to clear Alsace from the Vosges to the Rhine, including the Colmar Pocket.[44] Given the need to break the great stalemate of October, this is almost an absurd diversion of tremendous resources to an unimportant task. Clausewitz's most basic advice was, to the exclusion of everything else, concentrate all of one's power against the enemy's center of gravity. Marshall, the chiefs, and Eisenhower agreed the center of gravity was the Wehrmacht—and its destruction. For months the Allies struggled mightily but to little avail. The immediate operational objective was to engage and destroy 6SS Panzer Army. How did Eisenhower's deployment of 6th Army Group contribute to that objective?

One can understand the French national objective of clearing a province that historically had been in dispute. But that is just the type of sideshow Clausewitz admonished the strategist to avoid expending power on. The possessor of Alsace would have little to say about the ultimate slaying of the Nazi monster.

Except for the protection of Patton, little was done to tie 6th Army Group into theater strategy. Since the capture of the Parroy Forest and

Baccarat in early October, Patton's flank had been secured. By early November, Seventh Army represented a powerful force. The advance of VI Corps to Saint-Dié had not irrevocably committed either it or its parent army to the Vosges. XV Corps sat near Baccarat. It easily could have led Seventh Army to Saarburg on Patton's right and paralleled Third Army all the way to the Rhine. VI Corps could have followed Haislip as a powerful exploitation force. French II Corps could have guarded the Vosges and its passes all the way to Saverne. Any additional troops needed could have been taken from French I Corps and the attack on Belfort reduced proportionally.

In October, Third Army wasted most of its efforts around Metz. Had Third and Seventh Armies been yoked together in a secondary attack from Nancy–Lunéville–Saarburg and toward the Saar (see map 8.3), assignments would have more closely paralleled the initial outline of theater strategy. The 21st Army Group would concentrate on Antwerp, 12th Army Group the Aachen Gap and the Ruhr, and 6th Army Group the secondary attack across the Rhine toward the Saar. An obvious organizational change would have been to transfer all of Third Army, instead of just XV Corps, to 6th Army Group. Then 6th Army Group would make sense. After the failure of Market Garden, it was apparent that a long campaign would ensue and that Antwerp would not be available for some time to support it. Assigning the support of Third Army to Marseilles promised more tonnage earlier and lessened diversions from the main effort. We will return to this concept of a revised secondary effort when a possible Rhine crossing is discussed below.

Patton would have served under his classmate. He'd done so before. Patton penned in his diary, "I am not sure that, as the lesser of two evils, it might not be better to be in his [Devers] army group; he interferes less and is less timid than Bradley."[45]

If Eisenhower rejected this division of effort because he did not trust Devers, this was one of the most unfortunate mis-assignments in the ETO during the war. As the remainder of this chapter demonstrates, Devers executed his assignments in a competent manner. Even if Marshall had been right about Devers, if Ike distrusted the 6th Army Group commander, that was sufficient reason to assign him elsewhere. War is not conducted to be fair to the generals. It is prosecuted to win as quickly as possible in a manner that minimizes friendly casualties. All other interpersonal considerations are irrelevant. Marshall is the unselfish embodiment of this ideal. It is unfortunate that he did not better grasp the rift between two of his prodigies.

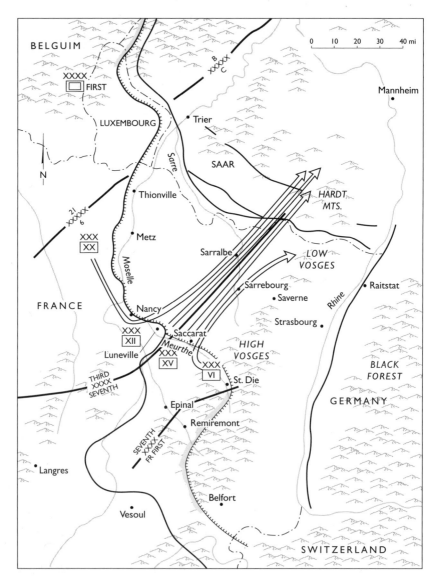

Map 8.3. Alternative Third/Seventh Army Plan for October

SIXTH ARMY GROUP'S NOVEMBER OPERATIONAL PLAN

Sixth Army Group retained the basic operational design it had followed since the end of September, except that the primary route of advance through the Vosges was now the Saverne Gap. VI Corps remained pointed toward Strasbourg. XV Corps was on its northern flank occupying the space between the Vosges and Patton. However de Lattre, CG First French Army, was itching to burst through the Belfort Gap and liberate Alsace.

Weather in the Vosges continued to be miserable. It rained almost every day. Frequently high winds whipped stinging cold droplets into exposed flesh. Snow appeared at higher elevations. Actual temperatures were not unbearable, but they made anyone living outdoors miserable. Temperatures ranged from 38 to 68 F. in October and 25–60 in November. In the latter half of October, only one day was suitable for air operations. No ground-support missions were flown from 5 to 19 November.

SHAEF's directive contemplated a Rhine crossing for 6th Army Group. SHAEF's directive for the November offensive, SGS 381, stated:

> 10. The mission of the Southern Group of Armies during the first and second phase is:
>   a. to advance in zone, secure crossings and deploy in strength across the Rhine.
>   b. to protect the southern flank of the Central Group of Armies [i.e., Bradley and Patton]. Initially this will involve denying Luneville to the enemy.[46]

Army group long-range planners began making studies of a crossing of the Rhine River near Rastatt, about 45 kilometers north of Strasbourg. This would be a very logical extension of the push to Strasbourg or continuation of Seventh Army's advance along the western face of the Low Vosges. If Seventh Army could blow through the Saverne Gap, a Rhine crossing appeared to be within reach.

SHAEF's directive specified start dates for the efforts of 12th and 21st Army Groups. Weather and logistics caused alterations in start dates that were much discussed. A measure of Ike's ambivalence regarding 6th Army Group was that at no time was a start date for Devers even mentioned by the supreme commander or SHAEF directive.

Devers planned to move Seventh Army via the Saverne and minor gaps through the mountains to gain both Strasbourg and access to Rhine crossing sites (map 8.4). Initially, Haislip's XV Corps would move in the direction of Saarburg. This was the move Balck most feared from Devers. Instead of continuing north, Haislip would swerve east and push through the main gap. VI Corps would continue through the minor gaps to the south. Initially, Seventh Army designated VI Corps as main effort. As the start date approached, the army staff adopted a more flexible plan that could shift weight between the two corps, depending on their relative success.

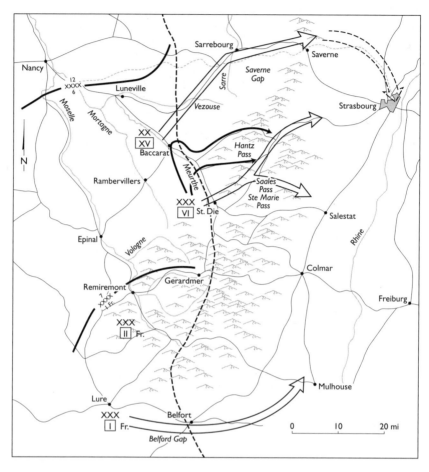

Map 8.4. Sixth Army Group November Offensive

De Lattre's army was also ready to liberate more of France. French First Army's plan opened with a limited attack by French II Corps into the High Vosges. While it might help VI Corps a little, this primarily was a feint. The main effort would be made by French I Corps a few days later. It would pierce the Belfort Gap and retake southern Alsace. The French attack would have to crack the German defensive line that ran through Belfort. Then the French would parallel the Rhine-Rhone Canal that flowed northeast toward Mulhouse before connecting with the river.

Devers estimated Patch would need about two weeks to break through the Saverne Gap onto the Alsatian plain. The French would need about the same time to break through at Belfort.[47] Beyond these first objectives, Devers projected a Rhine crossing above Strasbourg. With his troops on the east side of the Rhine, German First Army would be trapped in Lorraine between Patch and Patton. That was quite a dream. At least Devers was thinking in the right dimension.

Reading the reason for the drive on Saint-Dié is not hard. Balck and Wiese expected 6th Army Group's main effort would be through the Saverne Gap to Strasbourg.[48] Balck was responsible for everything from Luxembourg to the Swiss border. He was far more worried for his First Army defending against Patton than Nineteenth Army defending the Saverne and Belfort Gaps. To concentrate against the greater threat, Balck moved the inter-army border up to the Marne-Rhine Canal. This stretched Nineteenth Army even further. Balck was concerned that Patch would open a gap between the two defending armies. He did not think the French posed much of a threat. On the other hand, Wiese believed they would mount a major effort into the Belfort Gap.

Even the limited battles of October had pushed Wiese's Nineteenth Army beyond any normal limit. Wiese had no reserve to speak of. VI Corps was about to kick him out of the Vosges foothill position. Clausewitz warns about defense in mountains. In rugged terrain, it's tough to shift forces to meet alternating points of attack. Wiese might have written an endorsement to the old Prussian's proposition. As for reinforcements, Nineteenth Army stood at the bottom of the list. As long as Hodges and Patton pounded away on more critical sectors, he could expect nothing.

FRENCH FIRST ARMY ATTACKS

De Lattre's operation began on November 14th. Five days later the first patrol would stare across the Rhine and into Germany. The first 6th Army Group unit to reach the Rhine was French 1st Armored Division. For the November offensive First French Army contained:

I Corps	II Corps
2nd Moroccan Division	1st Infantry Division
9th Colonial Infantry Div	3rd Algerian Division
Groupe* Molle	
U.S. 13th Field Arty Bde	

1st Armored Division
5th Armored Division

*Brigade

In addition there were numerous regimental- and battalion-sized units. De Lattre initially held control of the two armored divisions at army level. He would release them to I Corps when the opportunity for exploitation became apparent. In this manner de Lattre kept more control over I Corps operations than was customary in the American Army.

For the most part French units were rested and up to strength. Third Algerian Division was an exception. It had been in continuous action in the High Vosges. A lot of semi-trained replacements were included in its ranks. French 5th Armored Division had not seen action.

De Lattre had another worry. He was under a lot of pressure to release troops for an operation to solidify the National Government's control over southwestern France. During the upcoming battle, he expected a call ordering him to divert armor in this direction.

Balck did not believe that the French would shift their main effort into the Belfort Gap. He thought they would remain committed to their earlier efforts in the mountains and focus on Colmar. Wiese thought just the opposite. Balck ordered Nineteenth Army to retain two of its best divisions in the mountains. A diversionary attack mounted by de Monsabert at the beginning of November reinforced Balck's convictions.[49] As a preliminary, de Lattre executed a complex deception plan to make it appear the main effort would remain in the mountains.

I Corps directed the main effort through the Belfort Gap to Mulhouse. De Lattre hoped a sharp blow would cause the German defenders to collapse. While this was a very important operation to liberate French territory, it is not central to our study, so we won't follow its tactical details.

By the end of November, French First Army had taken some 15,000 prisoners. French losses were high—1,300 dead, 4,500 wounded, and 4,500 non-battle casualties. Some French territory had been redeemed and a small portion of the Rhine uncovered. The northern limit of French advance became the southern limit of the Colmar Pocket.

SEVENTH ARMY TAKES STRASBOURG

Terrain in the Vosges Mountains was far more difficult than that which First Army fought through in the Stolberg Corridor and the Huertgen Forest. But the result was far different. Seventh Army did not face the best German field formations. But the defenders in the Huertgen were not Rundstedt's best either. So we will follow the tactical evolutions of Patch's troops.

At the beginning of the effort to break through the Saverne Gap, Seventh Army contained:

VI Corps	XV Corps
14th Armored Div (CCA)	Fr 2nd Armored Division
3rd Infantry Division	44th Infantry Division
36th Infantry Division	79th Infantry Division
100th Infantry Division	
103rd Infantry Division	
117th Cavalry Group	106th Cavalry Group

The 45ID was refitting after the hard fighting near Saint-Dié. Both 3rd and 36th Divisions could have used a similar respite. The 79ID had just finished sixteen days of rest and training after the bloody fight in the Parroy Forest on the flank of XII Corps of Patton's Third Army. Fourteenth Armored Division, 100ID, and 103ID were formations fresh off the boat from the United States. They were to have debarked in western France. Because of the shipping backup along the Channel coast, they were unloaded in Marseilles and assigned to Devers.

VI Corps was opposed by three volks divisions (16, 708, and 716) of LXIV Corps under Wiese's Nineteenth Army. The 708th Division was in good shape after having been sent to Czechoslovakia for reorganization and training. The 16VGD had been badly damaged in earlier fighting. The 716VGD was marginal at best. The 361VGD and 553VGD of First Army's LXXXIX Corps defended north and south of Saarburg respectively.

Operation Dogface continued until the first week of November. As supplies flowed through Marseilles, there was not the marked October cessation as on other fronts. VI Corps fed 100ID into the operation and gave 45ID a little rest. One Hundred Third "Cactus" Division provided a short breather for 3ID beginning on the 9th. In XV Corps's area, Leclerc's armor made a supporting attack. Forty-Fourth Infantry Division moved in to consolidate the ground.

For the November offensive, Patch planned to attack with two corps abreast. (See map 8.4.) The stronger VI Corps would continue to make the main effort from Saint-Dié through the minor passes on the shorter route to Strasbourg. XV Corps would make a secondary effort on the obvious axis of advance—the Saverne Gap. However, Seventh Army stood ready to switch the main effort to Haislip's corps if events warranted.

A small attack by 100ID preceded everything. It was to pull Germans into the northern sector of VI Corps and away from its intended route of advance. Then XV Corps would begin its attack. Initially Haislip's forces would advance in the direction of Saarburg. This would threaten a move up the southeastern portion of the Lorraine Gateway. Then it would turn east and make for the Saverne Gap. VI Corps would commence its drive two days after XV Corps. Again, the idea was to first draw off as many defenders as possible from the area of main effort.

Patch did an excellent job of coordinating the efforts of both his corps. In turn, the efforts of his two subordinates were well synchronized. Balck had set his inter-army-group boundary just south of the Saverne Gap. Patch wanted to tear open the inter-army boundary. Century Division's preliminary attack was designed to do this by dislocating the northernmost division in Nineteenth Army. As the Germans reacted, both of Patch's corps would begin their main efforts. Depending on what happened, either corps could then advance to Strasbourg.

Both corps commanders ensured their main assaults were penetrations, not frontal attacks. Instead of battering away at prepared German defenses, American infantry would slice through the four defensive belts on a very narrow front. Once they were through, follow-on units would envelop the defenders from the rear, widen the breach, and shatter the defense. As a recent historian observed, American forces would be used as "scalpels carving holes in the defenses . . . rather than battering rams."[50] Here the corps commanders were correct according to both the situation and the "book"—FM100-5.

XV Corps lead with 79ID. Haislip's plan envisioned the Cross of Lorraine Division penetrating to Saarburg on a small front. Then it would swing parallel to the Foothill Line, enveloping 553VGD. This would place the 79ID in Saarburg. Haislip estimated that German strength was insufficient to man the several continuous lines that had been laid out. Instead he expected to find individual strong points, placed in great depth, holding key ground. The defenders had few mobile reserves. If his lead division could get beyond the defensive belts, he thought, they would be able to move quickly. Haislip ordered his division commanders to stand ready to bypass defenders in order to keep up the momentum of the attack.[51] The 44ID generated a supporting attack to the north in order to pin more enemy down. French 2nd Armored Division, the Deuxième Blindée, would exploit any hole 79ID tore in German defenses. It would head east 15 kilometers on the road to Phalsbourg and then turn off on the road to Saverne.

Heavy rain gave way to blizzard. The entire XV Corps sector was covered. Many streams left their banks. Some roads and bridges disappeared into the dark water. Despite the weather, 79ID penetrated the lines of 708VGD. German troops began to melt away. Americans walked into Halloville and continued on in the direction of Saarburg. After some unorthodox maneuvers 44ID also made progress. By the 16th German commanders recognized their situation had become critical. The 553VGD retained a cohesive defense, but 708th was not faring well. Haislip began to push Deuxième Blindée forward.

Brooks recognized that the German defenses facing VI Corps were also weak and lacked depth.[52] He was concerned that 3ID would be too punched out after making the river crossing and their flanks too exposed to continue the exploitation. He decided to lead off with his two new divisions attacking north and south of his intended point of main effort. The 100ID began a supporting attack four days before the main effort. The Century Division would penetrate on a 4-kilometer front and then turn southeast to envelop 716VGD. Brooks wanted the bridges and road junction at Raon-l'Étape secured. This would prevent a gap from opening between VI and XV Corps to the north. Cactus Division would then take Saint-Dié, which was to the south of the intended Meurthe crossing. After a few days catching its breath as corps reserve, 3ID would make the corps's main effort. If 103ID was able, it would parallel 3ID to the south. The 36ID stood on the high ground overlooking Saint-Dié and the Taintrux Valley 7 kilometers from the Meurthe. It would cover the southern half of the corps sector and maintain contact with II French Corps of de Lattre's army to the south. The 36ID would get a small breather at the beginning of the operation. It did not have a mission to attack but would be prepared to join the corps attack on order.

Preliminary movements of 103ID allowed it to clear a triangular hill mass between Taintrux and Saint-Dié. Raon L'Etape would be 100ID's first fight. Instead of making a frontal assault on Raon-l'Étape across the Meurthe, the division commander, with Brooks's concurrence, decided to move north to Baccarat and cross the river on bridges already held by French 2AD, and then to attack Raon-l'Étape from the rear. On the 12th, two regiments made this enveloping maneuver while the third demonstrated across the river directly before Raon-l'Étape.

Unfortunately the Germans, survivors of 708VGD, had used the pause to construct new positions to defend to the north—the direction 100ID's two regiments attacked from. On the 14th, 100ID began a series of battalion-size attacks to penetrate these freshly constructed positions. The Century Division took several successive ridges that ran perpendicular to their axis of advance. This was tough, wooded country, and dogfaces fought in very bad weather. The ridges presented far worse obstacles than anything in the Huertgen. But the untried 100th did a fine job of breaking through newly prepared German positions. By the 16th they had gained key high ground that dominated Raon-l'Étape and the Plaine River Valley. The 708VGD counterattacked. But they didn't have the strength to beat the Century Division. By the 18th 100ID captured Raon-l'Étape.

The Winter Line that was to have held until April was ruptured in a few days. While 708VGD had already been beaten up in the fighting southwest of the Saverne Gap, the Century Division put in a good first performance. Its third regiment crossed the river and advanced another 3 kilometers. Now 100ID's attack was running out of punch. Elements of 716VGD occupied positions blocking further forward movement.

For a while Brooks considered deploying 14AD to exploit a breakthrough made by 100ID. The 716VGD's intact position dissuaded him. Century Division had accomplished its mission, however. It moved German focus from Saint-Dié and to the north, away from the main effort.

On the 19th 3ID began its attack by attempting to infiltrate across the Meurthe. Swift current of the flooded river, rather than enemy activity, frustrated this effort. Rapid water swamped the infantry's rubber rafts. That evening larger engineer boats were used to cross lead infantry platoons. The Germans didn't oppose the crossing. With security in place, engineers assembled a pair of footbridges and a light-vehicle bridge. By first light 3ID had five infantry battalions on the far bank. By 21 November both 100 and 3ID were making substantial progress.

To reinforce 3ID's successful crossing, Brooks altered his plan. Instead of a separate assault, he fed two regiments of 103ID into the 3ID bridgehead. Continually rising waters took out one of the foot bridges and made the vehicular bridge that had been installed impassable. These two Cactus Division regiments sought to envelop the defenders in the Foothill Line in front of their sister regiment near Saint-Dié. The Germans had the choice of running or being surrounded. They pulled back from the town. Brooks's offensive had splintered the Foothill Line with a few well-directed blows.

Despite local counterattacks, Haislip sensed the impending breakthrough. On the 18th, 44ID began to break into the tactical depth of 553VGD. Under assault from the Cross of Lorraine, 708VGD, the new boy on the line, began to collapse. The 79ID began to pick up speed. Leclerc's armor made ready to advance on secondary roads that bypassed Saarburg and then turn into the Saverne Gap.

Rapid XV Corps's maneuver created a 15-kilometer opening between Seventh Army's left flank and Third Army's right. Both Patch and Haislip estimated that the risk of a German reaction fast enough to take advantage of this opportunity was small. Rapid exploitation through the Saverne Gap was more than worth the risk. Haislip positioned his cavalry group to watch his open flank.

Like Haislip, VI Corps had already broken through, but had not cleared the mountain range. Brooks was on the verge of committing his exploitation force. However, he had only a single combat command of the inexperienced 14th Armored Division to fill the job.

Reversing the initial plan, Patch ordered Haislip to take the lead. On the 19th, even before his infantry had finished their final penetration of the forward German divisions, Haislip ordered Deuxième Blindée to shoot the gap. But the French weren't supposed to cover just the 35 kilometers to Saverne. Haislip had them ready to thrust all the way through the mountains and capture Strasbourg, 70 kilometers from their jump-off. By doing so he avoided a major inter-Allied problem. French troops, not American, would seize the Alsatian capital. "Leclerc" was the nom de guerre of Vicomte de Hauteclocque, a well-born patriot who became fugitive rather than be captured by the Germans in 1940. It was a gutsy, correct call. The 79ID was relieved of its mission to seize Saarburg so it could follow the French toward Saverne. The 44ID took Saarburg.

The 100ID was switched from VI to XV Corps. French 2AD advanced on two axes on minor approaches north of the Saverne Gap via Phalsbourg and La Petite Pierre. By this tactic, Leclerc intended to bypass the Germans blocking the main road that led through Saverne. His instincts were correct. By the 22nd, French armor was cleanly through the gap.

Haislip's two infantry divisions followed in van. They created a shield running east, west, and north of Strasbourg. Large bodies of Germans began to surrender. Each American division took thousands of prisoners. Leclerc moved too fast to bother with them. While each German formation initially defended well, they began to come apart when Americans got behind them. Battalion by battalion, their morale was failing. These makeshift units, many with Austrian fillers, did not have the cohesion the German Army was famous for.

French armor raced into the city from the north and west. Strasbourg fell on the 23rd. In ten days XV Corps had advanced 80 kilometers. French

2nd Armored covered the last 30 kilometers from Saverne to Strasbourg in a little over three hours. By comparison, Seventh Army had advanced only 20 kilometers in the forty-five days prior to the November offensive. Reporting the win to de Gaulle, Leclerc's cable stated, "We will not rest until the flag of France also flies over Paris and Strasbourg."

Why was Strasbourg so important to the French? The "lost provinces" of Alsace and Lorraine were part of the "disputed middle ground" between France and Germany that Charlemagne willed to his third son. Over the years, they had been annexed and re-annexed. In 1939 they were part of France. After the disgraceful collapse of French arms in 1940, Hitler incorporated them into the Reich. How would Americans feel if Black Jack's army had run away from Pancho Villa's bandits along the border and Villa seized Texas? Then what if the leaders of a British-dominated alliance ordered the U.S. Army to leave the Southwest to defend Montreal against the Germans while the skies over Texas were stained by the Mexican flag?

To the east lay the Rhine. A single armored division did not have the strength to cross it and hold Strasbourg. But the bridges over the Rhine at Kehl beckoned.

Sensing the enemy's complete withdrawal, Brooks ordered his corps to change over from attack to pursuit on the 21st. Ever the tanker, he wanted to begin exploitation as soon as he saw an opening. Despite maddening delays, VI Corps advanced 25 kilometers by the 24th. Americans captured another line of partially finished defensive positions and stockpiles of ammunition, barbed wire, and other construction materials.

Reasoned analysis allowed Haislip and Patch to ignore an open flank and achieve a major breakthrough. If only Collins and Hodges had reached a similar conclusion about the Huertgen Forest in September! Seventh Army had no reason to genuflect to the First.

Both Rundstedt and Balck realized the danger of the penetration.[53] Left unsealed, it created a major breach between German First and Nineteenth Armies. Patton's attack with XII Corps in the southern portion of Third Army's sector added to the gravity of the situation. German forces defending the Saar might be enveloped and destroyed, leaving an open road over the Rhine and into the Reich. German intelligence probably didn't know that Patch was already assembling DUKW amphibians to support a forced crossing.

Only a major counterattack to regain Saverne would end Balck's crisis. No German armored reserve worthy of mention existed. Rundstedt pleaded for OKW to release Panzer Lehr, which was near Muenster preparing for the Ardennes attack. Hitler acceded. It would have to move 500 kilometers in two days. Rundstedt ordered Balck to commit it en masse in an attack from north to south to seal off the American penetration at its base. Balck attempted to add what was left of 361VGD and the understrength and refitting 25PGD.

On Thanksgiving Day, Panzer Lehr clanked southward in two columns. It moved toward the opening gap between U.S. Third and Seventh Armies, seeking to hit the exposed northern flank of XV Corps. With great boldness, it attacked down the western face of the Vosges, rather than the eastern face still in German hands. Balck, the Army Group G commander, had not lost his nerve. But he did not have the troop strength to back up his audacious maneuver. Both of his army commanders, having a better grasp on the real situation, had little faith in his plan. First Army commander, General Knobelsdorff, who controlled the actions of Panzer Lehr, estimated the division would do well to hold what was left of his Saar Valley position.

This Panzer Lehr was not the same quality division the Allies had fought back in Normandy. Many of its fillers were semi-trained recruits. New tank crews especially were not trained to standard. Only half of Panzer Lehr's grenadiers and seventy panzers made the line of departure. Even this force attacked ten hours behind schedule. Nevertheless, Panzer Lehr, still in two columns, began punishing 106th Cavalry Group, guarding the gap on XV Corps's northern flank. After providing warning, the cavalry backed up.

Upon learning about the counterattack, Haislip stopped pushing additional units through the Saverne Gap and toward Strasbourg. En route east to create part of the "northern shield," 44ID was diverted to backstop the cavalry. But Haislip did not turn his forward spearhead back. Panzer Lehr forced one of 44ID's regiments back. The divisional commander moved his other forward regiment back so as not to give the panzers the opportunity to flank either of them.

Panzer Lehr's attack hit on the night of 23–24 down the 12th-6th Army Group boundary. Boundaries are notorious weak spots. More than likely, German intelligence had identified the weak seam. XII Corps was located northwest of the attacking Germans. Eddy's forces were making steady if unspectacular progress advancing toward the Saar River. Eddy was concerned that 4th Armored would become bogged in soggy open ground. To facilitate their advance he received permission to move 4AD through XV Corps's zone. Panzer Lehr wasn't the only armored division looking for an open flank. On the eve of Panzer Lehr's attack this placed the American armor in a fortuitous position. Fourth Armored saw an opportunity to bite Panzer Lehr in the flank. Brushing aside grenadiers from 361VGD, 4th Armored tore into the western column of Lehr's attack. Mud kept most German and American tanks roadbound. Seasoned American armored infantry proved more than a match for newly minted panzer grenadiers.

While 4AD chewed up the western column, the eastern one continued to advance against 44ID. Initially the forward American regiments had orders to withhold fire until the whereabouts of 4AD could be determined. When the panzers were almost upon them, an American artillery battalion commander, on his own initiative, opened fire. An aerial observer spotted a long column of vehicles backed up behind the American artillery strike. Additional guns were brought to bear. The shelling caused many German crews to abandon their vehicles. Fourth Armored so badly mauled the Lehr that it had to be withdrawn from action. The 25PGD was ordered up to backstop the panzers. Aside from presenting lucrative targets and threatening Ike's lunch plans with Naislip, the attack against XV Corps had no significant impact on Seventh Army's offensive.

NINETEENTH ARMY IN JEOPARDY

Nineteenth Army faced envelopment from both north and south. Haislip's thrust to Strasbourg opened a 30-kilometer gap between First and Nineteenth Armies: it is through this gap that the American columns headed to a Rhine crossing at Rastatt would have traveled. By the 24th Wiese believed his command faced collapse.[54] Six of his eight infantry divisions had been reduced to bloody stubs. Attacks by both U.S. Seventh and French First Armies had shattered his defenses—sparse and thin as they were. In comparison to Huertgen and Lorraine, defenses had been penetrated with comparative ease. The Germans as well as the Allies had designated it a low-priority sector. For the first time since mid-September, Allied soldiers could smell exploitation. Balck wanted to withdraw behind the Rhine, but he knew Hitler would not countenance surrendering what remained of Alsace. After all, it had been annexed into the Reich.[55] He was right. The fuehrer refused to even discuss the matter. But he did order his planners to look at an alternative to the Ardennes operation—an attack through Alsace and Lorraine.

For the first time in a long time, the Allies had undisputed control of the initiative. The German command apparatus was "incapable of keeping pace with the tempo of the Allied operations and was unable to respond effectively."[56] Finally the Americans had gotten inside of the German decision-making loop. The poorly coordinated counterattack against XV Corps was stark evidence of this. Balck was willing, but he did not have anything near a realistic view of the battlefield. Even if he had, he did not have the combat power to effectively counter the threats Devers's army group was presenting.

In order to prevent further incursion by VI Corps, Balck moved troops from south to north within the pocket that was forming around Colmar. Rundstedt was of the opposite opinion. He felt the French attacking up from Belfort were the larger threat. The field marshal recommended a tactical withdrawal northward to form a more compact defensive position. He requested an infantry and two additional panzer divisions from OKW. Not wanting to further impact forces concentrating for the Ardennes operation, Hitler refused. .

U.S. Seventh Army commanders had displayed excellent generalship. By coordinating the efforts of two corps, Patch had smashed a clean hole through the defenders. Bold action by Patch and Haislip had exploited through the snow and mountains all the way through the Rhine. Their efforts succeeded, while 12th Army Group stalled again. The leaders and soldiers of 6th Army Group had outfought the Germans. Patton wrote to his wife: "The Seventh Army and the French First Army seem to have made a monkey out of me."[57]

AN OPPORTUNITY TO EXPLOIT BEYOND THE RHINE

From top to bottom, Seventh Army commanders were full of vigor and ready to continue into Germany. Based upon preliminary plans and the speed with which the Saverne Gaps had been penetrated, Patch and Haislip were convinced XV Corps could easily seize a bridgehead across the Rhine at Rastatt.[58] Initially Devers and Patch planned a crossing between 10 and 20 December. But their troops were on a roll. The generals advanced the timetable into the first week in December. Although no one knew it, this would give the Rhine crossing a ten-day head start on Hitler's upcoming offensive in the Ardennes.

The concept of operations assigned the crossing itself to Haislip (map 8.5). XV Corps controlled four infantry divisions: 44, 100, 45, and 79. The more experienced units, 45ID and 79ID, were closest to the river and would have made the assault crossing. VI Corps would pass through the bridgehead and exploit up the east bank of the river. No layer caking here.

The exploitation would have commenced no later than the second week in December,[59] which placed it just prior to the Ardennes offensive. Brooks's corps contained 3, 36, and 103ID, elements of 14AD, and Deuxième Blindée. The 36ID, the southernmost division, was to have been withdrawn from Colmar containment operations by 30 November and coiled up for offensive action. By early December, 12th Armored Division became available to 6AG. Of course French First Army would have to slide north to cover the northern arc of the Colmar pocket covered by VI Corps.

The dashed arrows depict Devers's concept to bag German First Army and open the road for Patton. The deeper arrows would require more forces. Seventh Army began detailed planning for a Rastatt crossing. Back in October, a river crossing school was set up. DUKWs, bridges, ferries, and other specialized equipment were ordered forward. The Seventh Army engineer declared he was ready to support a two-division assault crossing of the Rhine.

During a conversation after the war Field Marshal von Rundstedt asked General Patch why the Americans didn't cross the Rhine north of Strasbourg when the Germans "had nothing to defend with." When Patch replied that he had the assault boats assembled and moved forward but that Ike had directed him north instead of east, Rundstedt replied: "For a young fellow, you are all right."[60]

While Devers, Patch, and their staffs feverously worked on plans to cross the Rhine, Bradley and Ike began a tour of the southern half of the ETO. First they met with Patton in Nancy. Horrible weather and river flooding had bogged his attempt at breakout through Lorraine. Third Army's offensive was crawling through the mud before strong triple-layered defenses. It was clear Patton was nowhere near breakthrough. While Ike and Bradley differed in the details, both agreed that Patton needed major assistance in order to get moving.

Patton had asked that XV Corps be returned to Third Army. He had a study prepared for his two seniors. Patton pointed out "that between Luneville and Thionville there was room for only one army, and there was just one natural corridor."[61] While Ike tended to agree, Bradley thought the change would take too much time. Instead, the 12th Army Group commander proposed to narrow Third Army's sector by moving the army-group boundary north. XV Corps, still under Patch's control, would have to take up the ground vacated by Third Army. Patton would then be able to better concentrate XII Corps.

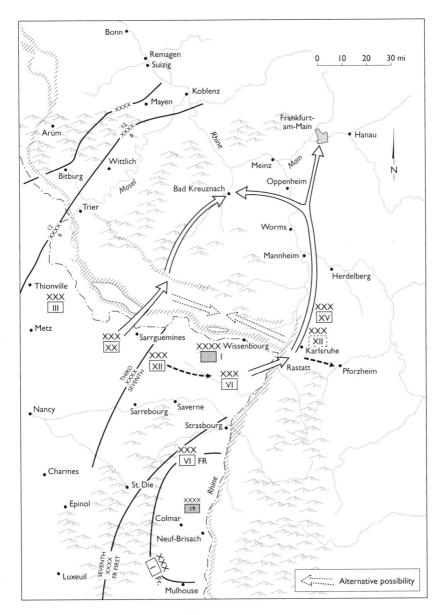

Map 8.5. Seventh Army East of the Rhine

Next Bradley and Eisenhower, joined by Patch and Devers, traveled to
Haislip's HQ at Saarburg. When the heavy brass arrived, Panzer Lehr was
only a handful of kilometers away. XV Corps headquarters troops were digging defensive positions. Haislip tried to wave the senior generals along. In
response to Haislip's pleadings, Eisenhower laughed and scolded, "Damnit,
Ham, you invited me for lunch and I'm not going to leave until I get it."[62]

While the snarling panzers didn't bother him, Ike was very upset to find
Haislip's staff busily preparing to cross the Rhine. "After some study of the
Seventh Army plans" Ike ordered all such activity to cease.[63] From the hip,
he issued verbal orders for XV Corps to travel back over the Vosges and support Patton's attack by paralleling it in the southern portion of Lorraine. This
would place Haislip partially in the area 4AD had been operating in. XV
Corps would have to attack up the length of the mountains themselves. This
adjustment was consistent with Bradley's thinking. The bestarred group traveled on to VI Corps HQ at Saint-Dié. General Brooks, elated at the progress
his corps was making, also was preparing for a Rhine crossing. Again Ike
halted further preparations.

Devers and Patch were stunned. Ike's instructions to Devers on 23 October were to seek a Rhine crossing and to deploy in strength.[64] SHAEF's 28
October directive stated the Allies would take "any opportunity" to gain a
bridgehead over the Rhine.[65]

Patton's presentation and Bradley's influence appear to have altered
Ike's opinion of what XV Corps was to do. In his 5 November diary entry,
Patton noted that Devers "would push XV Corps along on our Right" in
order to support Third Army's offensive.[66] Undoubtedly Devers believed he
had complied with Ike's instructions. However, as recounted above, a gap
was allowed to open between XII and XV Corps. Ike may have viewed his
orders to Haislip and Brooks as corrective action. If Ike did not want Devers
to take this latitude, he should have modified his instructions. Devers had
briefed SHAEF on his plan to move east through the Saverne Gap and
received approval. However, SHAEF failed to remain sufficiently informed
about frontline developments and to provide proper control.

Devers was determined to change his boss's mind.[67] After dinner at
6th Army Group HQ, Bradley, Devers, and Ike retired to Devers's office
to discuss strategy.[68] The discussion lasted into the early morning hours. At
times it became quite heated. Ike picked up on Bradley's recommendation
and ordered the inter-army-group boundary north. Now all of Seventh Army
would move north in support of Patton. The supreme commander would

countenance no Rhine crossing in 6th Army Group's zone. Furthermore, Ike proposed to transfer two divisions from Devers to Bradley.

Devers argued for permission to make a major effort over the Rhine. He stated Seventh Army, not the Third, should be reinforced. After all, Patton's effort had yet to bear fruit. The argument became very bitter. When he saw that Ike was not budging, Devers backed up a little and argued that Seventh Army advancing on the far side of the Rhine would do more to break Third Army free than simply supporting Patton's right flank west of the river. Bradley strongly disagreed with Devers. Omar opined that an assault against fixed fortifications on the east bank of the Rhine was foolhardy and would fail. Bradley was guessing. Devers retorted that Seventh Army patrols had already crossed the river and had peered into these works. They were devoid of defending troops. Devers had the facts, but to no avail.

The supreme commander was very concerned about remaining German units west of the Rhine wedged in between Patch and French First Army (the Colmar pocket; see map 8.5). Might not this force advance north into the flank of Seventh Army as Patch attempted to attack northeast? What was left of Wiese's Nineteenth Army wasn't about to bite anyone. Pressed from north and south, separated from German First Army, they were worried about saving their own hides.

Ike offered some salve. If Devers agreed to keep his troops on the west side of the Rhine, the supreme commander would not take away the two divisions he had earlier indicated would be transferred to Bradley. Instead, 6th Army Group would add an armored division due to arrive from the United States. One might infer that Ike had sandbagged a little in the initial proposal to move divisions north.

Ike was very sure-footed about his approach to Devers. Upon return to Shellburst (Ike's HQ), he wrote to General Marshall about the trip.[69] Eisenhower reiterated that the theater main effort remained up with First and Ninth Armies. With the adjustments Ike made to Devers's dispositions, Third and Seventh Armies would now attack the Siegfried Line west of the Rhine and in the vicinity of the Saar. The primary and secondary attacks remained in their established locations. However, he did not tell Marshall that a SHAEF staff study identified Patton's sector of attack as one of the best-defended sectors of the West Wall.[70] Meanwhile, the Rhine near Rastatt remained virtually unguarded.

Ike took Devers's criticism personally. He left the meeting very angry. Devers also was angry. He wondered if he would ever be included in Ike's inner circle. Devers felt that Eisenhower's decision not to press a Rhine crossing was a major error.[71] Both men owed their current commands to Marshall. But the already poor relationship between them became much worse. Devers began openly disparaging Eisenhower around 6th Army Group headquarters. That sealed his fate.

Professor Weigley states categorically, "Devers was wrong."[72] French First Army had "shot its bolt." True. Nineteenth Army elements within the Colmar pocket repeatedly rebuffed French attacks. But Nineteenth Army was in no shape to threaten Patch. On the other hand, Patch was ready to cross the Rhine.

Writing twelve years after Weigley, the official army historians, Jeffrey Clarke and Robert Ross Smith, communicate in a different tenor. "Eisenhower's decision not to exploit in some way the Belfort and Saverne penetrations to the Rhine is difficult to understand."[73]

Let's look at the situation a little more closely.

Because of the turmoil among the Combined Chiefs, that is, between Marshall and Brooke, Ike probably didn't have the freedom to re-designate his main effort from north to south. Even without this constraint, he probably wasn't disposed to do so. However, he probably had the latitude to move his secondary effort from Lorraine to Alsace.

Recall that the backbone of Ike's strategy was to draw the German army into decisive battle along the Rhine and kill it. That was the motivation for the two phases. Two thrusts were to prevent the Germans from piling up everything they had to oppose a single Allied avenue of attack.

The two biggest problems Ike's November strategy faced were a method to cross the Roer and some way to deal with Sixth Panzer Army. The main effort had deadlocked. However, there was no requirement that the thrust that killed the German Army in the field be also the main thrust line into Central Germany. Given the deadlock on the northern thrust, it was more than time to maneuver on the secondary one.

The primary purpose of a secondary attack is to facilitate the main effort. Patton's efforts had not caused Sixth Panzer Army to move.* Patch's penetration of the Saverne Gap had caused at least Panzer Lehr to displace southward and commit to an ineffective counterattack.

---

*The German buildup included both 5th and 6th Panzer Armies, but the 6th was the primary identification prior to the offensive's beginning.

The cornerstone of Ike's strategy was the destruction of the bulk of Germany's field army west of the Rhine. After pointing toward the Aachen Gap for two months, the Germans had pretty well got the idea. The Aachen approach was guarded by a strong force defending on generally broken terrain and emplaced in solid fortifications. Battering against Germans in pillboxes or in bunkers hidden in the woods was not going to accomplish that. Key to destruction of the German Army was destruction of Sixth Panzer Army. In the north, that wasn't going to happen west of the Roer. Nobody had any idea how to get over that small river with the big reservoirs. Sixth Panzer Army stood ready to chop off any spearhead that made it across the Roer. Instead of their being the hunted, the shape of the battlefield made the panzers the hunters. November required a reformulation of theater strategy.

Despite Devers's heated arguments, Eisenhower was not about to entertain a change in theater strategy. Compare this with his rapid endorsement of a major change when Montgomery proposed the Market Garden assault to cross the Rhine at Arnhem when the two commanders met in the back of Ike's B-25 at Brussels airport in early September.

Perhaps three alternative lines of reasoning can be advanced for Ike's seeming stubbornness. First, throughout a very frustrating fall, senior British generals had severely criticized Ike for not better concentrating Allied force in a northern thrust in September. Field Marshal Brooke led an effort to get the Combined Chiefs of Staff to *order* Eisenhower to do so. Ike was a brilliant observer of the limits of his own power and knew when not to exceed his grasp. Long before this inspection trip, he was welded to a strong effort in the north.

Second, Ike seemed more worried about the bulge west of the Rhine between Seventh Army's lunge to Strasbourg and the French Army's limited advance from the Belfort Gap. While Leclerc had shown great élan in taking Strasbourg, French First Army had dawdled in its cleanup of a 40-mile-wide, 25-mile-deep salient centered on the French town of Colmar. While this appears to have been a major topic of that heated conversation in Devers's office, it is probably the least likely explanation of Ike's decision. Ike thought defensively about the threat south of Strasbourg, while Devers looked aggressively at the hole in German defenses to the north that laid bare an approach to the Rhine. In fairness to the defensive-oriented argument, the existence of the Colmar Pocket badly stretched an already undersized 6th Army Group. Devers was confident that French First Army could take care of this salient. He stated, "The German Nineteenth Army has ceased to exist as a tactical force."[74] Failing to deliver on that estimate would become a major bone of contention between the two senior American generals well into 1945.

The third reason might have been Ike's fervent desire to keep most of the action under Bradley's control. In his later memoirs Bradley says as much. Eisenhower would have preferred to meld Seventh Army into Bradley's 12th Army Group and have Bradley conduct both the main effort and the secondary effort.[75] A school solution would have placed 12th Army Group in charge of the main effort and 6th Army Group conducting the secondary effort in the south. Something other than this seems to have been at work. Moving the secondary effort to a crossing at Rastatt, while consistent with the school solution, would have made even less sense if Ike retained Third Army under Bradley's control.

Ike relied heavily on his good friend Bradley. He could be depended on to carry out what the supreme commander wanted. Did Ike have similar confidence in Devers? Obviously not. Eisenhower was far too tactful to leave written adverse opinions of others behind. Perhaps the closest one can get is the confidential memo from Eisenhower to Marshall at the end of the war, where Ike gave his most honest assessment of the capabilities of his subordinates. The intent of the communication was to assist the chief in making plans for future assignments and promotions. Eisenhower wrote of General Devers: "The overall results he [Devers] and his organization produce are generally good, sometimes outstanding. But he has not, so far, produced among the seniors of the American organization here that feeling of trust and confidence that is so necessary to continued success."[76]

If Eisenhower turned down the Rastatt crossing opportunity because he did not trust Devers, then the appointment of that general to command 6th Army Group was one of the most egregious personnel decisions within the American Army in World War II. Ike had told his mentor, Marshall, that he could work with Devers as 6th Army Group commander. If he could not, then this error would lie at the feet of Eisenhower.

During their meeting, Ike began to bargain with the 6th Army Group commander. If Devers would desist from pressing the Rastatt crossing and stay on the west side of the Rhine, the supreme commander was prepared to cancel the transfer of two 6th Army Group divisions he had earlier indicated would be sent to Bradley. Instead, 6th Army Group would add an armored division due to arrive from the United States. One might infer that Ike had sandbagged a little in the initial proposal to move divisions north.

The obvious alternative was in Lorraine. In other words, recreate the tank battles around Arracourt, but on a larger scale. However, it would take more than the two corps that Patton had to execute this shift in strategy.

Seventh Army running amuck up the east side of the Rhine would certainly have been a cause for concern at OKW. If German First Army remained in place in Lorraine, it faced encirclement and destruction. If it withdrew, Patton got a free ride past the West Wall and into the Saar. He would be poised to strike deep into the heart of Germany. Despite delusions about his upcoming Ardennes offensive, Hitler would have had to do something about this threat. Sixth Panzer Army, or a reasonable portion thereof, would have to move south and away from Bradley's Queen. If Bradley ever figured out a way over the Roer, then his troops might have a chance to withstand a reduced German counterattack. If they could not, a successful campaign of destruction in Alsace-Lorraine and a victorious Seventh Army east of the Rhine headed toward Frankfurt was likely to change a lot of minds of those who previously argued that the only viable approach to Berlin was north of the Ruhr. After all, Napoleon's approach was via Lorraine–Frankfurt–Fulda Gap to Berlin. Here was a tremendous opportunity to execute the mission of the secondary attack by moving it less than 100 miles south in order to exploit a hole in Hitler's defenses.

If everyone on the Allied side from the North Sea to the Swiss border had worn the same color uniform and saluted the same national flag, shifting the main effort to the south might have been more easily agreed on. But the high-level squabbling between the American and British chiefs and between Monty and Ike rigidified strategic thinking. Everyone had to prove he was "right," "consistent," and "unwavering." This cacophony destroyed any unity of command on the Allied side. It robbed the Allies of any strategic agility whatsoever. Instead of allowing Eisenhower to be a field general, the political leadership ensured he would spend most of his energy holding a coalition together. This much simplified Rundstedt's problems and allowed Hitler to pursue his dream of offensive through the Ardennes.

Allowing Seventh Army to jump the Rhine and then maneuvering Third Army in a manner to complete the destruction of a German army would achieve a major objective that had eluded the allies for the better part of three months. The secondary attack had always focused on Mannheim as a probable crossing point. A crossing 70 kilometers to the south was a change in plans. It's about the same distance as that between Arnhem and Wesel. That arc split British Second from U.S. First Armies in early September. It is a significant distance. The ground east of the Rhine from Mannheim to Darmstadt is wooded and hilly—not the best tank country. Rastatt was not the ideal crossing site, but it was the only one the Allies had an immediate chance of taking. Seventh Army didn't have to race up a 100-kilometer corridor, hoping some paratroopers captured a string of bridges along the way. And Devers did not have to eschew any objective remotely near the importance of Antwerp to make the attempt.

A Rhine crossing at Rastatt was much less an alteration than Market Garden. In no way would the main effort in the north be impacted, lest the British marshals howl. No resources need be diverted from it. Devers's most probable subsequent axis of advance was due north toward Frankfurt. Stuttgart is 70 kilometers due east of the planned crossing site. German defensive problems would be compounded.

Sixth Army Group would have needed to prepare for a strong reaction. Given Balck's aggressiveness, he would have attempted to destroy the bridgehead by attacking down the *west* bank of the Rhine. At a minimum, forces equivalent to those that participated in the Nordwind counterattack in January might have been available. The west-bank attack force might have been built around XXXIX Panzer Corps (21 PzD, 25PGD, and 10SS PzD). Something akin to XII SS Corps (17SSPGD and 36ID), which made up the western wing of Nordwind, might have been slipped east to defend against Patch's forces attacking up the east bank of the Rhine. However, these units were only shadows of what their printed tables of organization and equipment described.

Fourth Armored Division repeatedly demonstrated what a meeting engagement in late 1944 between experienced Americans and rebuilt German formations looked like. When the Americans had the least bit of time to prepare in rolling country, they consistently inflicted heavy casualties on the Germans in mobile warfare. The same artillery concentration firing east in support of the Rhine crossing could traverse north and dismember a German attack. The corridor along the Rhine would be no empty quarter like the Ardennes. The Americans would be on guard and loaded for Panther.

The logical extension of a crossing at Rastatt would be to transfer Third Army to Devers. The encirclement and the pressure forces needed to be under one commander. With this change, Devers might have wanted to transfer another corps, perhaps Eddy's XII, to add weight to the forces on the east bank of the Rhine. Eddy's 4th Armored had already moved across the inter-army-group boundary to strike at Panzer Lehr. Patton could have held Lorraine with III Corps while XX Corps became the pressure force against German First Army along the Saar.

Again we have returned to the notion of 6th Army group running the secondary effort while 12th Army Group concentrated on the main effort north of the Ardennes. From the Ardennes north, there need to be no diminution in effort.

Patton had been looking to cross the Rhine farther north in Lorraine. That effort would cease as Third Army joined Seventh Army in a coordinated attack farther south. But Patton was farther from Darmstadt than Devers would be at Rastatt. And Third Army had yet to pierce the West Wall, let alone approach the Rhine. Part of Patton's force should have become the "direct pressure force" against German First Army while Seventh army sought to encircle and destroy it. In order to counter this offensive, 6 Panzer Army would have had to move several hundred kilometers. While it moved, Allied airpower would have had a field day. Attacking Americans would have more success in meeting engagements than in digging Germans out of the ground west of the Roer.

In Market Garden, Monty planned to advance east with a couple of divisions. A 6th Army Group attack would put at least two corps on the east bank. Balck did not have the forces to cover a thrust of this magnitude. In all probability, Nineteenth Army would have to be pulled back across the Rhine to defend Stuttgart.

But Ike wasn't ready to take on the risk of any of these alternatives in the south. Better than Devers, he recognized a crossing at Rastatt made no sense if 6th Army Group was not heavily reinforced. That meant shutting down something else that was scheduled, like Patton's offensive. It is hard to comprehend the huge strain he was under and to gauge the additional impact of the changes proposed by Devers.

Then again, that is what Eisenhower was promoted to do.

If Hitler persisted in his Ardennes offensive both antagonists would be pushing against a revolving door. Devers is attacking north and east while Hitler attacks west. Clausewitz advises, "Should the defender likewise be active, should he attack us at other points, we shall be able to gain victory only if we surpass him with energy and boldness."[77] Patton communicated a similar notion more forcefully: "I have never given a damn what the enemy was going to do or where he was. What I have known is what I have intended to do and then have done it."[78]

Early on during the Battle of the Bulge, Allied generals recognized that the German offensive would not reach the Meuse. If Fifth and Sixth Panzer Armies sent units to oppose a Rhine crossing, they would have made even a more modest Bulge. Bradley would have undoubtedly moved his headquarters north and retained control of the huge concentration of U.S. First and Ninth Armies assembled for Queen. The history of the Bulge records Collins's chafing at the bit and ready to counterattack while Monty pulled in the reins. One Hundred First Airborne Division still might have been surrounded in Bastogne. Instead of 4th Armored clanking up from the south to relieve Bastogne, it might have been 3rd Armored attacking from the north. The crises would have been very asymmetric. Devers would have had a German army surrounded in Lorraine. The Allies could risk a division with aerial resupply capability far easier than the Germans could risk an army under skies dominated by P-47s.

Devers would have been in position to push harder than Model. Balck would have nothing like the forces at Bradley's command to stop the American offensive. With a little fortitude, the Allied offensive would have caused the German one to withdraw in order to defend its homeland. Initiative most likely would have returned to Allied hands sooner with American armor over the Rhine. The subsequent campaign would have been several months ahead of the actual one that finished the Nazis.

But none of this happened. Ike declined to sanction a Rhine crossing as far south as Rastatt.

Notwithstanding the disagreement between Eisenhower and Devers, 6th Army Group moved quickly to comply with Ike's orders. Devers proved to be a loyal subordinate committed to the notion of unity of command. XV Corps moved back over the Low Vosges to support Patton. One can only imagine what the troops who fought hard to take the Saverne Gap must have thought when they marched through it in the "wrong" direction. The bulk of VI Corps moved south to contain or reduce the pocket. The 79ID moved north and prepared defensive positions between the Vosges and the Rhine.

Devers had finally broken the deadlock that had bound the entire theater since the beginning of October. Ike's decision threw away a major strategic opportunity that could have led to achievement of several major objectives. This was not a blind and useless leap into the Black Forest. It was an opportunity to destroy an entire German army west of the Rhine, cross that major barrier, and force commitment of German strategic reserves that would otherwise crush any budding attack in the Aachen Gap that Bradley might eke out.

Patton also disagreed with Ike's leashing of Devers. In a 24 November letter to his wife, Patton wrote, "I personally believe the VI Corps should have crossed the Rhine."[79] Bradley couldn't figure out how to get over the Roer, let alone the Rhine.

Ike's action was perplexing.

THE SQUABBLE CONTINUES

During the 28 November meeting at 21st Army Group TAC HQ at Zonhoven "Monty could barely hide his contempt of Ike."[80] Monty carried most of the conversation. Ike listened. The field marshal's theme: "We have failed, we have suffered a strategic reverse. We need a new plan." Again Monty sought control over the land campaign. Ike came to a full boil, but he held in the steam. Monty interpreted Ike's silence as agreement.

Monty continued to harp on his ideas in a 30 November letter to Ike. In part, it read:

> 4. In the new plan we must get away from the doctrine of attacking in so many places that nowhere are we strong enough to get decisive results. We must concentrate such strength on the main selected thrust that success will be certain. It is in this respect that we failed badly in the present operations.

Undoubtedly the field marshal was trying to help. Then again, no one ever accused him of being tactful. In the meantime the field marshal had written Brooke that Ike had agreed with his point of view.

Ike's reply in a letter to Montgomery dated 1 December was sharp: "There are certain things in your letter in which I do not concur. Your letter does state your conception and opinions as presented to me the other evening." "I do not agree that things have gone badly since Normandy."

Ike also threw it back at Monty. "If we had advanced from the beginning *as we had hoped* [i.e., cleared the Scheldt in early September], our maintenance services would have been in a position to supply us during the critical September say, when we actually reached the limit of our resources. . . . Even delivery of 500 tons at Brussels [in September] cost Bradley 3 divisions, the possession of which might have easily placed him on the Rhine in the Worms area."[81]

Ike also highlighted a basic difference in strategy between them. Eisenhower continued to concentrate on the enemy: "The Ruhr is an important place, but let us never forget for one second that our primary objective is to defeat the German forces that are barring our way into Germany. The

Ruhr itself was always given as a geographical objective, not only for its importance to Germany, but because it was believed that in that region the *German Forces* would be largely concentrated to meet our attacks."[82]

At Monty's request, Ike and senior SHAEF officers met a week later in Maastricht. The conference began with Eisenhower reviewing the campaign and its accomplishments to date. He read off German casualty lists. Then the supreme commander invited Monty's views. The field marshal stated there were two main factors required to win the war, and neither of them involved the number of German dead:

> First: The only real worthwhile objective on the western front is the Ruhr.
> If we cut it off from the rest of Germany the enemy capacity to continue the struggle must gradually peter out.
>   Second: It is essential that we force mobile war on the Germans.[83]

Monty went on to identify the need "to defeat decisively the enemy 6 Panzer Army."

The two leaders clashed on a basic element. Was the strategy to take a major economic zone or to draw the enemy into battle and destroy him?

Monty continued to emphasize that only operations made in the north made any sense. Of course he should command them all. However, even Monty suggested that U.S. First Army's effort be switched south of the Roer dams. No one seemed to want to take on the floodable moat.

Ike had begun to slightly modify his strategy. While he continued to designate operations north of the Ruhr as the main effort, he now intended to give a secondary attack in Patton's area more weight. The attack would seek a crossing around Worms-Mannheim and continue via Frankfurt toward Kassel. SHAEF planning staff issued a formal study detailing how either one or two corps (three to six divisions) could be swung from north of the Ardennes to the south or vice versa.[84] The maneuver would take about fourteen days. This was the main thrust line of Bradley's old American Plan. The area from the Roer through the Huertgen and the Ardennes would not see major offensive action.

Upon viewing the staff paper, Eisenhower said that such a maneuver was always a possibility but that he had no intention of ordering such a maneuver in the near future.[85] Apparently, Ike was solidly committed to the strategy of drawing the Wehrmacht to its destruction by threatening the Ruhr.

Monty was vociferous in his objectives. Later he wrote Brooke that it was now up to the chief of the Imperial General Staff to talk sense into the supreme commander.

On December 3 Eisenhower sent a long cable to the Combined Chiefs outlining the current situation.[86] Ike took full responsibility for the delay in opening Antwerp due to Market Garden. The Chiefs had been so concerned about the capture of that port they had considered giving Ike a direct order about taking it. Ike said he was ready to take any advantage of a crack in the Germans, "although it must be confessed that there is no basis on which to anticipate such an outcome." "The fighting qualities, particularly in defensive positions of the enemy continue to be good." Ike knew he was deadlocked. He planned to continue attrition warfare until some better opportunity appeared.

Ike told Bradley to give Patton the go-ahead to attack again in the Saar. In a departure from some earlier pondering, First Army would continue operations to gain the Roer dams. Second and 99th Divisions began to concentrate on the Elsenborn ridge at the northern extreme of the Ardennes and to prepare to attack toward the dams.

On 12 December Ike, Tedder, and the British chiefs of staff dined with Churchill back in England. Brooke invited Ike to reiterate his plan. Then he proceeded to tear it apart, especially for its lack of concentration. The chief of the Imperial Staff "became highly critical and extremely loud."[87] Churchill intervened. Appalled that senior British commanders were ganging up on his guest, Eisenhower, Churchill sided with Ike. Chagrined, Brooke realized he had lost.

But Hitler hadn't. On the 16th, under a tremendous bombardment, German panzers emerged from the early morning mist in the Ardennes.

Conclusion:
Unity of Command

A Cadet will not lie, steal, or cheat, nor will he tolerate anyone who does.

Honor Code

"For every objective, insure unity of effort under one responsible commander. This principle insures that all efforts are focused on a common goal."[1] Usually this definition is interpreted as "one boss for the job." But its implications run deeper. Unity of command is the tool required to see that all effort is focused on the one condition that causes the enemy to collapse. Virtually every military officer, including the senior commanders during the fall of 1944, emphatically supports unity of command. Yet the command environment during the Fall of Frustration was anything but unified. Eisenhower was the single boss. The campaign plan that Ike and his staff formulated was competent. As with most battle plans, there were plausible alternatives.

Once an operation begins, time literally is "of the essence." The minute taken to re-argue the best course of action may be the one "unforgiving minute" of hesitation that causes our destruction. Remember the enemy is trying to his utmost to do to you what you are trying to do to him. In addition to creating concentration of effort, unity of command improves our agility, our ability to react faster than our opponent. As Patton said, "Good is enemy of the best." A good plan executed in time is far preferable to the best plan conceived too late to catch the enemy. As we have seen, a smaller but more agile opponent can stop a stronger adversary. The contemporary term is getting inside the enemy's decision-making loop, which is the reason we spend so much on communication technology.

After having their views heard and after the boss made his decision, several of Eisenhower's seniormost lieutenants were unwilling to comply with their commander's intent. In September, by following their own ideas instead of SHAEF strategy, they wrecked any chances of ending the war before Christmas.

Anyone who has tried to get something done quickly within a large organization knows the usefulness of unity of command. Napoleon once said, "It is better to have one bad general than two good ones." When the council of war finishes, so does the debate. Juniors again become subordinates, whose sole task is to faithfully execute the intentions of their commander.

Asking senior officers to sublimate their personal and institutional egos sounds a little Pollyannaish. So does asking some dogface to advance in the direction of some people he doesn't know who are trying to kill him and who keep throwing hot metal at him. If the nation can ask the individual soldier to risk his life for his country, can't the nation ask the general to holster his ego? Our greatest general, George C. Marshall, did so without a prompt.

Contemporary warfare has become extremely complex. It takes a cast of thousands to control it, let alone fight it. Councils of war, committee work, have gained in importance. As long as military courtesy is observed, each officer should be, must be, allowed to air his or her views and the concerns of the organization that officer represents. Eisenhower was a master at conducting such councils. The solitary field marshal studying his maps in a private caravan had become an anachronism.

History demonstrates that the definition of unity of command needs a corollary:

Any subordinate who adopts an agenda that is inconsistent with EITHER *his commander's orders or* INTENT *is in* VIOLATION *of the principle of Unity of Command.*

Professional (as opposed to mercenary) armies exist because of the deeply held belief structures of their members. Adding this corollary to unity of command is the best way of inculcating a much-needed change in behavior. Military cadets need to hear this during their first lecture about the principles of war. Maybe it will inculcate the small voice that admonishes "the right thing to do" that all people need to hear from time to time.

Every officer expects his men to obey orders. How can any general think the same does not apply to him? History shows that a lot of them did. Patton was an astute student of why men fought. He would have been astonished to find some Third Army soldiers thought him a self-serving blowhard. If some guiding principle had directed him to more carefully examine his own motives, might not his army have accomplished even more? The mark of excellence is not what Third Army accomplished. It is how well it accomplished the mission assigned. Veterans of Seventh Army can easily hold their heads as high as those of the Third.

It isn't much different than having cadets "not lie, steal, or cheat, or tolerate anyone who does." That is too much to ask of the general population. A military officer is a member of a profession that stands far apart from those who might accept a lesser standard as "human nature."

The actions of senior Allied ground commanders in September of 1944 provide little to emulate. Eisenhower had an impossibly difficult job. Senior officers infected with victory disease eschewed good discipline as they grabbed for battle laurels. It was not a pretty sight. Almost-certain victory turned to defeat. The lesson is as important as it is distasteful. Behavior more akin to independent political satraps rather than loyal subordinate officers fractured what might have been a successful strategy.

We need no more seasons like the Fall of Frustration.

Notes

1. Culmination

The epigraph is from Blumenson, *Patton Papers*, p. 523.

1. Cable, Eisenhower to Bradley, 24 July 1944, SHAEF Papers.
2. Cable, Eisenhower to Bradley, 26 July 1944, SHAEF Papers.
3. Blumenson, *Breakout and Pursuit*, p. 217.
4. Ibid., p. 289.
5. Cable S556667, Eisenhower to Marshall and Combined Chiefs of Staff.
6. Letter, Montgomery to Eisenhower, 21 Feb. 1944, Eisenhower File on Montgomery, DDE Library.
7. FWD122614, Eisenhower to Marshall, 5 Aug. 1944, DDE Library.
8. M517 21, Army Group Directive 6, Aug. 1944, SHAEF Papers.
9. Blumenson, *Patton Papers*, Patton Diary, 9 Aug., p. 505.
10. Bradley, *Soldier's Story*, p. 377.
11. D'Este, *Eisenhower*, p. 521.
12. Blumenson, *Patton Papers*, Patton Diary, p. 521.
13. Blumenson, *Battle of the Generals*, p. 211.
14. FWD 12674, Eisenhower to Marshall, 7 Aug. 1944, SHAEF Papers.
15. Post Neptune Operations, 17 Aug. 1944, SHAEF File 18008, G3 Plans.
16. FM 100-5, pp. 6–8, 1993.
17. Eisenhower to Marshall, FWD 13792 4 Sept. 1944, SHAEF Papers.
18. Chandler and Ambrose, *Papers of Dwight David Eisenhower*, vol. 4, p. 1910. Hereafter, *Eisenhower Papers*.
19. Ambrose, *Supreme Commander*, p. 507.
20. Eisenhower, *Crusade in Europe*, p. 306.
21. Blumenson, *Patton Papers*, p. 533.
22. Weigley, *Eisenhower's Lieutenants*, p. 275.
23. Blumenson, *Breakout and Pursuit*, p. 679.
24. Ibid., p. 689.
25. Houston, *Hell on Wheels*, p. 265.
26. Ibid., p. 268.
27. Collins, *Lightning Joe*, p. 261.
28. Spearhead 3rd Armored Division, p. 89.
29. Collins, *Lightning Joe*, p. 263.
30. Spearhead, 3rd Armored Division, p. 88.
31. Ibid., p. 88.
32. Bradley, *Soldier's Story*, p. 408.
33. Marshall to Eisenhower, W29970 in Bland, Marshall Papers.
34. Farago, *Ordeal and Triumph*, p. 648.
35. Eisenhower, *Crusade in Europe*, p. 321.
36. Ruppenthal, *Logistical Support of the Armies*, vol. 1, p. 490.
37. Ibid., p. 483.

38. Ruppenthal, *Logistical Support of the Armies*, vol. 1, p. 487.

39. First Army Combat Journal for August, p. 49, Hodges files DDE Library.

40. Ambrose, *Supreme Commander*, p. 495.

41. Crosswell, *Chief of Staff*, p. 160.

42. Ambrose, *Eisenhower*, p. 343.

2. Logistics

The epigraph is from Eisenhower, *Crusade in Europe*, p. 292.

1. Ambrose, *Eisenhower, Soldier, General of the Army, President Elect*, p. 345.

2. Joint Publication 1-02 DoD Dictionary of Military Terms 1989, p. 211.

3. Cable S65533, Eisenhower to Somervell, p. 2281.

4. Ruppenthal, *Logistical Support of the Armies*, vol. 1, p. 318.

5. Bradley and Blair, *A General's Life*, p. 321. Hereafter Bradley, *General's Life*.

6. Huston, *Sinews of War*, p. 529.

7. Mayo, *Ordnance Department*, p. 295.

8. Ruppenthal, *Logistical Support of the Armies*, vol. 2, p. 116.

9. 3rd Armored Division AAR, Sept. 1944, quoted in MacDonald, *Siegfried Line Campaign*, p. 20.

10. Hughes, *Overlord: General Pete Quesada*, p. 235.

11. Marshall, *Men under Fire*, p. 149.

12. Ibid., p. 151.

13. Brownlee and Mullen, *Changing an Army*, p. 38.

14. D' Este, *Decision in Normandy*, p. 268.

15. Pogue, *Supreme Command*, p. 240.

16. Montgomery, *Normandy to the Baltic*.

17. Ruppenthal, *Logistical Support of the Armies*, vol. 2, p. 314.

18. Ibid., p. 46.

19. John Ellis, *Brute Force*, p. 399.

20. Ruppenthal, *Logistical Support of the Armies*, vol. 2, p. 262.

21. D' Este, *Eisenhower*, p. 590.

22. Ohl, *Supplying the Troops,* p. 227.

23. Eisenhower to Somervell, 27 Jan. and 19 March 1943, reported in Ohl, *Supplying the Troops*.

24. Ruppenthal, *Logistical Support of the Armies*, vol. 1, p. 267.

25. Ibid., vol. 2, p. 349.

26. Patton Diary, 25 Sept. entry, in Blumenson, *Patton Papers*, p. 557.

27. Ibid.

28. Smith, *Eisenhower's Six Great Decisions*, p. 266.

29. Huston, *Sinews of War*, p. 531.

30. Ibid., p. 533.

31. Ruppenthal, *Logistical Support of the Armies*, vol. 2, p. 349.

32. Ibid.

33. 1947 interview with Forrest Pogue, cited in D'Este, *Eisenhower*, p. 571.

34. Crosswell, *Chief of Staff*, p. 237.

35. Hughes diary cited in Crosswell, *Chief of Staff*, p. 269.

36. Crosswell, *Chief of Staff*, p. 270.

37. Interview of Marshall by Forrest Pogue, 13 November 1956, Marshall Library, Virginia Military Institute.

38. R.F. Ricarrdelli, "Information and Intelligence Revolution," *Military Review* 75 (Sept.–Oct. 1995): 83.

39. Ruppenthal, *Logistical Support of the Armies*, vol. 2, pp. 358–60.

40. Patton, *War as I Knew It*, p. 139.

41. Ruppenthal, *Logistical Support of the Armies*, vol. 2, pp. 18, 171.

42. Ibid., vol. 1, p. 306.

43. Moulton, *Battle for Antwerp*, p. 74.

44. Montgomery, *Normandy to the Baltic*, p. 214.

45. Ruppenthal, *Logistical Support of the Armies*, vol. 1, p. 436.

46. Ibid., p. 490.

47. Ibid., p. 482.

48. Ibid., vol. 2, p. 5.

49. Ibid., vol. 1, p. 509.

50. Ibid., p. 576.

51. MacDonald, *Siegfried Line Campaign*, p. 11.

52. Ruppenthal, *Logistical Support of the Armies*, vol. 1, p. 490.

53. Ibid., p. 491.

54. MacDonald, *Siegfried Line Campaign*, p. 12.

55. Ruppenthal, *Logistical Support of the Armies*, vol. 1, p. 492.

56. Ibid.

57. Montgomery, *Memoirs*, p. 245.

58. Ibid., 245–46.

59. MacDonald, *Siegfried Line Campaign*, p. 120.

60. Greenfield, *Command Decisions*, p. 423.

61. Bykofsky and Larson, *Transportation Corps*, p. 240.

62. Ruppenthal, *Logistical Support of the Armies*, vol. 1, p. 315.

63. Ibid., p. 488.

64. Ibid., p. 581.

65. FM 55-15, *Transportation Reference Data*, 28 Feb. 1968, p. 7-3.

66. Blumenson, *Breakout and Pursuit*, p. 690.

67. Ruppenthal, *Logistical Support of the Armies*, vol. 2, p. 140.

68. Bykofsky and Larson, *Transportation Corps: Operations Overseas*, p. 341.

69. Fuller, *A Military History of the Modern World*, p. 561.

70. Beck et al., *Corps of Engineers: The War against Germany*, p. 397.

71. Ibid., p. 398.

72. Ruppenthal, *Logistical Support of the Armies*, vol. 1, p. 218.

73. Patton, *War as I Knew It*, p. 142.

74. Letter, Eisenhower to Marshall, 24 Aug. 1944, 1910, p. 2094.

75. Ruppenthal, *Logistical Support of the Armies*, vol. 1, p. 324.

76. Beck et al., *Corps of Engineers*, p. 413.

77. Bykofsky and Larson, *Transportation Corps*, p. 329.

78. Ibid., p. 321.

79. Ibid., p. 331.

80. Ibid., p. 329.

81. Hamilton, *Monty: Final Years of the Field-Marshal*, 126n.

82. Blumenson, *Breakout and Pursuit*, p. 691.

83. FUSA AAR cited in MacDonald, *Siegfried Line Campaign*, p. 13.

84. Ruppenthal, *Logistical Support of the Armies*, p. 144, log.

85. Bykofsky and Larson, *Transportation Corps*, p. 240.

86. FUSA Rept of Opns cited in MacDonald, *Siegfried Line Campaign*, p. 12.

87. MacDonald, *Siegfried Line Campaign*, p. 13.

88. Bykofsky and Larson, *Transportation Corps*, 342.

89. Ruppenthal, *Logistical Support of the Armies*, vol. 1, p. 180.

90. Ibid., vol. 2, p. 4.

91. Ibid., vol. 1, p. 474.

92. Ibid., p. 187.

93. Ibid., p. 286.

94. Ibid., vol. 2, p. 5.

95. Ibid., p. 52.

96. 12AG AAR Sep 1944 cited in Ruppenthal, *Logistical Support of the Armies*, vol. 1; 12AG AAR Sep 1944 cited in Ruppenthal, *Logistical Support of the Armies*, vol. 1, p. 17.

97. Ruppenthal, *Logistical Support of the Armies*, vol. 2, p. 97.

98. Bykofsky and Larson, *Transportation Corps*, p. 310.

99. Ruppenthal, *Logistical Support of the Armies*, vol. 2, p. 46.

100. Ibid., pp. 18–20.

101. Kohn and Harahan, *Condensed Analysis of Ninth Air Force*, p. 36.

102. Ruppenthal, *Logistical Support of the Armies*, vol. 2, p. 247.

103. Patton, *War as I Knew It*, p. 139.

104. Ruppenthal, *Logistical Support of the Armies*, vol. 2, p. 267.

105. ST100-3 Battle Book 1 Apr. 1993, p. 6-1.
106. Ruppenthal, *Logistical Support of the Armies*, vol. 1, p. 537.
107. Ibid., p. 540.
108. Ibid., p. 538.
109. G4 12AG records, cited in ibid., p. 445.
110. Ruppenthal, *Logistical Support of the Armies*, vol. 1, p. 445.
111. Ibid., p. 447.
112. Ibid., p. 527.
113. Ibid., p. 540.
114. Bradley, *Soldier's Story*, p. 431.
115. Mayo, *Ordnance Department*, pp. 301–302.
116. FWD 12707 Eisenhower Papers IV, p. 2061.
117. Ruppenthal, *Logistical Support of the Armies*, vol. 1, p. 527.
118. Bykofsky and Larson, *Transportation Corps*, p. 309.
119. Ibid., p. 311.
120. Mayo, *Ordnance Department*, p. 302.
121. Bykofsky and Larson, *Transportation Corps*, p. 310.
122. Letter 12AG to COMZ 16 Sept., quoted in Ruppenthal, *Logistical Support of the Armies*, vol. 1, p. 543.
123. Ruppenthal, *Logistical Support of the Armies*, vol. 2, p. 258.
124. Ibid., p. 351.
125. Kohn and Harahan, Condensed Analysis of 9th Air Force, p. 31.
126. Hughes, *Overlord: General Pete Quesada*, p. 248.

3. SHAEF's Plan

The epigraph is from SHAEF SGS 322.011, CCCS Directive to SCAEF, para. 2, Task.
1. Advance to Breach Siegfried Line Appreciation SHAEF 17100.18 Ops(A), Eisenhower Library.
2. SHAEF records WO2190, Summarized in a memo, Bull to Smith, 18 May 1944.
3. D'Este, *Eisenhower*, p. 594.
4. Ellis, *Victory in the West*, vol. 2, *The Defeat of Germany*, p. 1.
5. Crosswell, *Chief of Staff*, p. 251.
6. D'Este, *Eisenhower*, p. 511.
7. D'Este, *Decision in Normandy*, p. 50.
8. D'Este, *Eisenhower*, p. 549.
9. Wilmot, *Struggle for Europe*, p. 465.
10. Montgomery, *Memoirs*, p. 235.
11. Letter Monty to Brooke, 14 Aug. 1944, cited in Hamilton, *Master of the Battlefield*, p. 791.
12. Bryant, *Triumph in the West*, p. 195.
13. Ibid., p. 254.
14. Hamilton, *Monty: Final Years of the Field-Marshal*, p. 722.
15. Brooke to Simpson, recounted in ibid., p. 799.
16. Sixsmith, *Eisenhower as Military Commander*, p. 216.
17. Ibid., p. 218.
18. *Parameters* 23, no. 3 (Autumn 1993): 6.
19. Clarke and Smith, *From the Riviera to the Rhine*, p. 228.
20. Wilmot, *Struggle for Europe*, pp. 468–69.
21. Ambrose, *Eisenhower: Soldier, General of the Army, President-Elect*, p. 70.
22. Ibid., p. 75.
23. D'Este, *Eisenhower*, p. 168.
24. Radio 2362, Marshall to Eisenhower, 16 Feb. 1943, Marshall Papers, vol. 3, p. 554.
25. Perry, *Partners in Command*, p. 77.
26. Eisenhower to Herbert Brees, 28 Feb. 1944, Eisenhower Papers #1573.
27. Taylor, *Principles of War*, p. 7, cited in Weigley, *Eisenhower's Lieutenants*, p. 6.
28. Crosswell, *Chief of Staff*, p. 54.

29. Weigley, *Eisenhower's Lieutenants*, p. 5.

30. Ambrose, *Eisenhower: Soldier, General of the Army, President-Elect*, p. 80.

31. Adjutant General's Report 1922, cited in Crosswell, *Chief of Staff*, p. 57.

32. Three quotes from Post–Overlord Planning, 18 May 144 Tab A, transmitted by SHAEF G3 MG Bull, SHAEF Papers "BIGOT."

33. Ibid.

34. Crosswell, *Chief of Staff*, p. 99.

35. Quoted in Ambrose, *Eisenhower: Soldier, General of the Army, President-Elect*, p. 130.

36. Gabel, *The U.S. Army GHQ Maneuvers of 1941*, p. 188.

37. Bradley, *Soldier's Story*, p. 354.

38. Bradley, *General's Life*, p. 130.

39. Farago, *Ordeal and Triumph*, p. 677.

40. Blumenson, *Patton Papers*, p. 537.

41. Cable S56677, Eisenhower to Marshall, 2 Aug. 1944, SHAEF Papers.

42. Cable FWD 12674, Eisenhower to Marshall, 7 Aug. 1944, SHAEF Papers.

43. Cable S 57189, Eisenhower to Marshall, 9 Aug. 1944, SHAEF Papers.

44. Chandler and Ambrose, *Eisenhower Papers*, Eisenhower to George Catlett Marshall, vol. 4, p. 1892.

45. SHAEF Planning Staff, Stabilization of the "Neptune" Operation, SHAEF Papers, BIGOT file.

46. SHAEF Planning Staff, Courses of Action After Capture of Lodgement Area, Section I Main Objective and axis of Advance, 3 May 1944, SHAEF Papers, BIGOT File.

47. Eisenhower, *Crusade in Europe*, pp. 227–28.

48. Eisenhower to Mamie Eisenhower, 11 Aug. 1944, Eisenhower Papers.

49. M518, M519, M522 SHAEF Papers.

50. D'Este, *Eisenhower*, p. 532.

51. Hobbs, *Dear General*, p. 172.

52. D'Este, *Decision in Normandy*, p. 309.

53. Crosswell, *Chief of Staff*, p. 150.

54. Ibid., p. 267.

55. Ibid., p. 275.

56. Ibid.

57. Ibid., p. 221.

58. Ibid., p. 222.

59. Montgomery, *Memoirs*, p. 231.

60. D'Este, *Patton*, p. 650.

61. Chandler and Ambrose, *Eisenhower Papers*, vol. 4, p. 2467.

62. Pogue, *Supreme Command*, p. 71.

63. Smith, *Eisenhower's Six Great Decisions*, p. 124.

64. Ibid., p. 221.

65. *Military Review* 75 (July–Aug. 1995): 8; see plan 1.

66. Crosswell, *Chief of Staff*, p. 149.

67. De'Este, *Eisenhower*, p. 555.

68. Memo, "Post Overlord Planning," from Bull to Chief of Staff (Smith), 18 May 1944, SHAEF Papers, BIGOT File.

69. Ibid.

70. Ellis, *Victory in the West*, vol. 2, p. 2.

71. 17 Aug., Monty to Brooke, in Hamilton, *Master of the Battlefield*, p. 798.

72. Ibid.

73. Montgomery, *Memoirs*, p. 239.

74. Ibid., p. 239.

75. Pogue, *Supreme Command*, p. 230.

76. Fuller, *Military History of the Modern World*, vol. 3, p. 577.

77. Quotations from Pogue, *Supreme Command*, pp. 244–45.

78. Ibid., p. 401.

79. Ibid., pp. 401–402.

80. Ibid.

81. Ellis, *Brute Force*, p. 394.

82. MacDonald, *Siegfried Line Campaign*, p. 393.

83. Ehrman, *Grand Strategy*, vol. 5, p. 379.

84. Ambrose, *Eisenhower: Soldier, General of the Army, President-Elect*, p. 343.

85. Ehrman, *History of the Second World War: Grand Strategy*, vol. 5, p. 379.

86. Ibid., p. 401.

87. Ambrose, *Eisenhower: Soldier, General of the Army, President-Elect*, p. 332.

88. Clausewitz, *Principles of War*, p. 362.

89. Quoted in MacDonald, *Mighty Endeavor*, p. 336.

90. Pogue, *Supreme Command*, p. 245.

91. Cable, Eisenhower to Marshal, 24 Aug. 1944, SHAEF Papers.

92. Eisenhower to Somervell, 30 Aug. 1944, Eisenhower Files, DDE Library.

93. Smith, *Eisenhower's Six Great Decisions*, pp. 83–84.

94. Letter, Eisenhower to Montgomery, 19 Aug. 1944, SHAEF Papers.

95. Chandler and Ambrose, *Eisenhower Papers*, Eisenhower to Marshall, 24 Aug. 1944.

96. Ruppenthal, *Logistical Support of the Armies*, vol. 2, pp. 10–11.

97. Chandler and Ambrose, *Eisenhower Papers*, Eisenhower to CCS, no. 1907, 22 Aug.

98. Gelb, *Ike and Monty*, p. 351.

99. Ibid., p. 11.

100. MacDonald, *Siegfried Line Campaign*, p. 8.

101. Wilmot, *Struggle for Europe*, p. 458.

102. Hamilton, *Master of the Battlefield*, p. 815.

103. Chandler and Ambrose, *Eisenhower Papers*, no. 1909, p. 2090.

104. Hamilton, *Master of the Battlefield*, p. 820.

105. Eisenhower, Message to Commanders, 29 Aug. 1944, SHAEF Papers.

106. From Montgomery papers, quoted in Hamilton, *Monty: Final Years of the Field-Marshal*, p. 3.

107. Lamb, *Montgomery in Europe*, p. 201.

108. Bradley, *General's Life*, p. 322.

109. Ibid., p. 323.

110. Blumenson, *Patton Papers*, p. 537.

111. MacDonald, *Siegfried Line Campaign*, p. 9.

112. Bradley, *Soldier's Story*, p. 400.

113. Bradley, *General's Life*, p. 317.

114. Moulton, *Battle for Antwerp*, p. 49.

115. Ambrose, *Eisenhower: Soldier, General of the Army, President-Elect*, p. 344.

116. Bryant, *Triumph in the West*, p. 213.

117. MacDonald, *Siegfried Line Campaign*, p. 10.

118. Ibid.

119. FWD13675, SHAEF Papers.

120. Liddel Hart, *History of the Second World War*, p. 590.

121. Smith, *Eisenhower's Six Great Decisions*, p. 88.

122. Ibid., p. 122.

123. Ibid., p. 182.

4. It Wasn't Arnhem versus Antwerp

The epigraph is from Montgomery, *Memoirs*, p. 242.

1. Montgomery, *Memoirs*, p. 235.

2. Letter, Montgomery to Brooke, 14 Aug. 1944, cited in Hamilton, *Master of the Battlefield*, p. 791.

3. Bryant, *Triumph in West*, p. 213n.

4. Montgomery, M520, SHAEF Papers.

5. D'Este, *Eisenhower*, p. 485.

6. Bluemenson, *Patton Papers*, p. 540, interview of 7 Sept..

7. Montgomery, M520, SHAEF Papers.

8. Ibid.

9. Montgomery, *Normandy to the Baltic*, p. 217.

10. Ibid., p. 214.

11. Ibid..

12. Eden, *Reckoning*, pp. 568–69.

13. Hamilton, *Monty: The Final Years of the Field-Marshal*, p. 126ff.

14. Graham, *Price of Command*, p. 179.

15. Wilmot, *Struggle for Europe*, p. 476.

16. Ambrose, *Eisenhower: Soldier, General of the Army, President-Elect*, p. 347.

17. In Hamilton, *Master of the Battlefield*, p. 18.

18. Montgomery, M523, SHAEF Papers.

19. Lecture, "The 21 Army Group in the Campaign in North-West Europe 1944—B 45," delivered by Montgomery, at the Royal United Service Institute, 3 Oct. 1945 (reprinted in the Institute's November Journal).

20. Stacy, *Operations in North-West Europe*, vol. 3, p. 32.

21. Montgomery, *Memoirs*, p. 256.

22. Ibid., p. 243.

23. Ibid., p. 244.

24. From Montgomery at TAC, personal for Eiesnhower M169, 6 Sept. 1944, SHAEF Papers.

25. John Ellis, *Brute Force*, p. 403.

26. Horrocks, *A Full Life*, p. 205.

27. Stacy, *Operations in North-west Europe*, vol. 3: *The Victory Campaign*, p. 301.

28. Montgomery to Eisenhower, 4 Sept., reported in Montgomery, *Memoirs*, p. 244.

29. Horrocks, *Corps Commander*, p. 69.

30. Lamb, *Montgomery in Europe*, p. 209.

31. Moulton, *Battle for Antwerp*, p. 39.

32. Interview, Roberts to Lamb, *Montgomery in Europe*, p. 201.

33. Lamb, *Montgomery in Europe*, p. 202.

34. Moulton, *Battle for Antwerp*, p. 68.

35. Horrocks, *A Full Life*, p. 205.

36. Ryan, *A Bridge Too Far*, p. 47.

37. Moulton, *Battle for Antwerp*, p. 41n.

38. Montgomery, *Memoirs*, p. 86.

39. Cited in Moulton, *Battle for Antwerp*, pp. 49–50.

40. Winterbotham, *Ultra Secret*, pp. 233–34.

41. Horrocks, *A Full Life*, recounted in Lamb, *Montgomery in Europe*, p. 202.

42. Horrocks, *A Full Life*, p. 319.

43. Montgomery, *Normandy to the Baltic*, p. 213.

44. Messenger, *Last Prussian*, p. 210.

45. Ryan, *A Bridge Too Far*, p. 58.

46. Wilmot, *Struggle for Europe*, p. 478.

47. Barnett, *Hitler's Generals*, p. 202.

48. MacDonald, *Battle of the Huertgen Forest*, p. 197.

49. Blumenson, *Breakout and Pursuit*, p. 678.

50. Liddell Hart, *Other Side of the Hill*, p. 429.

51. According to his chief of staff Blumentritt, cited in Ryan, *A Bridge Too Far*, p. 55.

52. Moulton, *Battle for Antwerp*, p. 68.

53. Ibid., p. 69.

54. Hamilton, *Master of the Battlefield*, p. 780.

55. Ibid., pp. 780–81.

56. Letter, Simonds to Stacy, Feb. 10, 1969, cited in Graham, *Price of Command*, p. 178.

57. Ellis, *Victory in the West*, vol. 2, p. 9.

58. Hamilton, *Master of the Battlefield: Monty's War Years*, p. 37.

59. Ibid., pp. 23–24.

60. Montgomery, *Normandy to the Baltic*, p. 214.

61. Moulton, *Battle for Antwerp*, p. 69.

62. Stacy, *Operations in North-West Europe*, vol. 3, p. 329.

63. GOC in C 1-0-4 of 9 Sept., quoted in Stacy, p. 330.

64. Interview of Eisenhower by Chester Wilmot, *Struggle for Europe*, pp. 48–49.

65. Ambrose, *Supreme Commander*, p. 516.

66. FWD14376, Eisenhower to Combined Chiefs of Staff, 9 Sept. 1944, SHAEF Papers.

67. Ambrose, *Supreme Commander*, p. 518.

68. Chester Wilmot's notes of a Montgomery interview, made 13 March 1946, state that Montgomery thought the Allies could not hope for much more than a bridgehead over the Rhine before the winter. However, this is inconsistent with the notion Monty expressed at the time that Antwerp's capacity couldn't be brought on line until the war ended.

69. Office Diary 11 Sept. 1944, SHAEF Papers.

70. Weigley, *Eisenhower's Lieutenants*, p. 281.

71. Ibid., p. 282.

72. Eisenhower to Montgomery, cable FWD 14758, SHAEF Papers.

73. Eisenhower Papers, p. 2135.

74. Cable from Brooke to Montgomery reported in Hamilton, *Monty: Final Years of the Field-Marshal*, pp. 53–54.

75. Montgomery, M525, SHAEF Papers.

76. John Ellis, *Brute Force*, p. 406.

77. FWD 14764, 13 Sept., addressed to Ike's army group and component commanders, SHAEF Papers.

78. FWD14764, SHAEF Papers.

79. Arnold, *Global Mission*, pp. 523–24.

80. Lamb, *Montgomery in Europe*, p. 215.

81. Pogue, *Supreme Command*, p. 281.

82. Crosswell, *Chief of Staff*, p. 257.

83. Ibid., p. 268.

84. Interview of Williams by Lamb, reported in Lamb, *Montgomery in Europe*, pp. 224, 262.

85. Eisenhower to Marshall, 14 Sept. 14, 1944, Eisenhower Files, DDE Library.

86. Ryan, *A Bridge Too Far*, p. 89.

87. Chandler and Ambrose, *Eisenhower Papers*, vol. 4, p. 2135.

88. Ibid., p. 113.

89. Eisenhower to Montgomery, Sept. 16, 1944, SHAEF Papers.

90. Urquhart, *Arnhem*, p. 4.

91. Bradley Commentaries USAMHI, cited in Hughes, p. 120.

92. Eisenhower to Marshall, March 29, 1944, Eisenhower papers.

93. Urquhart, *Arnhem*, p. 16.

94. Ibid.

95. Ellis, L. F., *Victory in the West*, p. 414.

96. MacDonald, *Siegfried Line Campaign*, p. 133.

97. Montgomery, *Normandy to the Baltic*, p. 228.

98. Ryan, *A Bridge Too Far*, p. 166.

99. All quotes, Ryan, *A Bridge Too Far*, p. 167.

100. Gavin, *On to Berlin*, p. 170.

101. John Ellis, *Brute Force*, p. 417.

102. Winterbotham, *Ultra Secret*, p. 236.

103. Lamb, *Montgomery in Europe*, p. 215.

104. Ibid., p. 213.

105. Moulton, *Battle for Antwerp*, p. 61.

106. Extract of Ramsay's diary, quoted in Hamilton, *Monty: Final Years of the Field-Marshal*, p. 104.

107. Ambrose, *Supreme Commander*, p. 524.

108. Ambrose interview with General Morgan, 17 July 1965.

109. Montgomery, M532, SHAEF Papers.

110. Montgomery, *Memoirs*, p. 266.

111. Wilmot, *Struggle for Europe*, p. 542.

112. Bryant, *Triumph in the West*, p. 219.

113. Wilmot, *Struggle for Europe*, p. 544.

5. Concentrate, General Bradley

1. 12th Army Group (AG) Admin Instructions 13, 27 Aug., cited in Blumenson, *Breakout and Pursuit*, p. 677.
2. First Army War Diary, 1–30 Sept., p. 1. Hodges Files, DDE Library.
3. Ibid., p. 3.
4. Ibid., p. 5.
5. Ibid.
6. *Spearhead in the West*, p. 88.
7. First Army War Diary, 1–30 Sept., p. 15.
8. Spearhead, p. 91.
9. 12AG Letter of Instructions #6, 25 Aug. 1944, Bradley Files, Military History Institute (MHI), Carlisle Barracks, Pa.
10. Bradley, *Soldier's Story*, p. 436.
11. Blumenson, *Patton Papers*, Patton Diary, p. 548.
12. Hansen Diary, 13 Sept. 1944, Bradley Papers, USMHI.
13. Bradley, *Soldier's Story*, p. 409.
14. Bradley, *General's Life*, p. 312.
15. Hogan, *Command Post at War*, p. 124.
16. Ibid., p. 288.
17. D'Este, *Eisenhower*, p. 548.
18. Memo for Record, 2 Sept. 44, Meeting of Supreme Commander and Commanders. MacDonald, *Siegfried Line Campaign*, p. 36.
19. 12AG Letter of Instructions dated 10 Sep but confirming oral orders issued earlier; Bradley Files, MHI.
20. Ibid.
21. Hansen diary, quoted in Hamilton, *Master of the Battlefield*, p. 59.
22. MacDonald, *Mighty Endeavor*, p. 332.
23. MacDonald, *Siegfried Line Campaign*, p. 37.
24. Diary entry 24 Sept. of Hodges's aide Maj. L. Sylvan. Hodges File, DDE Library, OMH Files.
25. MacDonald, *Time for Trumpets*, p. 187.
26. Bradley, *General's Life*, p. 95.
27. Pogue, *Organizer of Victory*, p. 647.
28. Bradley, *Soldier's Story*, p. 226.
29. Bolger, "Zero Defects," p. 69.
30. Currey, *Follow Me and Die*, p. 27.
31. Blumenson, *Patton Papers*, p. 486.
32. Sylvan Diary, 30 July 1944, Hodges file, DDE Library.
33. Hogan, *Command Post at War*, p. 289.
34. Bradley, *General's Life*, p. 223.
35. Ibid., p. 218.
36. Col. Cole Kingseed, "A Formidable Array of Warriors," *Army Magazine* (May 1996).
37. B. Gen. John G. Hill, G3, V Corps, interview cited in MacDonald, *Siegfried Line Campaign*, p. 22.
38. MacDonald, *Battle of the Huertgen Forest*, p. 8.
39. Bolger, "Zero Defects," p. 70.
40. Bradley, *General's Life*, p. 226.
41. Quesada interview, cited in Hughes, *Overlord*, p. 252.
42. Interview with B. Gen. T. C. Thorson, 12 Sep 1956, quoted in MacDonald, *Siegfried Line Campaign*, p. 619.
43. MacDonald, *Siegfried Line Campaign*, p. 619.
44. Crosswell, *Chief of Staff*, p. 285.
45. Ambrose, *Eisenhower: Soldier, General of the Army, President-Elect*, p. 566.
46. Brigadier Williams, Monty's intelligence officer, in Lamb, *Montgomery in Europe*, p. 311.
47. Allen, *Lucky Forward*, p. 13.
48. Thorson interview, p. 23, in MacDonald, *Siegfried Line Campaign*.
49. Eisenhower to Marshall, FWD 18934, April 11, 1945, Eisenhower Papers #2405, pp. 2596–98.
50. Bradley, *General's Life*, p. 472.
51. Bolger, "Zero Defects," p. 71.
52. Bradley, *General's Life*, p. 223.
53. D'Este, *Eisenhower*, p. 487.
54. Bradley, *General's Life*, p. 224.

55. MacDonald, *Battle of the Huertgen Forest*, p. 17.

56. MacDonald, *Siegfried Line Campaign*, p. 71.

57. Ibid., p. 37.

58. Bradley, *General's Life*, p. 324.

59. First Army estimate No. 28, 15 Sept. 1944, Hodges File, DDE Library.

60. Sylvan Diary, 15 Sept. 1944 Entry, Hodges File, DDE Library.

61. Collins, *Lightning Joe*, p. 271.

62. First Army War Journal, 12 Sept.

63. Collins, *Lightning Joe*, p. 267.

64. Ibid., p. 271.

65. Ibid., p. 269.

66. VII Corps G2 estimate, 10 Sep, cited in MacDonald, *Siegfried Line Campaign*, p. 38.

67. Weigley, *Eisenhower's Lieutenants*, p. 299.

68. First Army War Diary, Sept., p. 49.

69. MacDonald, *Battle of the Huertgen Forest*, p. 44.

70. Collins, *Lightning Joe*, p. 270.

71. Sylvan Diary, 17 Sept., Hodges files DDE Library.

72. Spearhead, p. 99.

73. MacDonald, *Battle of the Huertgen Forest*, p. 47.

74. First Army War Diary, 21 Sept., p. 57.

75. Clausewitz, *Principles of War*, p. 326.

76. MacDonald, *Siegfried Line Campaign*, p. 24.

77. Ibid., p. 619.

78. V Corps G2 estimate 11, 10 Sept. 1944, cited in MacDonald, *Siegfried Line Campaign*, p. 38.

79. MacDonald, *Siegfried Line Campaign*, p. 40.

80. First Army War Journal for Sept., p. 51.

81. Notes made by Rundstedt while a POW, reported in Messenger, *Last Prussian*, p. 206.

82. Beck et al., *Corps of Engineers*, p. 459.

83. Bradley, *Soldier's Story*, p. 401.

84. Bradley to Eisenhower, 12 Sept. 1944, SHAEF Papers, Bradley Files.

85. Eisenhower to Bradley, 15 Sept., SHAEF Papers.

86. First Army War Diary for September, Section 4 Supply, pp. 58–60.

87. FWD 14764, SHAEF Papers.

88. Eisenhower to Montgomery, 15 Sept., SHAEF Papers.

89. Eisenhower to Marshall, 14 Sept., SHAEF Papers.

90. Montgomery to Eisenhower, 18 Sept. 1944, Eisenhower–Montgomery correspondence in SHAEF Papers.

91. Bradley to Eisenhower, 21 Sept. 1944, SHAEF Papers.

92. Bradley, *Soldier's Story*, p. 332.

93. Order Army Group B to First Para Army 2230, 18 Sept. 1944, cited in MacDonald, *Siegfried Line Campaign*, p. 109.

94. Ibid., p. 109.

95. Montgomery to Eisenhower, 21 Sept., reported in Montgomery, *Memoirs*, pp. 252–53.

96. Factors Affecting Advance into Germany, SHAEF G3 Division 24, Sept. 1944, SHAEF Papers.

97. Minutes of meeting at SHAEF Forward, 22 Sept. 1944, SHAEF Papers.

98. Factors Affecting Advance into Germany, SHAEF G3 Division 24, Sept. 1944, SHAEF Papers.

99. Minutes of meeting at SHAEF Forward 22 Sept. 1944, SHAEF Papers.

100. Ibid.

101. Bradley, *Soldier's Story*, p. 425.

102. MacDonald, *Siegfried Line Campaign*, p. 251.

103. First Army War Dairy, October, p. 2.

104. MacDonald, *Siegfried Line Campaign*, p. 252.

105. Ibid.

106. First Army Directive, 29 Sept.,

cited in MacDonald, *Siegfried Line Campaign*, p. 285.

107. Ibid., p. 258.

108. First Army War Diary, October, p. 19.

109. Weigley, *Eisenhower's Lieutenants*, p. 360.

110. MacDonald, *Siegfried Line Campaign*, p. 266.

111. Ibid., p. 272.

112. Corlett to OCMH, 20 May 1956, reported in Macdonald, *Siegfried Line Campaign*, p. 278.

113. Weigley, *Eisenhower's Lieutenants*, p. 358.

114. 30ID Telephone Journal 7 Oct., cited in MacDonald, *Siegfried Line Campaign*, p. 279.

115. First Army War Diary, 13 Oct. 1944.

116. Corlett, "One Man's Story," p. 282.

117. Letter, Eisenhower to Marshall, 31 Aug. 1944, Eisenhower Papers #1925, pp. 2107–108.

118. Bolger, "Zero Defects," p. 71.

119. Collins, *Lightning Joe*, p. 277.

120. Cole, *Lorraine Campaign*, p. 296.

121. Collins, *Lightning Joe*, p. 269.

122. MacDonald, *Battle of the Huertgen Forest*, p. 63.

123. Miller, *A Dark and Bloody Ground*, p. 206.

124. Ellis, *Brute Force*, p. 431, quotes R. von Gersdorff, "Defense of the Siegfried Line," Pamphlet ETHINT-53 p. 7; see also Gavin, *On to Berlin*, p. 265.

125. MacDonald, *Battle of the Huertgen Forest*, pp. 44, 55.

126. Bolger, "Zero Defects," p. 71.

127. MacDonald, *Battle of the Huertgen Forest*, p. 88.

128. Collins, *Lightning Joe*, p. 273.

129. MacDonald, *Battle of the Huertgen Forest*, p. 196.

130. Weigley, *Eisenhower's Lieutenants*, p. 433.

131. Bradley, *General's Life*, p. 341.

132. Miller, *A Dark and Bloody Ground*, p. 206.

133. Bradley, *General's Life*, p. 341.

134. Collins, *Lightning Joe*, p. 274.

135. Beck et al., *Corps of Engineers*, p. 524.

136. Col. W. Heefner, "The Inch'on Landing," *Military Review* (March–April): 68.

137. *Conqueror: History of Ninth Army*, p. 98.

138. Coll, Keith, and Rosenthal, *Corps of Engineers*, p. 496.

139. FM 5-35 Engineers' Reference and Logistical Data 4/71, pp. 6-19, 6-23.

140. Beck et al., *Corps of Engineers*, p. 498.

141. Charles E. Wright, "Moselle Crossing at Cattenom," *Armored Cavalry Journal* (May–June 1948), reported in Rickard, *Patton at Bay*, p. 177.

142. Ambrose, *Supreme Commander*, p. 546.

143. Patton, *War as I Knew It*, p. 154.

144. MacDonald, *Siegfried Line Campaign*, p. 597.

145. Sylvan Diary, 9 Dec. 1944 entry.

146. *Conqueror: History of Ninth Army*, p. 94.

147. Ruppenthal, *Logistical Support of the Armies*, vol. 2, p. 7.

148. Blumenson, *Breakout and Pursuit*, p. 655.

149. Rust, *9th Air Force in World War II*, p. 115.

150. Blumenson, *Patton Papers*, p. 532.

151. Patton, *War as I Knew It*, p. 171.

152. VIII Corps, under the supervision of Ninth Army, took over this sector. Eddy's Corps finally was freed from Brest. 6th Armored Division was directed to Patton and 29ID to Corlett. VIII Corps retained but two divisions. Bradley, *General's Life*, p. 305.

6. Patton's Lorraine Campaign

The epigraph is from George Patton, *War as I Knew It*, p. 114.

1. Farago, *Ordeal and Triumph*, p. 559.
2. Essame, *Patton: A Study in Command*, p. 208.
3. Gavin, *On to Berlin*, p. 147.
4. Essame, *Patton: A Study in Command*, p. 211.
5. Nye, *Patton Mind*, p. 161.
6. Essame, *Patton: A Study in Command*, p. 258.
7. Ryan, *A Bridge Too Far*, p. 61.
8. Hamilton, *Master of the Battlefield*, p. 812.
9. Essame, *Patton: A Study in Command*, p. 190.
10. Blumenson, *Patton Papers*, p. 564.
11. Ibid., p. 561.
12. Nye, *Patton Mind*, p. 171.
13. Ibid., p. 182.
14. Bradley, *Soldier's Story*, p. 317.
15. Patton, *War as I Knew It*, p. 108.
16. Ibid., p. 111.
17. Blumenson, *Patton Papers*, p. 531, Patton Diary, 30 Aug.
18. Ibid., p. 545.
19. Bradley, *General's Life*, p. 308.
20. Blumenson, *Patton Papers*, p. 560, Patton Diary, 30 Sept.
21. Patton, *War as I Knew It*, p. 124.
22. Clarke and Smith, *Riviera to the Rhine*, p. 255.
23. Wyant, *Sandy Patch*, p. 156.
24. Ibid., p. 182.
25. Wallace, *Patton and His Third Army*, pp. 16–17.
26. Allen, *Lucky Forward*, chap. 2.
27. Blumenson, *Patton: The Man behind the Legend*, p. 231.
28. Cole, *Lorraine Campaign*, p. 45.
29. Ibid., p. 47.
30. Mellenthin, *Panzer Battles*, p. 321.
31. Ibid., p. 321.
32. Wilmot, *Struggle for Europe*, p. 473.
33. Winterbotham, *Ultra Secret*, p. 234.
34. Cole, *Lorraine Campaign*, p. 47.
35. TUSA G-2 Estimate 9, 28 Aug. 44, TUSA AAR, vol. 2.
36. Blumenson, *Patton Papers*, p. 589.
37. Ibid., p. 540.
38. Ibid., p. 589.
39. Operational Directive, 5 Sept. 1944, contained in Third Army AAR II.
40. Essame, *Patton: A Study in Command*, p. 214.
41. D'Este, *Patton*, p. 666.
42. XX Corps History, p. 109.
43. Ibid., p. 108.
44. 80ID G2 Journal, 4 Sept. 1944, cited in Cole, *Lorraine Campaign*, p. 62.
45. Operations FM 100-5, 1944, pp. 192–95.
46. Blumenson, *Patton Papers*, pp. 539–40.
47. Cole, *Lorraine Campaign*, p. 123.
48. XX Corps, p. 115.
49. Ibid., pp. 115–16.
50. XX Corps morning briefing, 14 Sept., quoted in Cole, *Lorraine Campaign*, p. 162.
51. 4th Armored Division History, p. 36.
52. Cole, *Lorraine Campaign*, p. 213.
53. Ibid., p. 213.
54. 21 AG suggestion, cited in SHAEF to 12AG FWD 14837, cited in Cole, *Lorraine Campaign*, p. 213.
55. Blumenson, *Patton Papers*, 12 Sept., Patton Diary, p. 547.
56. Patton, *War as I Knew It*, p. 124.
57. Blumenson, *Patton Papers*, Patton Diary 16 Sept., p. 549.
58. Outlined in XII Corps G3-intel summary 16 Sept., cited in Cole, *Lorraine Campaign*, p. 215.
59. Blumenson, *Patton Papers*, 12 Sept., Patton Diary, p. 549.

60. Tonnage figures, Cole, *Lorraine Campaign*, p. 210.

61. Blumenson, *Patton Papers*, p. 551, 18 Sept. diary entry.

62. Mellenthin, *Panzer Battles*, p. 314.

63. Ibid., p. 320.

64. Ibid., p. 315.

65. Ibid.

66. Ibid., p. 317.

67. Ibid., p. 320.

68. Blumenson, *Patton Papers*, Patton Diary, 25 Sept., pp. 559–60.

69. Patton, *War as I Knew It*, p. 135.

70. Koch G2, Intelligence for Patton, p. 53, cited in D'Este, *Patton*, p. 612.

71. Mellenthin, *Panzer Battles*, p. 322.

72. Blumenson, *Patton Papers*, p. 562.

73. Clausewitz, *Principles of War*, p. 595.

74. XX Corps, p. 145.

75. Bradley, *Soldier's Story*, p. 427.

76. Blumenson, *Patton Papers*, pp. 562–63.

77. Ibid., Patton Diary, p. 563.

7. November Rerun

1. Wilmot, *Struggle for Europe*, p. 539.

2. Crosswell, *Chief of Staff*, p. 262.

3. Oct. 23, Marshall to Eisenhower, Bland and Stevens, *Papers of George Catlett Marshall*, p. 636.

4. Pogue, *Supreme Command*, p. 307.

5. Montgomery, *Memoirs*, p. 254.

6. Montgomery to P. J. Grig, Secretary of State for War, 10 Oct. 1944, reprinted in Lamb, *Montgomery in Europe*, p. 283.

7. DDE To Early, 11/26/44, Eisenhower Papers.

8. Data from MS #P-065b Volks Grenadier Divisions and the Volkstrum, cited in MacDonald, *Siegfried Line Campaign*, p. 393.

9. Pogue, *Supreme Command*, p. 310.

10. Ruppenthal, *Logistical Support of the Armies*, vol. 2, p. 153.

11. Ibid., p. 255.

12. Ibid., pp. 239, 241.

13. Mayo, *Ordnance Department*, p. 302.

14. Ruppenthal, *Logistical Support of the Armies*, vol. 2, p. 256.

15. Ohl, *Supplying the Troops*, p. 238.

16. Cable S 63259, Eisenhower Papers, p. 2234.

17. Ruppenthal, *Logistical Support of the Armies*, vol. 2, p. 254.

18. Rust, *9th Air Force*, p. 119.

19. Ambrose, *Supreme Commander*, p. 542.

20. Eisenhower, *Crusade in Europe*, p. 323.

21. Pogue, *Supreme Command*, p. 311.

22. Bradley, *Soldier's Story*, p. 338.

23. Eisenhower, *Crusade in Europe*, p. 337.

24. Letter, Eisenhower to Montgomery, 1 Dec. 1944, Eisenhower Papers.

25. SHAEF SGS 381 Cable S64375 to army group, tactical air forces, and first Allied Airborne Army commanders, 28 Oct. 1944, SHAEF Papers. Quotes are from the order.

26. Patton, *War as I Knew It*, p. 143.

27. Cable s64375, 28 Oct. 1944, Eisenhower to his Principal Subordinates, SHAEF Papers.

28. Ambrose, *Eisenhower: Soldier, General of the Army, President-Elect*, p. 557.

29. Ambrose, *Supreme Commander*, p. 541.

30. Pogue, *Supreme Command*, p. 306.

31. Ambrose, *Eisenhower, Soldier, General, President Elect*, p. 556.

32. Eisenhower, *Crusade in Europe*, pp. 340–41.

33. MacDonald, *Siegfried Line Campaign*, p. 397.

34. HQ 12AG G2 Sec Weekly

Intelligence Summary 18, cited in Bradley, *General's Life*, p. 349.

35. MacDonald, *A Time for Trumpets*, pp. 430, 606.

36. Pogue, *Supreme Command*, p. 303.

37. *Conqueror: History of Ninth Army*, p. 65.

38. Ibid., p. 84.

39. MacDonald, *Siegfried Line Campaign*, p. 411.

40. *Conqueror: History of Ninth Army*, p. 65.

41. 12AG Weekly Intel summary 14, dated 13 Nov., cited in MacDonald, *Siegfried Line Campaign*, p. 394, talks of five divisions.

42. Bradley, *Soldier's Story*, p. 441.

43. Bradley, *General's Life*, p. 343.

44. Bradley, *Soldier's Story*, p. 439.

45. Ibid., p. 442.

46. MacDonald, *Siegfried Line Campaign*, p. 309.

47. Patton, *War as I Knew It*, p. 144.

48. 12th Army Group Letter of Instruction 10.

49. Hamilton, *Monty*, p. 129.

50. Montgomery, *Normandy to the Baltic*, p. 268.

51. Bradley to Montgomery, memo, 19 Nov., quoted in Hamilton, *Monty*, pp. 140–41.

52. MacDonald, *Siegfried Line Campaign*, p. 401.

53. Weigley, *Eisenhower's Lieutenants*, p. 422.

54. MacDonald, *Siegfried Line Campaign*, p. 401.

55. Bradley interview, cited in MacDonald, *Siegfried Line Campaign*, p. 402.

56. Weigley, *Eisenhower's Lieutenants*, p. 383.

57. Sylvan Diary of 16 Nov. 1944.

58. Rust, *9th Air Force in World War II*, p. 127.

59. MacDonald, *Siegfried Line Campaign*, p. 413.

60. Interview with DDE, cited in Ambrose, *Eisenhower: Soldier, General of the Army, President-Elect*, p. 114.

61. Blumenson, *Patton Papers*, p. 680.

62. In MacDonald, *Siegfried Line Campaign*, p. 406.

63. In ibid., p. 409.

64. Sylvan Diary entry, 16 Nov.

65. MacDonald, *Siegfried Line Campaign*, p. 379.

66. Bradley, *Soldier's Story*, p. 219.

67. Ruppenthal, *Logistical Support of the Armies*, vol. 2, p. 349.

68. Eisenhower's evaluation of senior officers, Eisenhower Papers 2271, p. 2467.

69. Bradley, *Soldier's Story*, p. 422.

70. Houston, *Hell on Wheels*, p. 303.

71. *Conqueror: History of Ninth Army*, p. 84.

72. MacDonald, *Siegfried Line Campaign*, p. 497.

73. Ibid., p. 522.

74. *Conqueror: History of Ninth Army*, pp. 82–83.

75. Ibid., p. 84.

76. Ibid., p. 85.

77. Ibid., p. 87.

78. MacDonald, *Siegfried Line Campaign*, p. 503.

79. OB WEST KTB, 16 Nov., cited in MacDonald, *Siegfried Line Campaign*, p. 530.

80. MacDonald, *Siegfried Line Campaign*, p. 530.

81. OB WEST KTB, 16 Oct. 44, cited in MacDonald, *Siegfried Line Campaign*, p. 547.

82. Houston, *Hell on Wheels*, p. 311.

83. Ibid.

84. Ibid., p. 313.

85. MacDonald, *Siegfried Line Campaign*, p. 537.

86. Ibid., p. 536.

87. *Conqueror: History of Ninth Army*, p. 91.

88. Rust, *9th Air Force in World War II*, p. 128.

89. MacDonald, *Siegfried Line Campaign*, p. 539.

90. Ibid., p. 558.

91. Weigley, *Eisenhower's Lieutenants*, p. 429.

92. MacDonald, *Siegfried Line Campaign*, p. 561, 29ID G2–G3 Journal, 23 Nov.

93. *Conqueror: History of Ninth Army*, p. 95.

94. MacDonald, *Siegfried Line Campaign*, p. 563.

95. Pogue, *Supreme Command*, p. 304.

96. SHAEF G3 memo, Advance into Germany after Occupation of the Ruhr, 24 Sept., SHAEF Papers.

97. 12th Army Group AAR V, cited in Cole, *Lorraine Campaign*, p. 299.

98. Weigley, *Eisenhower's Lieutenants*, p. 385.

99. Patton to Bradley, 19 Oct., cited by Cole, *Lorraine Campaign*, p. 300.

100. Bradley, *General's Life*, p. 343.

101. Patton, *War as I Knew It*, p. 163.

102. Farago, *Ordeal and Triumph*, p. 666.

103. Patton, *War as I Knew It*, p. 163.

104. Farago, *Ordeal and Triumph*, p. 685.

105. Cole, *Lorraine Campaign*, p. 300.

106. Ibid., p. 318.

107. Patton, *War as I Knew It*, p. 149.

108. Cole, *Lorraine Campaign*, p. 319.

109. Ibid., p. 318.

110. Cole, *Lorraine Campaign*.

111. Patton, *War as I Knew It*, p. 134.

112. Mellenthin, *Panzer Battles*, pp. 325–26.

113. Blumenson, *Patton Papers*, p. 574.

114. Cole, *Lorraine Campaign*, p. 428.

115. Ibid., p. 418.

116. Ibid., p. 449.

117. Ibid.

118. Ibid., p. 409.

119. Weigley, *Eisenhower's Lieutenants*, p. 398.

120. Cole, *Lorraine Campaign*, p. 502.

121. Patton, *War as I Knew It*, p. 163.

122. 95ID G3 Journal, 3 Dec. 44, cited in Cole, *Lorraine Campaign*, p. 517.

123. *Conqueror: History of Ninth Army*, p. 97.

124. MacDonald, *Siegfried Line Campaign*, p. 560.

125. Ibid., p. 600.

126. Pogue, *Supreme Command*, p. 317.

127. Eisenhower Papers, p. 2335.

128. Montgomery to Eisenhower, 30 Nov. 1944, SHAEF Papers.

129. Bradley, *General's Life*, p. 343.

130. Pogue, *Supreme Command*, p. 312.

131. Wilmot, *Struggle for Europe*, p. 613.

132. Bryant, *Triumph in the West*, p. 259.

133. Bradley, *General's Life*, p. 345.

134. Weigley, *Eisenhower's Lieutenants*, p. 729, and James, *A Time for Giants*, pp. 205–206, 234.

135. FM 100-5, 1993, p. 6-2.

8. Opportunity in the South

1. *Time*, 28 Aug. 1944, p. 24.

2. Clarke and Smith, *Riviera to the Rhine*, p. 207.

3. Bonn, *When the Odds Were Even*, p. 87.

4. Seventh Army Troop Operations 531, cited in Bonn, *When the Odds Were Even*.

5. Clarke and Smith, *Riviera to the Rhine*, p. 295.

6. Blumenson, *Patton Papers*, p. 41.

7. Pogue, *Organizer of Victory*, p. 374.

8. Gabel GHQ Army Maneuvers of 1941, p. 177.

9. Ibid., p. 188.

10. Blumenson, *Patton Papers*, p. 565.

11. Clarke and Smith, *Riviera to the Rhine*, p. 178.

12. Pogue, *Supreme Commander*, p. 340.

13. Pogue, *Organizer of Victory*, p. 119.

14. Bradley, *General's Life*, p. 210.

15. Blumenson, *Patton Papers*, Patton Diary, 21 Sept. 1944, p. 522.

16. Bradley, *Soldier's Story*, p. 210.

17. Clarke and Smith, *Riviera to the Rhine*, p. 323.

18. Strobridge and Nalty, "From the South Pass to the Brenner Pass," p. 41.

19. Truscott, *Command Missions*, p. 383.

20. Strobridge and Nalty, "From the South Pass to the Brenner Pass," p. 42.

21. Wyant, *Patch*, p. 3.

22. Ibid., p. 183.

23. Ibid., p. 147.

24. Ibid., p. 93.

25. Ibid., p. 94.

26. Ibid., p. 138.

27. Ibid., p. 300.

28. Clarke and Smith, *Riviera to the Rhine*, p. 198.

29. Mellenthin, *Panzer Battles*, p. 323.

30. Ibid., p. 322.

31. Eisenhower Papers, IV, pp. 2146–47.

32. Ibid., p. 2274.

33. Clarke and Smith, *Riviera to the Rhine*, p. 230.

34. Clarke and Smith, *Riviera to the Rhine*, p. 253.

35. Ibid., p. 231.

36. Ibid., p. 230.

37. Bonn, *When the Odds Were Even*, p. 77.

38. Cole, *Lorraine Campaign*, p. 304.

39. Wyant, *Patch*, p. 153.

40. Clarke and Smith, *Riviera to the Rhine*, p. 261.

41. Ibid., p. 351.

42. Ibid.

43. Letter to Jacob Loucks Devers, 23 Oct. 944, SHAEF Papers.

44. Clarke and Smith, *Riviera to the Rhine*, p. 353.

45. Blumenson, *Patton Papers*, Patton Diary, 7 December, p. 588.

46. SCS 381, 28 Oct. 1944, SHAEF Papers.

47. Devers's Diary, 11 and 12 Nov. 1944, Devers File, CMH.

48. Clarke and Smith, *Riviera to the Rhine*, p. 361.

49. Ibid., p. 411.

50. Bonn, *When the Odds Were Even*, p. 113.

51. Clarke and Smith, *Riviera to the Rhine*, p. 367.

52. Ibid., p. 388.

53. Ibid., pp. 377–78.

54. Ibid., p. 434.

55. Ibid.

56. Ibid.

57. Blumenson, *Patton Papers*, 20 Nov. letter Patton to his wife.

58. Clarke and Smith, *Riviera to the Rhine*, p. 442.

59. Ibid., p. 438.

60. *100ID News*, Feb. 1986, p. 2.

61. Patton, *War as I Knew It*, p. 169.

62. Hanson Diary, 24 Nov. entry, MHI Files.

63. Cole, *Lorraine Campaign*, p. 467.

64. Letter Eisenhower to Devers, 23 Oct., SHAEF Papers.

65. Directive to A GP Commanders SCAF 114, SHAEF Papers.

66. Blumenson, *Patton Papers*, Patton Diary, 5 Nov. 1944, p. 568.

67. Clarke and Smith, *Riviera to the Rhine*, p. 439.

68. Description of meeting from ibid., pp. 439–40.

69. Eisenhower to Marshall, 27 November 1944, SHAEF Files, DDE Library.

70. 27 November, Memorandum of Planning Staff, SHAEF Files, DDE Library.

71. Ibid., p. 442.

72. Weigley, *Eisenhower's Lieutenants*, p. 409.

73. Clarke and Smith, *Riviera to the Rhine*, p. 563.

74. Eisenhower, *Crusade in Europe*, p. 331.

75. Clarke and Smith, *From the Riviera to the Rhine*, p. 226.

76. Eisenhower to Marshall, in Chandler and Ambrose, *Eisenhower Papers*, vol. 4, pp. 2468–69.

77. Clausewitz, *Principles of War*, p. 328.

78. Blumenson, *Patton Papers*, Patton Diary.

79. Blumenson, *Patton Papers*, p. 583.

80. Ambrose, *Eisenhower: Soldier, General of the Army, President Elect*, p. 360.

81. Letter, Eisenhower to Montgomery, 1 Dec. 44, SHAEF Papers.

82. Eisenhower Papers, p. 2323.

83. Montgomery, *Memoirs*, p. 270.

84. Memorandum by Planning Staff, Possibilities of Mutual Reinforcement, 20 Nov. 1944, PS SHAEF (44) 66, SHAEF Papers.

85. Memo from Devers, CGT 370-31 Plans, December 1944, SHAEF Plans.

86. Cable S69334, Eisenhower to Combined Chiefs of Staff, 3 Dec. 1944.

87. Ambrose, *Eisenhower: Soldier, General of the Army, President-Elect*, p. 551.

Conclusion

1. FM 100-5, B3.

Bibliography

Allen, Robert S. *Lucky Forward: the History of Patton's Third U.S. Army.* New York, Vanguard Press, 1947.

Ambrose, Stephen. *Eisenhower: Soldier, General of the Army, President-Elect.* New York: Simon and Schuster, 1983.

———. *The Supreme Commander: The War Years of General Dwight D. Eisenhower.* Garden City, N.Y.: Doubleday, 1970.

Arnold, Henry Harley. *Global Mission.* New York: Harper and Row, 1949.

Barnett, Correlli, ed. *Hitler's Generals.* New York: Quill/William Morrow, 1989.

Bland, Larry, and Sharon Ritenour Stevens, eds. *The Papers of George Catlett Marshall.* Vol. 4. Baltimore, Md.: Johns Hopkins University Press, 1996.

Blumenson, Martin. *The Battle of the Generals: The Untold Story of the Falaise Pocket: The Campaign That Should Have Won World War II.* New York: William Morrow, 1993.

———. "A Deaf Ear to Clausewitz: Allied Operational Objectives in World War II," in *Parameters* 23, no. 2 (Summer 1993): 16–27.

———. *Patton: The Man behind the Legend, 1885–1945.* New York: William Morrow, 1985.

———, comp. and ed. *The Patton Papers 1885–1940.* 2 vols. Boston: Houghton Mifflin, 1972–74.

Bolger, D. P. "Zero Defects: Command Climate in First US Army 1944–45." *Military Review* 61 (May 1991): 61–73.

Bonn, Keith E. *When the Odds Were Even: The Vosges Mountains Campaign, October 1944–January 1945.* Novato, Calif.: Presidio Press, 1994.

Bradley, Omar. *A Soldier's Story.* New York: Holt, 1951.

Bradley, Omar, and Clay Blair. *A General's Life: An Autobiography.* New York: Simon and Schuster, 1983.

Brownlee, Romie L., and William J. Mullen III. *Changing an Army: An Oral History of General William E. Depuy.* Washington, D.C.: Center of Military History, U.S. Army, 1988.

Bryant, Arthur. *The Turn of the Tide: A History of the War Years Based on the Diaries of Field-Marshal Lord Alanbrooke, Chief of the Imperial General Staff.* New York: Doubleday, 1957.

———. *Triumph in the West: A History of the War Years Based on the Diaries of Field-Marshal Lord Alanbrooke, Chief of the Imperial General Staff.* New York: Doubleday, 1959.

Carell, Paul. *Invasion—They're Coming! The German Account of the Allied Landings and the 80 Days' Battle for France.* Trans. E. Osers. New York: Dutton, 1963.

Chandler, Alfred D., Jr., and Stephen E. Ambrose, eds. *The Papers of Dwight David Eisenhower: The War Years.* Vols. 4 and 5. Baltimore: Johns Hopkins Press, 1970.

Chant, Christopher, ed. *Hitler's Generals and Their Battles.* London: Salamander Books, 1977.

Clausewitz, Carl von. *Principles of War.* Reprinted in *Roots of Strategy,* vol. 2. Harrisburg, Pa.: Stackpole, 1987.

Collins, J. Lawton. *Lightning Joe: An Autobiography.* Baton Rouge: Louisiana State University Press, 1979.

Cooper, Matthew. *The German Army 1933–45: Its Political and Military Failure.* Reprint New York: Bonanza Books, 1984; New York: Stein and Day, 1978.

Corlett, Charles. "One Man's Story." Manuscript in file in U.S. Army Military History files, Army War College, Carlisle Barracks, Pa.

Cray, Ed. *General of the Army: George C. Marshall, Soldier and Statesman.* New York: Touchstone Books, 1990.

Crosswell, D. K. R. *The Chief of Staff: The Military Career of General Walter Bedell Smith.* New York: Greenwood Press, 1991.

Currey, Cecil B. *Follow Me and Die: The Destruction of an American Division in World War II.* New York: Stein and Day, 1984.

De Guingand, Francis W. *Operation Victory.* New York: Scribner's, 1947.

D'Este, Carlo. *Decision in Normandy.* New York: Dutton, 1983.

———. *Eisenhower: A Soldier's Life.* New York: Holt, 2002.

———. *Patton: A Genius for War.* New York: HarperCollins, 1995.

Doubler, Michael D. *Closing with the Enemy: How GIs Fought the War in Europe 1944–1945.* Lawrence: University Press of Kansas, 1994.

Eden, Anthony. *The Reckoning: The Memoirs of Anthony Eden, Earl of Avon.* Boston: Houghton Mifflin, 1965.

Ehrman, John. *History of the Second World War: Grand Strategy.* Vols. 5 and 6. London: Her Majesty's Stationery Office, 1956.

Eisenhower, D. D. *Crusade in Europe.* Garden City, N.Y.: Doubleday, 1948.

———. *Dear General: Eisenhower's Wartime Letters to Marshall.* Ed. Joseph Patrick Hobbs. Baltimore: Johns Hopkins Press, 1971.

———. *Report by the Supreme Commander to the Combined Chiefs of Staff on the Operations in Europe 6 June 1944 to 8 May 1945.* Washington, D.C.: U.S. Government Printing Office, 1946.

Ellis, John. *Brute Force: Allied Strategy and Tactics in the Second World War.* New York: Viking, 1990.

Ellis, L. F. *Victory in the West.* Vols. 1 and 2. London: Her Majesty's Stationery Office, 1962, 1968.

Essame, Hubert. *Patton: A Study in Command.* New York: Scribner, 1974.

Esposito, Vincent J., ed. *A Concise History of World War II.* New York: Praeger, 1964.

———, ed. *West Point Atlas of American Wars.* Vol. 2. New York: Praeger, 1959.

Farago, Ladislas. *Patton: Ordeal and Triumph.* New York: Obolensky, 1963.

Ferrell, Robert H., ed. *The Eisenhower Diaries.* New York: W. W. Norton, 1981.

Forty, George. *The Armies of George S. Patton.* London: Arms and Armour Press, 1996.

Fuller, J. F. C. *A Military History of the Western World.* Vol. 3. Minerva Press, 1957.

Gabel, Christopher R. *The U.S. Army GHQ Maneuvers of 1941*. Washington, D.C.: Center of Military History, U.S. Army, 1991.

Gavin, James N. *On to Berlin: Battles of an Airborne Commander, 1943–1946*. New York: Viking, 1978.

Gelb, Norman. *Ike and Monty: Generals at War*. New York: William Morrow, 1994.

Goerlitz, Walter. *History of the German General Staff*. Germany, 1952; English translation, New York: Barnes and Noble, 1995.

Graham, Dominick. *The Price of Command: A Biography of General Guy Simonds*. Toronto: Stoddart, 1993.

Greenfield, Kent Roberts, ed. *Command Decisions*. Reprint, Washington, D.C.: Office of Chief of Military History, 1960. See especially Ruppenthal, R. G. "Logistics and the Broad Front Strategy."

Harclerode, Peter. *Arnhem: A Tragedy of Errors*. London: Arms and Armour Press, 1994.

Hamilton, Nigel. *Master of the Battlefield: Monty's War Years 1942–1944*. New York: McGraw Hill, 1983.

————. *Monty: Final Years of the Field-Marshal, 1944–1976*. New York: McGraw Hill, 1987.

Handel, Michael J. *Masters of War: Classical Strategic Thought*. 3rd ed. London: Frank Cass Publishers, 2001.

Harvey, A. D. *Arnhem*. London: Cassell, 2001.

Hastings, Max. *Overlord: D-Day and the Battle for Normandy*. New York: Simon and Schuster, 1984.

Hirshson, Stanley P. *General Patton: A Soldier's Life*. New York: Harper Collins, 2002.

Hogan, David W. *A Command Post at War: First Army Headquarters in Europe 1943–1945*. Washington, D.C.: Center of Military History, U.S. Army, 2000.

Horne, Alistair, and David Montgomery. *Monty: The Lonely Leader 1944–1945*. London: MacMillan, 1994.

Horrocks, Brian. *Corps Commander*. London: Sidgwick and Jackson, 1977.

————. *A Full Life*. New York: Collins, 1960.

Houston, D. E. *Hell on Wheels: The 2d Armored Division*. Novato, California: Presidio, 1977.

Hughes, Thomas A. *Over Lord: General Pete Quesada and the Triumph of Tactical Air Power in WWII*. New York: Free Press, 1995.

Huston, James. *The Sinews of War: Army Logistics, 1775–1953*. Army Historical Series. Washington, D.C.: Government Printing Office, 1966.

Irving, David. *War between the Generals*. New York: Congdon and Latte's and St. Martin's Press, 1981.

James, D. Clayton. *A Time for Giants: Politics of the American High Command in World War II*. New York: Franklin Watts, 1987.

Keegan, John Grove. *Six Armies in Normandy: From D-Day to the Liberation of Paris*. New York: Penguin, 1983.

————, ed. *Churchill's Generals*. New York: Weidenfeld, Groves Press, 1991.

Lamb, Richard. *Montgomery in Europe 1943–1945: Success or Failure?* London: Buchan and Enright, 1987.

Liddell Hart, Basil H. *History of the Second World War*. New York: Putnam's Sons, 1970.

————. *The Other Side of the Hill*. London: Cassell, 1948.

MacDonald, Charles B. *The Battle of the Huertgen Forest*. New York: Jove, 1988 .

———. *Company Commander*. Washington, D.C.: Infantry Journal, 1947; reprint, New York: Ballentine, 1966.

———. *The Mighty Endeavor: American Armed Forces in the European Theater in World War II*. New York: Oxford University Press, 1969.

———. *A Time for Trumpets: The Untold Story of the Battle of the Bulge*. New York: William Morrow, 1985.

Marshall, George, ed. *Infantry in Battle*. Washington, D.C.: Infantry Journal, 1939; reprint, Ft. Leavenworth, Kans.: USCAGS, 1993.

Marshall, S. L. A. *Men against Fire*. Gloucester, Mass.: Peter Smith, 1947.

Mellenthin, F. W. von. *German Generals of World War II: As I saw Them*. Norman: University of Oklahoma Press, 1977.

———. *Panzer Battles: A Study of the Employment of Armor in the Second World War*. Ed. L. C. F. Turner; trans. H. Betzler. Norman: University of Oklahoma Press, 1956.

Messenger, Charles. *The Last Prussian: A Biography of Field Marshal Gerd Von Rundstedt, 1875–1953*. London: Brassey's (UK), 1991.

Miller, Edward G. *A Dark and Bloody Ground: The Hürtgen Forest and the Roer River Dams, 1944–1945*. College Station: Texas A&M University Press, 1995.

Montgomery, Bernard L. (Viscount Montgomery of Alamein). *The Memoirs of Field Marshal Montgomery*. Cleveland: World Publishing, 1958.

———. *Normandy to the Baltic: Twenty First Army Group*. Boston: Riverside Press, 1948.

Moulton, J. L. *Battle for Antwerp: The Liberation of the City and the Opening of the Scheldt, 1944*. New York: Hippocrene Books, 1978.

Nye, Roger H. *The Patton Mind*. Garden City Park, N.Y.: Avery Publishing, 1993.

Ohl, John Kennedy. *Supplying the Troops: General Somervell and American Logistics in WWII*. DeKalb : Northern Illinois University Press, 1994.

Parrish, Thomas. *The American Codebreakers: The U.S. Role in Ultra*. New York: Stein and Day, 1986; reprint, Chelsea, Mich.: Scarborough House, 1991.

Patton, George. *War as I Knew It*. Boston: Houghton Mifflin, 1947.

Perry, Mark. *Partners in Command: George Marshall and Dwight Eisenhower in War and Peace*. New York: Penguin Press, 2007.

Pogue, Forrest. *Organizer of Victory 1943–1945 George C. Marshall*. New York: Viking Press, 1973.

Province, Charles. *Patton's Third Army: A Daily Combat Diary*. New York: Hippocrene Books, 1992.

Rickard, John N. *Patton at Bay: The Lorraine Campaign, September to December, 1944*. Westport, Conn.: Praeger, 1999.

Rust, Kenn C. *The 9th Air Force in World War II*. Fallbrook, Calif.: Aero Publishers, 1967.

Ryan, Cornelius. *A Bridge Too Far*. New York: Popular Library, 1974.

Sixsmith, E. K. G. *Eisenhower as Military Commander*. New York: Da Capo, 1972.

Smith, Walter Bedell. *Eisenhower's Six Great Decisions: Europe, 1944–1945*. New York: Longmans, Green, 1956.

Stanton, Shelby. *Order of Battle U.S. Army, World War II*. Novato, Calif.: Presidio Press, 1984.

Stoler, Mark A. *Allies and Adversaries: The Joint Chiefs of Staff, the Grand Alliance, and U.S. Strategy in World War II*. Chapel Hill: University of North Carolina Press, 2000.

Strobridge, Truman R., and Bernard C. Nalty. "From the South Pass to the Brenner Pass: General Alexander M. Patch." *Military Review* 61 (June 1981): 41–48.

Truscott, Lucian K. *Command Missions: A Personal Story.* Novato, Calif.: Presidio, 1990.

Urquhart, R. E. *Arnhem.* London: Cassell Books, 1958.

Wallace, Brenton G. *Patton and His Third Army.* Harrisburg, Pa.: Military Service Publishing, 1946.

Warden, John A. *The Air Campaign: Planning for Combat.* Washington, D.C: Pergamon-Brassey's, 1989.

Weigley, Russel F. *The American Way of War: A History of United States Military Strategy and Policy.* New York: Macmillan, 1973.

———. *Eisenhower's Lieutenants: The Campaign of France and Germany, 1944–1945.* Bloomington: Indiana University Press, 1981.

Wilmot, Chester. *Struggle for Europe.* New York: Harper and Row, 1952.

Winterbotham, F. W. *The Ultra Secret.* New York: Harper and Brothers, 1974.

Wyant, William. *Sandy Patch.* New York: Praeger, 1991.

Unit Unofficial Histories

Conqueror: History of Ninth Army. 1946.

The Fourth Armored Division. Munich, 1946.

Spearhead in the West. 3rd Armored Division Darmstadt, 1945.

XX Corps. Unofficial Corps history prepared by Corps staff. Reprint, Halstead, Kans.: W.E.B.S., 1984

Official and Archival Sources

U.S. Army in World War II Series—European Theater of Operations; all published Washington, D.C.: Office of the Chief of Military History, Dept. of the Army.

Blumenson, Martin. *Breakout and Pursuit.* 1961.

Clarke, Jeffrey J., and Robert R. Smith. *Riviera to the Rhine.* 1993.

Cole, Hugh M. *The Lorraine Campaign.* 1950.

Harrison, G. A. *Cross-Channel Attack.* 1951.

MacDonald, Charles B. *The Siegfried Line Campaign.* 1963.

———. *The Last Offensive.* 1973.

Pogue, Forrest. *The Supreme Command.* 1954.

Ruppenthal, Roland G. *Logistical Support of the Armies.* Vols. 1 and 2. 1953 and 1954.

The Technical Services

Beck, Alfred M. et al. *The Corps of Engineers: The War against Germany.* 1985.

Bykofsky, Joseph, and Harold Larson. *The Transportation Corps: Operations Overseas.* 1957.

Coll, Blanche D., Jean E. Keith, and Herbert H. Rosenthal. *The Corps of Engineers: Troops and Equipment.* 1958.

Mayo, Lida. *Ordnance Department: On Beachhead and Battlefront.* 1968.

USAF Studies

Kohn, R. H., and J. P. Harahan, eds. *Condensed Analysis of the NINTH AIRFORCE in the European Theater of Operations*. RESTRICTED-1946, declassified and reprinted 1984.
Joint Publication 1-02 DoD Dictionary of Military Terms 1989.

Field Manuals

FM 5-35 Engineers' Reference and Logistical Data 4, 1971.
FM 7-20 Infantry Battalion, October 1944.
FM 17-32 Tank Company Tactics, 1944.
FM 17-33 Tank Battalion Tactics, November 1944.
FM 17-36 Employment of Tanks with Infantry, 1944.
FM 55-15 *Transportation Reference Data*, February 1968.

FM 100-5 Field Service Regulations Operations 1944.
FM 100-5 Field Service Regulations Operations 1949.
FM 100-5 Operations 1982.
FM 100-5 Operations 1993.

FM 101-10 Staff Officers' Field Manual, Organizational, Technical, and Logistical Data, 1949.
FM 101-10-1 Staff Officers' Field Manual, Organizational, Technical, and Logistical Data, July 1971.
FM 100-15 Field Service Regulations Larger Units, 1950.

Field Service Regulations 1920.
Field Service Regulations 1923.

ST100-3 Battle Book 1 April 93, Command and General Staff Text.

Eisenhower Library, Abiline, Kansas

Papers of Harold. R. Bull.
Papers of Dwight David Eisenhower.
　　SHAEF Office of Secretary of General Staff Accession 71-14 Papers (cited as SHAEF Papers).
　　Box 8, 9, 19 Weekly Intelligence Summaries.
　　Box 18 Directives to Subordinates.
　　Box 22, 23 Intelligence, G4 Reports.
　　Box 35 Directives for Air Forces.
　　Box 53, 54, 55, 77 Post Overlord Planning and Montgomery Directives.
Strategy of the Campaign in Western Europe 1944–45.
　　The General Board European Theater File 385/1 Study #1.
　　A69-Box 1.
12 Army Group Report of Operations.

First Army Report of Operations Hodges File.
Third Army Report of Operations.
Seventh Army Report of Operations.
Papers of Courtney Hodges A70-86.
  Box 25 First Army Journal.
  Box 28 G3 Summaries.
  Sylvan Diary.
Papers of Walter Bedell Smith.

Marshall Library, Virginia Military Institute, Lexington, Virginia

Papers of George C. Marshall.

U.S. Army Military History Institute (MHI), Carlisle Barracks, Pennsylvania

Papers of Jacob Devers.
  Devers Diary.
Papers of Omar Bradley.
  Hansen Diary.

British Official Sources

History of the Second World War Series, Her Majesty's Stationery Office, London:
GRAND STRATEGY
  Vol. 5, John Erhman, 1956.
  Vol. 6, John Erhman, 1956.
VICTORY IN THE WEST
  Vol. 1, Ellis, Allen, Robb, and Warhurst, 1962.
  Vol. 2, Ellis and Warhurst, 1968.

Canadian Official Sources

Stacy, C. P. *The Canadian Army 1939–45: An Official Historical Summary.* Ottawa: The
  King's Printer, 1948.
———. *Operations in North-west Europe.* Vol. 3: *The Victory Campaign 1944–45.*
  Ottawa: Ministry of National Defense, 1960.

Index

French First Army: 1st Armored Division, 222, 305; 5th Armored Division, 305–306; casualties, 306; combat capabilities, 288, 293–294, 299; combat operations, 297, 304, 314–316, 319–321; in North Africa, 293; organization and units, 305; as part of U.S. 6th Army, 290–291, 303
Fuller, J. F. C., 80
FWD13765, 81–82, 96–98, 107–109, 128, 146, 152–154, 238
FWD14827 14 Sept, 293–294

Gaffey, Hugh J., 207, 228, 271
Gale, Sir Humphrey M., 72–74, 125, 197
Gavin, James N., 137
Gay, Hobart R. ("Hap"), 198, 207, 231, 271
Gerhardt, Charles, 261, 264, 266, 268
German Army: Allied strategy for defeat, 62–63; Eisenhower objectives, 55, 67, 69–71; Falaise pocket disaster, 76; fighting ability, 16; leadership and tactics, 70; logistics regeneration, 53; Mortain counterattack, 5–6, 155, 207; "National Redoubt," 20; Nordwind counterattack, 324; rebuilding defensive capacity, 234; strategic reserves, 85–86
German Army Group B, 118, 160
German Army Group G, 6, 208, 230, 272–273, 292–293, 296, 298, 313
German Army units: Fifteenth Army, 90, 104, 110–115, 119, 125–126, 140–143, 245–246; First Army, 208, 273–278, 292, 296, 305, 312, 316, 323, 325; First Parachute Army, 16, 111, 114, 119, 122, 160, 177–178; LXXIV Corps, 15, 161, 246; Nineteenth Army, 208, 273, 285, 292, 295–299, 305–308, 312, 314–315, 319–321; Panzer Group West, 6; Panzer Lehr, 2, 160, 218, 276, 313–314, 318–320; Seventh Army, 6, 81, 160–162, 246; Sixth Panzer Army, 177, 241–243, 246–249, 264, 276, 281, 320–321, 326; XLVII Panzer Corps, 178, 243, 255, 263–267
German Eastern Front, 82, 85

German Luftwaffe, 53, 111, 119, 133–134, 166, 187, 209, 221, 241, 266
German West Wall (Siegfried Line): Allied logistics limitations, 10, 19–20, 238–239; as Allied objective, 96–97, 293–294; fortifications described, 149–150; Hitler's strategy for, 118; Patton's view of, 198, 201, 218; U.S. attacks on, 158, 168, 245, 249, 277–278, 319
German Western Front: Ardennes counteroffensive, 73; assessment of capabilities, 80–82; available divisions, 83; counterattack plans, 227–228; OKW decisions, 273, 276, 313, 315; reconstituting the Western Wall, 83–87; withdrawal to West Wall, 160–162. *See also* Battle of the Bulge
"Germany First" philosophy, 237
Gerow, Leonard ("Gee"), 64, 156, 169–171, 177, 189, 300
Gillem, Alvan, 257, 269
Grant, Ulysses S., 61, 63, 240–241
Guthrie, Sir Charles, 60

Haislip, Wade, 7, 205–206, 222, 289, 301, 308–315, 318
Hamilton, Nigel, 60, 122
Harmon, Ernst N., 187, 261, 264, 266
Hart, B. H. Liddell, 97–98
health and injuries: logistics and medical support, 25; weather impact on, 236. *See also* combat casualties
Hinds, John, 51
Hitler, Adolph: Ardennes counteroffensive, 177, 227–228, 323–325, 329; Army leadership changes, 76, 117; defense at Roer River, 255, 263–268, 279–281; defense of Metz, 220–232, 275; defensive strategy, 86–87, 111–112, 161, 166, 242–244; Normandy invasion response, 5–6, 47, 83; operational judgment, 197, 314–315; West Wall strategy, 83–84, 118–119, 242
HMS *Warsprite*, 143
Hobbs, Joseph P., 70, 183–187, 189

John A. Adams is author of *If Mahan Ran the Great Pacific War* (Indiana University Press, 2008). He is an airline executive and longtime business strategist with an interest in the use of economic principles to analyze history; as an avocation he has extensively researched military strategy and tactics.